Celtic Myths and Legends

Celtic Myths and Legends

by
Charles Squire

SIENA

This edition published and distributed by Parragon, 1998

Parragon
13 Whiteladies Road
Clifton
Bristol
BS8 1PB

ISBN 0 75252 676 6

A copy of the British Library Cataloguing-in-Publication Data
is available from the British Library.

Printed and bound in the EC

PREFACE

This book is what its author believes to be the only attempt yet made to put the English reader into possession, in clear, compact, and what it is hoped may prove agreeable, form, of the mythical, legendary, and poetic traditions of the earliest inhabitants of our islands who have left us written records—the Gaelic and the British Celts. It is true that admirable translations and paraphrases of much of Gaelic mythical saga have been recently published, and that Lady Charlotte Guest's translation of the *Mabinogion* has been placed within the reach of the least wealthy reader. But these books not merely each cover a portion only of the whole ground, but, in addition, contain little elucidatory matter. Their characters stand isolated and unexplained; and the details that would explain them must be sought for with considerable trouble in the lectures and essays of scholars to learned societies. The reader to whom this literature is entirely new is introduced, as it were, to numerous people of whose antecedents he knows nothing; and the effect is often disconcerting enough to make him lay down the volume in despair.

But here he will at last make the formal acquaintance of all the chief characters of Celtic myth: of the Gaelic gods and the giants against whom they struggled; of the "Champions of the Red Branch" of Ulster, heroes of a martial epopee almost worthy to be placed beside "the tale of Troy divine"; and of Finn and his Fenians. He will meet also with the divine and heroic personages of the ancient Britons: with their earliest gods, kin to the members of the Gaelic Pantheon; as well as with Arthur and his Knights, whom he will recognize as no mortal champions, but belonging to the same mythic company. Of all these mighty figures the histories will be briefly recorded, from the time of their unquestioned godhood, through their various transformations, to the last doubtful, dying recognition of them in the present day, as " fairies ". Thus the volume will form a kind of handbook to a subject of growing importance—the so-called "Celtic Renaissance", which is, after all, no more—and, indeed, no less—than an endeavour to refresh the vitality of English poetry at its most ancient native fount.

The book does not, of course, profess to be for Celtic scholars, to whom, indeed, its author himself owes all that is within it. It aims only at interesting the reader familiar with the mythologies of Greece, Rome, and Scandinavia in another, and a nearer, source of poetry. Its author's wish is to offer those who have fallen, or will fall, under the attraction of Celtic legend and romance, just such a volume as he himself would once have welcomed, and for which he sought in vain. It is his hope that, in choosing from the considerable, though scattered, translations and commentaries of students of Old Gaelic and Old Welsh, he has chosen wisely, and that his readers will be able, should they wish, to use his book as a stepping-stone to the authorities themselves. To that end it is wholly directed; and its marginal notes and short bibliographical appendix follow the same plan. They do not aspire to anything like completeness, but only to point out the chief sources from which he himself has drawn.

To acknowledge, as far as possible, such debts is now the author's pleasing duty. First and foremost, he has relied upon the volumes of M. H. d'Arbois de Jubainville's *Cours de Littérature celtique,* and the Hibbert Lectures for 1886 of John Rhys, Professor of Celtic in the University of Oxford, with their sequel entitled *Studies in the Arthurian Legend.* From the writings of Mr. Alfred Nutt he has also obtained much help. With regard to direct translations, it seems almost superfluous to refer to Lady Charlotte Guest's *Mabinogion* and Mr. W. F. Skene's *Four Ancient Books of Wales,* or to the work of such well-known Gaelic scholars as Mr. Eugene O'Curry, Dr. Kuno Meyer, Dr. Whitley Stokes, Dr. Ernest Windisch, Mr. Standish Hayes O'Grady (to mention no others), as contained in such publications as the *Revue Celtique,* the *Atlantis,* and the *Transactions of the Ossianic Society,* in Mr. O'Grady's *Silva Gadelica,* Mr. Nutt's *Voyage of Bran, Son of Febal,* and Miss Hull's *Cuchullin Saga.* But space is lacking to do justice to all. The reader is referred to the marginal notes and the Appendix for the works of these and other authors, who will no doubt pardon the use made of their researches to one whose sole object has been to gain a larger audience for the studies they have most at heart.

Finally, perhaps, a word should be said upon that vexed question, the transliteration of Gaelic. As yet there is no universal or consistent method of spelling. The author has therefore chosen the forms which seemed most familiar to himself, hoping in that way to best serve the uses of others.

CONTENTS

CHAP.   Page
I. THE INTEREST AND IMPORTANCE OF CELTIC
    MYTHOLOGY   1

II. THE SOURCES OF OUR KNOWLEDGE OF THE CELTIC
    MYTHOLOGY   8

III. WHO WERE THE "ANCIENT BRITONS"? . .   18

IV. THE RELIGION OF THE ANCIENT BRITONS AND
    DRUIDISM   31

THE GAELIC GODS AND THEIR STORIES

V. THE GODS OF THE GAELS   47

VI. THE GODS ARRIVE   65

VII. THE RISE OF THE SUN-GOD   78

VIII. THE GAELIC ARGONAUTS   89

IX. THE WAR WITH THE GIANTS   107

X. THE CONQUEST OF THE GODS BY MORTALS . .   119

XI. THE GODS IN EXILE   132

XII. THE IRISH ILIAD   153

XIII. SOME GAELIC LOVE-STORIES   184

XIV. FINN AND THE FENIANS   201

XV. THE DECLINE AND FALL OF THE GODS . .   227

THE BRITISH GODS AND THEIR STORIES

XVI. THE GODS OF THE BRITONS   251

XVII. THE ADVENTURES OF THE GODS OF HADES . .   278

XVIII. THE WOOING OF BRANWEN AND THE BEHEADING
    OF BRÂN   289

Contents

CHAP.   Page
XIX. THE WAR OF ENCHANTMENTS 298
XX. THE VICTORIES OF LIGHT OVER DARKNESS . . 305
XXI. THE MYTHOLOGICAL "COMING OF ARTHUR" . 312
XXII. THE TREASURES OF BRITAIN 336
XXIII. THE GODS AS KING ARTHUR'S KNIGHTS . . 354
XXIV. THE DECLINE AND FALL OF THE GODS . . 371

SURVIVALS OF THE CELTIC PAGANISM

XXV. SURVIVALS OF THE CELTIC PAGANISM INTO
MODERN TIMES 399

APPENDIX 419
INDEX 425
TABLE OF PRONUNCIATION FOR THE MORE DIFFICULT
WORDS 447

THE MYTHOLOGY OF THE
BRITISH ISLANDS

CHAPTER I

THE INTEREST AND IMPORTANCE OF CELTIC
MYTHOLOGY

It should hardly be necessary to remind the
reader of what profound interest and value to every
nation are its earliest legendary and poetical records.
The beautiful myths of Greece form a sufficing example. In threefold manner, they have influenced
the destiny of the people that created them, and of
the country of which they were the imagined theatre.
First, in the ages in which they were still fresh,
belief and pride in them were powerful enough to
bring scattered tribes into confederation. Secondly,
they gave the inspiration to sculptor and poet of an
art and literature unsurpassed, if not unequalled, by
any other age or race. Lastly, when "the glory
that was Greece" had faded, and her people had, by
dint of successive invasions, perhaps even ceased
to have any right to call themselves Hellenes, they
have passed over into the literatures of the modern

world, and so given to Greece herself a poetic
interest that still makes a petty kingdom of greater
account in the eyes of its compeers than many
others far superior to it in extent and resources.

This permeating influence of the Greek poetical
mythology, apparent in all civilized countries, has
acted especially upon our own. From almost the
very dawn of English literature, the Greek stories of
gods and heroes have formed a large part of the
stock-in-trade of English poets. The inhabitants of
Olympus occupy, under their better-known Latin
names, almost as great a space in English poetry as
they did in that of the countries to which they were
native. From Chaucer downwards, they have capti-
vated the imagination alike of the poets and their
hearers. The magic cauldron of classic myth fed,
like the Celtic "Grail", all who came to it for
sustenance.

At last, however, its potency became somewhat
exhausted. Alien and exotic to English soil, it
degenerated slowly into a convention. In the
shallow hands of the poetasters of the eighteenth
century, its figures became mere puppets. With
every wood a "grove", and every rustic maid a
"nymph", one could only expect to find Venus
armed with patch and powder-puff, Mars shouldering
a musket, and Apollo inspiring the versifier's own
trivial strains. The affectation killed—and fortunately killed—a mode of expression which had become obsolete. Smothered by just ridicule, and
abandoned to the commonplace vocabulary of the
inferior hack-writer, classic myth became a subject

which only the greatest poets could afford to handle.

But mythology is of such vital need to literature that, deprived of the store of legend native to southern Europe, imaginative writers looked for a fresh impulse. They turned their eyes to the North. Inspiration was sought, not from Olympus, but from Asgard. Moreover, it was believed that the fount of primeval poetry issuing from Scandinavian and Teutonic myth was truly our own, and that we were rightful heirs of it by reason of the Anglo-Saxon in our blood. And so, indeed, we are; but it is not our sole heritage. There must also run much Celtic —that is, truly British—blood in our veins.[1] And Matthew Arnold was probably right in asserting that, while we owe to the Anglo-Saxon the more practical qualities that have built up the British Empire, we have inherited from the Celtic side that poetic vision which has made English literature the most brilliant since the Greek.[2]

We have the right, therefore, to enter upon a new spiritual possession. And a splendid one it is! The Celtic mythology has little of the heavy crudeness that repels one in Teutonic and Scandinavian story.

[1] "There is good ground to believe", writes Mr. E. W. B. Nicholson, M.A., the librarian of the Bodleian Library, in the preface to his recently-published *Keltic Researches*, "that Lancashire, West Yorkshire, Staffordshire, Worcestershire, Warwickshire, Leicestershire, Rutland, Cambridgeshire, Wiltshire, Somerset, and part of Sussex, are as Keltic as Perthshire and North Munster; that Cheshire, Shropshire, Herefordshire, Monmouthshire, Gloucestershire, Devon, Dorset, Northamptonshire, Huntingdonshire, and Bedfordshire are more so—and equal to North Wales and Leinster; while Buckinghamshire and Hertfordshire exceed even this degree and are on a level with South Wales and Ulster. Cornwall, of course, is more Keltic than any other English county, and as much so as Argyll. Inverness-shire, or Connaught." [2] *The Study of Celtic Literature.*

It is as beautiful and graceful as the Greek; and, unlike the Greek, which is the reflection of a clime and soil which few of us will ever see, it is our own. Divinities should, surely, seem the inevitable outgrowth of the land they move in! How strange Apollo would appear, naked among icebergs, or fur-clad Thor striding under groves of palms! But the Celtic gods and heroes are the natural inhabitants of a British landscape, not seeming foreign and out-of-place in a scene where there is no vine or olive, but "shading in with" our homely oak and bracken, gorse and heath.

Thus we gain an altogether fresh interest in the beautiful spots of our own islands, especially those of the wilder and more mountainous west, where the older inhabitants of the land lingered longest. Saxon conquest obliterated much in Eastern Britain, and changed more; but in the West of England, in Wales, in Scotland, and especially in legend-haunted Ireland, the hills and dales still keep memories of the ancient gods of the ancient race. Here and there in South Wales and the West of England are regions—once mysterious and still romantic—which the British Celts held to be the homes of gods or outposts of the Other World. In Ireland, not only is there scarcely a place that is not connected in some way with the traditionary exploits of the "Red Branch Champions", or of Finn and his mighty men, but the old deities are still remembered, dwarfed into fairies, but keeping the same attributes and the same names as of yore. Wordsworth's complaint[1]

---

[1] In a sonnet written in 1801.

that, while Pelion and Ossa, Olympus and Parnassus are "in immortal books enrolled", not one English mountain, "though round our sea-girt shore they rise in crowds", had been "by the Celestial Muses glorified" doubtless seemed true to his own generation. Thanks to the scholars who have unveiled the ancient Gaelic and British mythologies, it need not be so for ours. On Ludgate Hill, as well as on many less famous eminences, once stood the temple of the British Zeus. A mountain not far from Bettws-y-Coed was the British Olympus, the court and palace of our ancient gods.

It may well be doubted, however, whether Wordsworth's contemporaries would have welcomed the mythology which was their own by right of birth as a substitute for that of Greece and Rome. The inspiration of classic culture, which Wordsworth was one of the first to break with, was still powerful. How some of its professors would have held their sides and roared at the very notion of a British mythology! Yet, all the time, it had long been secretly leavening English ideas and ideals, none the less potently because disguised under forms which could be readily appreciated. Popular fancy had rehabilitated the old gods, long banned by the priests' bell, book, and candle, under various disguises. They still lived on in legend as kings of ancient Britain reigning in a fabulous past anterior to Julius Caesar—such were King Lud, founder of London; King Lear, whose legend was immortalized by Shakespeare; King Brennius, who conquered Rome; as well as many others who will be found filling parts in old drama. They still lived on as long-dead saints of the early churches of Ireland and Britain, whose wonderful attributes and adventures are, in many cases, only those of their original namesakes, the old gods, told afresh. And they still lived on in another, and a yet more potent, way. Myths of Arthur and his cycle of gods passed into the hands of the Norman story-tellers, to reappear as romances of King Arthur and his Knights of the Table Round. Thus spread over civilized Europe, their influence was immense. Their primal poetic impulse is still resonant in our literature; we need only instance Tennyson and Swinburne as minds that have come under its sway.

This diverse influence of Celtic mythology upon English poetry and romance has been eloquently set forth by Mr. Elton in his *Origins of English History*. "The religion of the British tribes", he writes, "has exercised an important influence upon literature. The mediæval romances and the legends which stood for history are full of the 'fair humanities' and figures of its bright mythology. The elemental powers of earth and fire, and the spirits which haunted the waves and streams appear again as kings in the Irish Annals, or as saints and hermits in Wales. The Knights of the Round Table, Sir Kay and Tristrem and the bold Sir Bedivere, betray their mighty origin by the attributes they retained as heroes of romance. It was a goddess, '*Dea quaedam phantastica*', who bore the wounded Arthur to the peaceful valley. 'There was little sunlight on its woods and streams, and the nights were dark

and gloomy for want of the moon and stars.' This
is the country of Oberon and of Sir Huon of Bordeaux. It is the dreamy forest of Arden. In an
older mythology, it was the realm of a King of
Shadows, the country of Gwyn ap Nudd, who rode
as Sir Guyon in the ' Fairie Queene '—

> And knighthood took of good Sir Huon's hand,
> When with King Oberon he came to Fairyland '."[1]

To trace Welsh and Irish kings and saints and
hermits back to "the elemental powers of earth
and fire, and the spirits that haunted the woods
and streams" of Celtic imagination, and to disclose
primitive pagan deities under the mediæval and
Christian trappings of "King Arthur's Knights" will
necessarily fall within the scope of this volume.
But meanwhile the reader will probably be asking
what evidence there is that apocryphal British kings
like Lear and Lud, and questionable Irish saints
like Bridget are really disguised Celtic divinities, or
that the Morte D'Arthur, with its love of Launcelot
and the queen, and its quest of the Holy Grail, was
ever anything more than an invention of the Norman
romance-writers. He will demand to know what
facts we really possess about this supposed Celtic
mythology alleged to have furnished their prototypes,
and of what real antiquity and value are our authorities upon it.

The answer to his question will be found in the
next chapter.

---

[1] Elton: *Origins of English History*. chap. x.

CHAPTER II

We may begin by asserting with confidence that
Mr. Elton has touched upon a part only of the
material on which we may draw, to reconstruct
the ancient British mythology.   Luckily, we are
not wholly dependent upon the difficult tasks of
resolving the fabled deeds of apocryphal Irish and
British kings who reigned earlier than St. Patrick
or before Julius Caesar into their original form of
Celtic myths, of sifting the attributes and miracles
of doubtfully historical saints, or of separating the
primitive pagan elements in the legends of Arthur
and his Knights from the embellishments added by
the romance-writers.   We have, in addition to these
—which we may for the present put upon one side as
secondary—sources, a mass of genuine early writings
which, though post-Christian in the form in which
they now exist, none the less descend from the preceding pagan age.   These are contained in vellum
and parchment manuscripts long preserved from
destruction in mansions and monasteries in Ireland,
Scotland, and Wales, and only during the last century brought to light, copied, and translated by the
patient labours of scholars who have grappled with

the long-obsolete dialects in which they were trans-scribed.

Many of these volumes are curious miscellanies. Usually the one book of a great house or monastic community, everything was copied into it that the scholar of the family or brotherhood thought to be best worth preserving. Hence they contain matter of the most diverse kind. There are translations of portions of the Bible and of the classics, and of such then popular books as Geoffrey of Monmouth's and Nennius' Histories of Britain; lives of famous saints, together with works attributed to them; poems and romances of which, under a thin disguise, the old Gaelic and British gods are the heroes; together with treatises on all the subjects then studied—grammar, prosody, law, history, geography, chronology, and the genealogies of important chiefs.

The majority of these documents were put together during a period which, roughly speaking, lasted from the beginning of the twelfth century to the end of the sixteenth. In Ireland, in Wales, and, apparently, also in Scotland, it was a time of literary revival after the turmoils of the previous epoch. In Ireland, the Norsemen, after long ravaging, had settled peacefully down, while in Wales, the Norman Conquest had rendered the country for the first time comparatively quiet. The scattered remains of history, lay and ecclesiastical, of science, and of legend were gathered together.

Of the Irish manuscripts, the earliest, and, for our purposes, the most important, on account of the great store of ancient Gaelic mythology which, in spite of its dilapidated condition, it still contains, is in the possession of the Royal Irish Academy. Unluckily, it is reduced to a fragment of one hundred and thirty-eight pages, but this remnant preserves a large number of romances relating to the old gods and heroes of Ireland. Among other things, it contains a complete account of the epical saga called the *Táin Bó Chuailgné*, the " Raiding of the Cattle of Cooley ", in which the hero, Cuchulainn, performed his greatest feats. This manuscript is called the Book of the Dun Cow, from the tradition that it was copied from an earlier book written upon the skin of a favourite animal belonging to Saint Ciaran, who lived in the seventh century. An entry upon one of its pages reveals the name of its scribe, one Maelmuiri, whom we know to have been killed by robbers in the church of Clonmacnois in the year 1106.

Far more voluminous, and but little less ancient, is the Book of Leinster, said to have been compiled in the early part of the twelfth century by Finn mac Gorman, Bishop of Kildare. This also contains an account of Cuchulainn's mighty deeds which supplements the older version in the Book of the Dun Cow. Of somewhat less importance from the point of view of the student of Gaelic mythology come the Book of Ballymote and the Yellow Book of Lecan, belonging to the end of the fourteenth century, and the Books of Lecan and of Lismore, both attributed to the fifteenth. Besides these six great collections, there survive many other manuscripts which also contain ancient mythical lore. In one of these, dating from the fifteenth century, is to be found the story of the Battle of Moytura, fought between the gods of Ireland and their enemies, the Fomors, or demons of the deep sea.

The Scottish manuscripts, preserved in the Advocates' Library at Edinburgh, date back in some cases as far as the fourteenth century, though the majority of them belong to the fifteenth and sixteenth. They corroborate the Irish documents, add to the Cuchulainn saga, and make a more special subject of the other heroic cycle, that which relates the not less wonderful deeds of Finn, Ossian, and the Fenians. They also contain stories of other characters, who, more ancient than either Finn or Cuchulainn, are the Tuatha Dé Danann, the god-tribe of the ancient Gaels.

The Welsh documents cover about the same period as the Irish and the Scottish. Four of these stand out from the rest, as most important. The oldest is the Black Book of Caermarthen, which dates from the third quarter of the twelfth century; the Book of Aneurin, which was written late in the thirteenth; the Book of Taliesin, assigned to the fourteenth; and the Red Book of Hergest, compiled by various persons during that century and the one following it. The first three of these " Four Ancient Books of Wales" are small in size, and contain poems attributed to the great traditional bards of the sixth century, Myrddin, Taliesin, and Aneurin. The last—the Red Book of Hergest—is far larger. In it are to be found Welsh translations of the British Chronicles; the oft-mentioned Triads, verses celebrating famous traditionary persons or things;

ancient poems attributed to Llywarch Hên; and, of priceless value to any study of our subject, the so-called Mabinogion, stories in which large portions of the old British mythology are worked up into romantic form.

The whole bulk, therefore, of the native literature bearing upon the mythology of the British Islands may be attributed to a period which lasted from the beginning of the twelfth century to the end of the sixteenth. But even the commencement of this era will no doubt seem far too late a day to allow authenticity to matter which ought to have vastly preceded it. The date, however, merely marks the final redaction of the contents of the manuscripts into the form in which they now exist, without bearing at all upon the time of their authorship. Avowedly copies of ancient poems and tales from much older manuscripts, the present books no more fix the period of the original composition of their contents than the presence of a portion of the *Canterbury Tales* in a modern anthology of English poetry would assign Chaucer to the present year of grace.

This may be proved both directly and inferentially.[1] In some instances—as in that of an elegy upon Saint Columba in the Book of the Dun Cow—the dates of authorship are actually given. In others, we may depend upon evidence which, if not quite so absolute, is nearly as convincing. Even where the writer does not state that he is copying from older manu-

---

[1] Satisfactory summaries of the evidence for the dates of both the Gaelic and Welsh legendary material will be found in pamphlets No. 8 and 11 of Mr. Nutt's *Popular Studies in Mythology, Romance, and Folklore.*

scripts, it is obvious that this must have been the case, from the glosses in his version. The scribes of the earlier Gaelic manuscripts very often found, in the documents from which they themselves were copying, words so archaic as to be unintelligible to the readers of their own period. To render them comprehensible, they were obliged to insert marginal notes which explained these obsolete words by reference to other manuscripts more ancient still. Often the mediæval copyists have ignorantly moved these notes from the margin into the text, where they remain, like philological fossils, to give evidence of previous forms of life. The documents from which they were taken have perished, leaving the mediæval copies as their sole record. In the Welsh Mabinogion the same process is apparent. Peculiarities in the existing manuscripts show plainly enough that they must have been copied from some more archaic text. Besides this, they are, as they at present stand, obviously made up of earlier tales pieced together. Almost as clearly as the Gaelic manuscripts, the Welsh point us back to older and more primitive forms.

The ancient legends of the Gael and the Briton are thus shown to have been no mere inventions of scholarly monks in the Middle Ages. We have now to trace, if possible, the date, not necessarily of their first appearance on men's lips, but of their first redaction into writing in approximately the form in which we have them now.

Circumstantial evidence can be adduced to prove that the most important portions both of Gaelic

and British early literature can be safely relegated
to a period of several centuries prior to their now-
existing record. Our earliest version of the episode
of the *Táin Bó Chuailgné*, which is the nucleus and
centre of the ancient Gaelic heroic cycle of which
Cuchulainn, *fortissimus heros Scotorum*, is the principal figure, is found in the twelfth-century Book of
the Dun Cow. But legend tells us that at the beginning of the seventh century the Saga had not
only been composed, but had actually become so
obsolete as to have been forgotten by the bards.
Their leader, one Senchan Torpeist, a historical
character, and chief bard of Ireland at that time,
obtained permission from the Saints to call Fergus,
Cuchulainn's contemporary, and a chief actor in the
" Raid", from the dead, and received from the resur-
rected hero a true and full version. This tradition,
dealing with a real personage, surely shows that the
story of the *Táin* was known before the time of
Senchan, and probably preserves the fact, either
that his version of Cuchulainn's famous deeds
became the accepted one, or that he was the first
to reduce it to writing. An equally suggestive consideration approximately fixes for us the earliest
redaction of the Welsh mythological prose tales
called the " Mabinogion", or, more correctly speaking, the " Four Branches of the Mabinogi ".[1] In
none of these is there the slightest mention, or
apparently the least knowledge, of Arthur, around
whom and whose supposed contemporaries centres
the mass of British legend as it was transmitted by

[1] Rhys: *Studies in the Arthurian Legend*, chap. 1

the Welsh to the Normans. These mysterious mythological records must in all probability, therefore, antedate the Arthurian cycle of myth, which was already being put into form in the sixth century. On the other hand, the characters of the "Four Branches" are mentioned without comment —as though they were personages with whom no one could fail to be familiar—in the supposed sixth-century poems contained in those "Four Ancient Books of Wales" in which are found the first meagre references to the British hero.

Such considerations as these throw back, with reasonable certainty, the existence of the Irish and Welsh poems and prose tales, in something like their present shape, to a period antedating the seventh century.

But this, again, means only that the myths, traditions, and legends were current at that to us early, but to them, in their actual substance, late date, in literary form. A mythology must always be far older than the oldest verses and stories that celebrate it. Elaborate poems and sagas are not made in a day, or in a year. The legends of the Gaelic and British gods and heroes could not have sprung, like Athena from the head of Zeus, full-born out of some poet's brain. The bard who first put them into artistic shape was setting down the primitive traditions of his race. We may therefore venture to describe them as not of the twelfth century or of the seventh, but as of a prehistoric and immemorial antiquity.

Internal evidence bears this out. An examination

of both the Gaelic and British legendary romances
shows, under embellishing details added by later
hands, an inner core of primeval thought which
brings them into line with the similar ideas of other
races in the earliest stage of culture. Their "local
colour" may be that of their last "editor", but their
"plots" are pre-mediæval, pre-Christian, pre-historic.
The characters of early Gaelic legend belong to the
same stamp of imagination that created Olympian
and Titan, Æsir and Jötun. We must go far to
the back of civilized thought to find parallels to such
a story as that in which the British sun-god, struck
by a rival in love with a poisoned spear, is turned
into an eagle, from whose wound great pieces of
carrion are continually falling.[1]

This aspect of the Celtic literary records was
clearly seen, and eloquently expressed, by Matthew
Arnold in his *Study of Celtic Literature*.[2] He was
referring to the Welsh side, but his image holds
good equally for the Gaelic. "The first thing that
strikes one", he says, "in reading the *Mabinogion* is
how evidently the mediæval story-teller is pillaging
an antiquity of which he does not fully possess the
secret: he is like a peasant building his hut on the
site of Halicarnassus or Ephesus; he builds, but
what he builds is full of materials of which he knows
not the history, or knows by a glimmering tradition
merely: stones 'not of this building', but of an older
architecture, greater, cunninger, more majestical."
His heroes "are no mediæval personages: they belong to an older, pagan, mythological world". So,

---

[1] See chap. XVI of this book—"The Gods of the Britons".   [2] Lecture II.

too, with the figures, however euhemerized, of the three great Gaelic cycles: that of the Tuatha Dé Danann, of the Heroes of Ulster, of Finn and the Fenians. Their divinity outshines their humanity; through their masks may be seen the faces of gods.

Yet, gods as they are, they had taken on the semblance of mortality by the time their histories were fixed in the form in which we have them now. Their earliest records, if those could be restored to us, would doubtless show them eternal and undying, changing their shapes at will, but not passing away. But the post-Christian copyists, whether Irish or Welsh, would not countenance this. Hence we have the singular paradox of the deaths of Immortals. There is hardly one of the figures of either the Gaelic or the British Pantheon whose demise is not somewhere recorded. Usually they fell in the unceasing battles between the divinities of darkness and of light. Their deaths in earlier cycles of myth, however, do not preclude their appearance in later ones. Only, indeed, with the closing of the lips of the last mortal who preserved his tradition can the life of a god be truly said to end.

CHAPTER III

But, before proceeding to recount the myths of the "Ancient Britons", it will be well to decide what people, exactly, we mean by that loose but convenient phrase. We have, all of us, vague ideas of Ancient Britons, recollected, doubtless, from our school - books. There we saw their pictures as, painted with woad, they paddled coracles, or drove scythed chariots through legions of astonished Romans. Their Druids, white-bearded and wearing long, white robes, cut the mistletoe with a golden sickle at the time of the full moon, or, less innocently employed, made bonfires of human beings shut up in gigantic figures of wicker-work.

Such picturesque details were little short of the sum-total, not only of our own knowledge of the subject, but also of that of our teachers. Practically all their information concerning the ancient inhabitants of Britain was taken from the Commentaries of Julius Caesar. So far as it went, it was no doubt correct; but it did not go far. Caesar's interest in our British ancestors was that of a general who was his own war-correspondent rather than that of an exhaustive and painstaking scientist. It has been reserved for modern archæologists, philologists, and ethnologists to give us a fuller account of the Ancient Britons.

The inhabitants of our islands previous to the Roman invasion are generally described as "Celts". But they must have been largely a mixed race; and the people with whom they mingled must have modified to some—and perhaps to a large—extent their physique, their customs, and their language.

Speculation has run somewhat wild over the question of the composition of the Early Britons. But out of the clash of rival theories there emerges one—and one only—which may be considered as scientifically established. We have certain proof of two distinct human stocks in the British Islands at the time of the Roman Conquest; and so great an authority as Professor Huxley has given his opinion that there is no evidence of any others.[1]

The earliest of these two races would seem to have inhabited our islands from the most ancient times, and may, for our purpose, be described as aboriginal. It was the people that built the "long barrows"; and which is variously called by ethnologists the Iberian, Mediterranean, Berber, Basque, Silurian, or Euskarian race. In physique it was short, swarthy, dark-haired, dark-eyed, and long-skulled; its language belonged to the class called "Hamitic", the surviving types of which are found among the Gallas, Abyssinians, Berbers, and other North African tribes; and it seems to have come originally from some part either of Eastern, Northern, or Central Africa. Spreading thence, it was

---

[1] Huxley: *On Some Fixed Points in British Ethnology.* 1871.

probably the first people to inhabit the Valley of the Nile, and it sent offshoots into Syria and Asia Minor. The earliest Hellenes found it in Greece under the name of "Pelasgoi"; the earliest Latins in Italy, as the "Etruscans"; and the Hebrews in Palestine, as the "Hittites". It spread northward through Europe as far as the Baltic, and westward, along the Atlas chain, to Spain, France, and our own islands.[1] In many countries it reached a comparatively high level of civilization, but in Britain its development must have been early checked. We can discern it as an agricultural rather than a pastoral people, still in the Stone Age, dwelling in totemistic tribes on hills whose summits it fortified elaborately, and whose slopes it cultivated on what is called the "terrace system", and having a primitive culture which ethnologists think to have much resembled that of the present hill-tribes of Southern India.[2] It held our islands till the coming of the Celts, who fought with the aborigines, dispossessed them of the more fertile parts, subjugated them, even amalgamated with them, but certainly never extirpated them. In the time of the Romans they were still practically independent in South Wales. In Ireland they were long unconquered, and are found as allies rather than serfs of the Gaels, ruling their own provinces, and preserving their own customs and religion. Nor, in spite of all the successive invasions of Great Britain and Ireland,

[1] Sergi: *The Mediterranean Race.*
[2] Gomme: *The Village Community.* Chap. IV—"The non-Aryan Elements in the English Village Community".

are they yet extinct, or so merged as to have lost their type, which is still the predominant one in many parts of the west both of Britain and Ireland, and is believed by some ethnologists to be generally upon the increase all over England.

The second of the two races was the exact opposite to the first. It was the tall, fair, light-haired, blue- or gray-eyed, broad-headed people called, popularly, the "Celts", who belonged in speech to the "Aryan" family, their language finding its affinities in Latin, Greek, Teutonic, Slavic, the Zend of Ancient Persia, and the Sanscrit of Ancient India. Its original home was probably somewhere in Central Europe, along the course of the upper Danube, or in the region of the Alps. The "round barrows" in which it buried its dead, or deposited their burnt ashes, differ in shape from the "long barrows" of the earlier race. It was in a higher stage of culture than the "Iberians", and introduced into Britain bronze and silver, and, perhaps, some of the more lately domesticated animals.

Both Iberians and Celts were divided into numerous tribes, but there is nothing to show that there was any great diversity among the former. It is otherwise with the Celts, who were separated into two main branches which came over at different times. The earliest were the Goidels, or Gaels; the second, the Brythons, or Britons. Between these two branches there was not only a dialectical, but probably, also, a considerable physical difference. Some anthropologists even postulate a different shape of skull. Without necessarily admitting this,

there is reason to suppose a difference of build and
of colour of hair.   With regard to this, we have the
evidence of Latin writers—of Tacitus,[1] who tells us
that the "Caledonians" of the North differed from
the Southern Britons in being larger-limbed and
redder-haired, and of Strabo,[2] who described the
tribes in the interior of Britain as taller than the
Gaulish colonists on the coast, with hair less yellow
and limbs more loosely knit.   Equally do the classic
authorities agree in recognizing the "Silures" of
South Wales as an entirely different race from any
other in Britain.   The dark complexions and curly
hair of these Iberians seemed to Tacitus to prove
them immigrants from Spain.[3]

Professor Rhys also puts forward evidence to
show that the Goidels and the Brythons had already
separated before they first left Gaul for our islands.[4]
He finds them as two distinct peoples there.   We
do not expect so much nowadays from "the merest
school-boy" as we did in Macaulay's time, but even
the modern descendant of that paragon could probably tell us that all Gaul was divided into three
parts, one of which was inhabited by the Belgae,
another by the Aquitani, and the third by those
who called themselves Celtae, but were termed
Galli by the Romans; and that they all differed
from one another in language, customs, and laws.[5]
Of these, Professor Rhys identifies the Belgae with
the Brythons, and the Celtae with the Goidels, the

[1] Tacitus: *Agricola*, chap. XI.   [2] Strabo: *Geographica*, Book IV, chap. v.
[3] Tacitus, *op. cit.*
[4] Rhys: *The Early Ethnology of the British Islands. Scottish Review.* April,
1890.   [5] Caesar: *De Bello Gallico*, Book I, chap. I.

third people, the Aquitani, being non-Celtic and
non-Aryan, part of the great Hamitic-speaking
Iberian stock.[1]   The Celtae, with their Goidelic
dialect of Celtic, which survives to-day in the Gaelic
languages of Ireland, Scotland, and the Isle of Man,
were the first to come over to Britain, pushed forward, probably, by the Belgae, who, Caesar tells us,
were the bravest of the Gauls.[2]   Here they conquered the native Iberians, driving them out of the
fertile parts into the rugged districts of the north
and west.   Later came the Belgae themselves,
compelled by press of population; and they, bringing better weapons and a higher civilization, treated
the Goidels as those had treated the Iberians.
Thus harried, the Goidels probably combined with
the Iberians against what was now the common foe,
and became to a large degree amalgamated with
them.   The result was that during the Roman
domination the British Islands were roughly divided
with regard to race as follows: The Brythons, or
second Celtic race, held all Britain south of the
Tweed, with the exception of the extreme west,
while the first Celtic race, the Goidelic, had most
of Ireland, as well as the Isle of Man, Cumberland,
the West Highlands, Cornwall, Devon, and North
Wales.   North of the Grampians lived the Picts,
who were probably more or less Goidelicized Iberians, the aboriginal race also holding out, unmixed,
in South Wales and parts of Ireland.

It is now time to decide what, for the purposes
of this book, it will be best to call the two different

---

[1] Rhys: *Scottish Review.* April, 1890.   [2] Op. Caesar, *op. cit.*

branches of the Celts, and their languages. With such familiar terms as "Gael" and "Briton", "Gaelic" and "British", ready to our hands, it seems pedantic to insist upon the more technical "Goidel" and "Brython", "Goidelic" and "Brythonic". The difficulty is that the words "Gael" and "Gaelic" have been so long popularly used to designate only the modern "Goidels" of Scotland and their language, that they may create confusion when also applied to the people and languages of Ireland and the Isle of Man. Similarly, the words "Briton" and "British" have come to mean, at the present day, the people of the whole of the British Islands, though they at first only signified the inhabitants of England, Central Wales, the Lowlands of Scotland, and the Brythonic colony in Brittany. However, the words "Goidel" and "Brython", with their derivatives, are so clumsy that it will probably prove best to use the neater terms. In this volume, therefore, the "Goidels" of Ireland, Scotland, and the Isle of Man are our "Gaels" and the "Brythons" of England and Wales are our "Britons".

We get the earliest accounts of the life of the inhabitants of the British Islands from two sources. The first is a foreign one, that of the Latin writers. But the Romans only really knew the Southern Britons, whom they describe as similar in physique and customs to the Continental Gauls, with whom, indeed, they considered them to be identical.[1] At the time they wrote, colonies of Belgae were still

---

[1] Tacitus: *Agricola*, chap. XI.

settling upon the coasts of Britain opposite to Gaul.[1]
Roman information grew scantier as it approached
the Wall, and of the Northern tribes they seem to
have had only such knowledge as they gathered
through occasional warfare with them. They describe
them as entirely barbarous, naked and tattooed,
living by the chase alone, without towns, houses,
or fields, without government or family life, and regarding iron as an ornament of value, as other, more
civilized peoples regarded gold.[2]   As for Ireland,
it never came under their direct observation, and we
are entirely dependent upon its native writers for
information as to the manners and customs of the
Gaels.   It may be considered convincing proof of
the authenticity of the descriptions of life contained
in the ancient Gaelic manuscripts that they corroborate so completely the observations of the Latin
writers upon the Britons and Gauls.   Reading the
two side by side, we may largely reconstruct the
common civilization of the Celts.

Roughly speaking, one may compare it with the
civilization of the Greeks, as described by Homer.[3]
Both peoples were in the tribal and pastoral stage
of culture, in which the chiefs are the great cattle-
owners round whom their less wealthy fellows gather.
Both wear much the same attire, use the same kind
of weapons, and fight in the same manner—from
the war-chariot, a vehicle already obsolete even in
Ireland by the first century of the Christian era.

---

[1] Caesar : *De Bellico Gallico*, Book V, chap. XII.

[2] Elton : *Origins of English History*, chap. VII.

[3] See " *La Civilisation des Celtes et celle de l'Épopée Homérique*", by M. d'Arbois
de Jubainville, *Cours de Littérature Celtique*, Vol. VI.

Battles are fought single-handed between chiefs, the ill-armed common people contributing little to their result, and less to their history. Such chiefs are said to be divinely descended—sons, even, of the immortal gods. Their tremendous feats are sung by the bards, who, like the Homeric poets, were privileged persons, inferior only to the war - lord. Ancient Greek and Ancient Celt had very much the same conceptions of life, both as regards this world and the next.

We may gather much detailed information of the early inhabitants of the British Islands from our various authorities.[1] Their clothes, which consisted, according to the Latin writers, of a blouse with sleeves, trousers fitting closely round the ankles, and a shawl or cloak, fastened at the shoulder with a brooch, were made either of thick felt or of woven cloth dyed with various brilliant colours. The writer Diodorus tells us that they were crossed with little squares and lines, "as though they had been sprinkled with flowers". They were, in fact, like "tartans", and we may believe Varro, who tells us that they "made a gaudy show". The men alone seem to have worn hats, which were of soft felt, the women's hair being uncovered, and tied in a knot behind. In time of battle, the men also dispensed with any head-covering, brushing their abundant hair forward into a thick mass, and dyeing it red with a soap made of goat's fat and beech ashes, until they looked (says Cicero's tutor Posidonius, who visited Britain about

[1] See Elton: *Origins of English History*, chap. VII.

110 B.C.) less like human beings than wild men of the woods. Both sexes were fond of ornaments, which took the form of gold bracelets, rings, pins, and brooches, and of beads of amber, glass, and jet. Their knives, daggers, spear-heads, axes, and swords were made of bronze or iron; their shields were the same round target used by the Highlanders at the battle of Culloden; and they seem also to have had a kind of lasso to which a hammer-shaped ball was attached, and which they used as the Gauchos of South America use their *bola*. Their war-chariots were made of wicker, the wooden wheels being armed with sickles of bronze. These were drawn either by two or four horses, and were large enough to hold several persons in each. Standing in these, they rushed along the enemy's lines, hurling darts, and driving the scythes against all who came within reach. The Romans were much impressed by the skill of the drivers, who "could check their horses at full speed on a steep incline, and turn them in an instant, and could run along the pole, and stand on the yoke, and then get back into their chariots again without a moment's delay".[1]

With these accounts of the Roman writers we may compare the picture of the Gaelic hero, Cuchulainn, as the ancient Irish writers describe him dressed and armed for battle. Glorified by the bard, he yet wears essentially the same costume and equipment which the classic historians and geographers described more soberly. "His gorgeous raiment that he wore in great conventions"

---

[1] Caesar: *De Bello Gallico*, Book IV, chap. XXXIII.

consisted of "a fair crimson tunic of five plies and
fringed, with a long pin of white silver, gold-enchased
and patterned, shining as if it had been a luminous
torch which for its blazing property and brilliance
men might not endure to see. Next his skin, a
body-vest of silk, bordered and fringed all round
with gold, with silver, and with white bronze, which
vest came as far as the upper edge of his russet-
coloured kilt. . . . About his neck were a hundred
linklets of red gold that flashed again, with pendants
hanging from them. His head-gear was adorned
with a hundred mixed carbuncle jewels, strung."
He carried "a trusty special shield, in hue dark
crimson, and in its circumference armed with a pure
white silver rim. At his left side a long and golden-
hilted sword. Beside him, in the chariot, a lengthy
spear; together with a keen, aggression - boding
javelin, fitted with hurling thong, with rivets of
white bronze."[1] Another passage of Gaelic saga
describes his chariot. It was made of fine wood,
with wicker-work, moving on wheels of white bronze.
It had a high rounded frame of creaking copper,
a strong curved yoke of gold, and a pole of white
silver, with mountings of white bronze. The yellow
reins were plaited, and the shafts were as hard and
straight as sword-blades.[2]

In like manner the ancient Irish writers have
made glorious the halls and fortresses of their
mythical kings. Like the palaces of Priam, of
Menelaus, and of Odysseus, they gleam with gold

[1] From the *Táin Bó Chuailgné*. The translator is Mr. Standish Hayes O'Grady.
[2] *Tochmarc Emire*—the *Wooing of Emer*—an old Irish romance.

and gems. Conchobar,[1] the legendary King of Ulster in its golden age, had three such "houses" at Emain Macha. Of the one called the "Red Branch", we are told that it contained nine compartments of red yew, partitioned by walls of bronze, all grouped around the king's private chamber, which had a ceiling of silver, and bronze pillars adorned with gold and carbuncles.[2] But the far less magnificent accounts of the Latin writers have, no doubt, more truth in them than such lavish pictures. They described the Britons they knew as living in villages of bee-hive huts, roofed with fern or thatch, from which, at the approach of an enemy, they retired to the local *dún*. This, so far from being elaborate, merely consisted of a round or oval space fenced in with palisades and earthworks, and situated either upon the top of a hill or in the midst of a not easily traversable morass.[3] We may see the remains of such strongholds in many parts of England—notable ones are the "castles" of Amesbury, Avebury, and Old Sarum in Wiltshire, Saint Catherine's Hill, near Winchester, and Saint George's Hill, in Surrey—and it is probable that, in spite of the Celtic praisers of past days, the "palaces" of Emain Macha and of Tara were very like them.

The Celtic customs were, like the Homeric, those of the primitive world. All land (though it may have theoretically belonged to the chief) was cultivated in common. This community of possessions

---

[1] Sometimes spelt "Conachar", and pronounced *Conhower* or *Connor*.
[2] The *Wooing of Emer*.
[3] Caesar: *De Bello Gallico*, Book V, chap. XXI, and various passages in Book VII.

is stated by Caesar[1] to have extended to their wives; but the imputation cannot be said to have been proved.   On the contrary, in the stories of both branches of the Celtic race, women seem to have taken a higher place in men's estimation, and to have enjoyed far more personal liberty, than among the Homeric Greeks.   The idea may have arisen from a misunderstanding of some of the curious Celtic customs.   Descent seems to have been traced through the maternal rather than through the paternal line, a very un-Aryan procedure which some believe to have been borrowed from another race. The parental relation was still further lessened by the custom of sending children to be brought up outside the family in which they were born, so that they had foster-parents to whom they were as much, or even more, attached than to their natural ones.

Their political state, mirroring their family life, was not less primitive.   There was no central tribunal.   Disputes were settled within the families in which they occurred, while, in the case of graver injuries, the injured party or his nearest relation could kill the culprit or exact a fine from him.   As families increased in number, they became petty tribes, often at war with one another.   A defeated tribe had to recognize the sovereignty of the head man of the conquering tribe, and a succession of such victories exalted him into the position of a chief of his district.   But even then, though his decision was the whole of the law, he was little more than the mouthpiece of public opinion.

[1] *Ibid.*, chap. XIV.

CHAPTER IV

THE RELIGION OF THE ANCIENT BRITONS AND
DRUIDISM

The ancient inhabitants of Britain—the Gaelic and British Celts—have been already described as forming a branch of what are roughly called the "Aryans". This name has, however, little reference to race, and really signifies the speakers of a group of languages which can be all shown to be connected, and to descend remotely from a single source —a hypothetical mother-tongue spoken by a hypothetical people which we term "Aryan", or, more correctly, "Indo-European". This primeval speech, evolved, probably, upon some part of the great plain which stretches from the mountains of Central Europe to the mountains of Central Asia, has spread, superseding, or amalgamating with the tongues of other races, until branches of it are spoken over almost the whole of Europe and a great portion of Asia. All the various Latin, Greek, Slavic, Teutonic, and Celtic languages are "Aryan", as well as Persian and other Asiatic dialects derived from the ancient "Zend", and the numerous Indian languages which trace their origin to Sanscrit.

Not very long ago, it was supposed that this

common descent of language involved a common descent of blood. A real brotherhood was enthusiastically claimed for all the principal European nations, who were also invited to recognize Hindus and Persians as their long-lost cousins. Since then, it has been conceded that, while the Aryan speech survived, though greatly modified, the Aryan blood might well have disappeared, diluted beyond recognition by crossing with the other races whom the Aryans conquered, or among whom they more or less peacefully settled. As a matter of fact, there are no European nations—perhaps no people at all except a few remote savage tribes—which are not made up of the most diverse elements. Aryan and non-Aryan long ago blended inextricably, to form by their fusion new peoples.

But, just as the Aryan speech influenced the new languages, and the Aryan customs the new civilizations, so we can still discern in the religions of the Aryan-speaking nations similar ideas and expressions pointing to an original source of mythological conceptions. Hence, whether we investigate the mythology of the Hindus, the Greeks, the Teutons, or the Celts, we find the same mythological groundwork. In each, we see the powers of nature personified, and endowed with human form and attributes, though bearing, with few exceptions, different names. Like the Vedic brahmans, the Greek and Latin poets, and the Norse scalds, the Celtic bards —whether Gaels or Britons—imagined the sky, the sun, the moon, the earth, the sea, and the dark underwo.ld, as well as the mountains, tne streams, and the woods, to be ruled by beings like their own chiefs, but infinitely more powerful; every passion, as War and Love, and every art, as Poetry and Smithcraft, had its divine founder, teacher, and exponent; and of all these deities and their imagined children, they wove the poetical and allegorical romances which form the subject of the present volume.

Like other nations, too, whether Aryan or non-Aryan, the Celts had, besides their mythology, a religion. It is not enough to tell tales of shadowy gods; they must be made visible by sculpture, housed in groves or temples, served with ritual, and propitiated with sacrifices, if one is to hope for their favours. Every cult must have its priests living by the altar.

The priests of the Celts are well-known to us by name as the "Druids"—a word derived from a root DR which signifies a tree, and especially the oak, in several Aryan languages.[1] This is generally—though not by all scholars—taken as proving that they paid an especial veneration to the king of trees. It is true that the mistletoe—that strange parasite upon the oak—was prominent among their "herbs of power", and played a part in their ritual;[2] but this is equally true of other Aryan nations. By the Norse it was held sacred to the god Balder, while the Romans believed it to be the "golden bough" that gave access to Hades.[3]

---

[1] See Schrader: *Prehistoric Antiquities of the Aryan Peoples*, pp. 138, 272.
[2] A description of the Druidical cult of the mistletoe is given by Pliny: *Natural History*, XVI, chap. xcv.   [3] See Frazer: *The Golden Bough*, chap. IV.

The accounts both of the Latin and Gaelic writers give us a fairly complete idea of the nature of the Druids, and especially of the high estimation in which they were held. They were at once the priests, the physicians, the wizards, the diviners, the theologians, the scientists, and the historians of their tribes. All spiritual power and all human knowledge were vested in them, and they ranked second only to the kings and chiefs. They were freed from all contribution to the State, whether by tribute or service in war, so that they might the better apply themselves to their divine offices. Their decisions were absolutely final, and those who disobeyed them were laid under a terrible excommunication or "boycott".[1] Classic writers tell us how they lorded it in Gaul, where, no doubt, they borrowed splendour by imitating their more civilized neighbours. Men of the highest rank were proud to cast aside the insignia of mere mortal honour to join the company of those who claimed to be the direct mediators with the sky-god and the thunder-god, and who must have resembled the ecclesiastics of mediæval Europe in the days of their greatest power, combining, like them, spiritual and temporal dignities, and possessing the highest culture of their age. Yet it was not among these Druids of Gaul, with their splendid temples and vestments and their elaborate rituals, that the metropolis of Druidism was to be sought. We learn from Caesar that the Gallic Druids be-

---

[1] Caesar: *De Bello Gallico*, Book VI, chaps. XIII, XIV. But for a full exposition of what is known of the Druids the reader is referred to M. d'Arbois de Jubainville's *Introduction à l'étude de la Littérature Celtique*, Vol. I of his *Cours de Littérature Celtique*.

lieved their religion to have come to them, originally, from Britain, and that it was their practice to send their "theological students" across the Channel to learn its doctrines at their purest source.[1]   To trace a cult backwards is often to take a retrograde course in culture, and it was no doubt in Britain—which Pliny the Elder tells us "might have taught magic to Persia"[2]— that the sufficiently primitive and savage rites of the Druids of Gaul were preserved in their still more savage and primitive forms.   It is curious corroboration of this alleged British origin of Druidism that the ancient Irish also believed their Druidism to have come from the sister island.   Their heroes and seers are described as only gaining the highest knowledge by travelling to Alba.[3]   However this may be, we may take it as certain that this Druidism was the accepted religion of the Celtic race.

Certain scholars look deeper for its origin, holding its dark superstitions and savage rites to bear the stamp of lower minds than those of the poetic and manly Celts.   Professor Rhys inclines to see three forms of religion in the British Islands at the time of the Roman invasion: the "Druidism" of the Iberian aborigines; the pure polytheism of the Brythons, who, having come later into the country, had mixed but little with the natives; and the mingled Aryan and non-Aryan cults of the Goidels, who were already largely amalgamated with them.[4]

[1] Caesar: *De Bello Gallico*, Book VI, chap. XIII.
[2] Pliny: *Natural History*, XXX.
[3] See chap. XII, *The Irish Iliad*.
[4] Rhys: *Celtic Britain*, chap. II.   See also Gomme: *Ethnology in Folk-lore*, pp. 58–62; *Village Community*, p. 104.

But many authorities dissent from this view, and, indeed, we are not obliged to postulate borrowing from tribes in a lower state of culture, to explain primitive and savage features underlying a higher religion. The "Aryan" nations must have passed, equally with all others, through a state of pure savagery; and we know that the religion of the Greeks, in many respects so lofty, sheltered features and legends as barbarous as any that can be attributed to the Celts.[1]

Of the famous teaching of the Druids we know little, owing to their habit of never allowing their doctrines to be put into writing. Caesar, however, roughly records its scope. "As one of their leading dogmas", he says, "they inculcate this: that souls are not annihilated, but pass after death from one body to another, and they hold that by this teaching men are much encouraged to valour, through disregarding the fear of death. They also discuss and impart to the young many things concerning the heavenly bodies and their movements, the size of the world and of our earth, natural science, and of the influence and power of the immortal gods."[2] The Romans seem to have held their wisdom in some awe, though it is not unlikely that the Druids themselves borrowed whatever knowledge they may have had of science and philosophy from the classical culture. That their creed of transmigration was not, however, merely taken over from the Greeks seems certain from its appearance in the

---

[1] Abundant evidence of this is contained in Pausanias' *Description of Greece.*
[2] Caesar: *De Bello Gallico*, Book VI, chap. XIV.

ancient Gaelic myths. Not only the "shape-shift-ing" common to the magic stories of all nations, but actual reincarnation was in the power of privileged beings. The hero Cuchulainn was urged by the men of Ulster to marry, because they knew "that his rebirth would be of himself",[1] and they did not wish so great a warrior to be lost to their tribe. Another legend tells how the famous Finn mac Coul was reborn, after two hundred years, as an Ulster king called Mongan.[2]

Such ideas, however, belonged to the metaphysical side of Druidism. Far more important to the prac-tical primitive mind are ritual and sacrifice, by the due performance of which the gods are persuaded or compelled to grant earth's increase and length of days to men. Among the Druids, this humouring of the divinities took the shape of human sacrifice, and that upon a scale which would seem to have been unsurpassed in horror even by the most savage tribes of West Africa or Polynesia. "The whole Gaulish nation", says Caesar, "is to a great degree devoted to superstitious rites; and on this account those who are afflicted with severe diseases, or who are engaged in battles and dangers, either sacrifice human beings for victims, or vow that they will immolate themselves, and these employ the Druids as ministers for such sacrifices, because they think that, unless the life of man be repaid for the life of man, the will of the immortal gods cannot be

[1] The *Wooing of Emer.*
[2] It is contained in the Book of the Dun Cow, and has been translated or com-mented upon by Eugene O'Curry (*Manners and Customs of the Ancient Irish*), De Jubainville (*Cycle Mythologique Irlandais*), and Nutt (*Voyage of Bran*).

appeased. They also ordain national offerings of the
same kind. Others make wicker-work images of
vast size, the limbs of which they fill with living men
and set on fire."[1]

We find evidence of similarly awful customs in
pagan Ireland. Among the oldest Gaelic records
are tracts called *Dinnsenchus*, in which famous places
are enumerated, together with the legends relating
to them. Such topographies are found in several of
the great Irish mediæval manuscripts, and therefore,
of course, received their final transcription at the
hands of Christian monks. But these ecclesiastics
rarely tampered with compositions in elaborate
verse. Nor can it be imagined that any monastic
scribe could have invented such a legend as this one
which describes the practice of human sacrifice among
the ancient Irish. The poem (which is found in the
Books of Leinster, of Ballymote, of Lecan, and in a
document called the Rennes MS.)[2] records the reason
why a spot near the present village of Ballymagauran,
in County Cavan, received the name of Mag Slecht,
the " Plain of Adoration ".

> " Here used to be
> A high idol with many fights,
> Which was named the Cromm Cruaich;
> It made every tribe to be without peace.

> " 'T was a sad evil!
> Brave Gaels used to worship it.

---

[1] Caesar: *De Bello Gallico*, Book VI, chap. XVI.

[2] The following translation was made by Dr. Kuno Meyer, and appears as
Appendix B to Nutt's *Voyage of Bran*. Three verses, here omitted, will be found
later as a note to chap. XII—" The Irish Iliad ".

From it they would not without tribute ask
To be satisfied as to their portion of the hard world.

" He was their god,
The withered Cromm with many mists,
The people whom he shook over every host,
The everlasting kingdom they shall not have.

" To him without glory
They would kill their piteous, wretched offspring
With much wailing and peril,
To pour their blood around Cromm Cruaich.

" Milk and corn
They would ask from him speedily
In return for one-third of their healthy issue:
Great was the horror and the scare of him.

" To him
Noble Gaels would prostrate themselves,
From the worship of him, with many manslaughters,
The plain is called " Mag Slecht".

    .   .   .   .   .   .

" They did evil,
They beat their palms, they pounded their bodies,
Wailing to the demon who enslaved them,
They shed falling showers of tears.

    .   .   .   .   .   .

" Around Cromm Cruaich
There the hosts would prostrate themselves;
Though he put them under deadly disgrace,
Their name clings to the noble plain.

" In their ranks (stood)
Four times three stone idols;
To bitterly beguile the hosts,
The figure of the Cromm was made of gold.

" Since the rule
Of Herimon[1], the noble man of grace,
There was worshipping of stones
Until the coming of good Patrick of Macha.

" A sledge-hammer to the Cromm
He applied from crown to sole,
He destroyed without lack of valour
The feeble idol which was there."

Such, we gather from a tradition which we may
deem authentic, was human sacrifice in early Ireland.
According to the quoted verse, one third of the
healthy children were slaughtered, presumably every
year, to wrest from the powers of nature the grain
and grass upon which the tribes and their cattle sub-
sisted.   In a prose *dinnsenchus* preserved in the
Rennes MS.,[2] there is a slight variant.   " 'T is
there", (at Mag Slecht), it runs, " was the king idol
of Erin, namely the Crom Croich, and around him
were twelve idols made of stones, but he was of
gold.   Until Patrick's advent he was the god of
every folk that colonized Ireland.   To him they
used to offer the firstlings of every issue and the
chief scions of every clan."   The same authority
also tells us that these sacrifices were made at
" Hallowe'en", which took the place, in the Christian calendar, of the heathen *Samhain*—" Summer's
End " — when the sun's power waned, and the
strength of the gods of darkness, winter, and the
underworld grew great.

---

[1] The first King of the Milesians.   The name is more usually spelt Eremon.
[2] The Rennes *Dinnsenchus* has been translated by Dr. Whitley Stokes in Vol. XVI
of the *Revue Celtique*.

Who, then, was this bloodthirsty deity? His name, *Cromm Cruaich*, means the "Bowed One of the Mound", and was evidently applied to him only after his fall from godhead. It relates to the tradition that, at the approach of the all-conquering Saint Patrick, the "demon" fled from his golden image, which thereupon sank forward in the earth in homage to the power that had come to supersede it.[1] But from another source we glean that the word *cromm* was a kind of pun upon *cenn*, and that the real title of the "king idol of Erin" was *Cenn Cruaich*, "Head" or "Lord" of the Mound. Professor Rhys, in his *Celtic Heathendom*,[2] suggests that he was probably the Gaelic heaven-god, worshipped, like the Hellenic Zeus, upon "high places", natural or artificial. At any rate, we may see in him the god most revered by the Gaels, surrounded by the other twelve chief members of their Pantheon.

It would appear probable that the Celtic State worship was what is called "solar". All its chief festivals related to points in the sun's progress, the equinoxes having been considered more important than the solstices. It was at the spring equinox (called by the Celts "Beltaine"[3]) in every nineteenth year that, we learn from Diodorus the Sicilian, a writer contemporary with Julius Caesar, Apollo himself appeared to his worshippers, and was seen harping and dancing in the sky until the rising of the Pleiades.[4] The other corresponding festival was

---

[1] Told in the Tripartite Life of Saint Patrick, a fifteenth-century combination of three very ancient Gaelic MSS.

[2] The *Hibbert Lectures* for 1886. Lecture II—"The Zeus of the Insular Celts".

[3] Pronounced *Baltinna*. [4] *Diodorus Siculus*: Book II, chap. III

"Samhain"[1], the autumn equinox. As Beltaine marked the beginning of summer, so Samhain recorded its end. The summer solstice was also a great Celtic feast. It was held at the beginning of August in honour of the god called Lugus by the Gauls, Lugh by the Gaels, and Lleu by the Britons —the pan-Celtic Apollo, and, probably, when the cult of the war-god had fallen from its early prominence, the chief figure of the common Pantheon.

It was doubtless at Stonehenge that the British Apollo was thus seen harping and dancing. That marvellous structure well corresponds to Diodorus's description of a "magnificent temple of Apollo" which he locates "in the centre of Britain". "It is a circular enclosure," he says, "adorned with votive offerings and tablets with Greek inscriptions suspended by travellers upon the walls. The rulers of the temple and city are called 'Boreadæ'[2], and they take up the government from each other according to the order of their tribes. The citizens are given up to music, harping and chanting in honour of the sun."[3] Stonehenge, therefore, was a sacred religious centre, equally revered by and equally belonging to all the British tribes—a Rome or Jerusalem of our ancient paganism.

The same great gods were, no doubt, adored by all the Celts, not only of Great Britain and Ireland, but of Continental Gaul as well. Sometimes they can be traced by name right across the ancient

---

[1] Pronounced *Sowin*.
[2] It has been suggested that this title is an attempt to reproduce the ancient British word for "bards".   [3] *Diodorus Siculus*: Book II, chap. III.

Celtic world. In other cases, what is obviously the same personified power of nature is found in various places with the same attributes, but with a different title. Besides these, there must have been a multitude of lesser gods, worshipped by certain tribes alone, to whom they stood as ancestors and guardians. " I swear by the gods of my people", was the ordinary oath of a hero in the ancient Gaelic sagas. The aboriginal tribes must also have had their gods, whether it be true or not that their religion influenced the Celtic Druidism. Professor Rhys inclines to see in the *genii locorum*, the almost nameless spirits of well and river, mountain and wood—shadowy remnants of whose cults survive today,—members of a swarming Pantheon of the older Iberians.[1] These local beings would in no way conflict with the great Celtic nature-gods, and the two worships could exist side by side, both even claiming the same votary. It needs the stern faith of monotheism to deny the existence of the gods of others. Polytheistic nations have seldom or never risen to such a height. In their dealings with a conquered people, the conquerors naturally held their own gods to be the stronger. Still, it could not be denied that the gods of the conquered were upon their own ground; they knew, so to speak, the country, and might have unguessed powers of doing evil! What if, to avenge their worshippers and themselves, they were to make the land barren and useless to the conquerors? So that conquering pagan nations have usually been quite ready to stretch out the hand of

[1] *Hibbert Lectures*, 1886. Lecture I—" The Gaulish Pantheon"

welcome to the deities of their new subjects, to propitiate them by sacrifice, and even to admit them
within the pale of their own Pantheon.

This raises the question of the exact nationality of
the gods whose stories we are about to tell. Were
they all Aryan, or did any of the greater aboriginal
deities climb up to take their place among the Gaelic
tribe of the goddess Danu, or the British children
of the goddess Dôn? Some of the Celtic gods have
seemed to scholars to bear signs of a non-Aryan
origin.[1] The point, however, is at present very
obscure. Neither does it much concern us. Just
as the diverse deities of the Greeks—some Aryan
and Hellenic, some pre-Aryan and Pelasgian, some
imported and Semitic—were all gathered into one
great divine family, so we may consider as members
of one national Olympus all these gods whose
legends make up "The Mythology of the British
Islands".

[1] See Rhys: *Lectures on Welsh Philology*, pp. 426, 552, 653.

THE GAELIC GODS AND THEIR STORIES

CHAPTER V

THE GODS OF THE GAELS

Of the two Celtic races that settled in our islands, it is the earlier, the Gaels, that has best preserved its old mythology. It is true that we have in few cases such detailed account of the Gaelic gods as we gain of the Hellenic deities from the Greek poets, of the Indian Devas from the Rig Veda, or of the Norse Æsir from the Eddas. Yet none the less may we draw from the ancient Irish manuscripts quite enough information to enable us to set forth their figures with some clearness. We find them, as might have been anticipated, very much like the divine hierarchies of other Aryan peoples.

We also find them separated into two opposing camps, a division common to all the Aryan religions. Just as the Olympians struggled with the Giants, the Æsir fought the Jötuns, and the Devas the Asuras, so there is warfare in the Gaelic spiritual world between two superhuman hosts. On one side are ranged the gods of day, light, life, fertility, wisdom, and good; on the other, the demons of night, darkness, death, barrenness, and evil. The first were the great spirits symbolizing the beneficial aspects of nature and the arts and intelligence of man; the second were the hostile powers thought to be behind such baneful manifestations as storm and

fog, drought and disease. The first are ranged as
a divine family round a goddess called Danu, from
whom they took their well-known name of *Tuatha
Dé Danann*,[1] "Tribe" or "Folk of the Goddess
Danu". The second owned allegiance to a female
divinity called Domnu; their king, Indech, is described as her son, and they are all called "Domnu's
gods". The word "Domnu" appears to have signified the abyss or the deep sea,[2] and the same
idea is also expressed in their better-known name of
"Fomors", derived from two Gaelic words meaning
"under sea".[3] The waste of water seems to have
always impressed the Celts with the sense of primeval ancientness; it was connected in their minds
with vastness, darkness, and monstrous births—the
very antithesis of all that was symbolized by the
earth, the sky, and the sun.

Therefore the Fomors were held to be more
ancient than the gods, before whom they were,
however, destined to fall in the end. Offspring of
"Chaos and Old Night", they were, for the most
part, huge and deformed. Some had but one arm
and one leg apiece, while others had the heads of
goats, horses, or bulls.[4] The most famous, and
perhaps the most terrible of them all was Balor,
whose father is said to have been one Buarainech,
that is, the "cow-faced",[5] and who combined in himself the two classical rôles of the Cyclops and the
Medusa. Though he had two eyes, one was always

---

[1] Pronounced *Toodha dae donnann.*
[2] Rhys: *Hibbert Lectures,* 1886. **Lecture VI**—"Gods, Demons, and Heroes".
[3] *Ibid.*   [4] De Jubainville: *Le Cycle Mythologique Irlandais,* chap. V.
[5] De Jubainville: *Cycle Mythologique Irlandais,* chap. IX.

kept shut, for it was so venomous that it slew anyone on whom its look fell. This malignant quality
of Balor's eye was not natural to him, but was the
result of an accident. Urged by curiosity, he once
looked in at the window of a house where his
father's sorcerers were preparing a magic potion,
and the poisonous smoke from the cauldron reached
his eye, infecting it with so much of its own deadly
nature as to make it disastrous to others. Neither
god nor giant seems to have been exempt from its
dangers; so that Balor was only allowed to live on
condition that he kept his terrible eye shut. On
days of battle he was placed opposite to the enemy,
the lid of the destroying eye was lifted up with a
hook, and its gaze withered all who stood before it.
The memory of Balor and his eye still lingers in
Ireland : the " eye of Balor" is the name for what
the peasantry of other countries call the " evil eye";
stories are still told of *Balar Beimann*, or " Balor of
the Mighty Blows"; and " Balor's Castle" is the name
of a curious cliff on Tory Island. This island, off
the coast of Donegal, was the Fomorian outpost
upon earth, their real abode being in the cold depths
of the sea.

This rule, however, as to the hideousness of the
Fomors had its exceptions. Elathan, one of their
chiefs, is described in an old manuscript as of
magnificent presence — a Miltonic prince of darkness. "A man of fairest form," it says, "with
golden hair down to his shoulders. He wore a
mantle of gold braid over a shirt interwoven with
threads of gold. Five golden necklaces were round

his neck, and a brooch of gold with a shining precious stone thereon was on his breast. He carried two silver spears with rivets of bronze, and his sword was golden-hilted and golden-studded."[1] Nor was his son less handsome. His name was Bress, which means "beautiful", and we are told that every beautiful thing in Ireland, "whether plain, or fortress, or ale, or torch, or woman, or man", was compared with him, so that men said of them, "that is a Bress".[2]

Balor, Bress, and Elathan are the three Fomorian personages whose figures, seen through the mists of antiquity, show clearest to us. But they are only a few out of many, nor are they the oldest. We can learn, however, nothing but a few names of any ancestors of the Gaelic giants. This is equally true of the Gaelic gods. Those we know are evidently not without parentage, but the names of their fathers are no more than shadows following into oblivion the figures they designated. The most ancient divinity of whom we have any knowledge is Danu herself, the goddess from whom the whole hierarchy of gods received its name of Tuatha Dé Danann. She was also called Anu or Ana, and her name still clings to two well-known mountains near Killarney, which, though now called simply "The Paps", were known formerly as the "Paps of Ana".[3] She was the

---

[1] From the fifteenth-century Harleian MS. in the British Museum, numbered 5280, and called the *Second Battle of Moytura*.   [2] Harleian MS. 5280.

[3] "In Munster was worshipped the goddess of prosperity, whose name was Ana, and from her are named the Two Paps of Ana over Luachair Degad." From *Coir Anmann*, the *Choice of Names*, a sixteenth-century tract, published by Dr. Whitley Stokes in *Irische Texte*.

universal mother; "well she used to cherish the gods", says the commentator of a ninth-century Irish glossary.[1] Her husband is never mentioned by name, but one may assume him, from British analogies, to have been Bilé, known to Gaelic tradition as a god of Hades, a kind of Celtic Dis Pater from whom sprang the first men. Danu herself probably represented the earth and its fruitfulness, and one might compare her with the Greek Demeter. All the other gods are, at least by title, her children. The greatest of these would seem to have been Nuada, called *Argetlám*, or "He of the Silver Hand". He was at once the Gaelic Zeus, or Jupiter, and their war-god; for among primitive nations, to whom success in war is all-important, the god of battles is the supreme god.[2] Among the Gauls, Camulus, whose name meant "Heaven",[3] was identified by the Romans with Mars; and other such instances come readily to the mind. He was possessed of an invincible sword, one of the four chief treasures of the Tuatha Dé Danann, over whom he was twice king; and there is little doubt that he was one of the most important gods of both the Gaels and the Britons, for his name is spread over the whole of the British Isles, which we may surmise the Celts conquered under his auspices. We may picture him as a more savage Mars, delighting in battle and slaughter, and worshipped, like his Gaulish affinities, Teutates and Hesus, of whom the

[1] Attributed to Cormac, King-Bishop of Cashel.
[2] Rhys: *Hibbert Lectures*, 1886—"The Zeus of the Insular Celts".
[3] Rhys: *Hibbert Lectures*, 1886—"The Gaulish Pantheon".

Latin poet Lucan tells us, with human sacrifices, shared in by his female consorts, who, we may imagine, were not more merciful than himself, or than that Gaulish Taranis whose cult was "no gentler than that of the Scythian Diana", and who completes Lucan's triad as a fit companion to the "pitiless Teutates" and the "horrible Hesus".[1] Of these warlike goddesses there were five—Fea, the "Hateful", Nemon, the "Venomous", Badb, the "Fury", Macha, a personification of "battle", and, over all of them, the Morrígú, or "Great Queen". This supreme war-goddess of the Gaels, who resembles a fiercer Herê, perhaps symbolized the moon, deemed by early races to have preceded the sun, and worshipped with magical and cruel rites. She is represented as going fully armed, and carrying two spears in her hand. As with Arês[2] and Poseidon[3] in the "Iliad", her battle-cry was as loud as that of ten thousand men. Wherever there was war, either among gods or men, she, the great queen, was present, either in her own shape or in her favourite disguise, that of a "hoodie" or carrion crow. An old poem shows her inciting a warrior:

> " Over his head is shrieking
>   A lean hag, quickly hopping
> Over the points of the weapons and shields;
>   She is the gray-haired Morrígú".[4]

With her, Fea and Nemon, Badb and Macha also

---

[1] *Pharsalia*, Book I, l. 444, &c.:

    " Et quibus immitis placatur sanguine diro
      Teutates, horrensque feris altaribus Hesus;
      Et Taranis Scythicae non mitior ara Dianae ".

[2] *Iliad*, Book V.   [3] *Op. cit.*, Book XIV.   [4] It commemorates the battle of Magh Rath.

hovered over the fighters, inspiring them with the madness of battle. All of these were sometimes called by the name of " Badb"[1]. An account of the Battle of Clontarf, fought by Brian Boru, in 1014, against the Norsemen, gives a gruesome picture of what the Gaels believed to happen in the spiritual world when battle lowered and men's blood was aflame. "There arose a wild, impetuous, precipitate, mad, inexorable, furious, dark, lacerating, merciless, combative, contentious *badb*, which was shrieking and fluttering over their heads. And there arose also the satyrs, and sprites, and the maniacs of the valleys, and the witches and goblins and owls, and destroying demons of the air and firmament, and the demoniac phantom host; and they were inciting and sustaining valour and battle with them." When the fight was over, they revelled among the bodies of the slain; the heads cut off as barbaric trophies were called " Macha's acorn crop". These grim creations of the savage mind had immense vitality. While Nuada, the supreme war-god, vanished early out of the Pantheon—killed by the Fomors in the great battle fought between them and the gods—Badb and the Morrígú lived on as late as any of the Gaelic deities. Indeed, they may be said to still survive in the superstitious dislike and suspicion shown in all Celtic-speaking countries for their *avatar*, the hoodie-crow.[2]

After Nuada, the greatest of the gods was the

[1] The word is approximately pronounced *Bive* or *Bibe*.
[2] For a full account of these beings see a paper by Mr. W. M. Hennessey in Vol. I of the *Revue Celtique*, entitled " The Ancient Irish Goddess of War".

Dagda, whose name seems to have meant the "Good God".[1] The old Irish tract called "The Choice of Names" tells us that he was a god of the earth; he had a cauldron called "The Undry", in which everyone found food in proportion to his merits, and from which none went away unsatisfied. He also had a living harp; as he played upon it, the seasons came in their order—spring following winter, and summer succeeding spring, autumn coming after summer, and, in its turn, giving place to winter. He is represented as of venerable aspect and of simple mind and tastes, very fond of porridge, and a valiant consumer of it. In an ancient tale we have a description of his dress. He wore a brown, low-necked tunic which only reached down to his hips, and, over this, a hooded cape which barely covered his shoulders. On his feet and legs were horse-hide boots, the hairy side outwards. He carried, or, rather, drew after him on a wheel, an eight-pronged war-club, so huge that eight men would have been needed to carry it; and the wheel, as he towed the whole weapon along, made a track like a territorial boundary.[2] Ancient and gray-headed as he was, and sturdy porridge-eater, it will be seen from this that he was a formidable fighter. He did great deeds in the battle between the gods and the Fomors, and, on one occasion, is even said to have captured single-handed a hundred-legged and four-headed monster called Mata, dragged him to the "Stone of Benn", near the Boyne, and killed him there.

---

[1] De Jubainville: *Le Cycle Mythologique.* Rhys: *Hibbert Lectures,* p. 154. The *Coir Anmann,* however, translates it "Fire of God".

[2] *The Second Battle of Moytura.* Harleian MS. 5280.

The Dagda's wife was called Boann. She was connected in legend with the River Boyne, to which she gave its name, and, indeed, its very existence.[1] Formerly there was only a well[2], shaded by nine magic hazel-trees. These trees bore crimson nuts, and it was the property of the nuts that whoever ate of them immediately became possessed of the knowledge of everything that was in the world. The story is, in fact, a Gaelic version of the Hebrew myth of "the Tree of the Knowledge of Good and Evil". One class of creatures alone had this privilege—divine salmon who lived in the well, and swallowed the nuts as they dropped from the trees into the water, and thus knew all things, and appear in legend as the "Salmons of Knowledge". All others, even the highest gods, were forbidden to approach the place. Only Boann, with the proverbial woman's curiosity, dared to disobey this fixed law. She came towards the sacred well, but, as she did so, its waters rose up at her, and drove her away before them in a mighty, rushing flood. She escaped; but the waters never returned. They made the Boyne; and as for the all-knowing inhabitants of the well, they wandered disconsolately through the depths of the river, looking in vain for their lost nuts. One of these salmon was afterwards eaten by the famous Finn mac Coul, upon whom all its omniscience descended.[3] This way of accounting for the existence of a river is a favourite one in Irish legend. It is told also of the Shannon, which burst,

[1] The story is told in the Book of Leinster.   [2] Now called "Trinity Well".
[3] See chap. XIV—"Finn and the Fenians".

like the Boyne, from an inviolable well, to pursue another presumptuous nymph called Sinann, a grand-daughter of the sea-god Lêr.[1]

The Dagda had several children, the most important of whom are Brigit, Angus, Mider, Ogma, and Bodb the Red. Of these, Brigit will be already familiar to English readers who know nothing of Celtic myth. Originally she was a goddess of fire and the hearth, as well as of poetry, which the Gaels deemed an immaterial, supersensual form of flame. But the early Christianizers of Ireland adopted the pagan goddess into their roll of saint-ship, and, thus canonized, she obtained immense popularity as Saint Bridget, or Bride.[2]

Angus was called *Mac Oc*, which means the "Son of the Young", or, perhaps, the "Young God". This most charming of the creations of the Celtic mythology is represented as a Gaelic Eros, an eternally youthful exponent of love and beauty. Like his father, he had a harp, but it was of gold, not oak, as the Dagda's was, and so sweet was its music that no one could hear and not follow it. His kisses became birds which hovered invisibly over the young men and maidens of Erin, whispering thoughts of love into their ears. He is chiefly connected with the banks of the Boyne, where he had a "brugh", or fairy palace; and many stories are told of his exploits and adventures.

Mider, also the hero of legends, would seem to have been a god of the underworld, a Gaelic

---

[1] Book of Leinster. A paraphrase of the story will be found in O'Curry's *Manners and Customs of the Ancient Irish*, Vol. II, p. 143.

[2] See chap. xv—"The Decline and Fall of the Gods".

Pluto. As such, he was connected with the Isle of Falga—a name for what was otherwise, and still is, called the Isle of Man—where he had a stronghold in which he kept three wonderful cows and a magic cauldron. He was also the owner of the "Three Cranes of Denial and Churlishness", which might be described flippantly as personified "gentle hints". They stood beside his door, and when anyone approached to ask for hospitality, the first one said: "Do not come! do not come!" and the second added: "Get away! get away!" while the third chimed in with: "Go past the house! go past the house!"[1] These three birds were, however, stolen from Mider by Aitherne, an avaricious poet, to whom they would seem to have been more appropriate than to their owner, who does not otherwise appear as a churlish and illiberal deity.[2] On the contrary, he is represented as the victim of others, who plundered him freely. The god Angus took away his wife Etain,[3] while his cows, his cauldron, and his beautiful daughter Blathnat were carried off as spoil by the heroes or demi-gods who surrounded King Conchobar in the golden age of Ulster.

Ogma, who appears to have been also called Cermait, that is, the "honey-mouthed", was the god of literature and eloquence. He married Etan, the daughter of Diancecht, the god of medicine, and had several children, who play parts more or less prominent in the mythology of the Gaelic Celts. One of them was called Tuirenn, whose

---

[1] Rhys: *Hibbert Lectures*, p. 331.   [2] Rhys: *Hibbert Lectures*, p. 331.
[3] See chap. XI—"The Gods in Exile".

three sons murdered the father of the sun-god, and were compelled, as expiation, to pay the greatest fine ever heard of—nothing less than the chief treasures of the world.[1]   Another son, Cairpré, became the professional bard of the Tuatha Dé Danann, while three others reigned for a short time over the divine race.   As patron of literature, Ogma was naturally credited with having been the inventor of the famous *Ogam* alphabet.   This was an indigenous script of Ireland, which spread afterwards to Great Britain, inscriptions in ogmic characters having been found in Scotland, the Isle of Man, South Wales, Devonshire, and at Silchester in Hampshire, the Roman city of Calleva Attrebatum.   It was originally intended for inscriptions upon upright pillar-stones or upon wands, the equivalents for letters being notches cut across, or strokes made upon one of the faces of the angle, the alphabet running as follows:

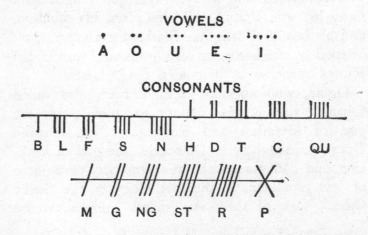

VOWELS

A   O   U   E   I

CONSONANTS

B   L   F   S   N   H   D   T   C   QU

M   G   NG   ST   R   P

[1] See chap. VIII—"The Gaelic Argonauts".

When afterwards written in manuscript, the strokes were placed over, under, or through a horizontal line, in the manner above; and the vowels were represented by short lines instead of notches, as:

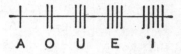

A good example of an ogmic inscription is given in Professor Rhys's *Hibbert Lectures.* It comes from a pillar on a small promontory near Dunmore Head, in the west of Kerry, and, read horizontally, reads:

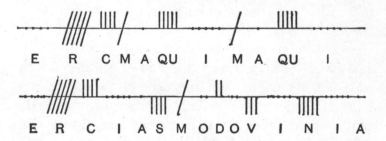

ERC, THE SON OF THE SON OF ERCA (DESCENDANT OF) MODOVINIA.[1]

The origin of this alphabet is obscure. Some authorities consider it of great antiquity, while others believe it entirely post-Christian. It seems, at any rate, to have been based upon, and consequently to presuppose a knowledge of, the Roman alphabet.

Ogma, besides being the patron of literature, was the champion, or professional strong man of the Tuatha Dé Danann. His epithet is *Grianainech,*

[1] Rhys: *Hibbert Lectures,* p. 524.

that is, the "Sunny-faced", from his radiant and shining countenance.

The last of the Dagda's more important children is Bodb[1] the Red, who plays a greater part in later than in earlier legend. He succeeded his father as king of the gods. He is chiefly connected with the south of Ireland, especially with the Galtee Mountains, and with Lough Dearg, where he had a famous *sídh*, or underground palace.

The Poseidon of the Tuatha Dé Danann Pantheon was called Lêr, but we hear little of him in comparison with his famous son, Manannán, the greatest and most popular of his many children. Manannán mac Lir[2] was the special patron of sailors, who invoked him as "God of Headlands", and of merchants, who claimed him as the first of their guild. His favourite haunts were the Isle of Man, to which he gave his name, and the Isle of Arran, in the Firth of Clyde, where he had a palace called "Emhain of the Apple-Trees". He had many famous weapons —two spears called "Yellow Shaft" and "Red Javelin", a sword called "The Retaliator", which never failed to slay, as well as two others known as the "Great Fury" and the "Little Fury". He had a boat called "Wave-sweeper", which propelled and guided itself wherever its owner wished, and a horse called "Splendid Mane", which was swifter than the spring wind, and travelled equally fast on land or over the waves of the sea. No weapon could hurt him through his magic mail and breast-plate, and on his helmet there shone two magic jewels

---

[1] Pronounced *Bove*.   [2] Lêr—genitive Lir.

bright as the sun. He endowed the gods with the mantle which made them invisible at will, and he fed them from his pigs, which, like the boar Sæhrimnir, in the Norse Valhalla, renewed themselves as soon as they had been eaten. Of these, no doubt, he made his "Feast of Age", the banquet at which those who ate never grew old. Thus the people of the goddess Danu preserved their immortal youth, while the ale of Goibniu the Smith-God bestowed invulnerability upon them. It is fitting that Manannán himself should have been blessed beyond all the other gods with inexhaustible life; up to the latest days of Irish heroic literature his luminous figure shines prominent, nor is it even yet wholly forgotten.

Goibniu, the Gaelic Hephaestus, who made the people of the goddess Danu invulnerable with his magic drink, was also the forger of their weapons. It was he who, helped by Luchtainé, the divine carpenter, and Credné, the divine bronze-worker, made the armoury with which the Tuatha Dé Danann conquered the Fomors. Equally useful to them was Diancecht, the god of medicine.[1] It was he who once saved Ireland, and was indirectly the cause of the name of the River Barrow. The Morrígú, the heaven-god's fierce wife, had borne a son of such terrible aspect that the physician of the gods, foreseeing danger, counselled that he should be destroyed in his infancy. This was done; and Diancecht opened the infant's heart, and found

---

[1] Pronounced *Dianket*. His name is explained, both in the *Choice of Names* and in Cormac's *Glossary*, as meaning "God of Health".

within it three serpents, capable, when they grew to full size, of depopulating Ireland. He lost no time in destroying these serpents also, and burning them into ashes, to avoid the evil which even their dead bodies might do. More than this, he flung the ashes into the nearest river, for he feared that there might be danger even in them; and, indeed, so venomous were they that the river boiled up and slew every living creature in it, and therefore has been called " Barrow" (boiling) ever since.[1]

Diancecht had several children, of whom two followed their father's profession. These were Miach and his sister Airmid. There were also another daughter, Etan, who married Cermait (or Ogma), and three other sons called Cian, Cethé, and Cu. Cian married Ethniu, the daughter of Balor the Fomor, and they had a son who was the crowning glory of the Gaelic Pantheon—its Apollo, the Sun-God,—Lugh[2], called *Lamhfada*[3], which means the "Long-handed", or the "Far-shooter". It was not, however, with the bow, like the Apollo of the Greeks, but with the rod-sling that Lugh performed his feats; his worshippers sometimes saw the terrible weapon in the sky as a rainbow, and the Milky Way was called "Lugh's Chain". He also had a magic spear, which, unlike the rod-sling, he had no need to wield, himself; for it was alive, and thirsted so for blood that only by steeping its head in a sleeping-draught of pounded poppy leaves could it be kept at rest. When battle was near, it

---

[1] Standish O'Grady: *The Story of Ireland*, p. 17.
[2] Pronounced *Luga* or *Loo*.
[3] Pronounced *Lavăda*.

was drawn out; then it roared, and struggled against its thongs; fire flashed from it; and, once slipped from the leash, it tore through and through the ranks of the enemy, never tired of slaying. Another of his possessions was a magic hound which an ancient poem,[1] attributed to the Fenian hero, Caoilte, calls—

> "That hound of mightiest deeds,
> Which was irresistible in hardness of combat,
> Was better than wealth ever known,
> A ball of fire every night.

> "Other virtues had that beautiful hound
> (Better this property than any other property),
> Mead or wine would grow of it,
> Should it bathe in spring water."

This marvellous hound, as well as the marvellous spear, and the indestructible pigs of Manannán were obtained for Lugh by the sons of Tuirenn as part of the blood-fine he exacted from them for the murder of his father Cian.[2] A hardly less curious story is that which tells how Lugh got his name of the *Ioldanach*, or the "Master of All Arts".[3]

These are, of course, only the greater deities of the Gaelic Pantheon, their divinities which answered to such Hellenic figures as Demeter, Zeus, Herê, Cronos, Athena, Eros, Hades, Hermes, Hephaestus, Aesculapius, and Apollo. All of them had many descendants, some of whom play prominent parts

---

[1] Translated by O'Curry in *Atlantis*, Vol. III, from the Book of Lismore.
[2] Chap. VIII—"The Gaelic Argonauts".
[3] Chap. VII—"The Rise of the Sun-God".

in the heroic cycles of the " Red Branch of Ulster '
and of the " Fenians ".   In addition to these, there
must have been a multitude of lesser gods who
stood in much the same relation to the great gods
as the rank and file of tribesmen did to their chiefs.
Most of these were probably local deities of the
various clans—the gods their heroes swore by.   But
it is also possible that some may have been divinities of the aboriginal race.   Professor Rhys thinks
that he can still trace a few of such Iberian gods by
name, as Nêt, Ri or Roi, Corb, and Beth.[1]   But
they play no recognizable part in the stories of the
Gaelic gods.

[1] Rhys: *Celtic Britain*, chap. VII.

CHAPTER VI

THE GODS ARRIVE

The people of the goddess Danu were not the first divine inhabitants of Ireland. Others had been before them, dwellers in "the dark backward and abysm of time". In this the Celtic mythology resembles those of other nations, in almost all of which we find an old, dim realm of gods standing behind the reigning Pantheon. Such were Cronos and the Titans, dispossessed by the Zeus who seemed, even to Hesiod, something of a *parvenu* deity. Gaelic tradition recognizes two divine dynasties anterior to the Tuatha Dé Danann. The first of these was called "The Race of Partholon". Its head and leader came—as all gods and men came, according to Celtic ideas—from the Other World, and landed in Ireland with a retinue of twenty-four males and twenty-four females upon the first of May, the day called "Beltaine", sacred to Bilé, the god of death. At this remote time, Ireland consisted of only one treeless, grassless plain, watered by three lakes and nine rivers. But, as the race of Partholon increased, the land stretched, or widened, under them—some said miraculously, and others, by the labours of Partholon's people. At any rate, during the three hundred years they dwelt there, it grew from one plain to four, and acquired seven new lakes; which was fortunate, for the race of Partholon increased from forty-eight members to five thousand, in spite of battles with the Fomors.

These would seem to have been inevitable. Whatever gods ruled, they found themselves in eternal opposition to the not-gods—the powers of darkness, winter, evil, and death. The race of Partholon warred against them with success. At the Plain of Ith, Partholon defeated their leader, a gigantic demon called Cichol the Footless, and dispersed his deformed and monstrous host. After this there was quiet for three hundred years. Then —upon the same fatal first of May—there began a mysterious epidemic, which lasted a week, and destroyed them all. In premonition of their end, they foregathered upon the original, first-created plain— then called *Sen Mag*, or the "Old Plain",—so that those who survived might the more easily bury those that died. Their funeral-place is still marked by a mound near Dublin, called "Tallaght" in the maps, but formerly known as *Tamlecht Muintre Partholain*, the "Plague-grave of Partholon's People". This would seem to have been a development of the very oldest form of the legend— which knew nothing of a plague, but merely represented the people of Partholon as having returned, after their sojourn in Ireland, to the other world, whence they came—and is probably due to the gradual euhemerization of the ancient gods into ancient men.

Following the race of Partholon, came the race

of Nemed, which carried on the work and traditions of its forerunner. During its time, Ireland again enlarged herself, to the extent of twelve new plains and four more lakes. Like the people of Partholon, the race of Nemed struggled with the Fomors, and defeated them in four consecutive battles. Then Nemed died, with two thousand of his people, from an epidemic, and the remnant, left without their leader, were terribly oppressed by the Fomors. Two Fomorian kings — Morc, son of Dela, and Conann, son of Febar—had built a tower of glass upon Tory Island, always their chief stronghold, and where stories of them still linger, and from this vantage-point they dictated a tax which recalls that paid, in Greek story, to the Cretan Minotaur. Two-thirds of the children born to the race of Nemed during the year were to be delivered up on each day of Samhain. Goaded by this to a last desperate effort, the survivors of Nemed's people attacked the tower, and took it, Conann perishing in the struggle. But their triumph was short. Morc, the other king, collected his forces, and inflicted such a slaughter upon the people of Nemed that, out of the sixteen thousand who had assembled for the storming of the tower, only thirty survived. And these returned whence they came, or died—the two acts being, mythologically speaking, the same.[1]

One cannot help seeing a good deal of similarity between the stories of these two mythical invasions of Ireland. Especially noticeable is the account of

---

[1] De Jubainville: *Cycle Mythologique*, chap. v.

the epidemic which destroyed all Partholon's people
and nearly all of Nemed's. Hence it has been held
that the two legends are duplicates, and that there
was at first only one, which has been adapted somewhat differently by two races, the Iberians and the
Gaels. Professor Rhys considers[1] the account of
Nemed to have been the original Celtic one, and
the Partholon story, the version of it which the
native races made to please themselves. The name
"Partholon", with its initial *p*, is entirely foreign to
the genius of Gaelic speech. Moreover, Partholon
himself is given, by the early chroniclers, ancestors
whose decidedly non-Aryan names reappear afterwards as the names of Fir Bolg chiefs. Nemed was
later than Partholon in Ireland, as the Gaels, or "Milesians", were later than the Iberians, or "Fir Bolgs".

These "Fir Bolgs" are found in myth as the
next colonizers of Ireland. Varying traditions say
that they came from Greece, or from "Spain"—
which was a post - Christian euphemism for the
Celtic Hades.[2] They consisted of three tribes,
called the "Fir Domnann" or "Men of Domnu",
the "Fir Gaillion" or "Men of Gaillion", and the
"Fir Bolg" or "Men of Bolg"; but, in spite of the
fact that the first-named tribe was the most important, they are usually called collectively after
the last. Curious stories are told of their life in
Greece, and how they came to Ireland; but these
are somewhat factitious, and obviously do not belong to the earliest tradition.

[1] Rhys: "The Mythographical Treatment of Celtic Ethnology", *Scottish Review*, Oct. 1890.

[2] De Jubainville: *Cycle Mythologique*, chap. v. Rhys: *Hibbert Lectures*, pp. 90, 91.

In the time of their domination they had, we are told, partitioned Ireland among them: the Fir Bolg held Ulster; the Fir Domnann, divided into three kingdoms, occupied North Munster, South Munster, and Connaught; while the Fir Gaillion owned Leinster. These five provinces met at a hill then called "Balor's Hill", but afterwards the "Hill of Uisnech". It is near Rathconrath, in the county of West Meath, and was believed, in early times, to mark the exact centre of Ireland. They held the country from the departure of the people of Nemed to the coming of the people of the goddess Danu, and during this period they had nine supreme kings. At the time of the arrival of the gods, their king's name was Eochaid[1] son of Erc, surnamed "The Proud".

We have practically no other details regarding their life in Ireland. It is obvious, however, that they were not really gods, but the pre-Aryan race which the Gaels, when they landed in Ireland, found already in occupation. There are many instances of peoples at a certain stage of culture regarding tribes in a somewhat lower one as semi-divine, or, rather, half-diabolical.[2] The suspicion and fear with which the early Celts must have regarded the savage aborigines made them seem "larger than human". They feared them for the weird magical rites which they practised in their inaccessible forts among the hills, amid storms and mountain mists. The Gaels, who held themselves to be the children of light, deemed these "dark Iberians" children of

---

[1] Pronounced *Ecca* or *Eohee*.

[2] Gomme: *Ethnology in Folklore*, chap. III—"The Mythic Influence of a Conquered Race".

the dark. Their tribal names seem to have been, in several instances, founded upon this idea. There were the *Corca-Oidce* (" People of Darkness ") and the *Corca-Duibhne* (" People of the Night "). The territory of the western tribe of the *Hi Dorchaide* (" Sons of Dark ") was called the " Night Country ".[1] The Celts, who held their own gods to have preceded them into Ireland, would not believe that even the Tuatha Dé Danann could have wrested the land from these magic-skilled Iberians without battle.

They seem also to have been considered as in some way connected with the Fomors. Just as the largest Iberian tribe was called the " Men of Domnu ", so the Fomors were called the " Gods of Domnu ", and Indech, one of their kings, is a "son of Domnu ". Thus eternal battle between the gods, children of Danu, and the giants, children of Domnu, would reflect, in the supernatural world, the perpetual warfare between invading Celt and resisting Iberian. It is shadowed, too, in the later heroic cycle. The champions of Ulster, Aryans and Gaels *par excellence*, have no such bitter enemies as the Fir Domnann of Munster and the Fir Gaillion of Leinster. A few scholars would even see in the later death-struggle between the High King of Ireland and his rebellious Fenians the last historic or mythological adumbration of racial war.[2]

The enemies alike of Fir Bolg and Fomor, the

---

[1] Elton: *Origins of English History,* note to p. 136.

[2] It has been contended that the Fenians were originally the gods or heroes of an aboriginal people in Ireland, the myths about them representing the pre-Celtic and pre-Aryan ideal, as the sagas of the Red Branch of Ulster embodied that of the Celtic Aryans. The question, however, is as yet far from being satisfactorily solved.

Tuatha Dé Danann, gods of the Gaels, were the next to arrive. What is probably the earliest account tells us that they came from the sky. Later versions, however, give them a habitation upon earth—some say in the north, others in the "southern isles of the world". They had dwelt in four mythical cities called Findias, Gorias, Murias, and Falias, where they had learned poetry and magic—to the primitive mind two not very dissimilar things—and whence they had brought to Ireland their four chief treasures. From Findias came Nuada's sword, from whose stroke no one ever escaped or recovered; from Gorias, Lugh's terrible lance; from Murias, the Dagda's cauldron; and from Falias, the Stone of Fál, better known as the "Stone of Destiny", which afterwards fell into the hands of the early kings of Ireland. According to legend, it had the magic property of uttering a human cry when touched by the rightful King of Erin. Some have recognized in this marvellous stone the same rude block which Edward I brought from Scone in the year 1300, and placed in Westminster Abbey, where it now forms part of the Coronation Chair. It is a curious fact that, while Scottish legend asserts this stone to have come to Scotland from Ireland, Irish legend should also declare that it was taken from Ireland to Scotland. This would sound like conclusive evidence, but it is none the less held by leading modern archæologists—including Dr. W. F. Skene, who has published a monograph on the subject[1]—that the Stone of Scone and the Stone of

---

[1] *The Coronation Stone*, by William Forbes Skene.

Tara were never the same. Dr. Petrie identifies the real *Lia Fáil* with a stone which has always remained in Ireland, and which was removed from its original position on Tara Hill, in 1798, to mark the tomb of the rebels buried close by under a mound now known as "the Croppies' grave".[1]

Whether the Tuatha Dé Danann came from earth or heaven, they landed in a dense cloud upon the coast of Ireland on the mystic first of May without having been opposed, or even noticed by the people whom it will be convenient to follow the manuscript authorities in calling the "Fir Bolgs".[2] That those might still be ignorant of their coming, the Morrígú, helped by Badb and Macha, made use of the magic they had learned in Findias, Gorias, Murias, and Falias. They spread "druidically-formed showers and fog-sustaining shower-clouds" over the country, and caused the air to pour down fire and blood upon the Fir Bolgs, so that they were obliged to shelter themselves for three days and three nights. But the Fir Bolgs had druids of their own, and, in the end, they put a stop to these enchantments by counter-spells, and the air grew clear again.

The Tuatha Dé Danann, advancing westward, had reached a place called the "Plain of the Sea", in Leinster, when the two armies met. Each sent out a warrior to parley. The two adversaries ap-

---

[1] See *History and Antiquities of Tara Hill.*

[2] Our authorities for the details of this war between the Tuatha Dé Danann and the Fir Bolgs are the opening verses of the Harleian MS. 5280, as translated by Stokes and De Jubainville, and Eugene O'Curry's translations, in his *MS. Materials of Ancient Irish History* and his *Manners and Customs of the Ancient Irish*, from a manuscript preserved at Trinity College, Dublin.

proached each other cautiously, their eyes peeping over the tops of their shields. Then, coming gradually nearer, they spoke to one another, and the desire to examine each other's weapons made them almost friends.

The envoy of the Fir Bolgs looked with wonder at the " beautifully-shaped, thin, slender, long, sharp-pointed spears " of the warrior of the Tuatha Dé Danann, while the ambassador of the tribe of the goddess Danu was not less impressed by the lances of the Fir Bolgs, which were " heavy, thick, point-less, but sharply-rounded ". They agreed to ex-change weapons, so that each side might, by an examination of them, be able to come to some opinion as to its opponent's strength. Before part-ing, the envoy of the Tuatha Dé Danann offered the Fir Bolgs, through their representative, peace, with a division of the country into two equal halves.

The Fir Bolg envoy advised his people to accept this offer. But their king, Eochaid, son of Erc, would not. " If we once give these people half," he said, " they will soon have the whole."

The people of the goddess Danu were, on the other hand, very much impressed by the sight of the Fir Bolgs' weapons. They decided to secure a more advantageous position, and, retreating farther west into Connaught, to a plain then called Nia, but now Moytura, near the present village of Cong, they drew up their line at its extreme end, in front of the pass of Balgatan[1], which offered a retreat in case of defeat.

[1] Now called Benlevi.

The Fir Bolgs followed them, and encamped on the nearer side of the plain. Then Nuada, King of the Tuatha Dé Danann, sent an ambassador offering the same terms as before. Again the Fir Bolgs declined them.

" Then when ", asked the envoy, " do you intend to give battle?"

" We must have a truce," they said, " for we want time to repair our armour, burnish our helmets, and sharpen our swords. Besides, we must have spears like yours made for us, and you must have spears like ours made for you."

The result of this chivalrous, but, to modern ideas, amazing, parley was that a truce of one hundred and five days was agreed upon.

It was on Midsummer Day that the opposing armies at last met. The people of the goddess Danu appeared in "a flaming line", wielding their " red-bordered, speckled, and firm shields ". Opposite to them were ranged the Fir Bolgs, "sparkling, brilliant, and flaming, with their swords, spears, blades, and trowel-spears ". The proceedings began with a kind of deadly hurley-match, in which thrice nine of the Tuatha Dé Danann played the same number of the Fir Bolgs, and were defeated and killed. Then followed another parley, to decide how the battle should be carried on, whether there should be fighting every day or only on every second day. Moreover, Nuada obtained from Eochaid an assurance that the battles should always be fought with equal numbers, although this was, we are told, "very disagreeable to the Fir Bolg king, because he had largely the advantage in the numbers of his army". Then warfare recommenced with a series of single combats, like those of the Greeks and Trojans in the " Iliad". At the end of each day the conquerors on both sides went back to their camps, and were refreshed by being bathed in healing baths of medicinal herbs.

So the fight went on for four days, with terrible slaughter upon each side. A Fir Bolg champion called Sreng fought in single combat with Nuada, the King of the Gods, and shore off his hand and half his shield with one terrific blow. Eochaid, the King of the Fir Bolgs, was even less fortunate than Nuada; for he lost his life. Suffering terribly from thirst, he went, with a hundred of his men, to look for water, and was followed, and pursued as far as the strand of Ballysadare, in Sligo. Here he turned to bay, but was killed, his grave being still marked by a tumulus. The Fir Bolgs, reduced at last to three hundred men, demanded single combat until all upon one side were slain. But, sooner than consent to this, the Tuatha Dé Danann offered them a fifth part of Ireland, whichever province they might choose. They agreed, and chose Connaught, ever afterwards their especial home, and where, until the middle of the seventeenth century, men were still found tracing their descent from Sreng.

The whole story has a singularly historical, curiously unmythological air about it, which contrasts strangely with the account of the other battle of the same name which the Tuatha Dé Danann waged

afterwards with the Fomors. The neighbourhood
of Cong still preserves both relics and traditions of
the fight. Upon the plain of " Southern Moytura "
(as it is called, to distinguish it from the " Northern
Moytura " of the second battle) are many circles
and tumuli. These circles are especially numerous
near the village itself; and it is said that there were
formerly others, which have been used for making
walls and dykes. Large cairns of stones, too, are
scattered over what was certainly once the scene of
a great battle.[1] These various prehistoric monuments each have their still - told story; and Sir
William Wilde, as he relates in his *Lough Corrib*,[2]
was so impressed by the unexpected agreement
between the details of the legendary battle, as he
read them in the ancient manuscript, and the traditions still attaching to the mounds, circles, and
cairns, that he tells us he could not help coming to
the conclusion that the account was absolutely historical. Certainly the coincidences are curious.
His opinion was that the "Fir Bolgs" were a colony
of Belgæ, and that the "Tuatha Dé Danann" were
Danes. But the people of the goddess Danu are
too obviously mythical to make it worth while to
seek any standing-ground for them in the world of
reality. In their superhuman attributes, they are
quite different from the Fir Bolgs. In the epical
cycle it is made as clear that the Tuatha Dé Danann are divine beings as it is that the Fir Bolg, the
Fir Domnann, and the Fir Gaillion stand on exactly

[1] See Dr. James Fergusson: *Rude Stone Monuments*, pp. 177–180.
[2] *Lough Corrib, Its Shores and Islands*, by Sir William R. Wilde, chap. VIII

the same footing as the men of Ulster. Later
history records by what Milesian kings and on what
terms of rack-rent the three tribes were allowed
settlements in other parts of Ireland than their
native Connaught. They appear in ancient, mediæval, and almost modern chronicles as the old race
of the land. The truth seems to be that the whole
story of the war between the gods and the Fir
Bolgs is an invention of comparatively late times.
In the earliest documents there is only one battle of
Moytura, fought between the people of the goddess
Danu and the Fomors. The idea of doubling it
seems to date from after the eleventh century;[1] and
its inventor may very well have used the legends
concerning this battle - field, where two unknown
armies had fought in days gone by, in compiling
his story. It never belonged to the same genuine
mythological stratum as the legend of the original
battle fought by the Tuatha Dé Danann, the gods
of the Gaels, against the Fomors, the gods of the
Iberians.

[1] De Jubainville: *Cycle Mythologique Irlandais*, p. 156.

CHAPTER VII

THE RISE OF THE SUN-GOD[1]

It was as a result of the loss of his hand in this battle with the Fir Bolgs that Nuada got his name of *Argetlám*, that is, the "Silver Handed". For Diancecht, the physician of the Tuatha Dé Danann, made him an artificial hand of silver, so skilfully that it moved in all its joints, and was as strong and supple as a real one. But, good as it was of its sort, it was a blemish; and, according to Celtic custom, no maimed person could sit upon the throne. Nuada was deposed; and the Tuatha Dé Danann went into council to appoint a new king.

They agreed that it would be a politic thing for them to conciliate the Fomors, the giants of the sea, and make an alliance with them. So they sent a message to Bress, the son of the Fomorian king, Elathan, asking him to come and rule over them. Bress accepted this offer; and they made a marriage between him and Brigit, the daughter of the Dagda. At the same time, Cian[2], the son of Diancecht, the physician of the Tuatha Dé Danann, married

---

[1] The principal sources of information for this chapter are the Harleian MS. 5280 entitled *The Second Battle of Moytura*, of which translations have been made by Dr. Whitley Stokes in the *Revue Celtique* and M. de Jubainville in his *L'Épopée Celtique en Irlande*, and Eugene O'Curry's translation in Vol. IV. of *Atlantis* of the *Fate of the Children of Tuirenn*.   [2] Pronounced *Kian*.

Ethniu, the daughter of the Fomor, Balor. Then Bress was made king, and endowed with lands and a palace; and he, on his part, gave hostages that he would abdicate if his rule ever became unpleasing to those who had elected him.

But, in spite of all his fair promises, Bress, who belonged in heart to his own fierce people, began to oppress his subjects with excessive taxes. He put a tax upon every hearth, upon every kneading-trough, and upon every quern, as well as a poll-tax of an ounce of gold upon every member of the Tuatha Dé Danann. By a crafty trick, too, he obtained the milk of all their cattle. He asked at first only for the produce of any cows which happened to be brown and hairless, and the people of the goddess Danu granted him this cheerfully. But Bress passed all the cattle in Ireland between two fires, so that their hair was singed off, and thus obtained the monopoly of the main source of food. To earn a livelihood, all the gods, even the greatest, were now forced to labour for him. Ogma, their champion, was sent out to collect firewood, while the Dagda was put to work building forts and castles.

One day, when the Dagda was at his task, his son, Angus, came to him. "You have nearly finished that castle," he said. "What reward do you intend to ask from Bress when it is done?" The Dagda replied that he had not yet thought of it. "Let me give you some advice," said Angus. "Ask Bress to have all the cattle in Ireland gathered together upon a plain, so that you can pick out one for yourself. He will consent to that. Then choose the black-maned heifer called ' Ocean '."

The Dagda finished building the fort, and then went to Bress for his reward. " What will you have?" asked Bress. " I want all the cattle in Ireland gathered together upon a plain, so that I may choose one of them for myself." Bress did this; and the Dagda took the black-maned heifer Angus had told him of. The king, who had expected to be asked very much more, laughed at what he thought was the Dagda's simplicity. But Angus had been wise; as will be seen hereafter.

Meanwhile Bress was infuriating the people of the goddess Danu by adding avarice to tyranny. It was for kings to be liberal to all-comers, but at the court of Bress no one ever greased his knife with fat, or made his breath smell of ale. Nor were there ever any poets or musicians or jugglers or jesters there to give pleasure to the people; for Bress would distribute no largess. Next, he cut down the very subsistence of the gods. So scanty was his allowance of food that they began to grow weak with famine. Ogma, through feebleness, could only carry one-third of the wood needed for fuel; so that they suffered from cold as well as from hunger.

It was at this crisis that two physicians, Miach, the son, and Airmid, the daughter, of Diancecht, the god of medicine, came to the castle where the dispossessed King Nuada lived. Nuada's porter, blemished, like himself (for he had lost an eye), was sitting at the gate, and on his lap was a cat curled up asleep. The porter asked the strangers who they were. "We are good doctors," they said. "If that is so," he replied, "perhaps you can give me a new eye." "Certainly," they said, "we could take one of the eyes of that cat, and put it in the place where your lost eye used to be." "I should be very pleased if you would do that," answered the porter, So Miach and Airmid removed one of the cat's eyes, and put it in the hollow where the man's eye had been.

The story goes on to say that this was not wholly a benefit to him; for the eye retained its cat's nature, and, when the man wished to sleep at nights, the cat's eye was always looking out for mice, while it could hardly be kept awake during the day. Nevertheless, he was pleased at the time, and went and told Nuada, who commanded that the doctors who had performed this marvellous cure should be brought to him.

As they came in, they heard the king groaning, for Nuada's wrist had festered where the silver hand joined the arm of flesh. Miach asked where Nuada's own hand was, and they told him that it had been buried long ago. But he dug it up, and placed it to Nuada's stump; he uttered an incantation over it, saying: "Sinew to sinew, and nerve to nerve be joined!" and in three days and nights the hand had renewed itself and fixed itself to the arm, so that Nuada was whole again.

When Diancecht, Miach's father, heard of this he was very angry to think that his son should have excelled him in the art of medicine. He sent for him, and struck him upon the head with a sword, cutting the skin, but not wounding the flesh. Miach easily healed this. So Diancecht hit him again, this time to the bone. Again Miach cured himself. The third time his father smote him, the sword went right through the skull to the membrane of the brain, but even this wound Miach was able to leech. At the fourth stroke, however, Diancecht cut the brain in two, and Miach could do nothing for that. He died, and Diancecht buried him. And upon his grave there grew up three hundred and sixty-five stalks of grass, each one a cure for any illness of each of the three hundred and sixty-five nerves in a man's body. Airmid, Miach's sister, plucked all these very carefully, and arranged them on her mantle according to their properties. But her angry and jealous father overturned the cloak, and hopelessly confused them. If it had not been for that act, says the early writer, men would know how to cure every illness, and would so be immortal.

The healing of Nuada's blemish happened just at the time when all the people of the goddess Danu had at last agreed that the exactions and tyranny of Bress could no longer be borne. It was the insult he put upon Cairpré, son of Ogma the god of literature, that caused things to come to this head. Poets were always held by the Celts in great honour; and when Cairpré, the bard of the Tuatha Dé Danann, went to visit Bress, he expected to be treated with much consideration, and fed at the king's own table. But, instead of doing so, Bress lodged him in a small, dark room where there was no fire, no bed, and no furniture except a mean table on which small cakes of dry bread were put on a little dish for his food. The next morning, Cairpré rose early and left the palace without having spoken to Bress. It was the custom of poets when they left a king's court to utter a panegyric on their host, but Cairpré treated Bress instead to a magical satire. It was the first satire ever made in Ireland, and seems to us to bear upon it all the marks of an early effort. Roughly rendered, it said:

> " No meat on the plates,
>   No milk of the cows;
>   No shelter for the belated;
>   No money for the minstrels:
>   May Bress's cheer be what he gives to others!"

This satire of Cairpré's was, we are assured, so virulent that it caused great red blotches to break out all over Bress's face. This in itself constituted a blemish such as should not be upon a king, and the Tuatha Dé Danann called upon Bress to abdicate and let Nuada take the throne again.

Bress was obliged to do so. He went back to the country of the Fomors, underneath the sea, and complained to his father Elathan, its king, asking him to gather an army to reconquer his throne. The Fomors assembled in council — Elathan, Tethra, Balor, Indech, and all the other warriors and chiefs—and they decided to come with a great host, and take Ireland away, and put it under the sea where the people of the goddess Danu would never be able to find it again.

At the same time, another assembly was also

being held at Tara, the capital of the Tuatha Dé
Danann. Nuada was celebrating his return to the
throne by a feast to his people. While it was at its
height, a stranger clothed like a king came to the
palace gate. The porter asked him his name and
errand.

"I am called Lugh," he said. "I am the grandson of Diancecht by Cian, my father, and the grandson of Balor by Ethniu, my mother."

"But what is your profession?" asked the porter;
"for no one is admitted here unless he is a master
of some craft."

"I am a carpenter," said Lugh.

"We have no need of a carpenter. We already
have a very good one; his name is Luchtainé.

"I am an excellent smith," said Lugh.

"We do not want a smith. We have a very
good one; his name is Goibniu."

"I am a professional warrior," said Lugh.

"We have no need of one. Ogma is our champion."

"I am a harpist," said Lugh.

"We have an excellent harpist already."

"I am a warrior renowned for skilfulness rather
than for mere strength."

"We already have a man like that."

"I am a poet and tale-teller," said Lugh.

"We have no need of such. We have a most
accomplished poet and tale-teller."

"I am a sorcerer," said Lugh.

"We do not want one. We have numberless
sorcerers and druids."

" I am a physician," said Lugh.

" Diancecht is our physician."

" I am a cup-bearer," said Lugh.

" We already have nine of them."

" I am a worker in bronze."

" We have no need of you. We already have a worker in bronze. His name is Credné."

" Then ask the king," said Lugh, " if he has with him a man who is master of all these crafts at once, for, if he has, there is no need for me to come to Tara."

So the door-keeper went inside, and told the king that a man had come who called himself Lugh the *Ioldanach*[1], or the " Master of all Arts ", and that he claimed to know everything.

The king sent out his best chess-player to play against the stranger. Lugh won, inventing a new move called " Lugh's enclosure ".

Then Nuada invited him in. Lugh entered, and sat down upon the chair called the " sage's seat ", kept for the wisest man.

Ogma, the champion, was showing off his strength. Upon the floor was a flagstone so large that four-score yokes of oxen would have been needed to move it. Ogma pushed it before him along the hall, and out at the door. Then Lugh rose from his chair, and pushed it back again. But this stone, huge as it was, was only a portion broken from a still greater rock outside the palace. Lugh picked it up, and put it back into its place.

The Tuatha Dé Danann asked him to play the

[1] Pronounced *Ildāna*.

harp to them. So he played the "sleep-tune", and the king and all his court fell asleep, and did not wake until the same hour of the following day. Next he played a plaintive air, and they all wept. Lastly, he played a measure which sent them into transports of joy.

When Nuada had seen all these numerous talents of Lugh, he began to wonder whether one so gifted would not be of great help against the Fomors. He took counsel with the others, and, by their advice, lent his throne to Lugh for thirteen days, taking the "sage's seat" at his side.

Lugh summoned all the Tuatha Dé Danann to a council.

"The Fomors are certainly going to make war on us," he said. "What can each of you do to help?"

Diancecht the Physician said: "I will completely cure everyone who is wounded, provided his head is not cut off, or his brain or spinal marrow hurt."

"I," said Goibniu the Smith, "will replace every broken lance and sword with a new one, even though the war last seven years. And I will make the lances so well that they shall never miss their mark, or fail to kill. Dulb, the smith of the Fomors, cannot do as much as that. The fate of the fighting will be decided by my lances."

"And I," said Credné the Bronze-worker, "will furnish all the rivets for the lances, the hilts for the swords, and the rims and bosses for the shields."

"And I," said Luchtainé the Carpenter, "will provide all the shields and lance-shafts."

Ogma the Champion promised to kill the King of the Fomors, with thrice nine of his followers, and to capture one-third of his army.

"And you, O Dagda," said Lugh, "what will you do?"

"I will fight," said the Dagda, "both with force and craft. Wherever the two armies meet, I will crush the bones of the Fomors with my club, till they are like hailstones under a horse's feet."

"And you, O Morrígú?" said Lugh.

"I will pursue them when they flee," she replied. "And I always catch what I chase."

"And you, O Cairpré, son of Etan?" said Lugh to the poet, "what can you do?"

"I will pronounce an immediately-effective curse upon them; by one of my satires I will take away all their honour, and, enchanted by me, they shall not be able to stand against our warriors."

"And ye, O sorcerers, what will ye do?"

"We will hurl by our magic arts," replied Mathgan, the head sorcerer, "the twelve mountains of Ireland at the Fomors. These mountains will be Slieve League, Denna Ulad, the Mourne Mountains, Bri Ruri, Slieve Bloom, Slieve Snechta, Slemish, Blai-Sliab, Nephin, Sliab Maccu Belgodon, Segais[1], and Cruachan Aigle[2]".

Then Lugh asked the cup-bearers what they would do.

"We will hide away by magic," they said, "the twelve chief lakes and the twelve chief rivers of Ireland from the Fomors, so that they shall not be

---

[1] The Curlieu Hills, between Roscommon and Sligo.   [2] Croagh Patrick.

able to find any water, however thirsty they may be; those waters will conceal themselves from the Fomors so that they shall not get a drop, while they will give drink to the people of the goddess Danu as long as the war lasts, even if it last seven years." And they told Lugh that the twelve chief lakes were Lough Derg, Lough Luimnigh[1], Lough Corrib, Lough Ree, Lough Mask, Strangford Lough, Lough Læig, Lough Neagh, Lough Foyle, Lough Gara, Lough Reagh, and Márloch, and that the twelve chief rivers were the Bush, the Boyne, the Bann, the Nem, the Lee, the Shannon, the Moy, the Sligo, the Erne, the Finn, the Liffey, and the Suir.

Finally, the Druid, Figol, son of Mamos, said: " I will send three streams of fire into the faces of the Fomors, and I will take away two-thirds of their valour and strength, but every breath drawn by the people of the goddess Danu will only make them more valorous and strong, so that even if the fighting lasts seven years, they will not be weary of it."

All decided to make ready for a war, and to give the direction of it to Lugh.

[1] The estuary of the Shannon.

CHAPTER VIII

THE GAELIC ARGONAUTS

The preparations for this war are said to have lasted seven years. It was during the interval that there befel an episode which might almost be called the "Argonautica" of the Gaelic mythology.[1]

In spite of the dethronement of Bress, the Fomors still claimed their annual tribute from the tribe of the goddess Danu, and sent their tax-gatherers, nine times nine in number, to "Balor's Hill" to collect it. But, while they waited for the gods to come to tender their submission and their subsidy, they saw a young man approaching them. He was riding upon "Splendid Mane", the horse of Manannán son of Lêr, and was dressed in Manannán's breast-plate and helmet, through which no weapon could wound their wearer, and he was armed with sword and shield and poisoned darts. "Like to the setting sun", says the story, "was the splendour of his countenance and his forehead, and they were not able to look in his face for the greatness of his splendour." And no wonder! for he was Lugh the Far-shooter, the new-come sun-god of the Gaels. He fell upon

---

[1] This story of the *Fate of the Children of Tuirenn* is mentioned in the ninth-century "Cormac's Glossary". It is found in various Irish and Scottish MSS., including the Book of Lecan. The present re-telling is from Eugene O'Curry's translation, published in *Atlantis*, Vol. IV.

the Fomorian tax-gatherers, killing all but nine of them, and these he only spared that they might go back to their kinsmen and tell how the gods had received them.

There was consternation in the under-sea country. "Who can this terrible warrior be?" asked Balor. "I know," said Balor's wife; "he must be the son of our daugher Ethniu; and I foretell that, since he has cast in his lot with his father's people, we shall never bear rule in Erin again."

The chiefs of the Fomors saw that this slaughter of their tax-gatherers signified that the Tuatha Dé Danann meant fighting. They held a council to debate on it. There came to it Elathan and Tethra and Indech, kings of the Fomors; Bress himself, and Balor of the stout blows; Cethlenn the crooked tooth, Balor's wife; Balor's twelve white-mouthed sons; and all the chief Fomorian warriors and druids.

Meanwhile, upon earth, Lugh was sending messengers all over Erin to assemble the Tuatha Dé Danann. Upon this errand went Lugh's father Cian, who seems to have been a kind of lesser solar deity,[1] son of Diancecht, the god of medicine. As Cian was going over the plain of Muirthemne,[2] he saw three armed warriors approaching him, and, when they got nearer, he recognized them as the three sons of Tuirenn, son of Ogma, whose names were Brian, Iuchar, and Iucharba. Between these three and Cian, with his brothers Cethé and Cu,

---

[1] Rhys: *Hibbert Lectures*, pp. 390-396.

[2] A part of County Louth, between the Boyne and Dundalk. The heroic cycle connects it especially with Cuchulainn. Pronounced *Mürthemna* or *Mürhevna*.

there was, for some reason, a private enmity. Cian saw that he was now at a disadvantage. "If my brothers were with me," he said to himself, "what a fight we would make; but, as I am alone, it will be best for me to conceal myself." Looking round, he saw a herd of pigs feeding on the plain. Like all the gods, he had the faculty of shape-shifting; so, striking himself with a magic wand, he changed himself into a pig, joined the herd, and began feeding with them.

But he had been seen by the sons of Tuirenn. "What has become of the warrior who was walking on the plain a moment ago?" said Brian to his brothers. "We saw him then," they replied, "but we do not know where he is now." "Then you have not used the proper vigilance which is needed in time of war," said the elder brother. "However, I know what has become of him. He has struck himself with a druidical wand, and changed himself into a pig, and there he is, in that herd, rooting up the ground, just like all the other pigs. I can also tell you who he is. His name is Cian, and you know that he is no friend of ours."

"It is a pity that he has taken refuge among the pigs," they replied, "for they belong to some one of the Tuatha Dé Danann, and, even if we were to kill them all, Cian might still escape us."

Again Brian reproached his brothers. "You are very ignorant," he said, "if you cannot distinguish a magical beast from a natural beast. However, I will show you." And thereupon he struck his two brothers with his own wand of shape-changing, and turned them into two swift, slender hounds, and set them upon the pigs.

The magic hounds soon found the magic pig, and drove it out of the herd on to the open plain. Then Brian threw his spear, and hit it. The wounded pig came to a stop. "It was an evil deed of yours, casting that spear," it cried, in a human voice, "for I am not a pig, but Cian, son of Diancecht. So give me quarter."

Iuchar and Iucharba would have granted it, and let him go; but their fiercer brother swore that Cian should be put an end to, even if he came back to life seven times. So Cian tried a fresh ruse. "Give me leave", he asked, "only to return to my own shape before you slay me." "Gladly," replied Brian, "for I would much rather kill a man than a pig."

So Cian spoke the befitting spell, cast off his pig's disguise, and stood before them in his own shape. "You will be obliged to spare my life now," he said. "We will not," replied Brian. "Then it will be the worst day's work for all of you that you ever did in your lives," he answered; "for, if you had killed me in the shape of a pig, you would only have had to pay the value of a pig, but if you kill me now, I tell you that there never has been, and there never will be, anyone killed in this world for whose death a greater blood-fine will be exacted than for mine."

But the sons of Tuirenn would not listen to him. They slew him, and pounded his body with stones until it was a crushed mass. Six times they tried to bury him, and the earth cast him back in horror; but, the seventh time, the mould held him, and they put stones upon him to keep him down. They left him buried there, and went to Tara.

Meanwhile Lugh had been expecting his father's return. As he did not come, he determined to go and look for him. He traced him to the Plain of Muirthemne, and there he was at fault. But the indignant earth itself, which had witnessed the murder, spoke to Lugh, and told him everything. So Lugh dug up his father's corpse, and made certain how he had come to his death; then he mourned over him, and laid him back in the earth, and heaped a barrow over him, and set up a pillar with his name on it in " ogam ".[1]

He went back to Tara, and entered the great hall. It was filled with the people of the goddess Danu, and among them Lugh saw the three sons of Tuirenn. So he shook the " chiefs' chain ", with which the Gaels used to ask for a hearing in an assembly, and when all were silent, he said:

" People of the goddess Danu, I ask you a question. What would be the vengeance that any of you would take upon one who had murdered his father?"

A great astonishment fell upon them, and Nuada, their king, said: " Surely it is not your father that has been murdered?"

" It is," replied Lugh. " And I am looking at

---

[1] There is known to have been a hill called Ard Chein (Cian's Mound) in the district of Muirthemne, and O'Curry identifies it tentatively with one now called Dromslian.

those who murdered him; and they know how they did it better than I do."

"Then Nuada declared that nothing short of hewing the murderer of his father limb from limb would satisfy him, and all the others said the same, including the sons of Tuirenn.

"The very ones who did the deed say that," cried Lugh. "Then let them not leave the hall till they have settled with me about the blood-fine to be paid for it."

"If it was I who had killed your father," said the king, "I should think myself lucky if you were willing to accept a fine instead of vengeance."

The sons of Tuirenn took counsel together in whispers. Iuchar and Iucharba were in favour of admitting their guilt, but Brian was afraid that, if they confessed, Lugh would withdraw his offer to accept a fine, and would demand their deaths. So he stood out, and said that, though it was not they who had killed Cian, yet, sooner than remain under Lugh's anger, as he suspected them, they would pay the same fine as if they had.

"Certainly you shall pay the fine," said Lugh, "and I will tell you what it shall be. It is this: three apples; and a pig's-skin; and a spear; and two horses and a chariot; and seven pigs; and a hound-whelp; and a cooking-spit; and three shouts on a hill: that is the fine, and, if you think it is too much, I will remit some of it, but, if you do not think it is too much, then pay it."

"If it were a hundred times that," replied Brian, "we should not think it too much. Indeed, it seems so little that I fear there must be some treachery concealed in it."

"I do not think it too little," replied Lugh. "Give me your pledge before the people of the goddess Danu that you will pay it faithfully, and I will give you mine that I will ask no more."

So the sons of Tuirenn bound themselves before the Tuatha Dé Danann to pay the fine to Lugh.

When they had sworn, and given sureties, Lugh turned to them again. "I will now", he said, "explain to you the nature of the fine you have pledged yourselves to pay me, so that you may know whether it is too little or not." And, with foreboding hearts, the sons of Tuirenn set themselves to listen.

"The three apples that I have demanded," he began, "are three apples from the Garden of the Hesperides, in the east of the world. You will know them by three signs. They are the size of the head of a month-old child, they are of the colour of burnished gold, and they taste of honey. Wounds are healed and diseases cured by eating them, and they do not diminish in any way by being eaten. Whoever casts one of them hits anything he wishes, and then it comes back into his hand. I will accept no other apples instead of these. Their owners keep them perpetually guarded because of a prophecy that three young warriors from the west of the world will come to take them by force, and, brave as you may be, I do not think that you will ever get them.

"The pig's-skin that I have demanded is the

pig's-skin of Tuis, King of Greece. It has two
virtues: its touch perfectly cures all wounded or
sick persons if only there is any life still left in
them; and every stream of water through which it
passes is turned into wine for nine days. I do not
think that you will get it from the King of Greece,
either with his consent or without it.

"And can you guess what spear it is that I have
demanded?" asked Lugh. "We cannot," they said.
" It is the poisoned spear of Pisear[1], King of Persia;
it is irresistible in battle; it is so fiery that its blade
must always be held under water, lest it destroy the
city in which it is kept. You will find it very difficult
to obtain.

"And the two horses and the chariot are the two
wonderful horses of Dobhar[2], King of Sicily, which
run equally well over land and sea; there are no
other horses in the world like them, and no other
vehicle equal to the chariot.

"And the seven pigs are the pigs of Easal[3],
King of the Golden Pillars; though they may be
killed every night, they are found alive again the
next day, and every person that eats part of them
can never be afflicted with any disease.

"And the hound-whelp I claim is the hound-
whelp of the King of Ioruaidhe[4]; her name is
Failinis; every wild beast she sees she catches at
once. It will not be easy for you to secure her.

"The cooking-spit which you must get for me is
one of the cooking-spits of the women of the Island

---

1 Pronounced *Pēsar.*   2 Pronounced *Dobar.*
3 Pronounced *Asal.*   4 Pronounced *Irōda.*

of Fianchuivé[1], which is at the bottom of the sea, between Erin and Alba.

"You have also pledged yourselves to give three shouts upon a hill. The hill upon which they must be given is the hill called Cnoc Miodhchaoin[2], in the north of Lochlann[3]. Miodhchaoin and his sons do not allow shouts to be given on that hill; besides this, it was they who gave my father his military education, and, even if I were to forgive you, they would not; so that, though you achieve all the other adventures, I think that you will fail in this one.

"Now you know what sort of a fine it is that you have bargained to pay me," said Lugh.

And fear and astonishment fell upon the sons of Tuirenn.

This tale is evidently the work of some ancient Irish story-teller who wished to compile from various sources a more or less complete account of how the Gaelic gods obtained their legendary possessions. The spear of Pisear, King of Persia, is obviously the same weapon as the lance of Lugh, which another tradition describes as having been brought by the Tuatha Dé Danann from their original home in the city of Gorias;[4] Failinis, the whelp of the King of Ioruaidhe, is Lugh's "hound of mightiest deeds", which was irresistible in battle, and which turned any running water it bathed in into wine,[5] a property here transferred to the magic pig's-skin of King Tuis: the seven swine of the King of the

[1] Pronounced *Fincára*. [2] The *Hill* (cnoc) *of Midkēna*.
[3] A mythical country inhabited by Fomors.
[4] See chap. VI—"The Gods Arrive". [5] *Ibid.*
(B 219) G

Golden Pillars must be the same undying porkers from whose flesh Manannán mac Lir made the "Feast of Age" which preserved the eternal youth of the gods;[1] it was with horses and chariot that ran along the surface of the sea that Manannán used to journey to and fro between Erin and the Celtic Elysium in the West;[2] the apples that grew in the Garden of the Hesperides were surely of the same celestial growth as those that fed the inhabitants of that immortal country;[3] while the cooking-spit reminds us of three such implements at Tara, made by Goibniu and associated with the names of the Dagda and the Morrígú.[4]

The burden of collecting all these treasures was placed upon the shoulders of the three sons of Tuirenn.

They consulted together, and agreed that they could never hope to succeed unless they had Manannán's magic horse, "Splendid Mane", and Manannán's magic coracle, "Wave-sweeper". But both these had been lent by Manannán to Lugh himself. So the sons of Tuirenn were obliged to humble themselves to beg them from Lugh. The sun-god would not lend them the horse, for fear of making their task too easy, but he let them have the boat, because he knew how much the spear of Pisear and the horses of Dobhar would be needed in the coming war with the Fomors. They bade farewell to their father, and went down to the shore and put out to sea, taking their sister with them.

---

[1] See chap. VI—"The Gods Arrive".   [2] See chap. XI—"The Gods in Exile".
[3] *Ibid.*   [4] Petrie: *Hist. and Antiq. of Tara Hill.*

"Which portion of the fine shall we seek first?" said the others to Brian. "We will seek them in the order in which they were demanded," he replied. So they directed the magic boat to sail to the Garden of the Hesperides, and presently they arrived there.

They landed at a harbour, and held a council of war. It was decided that their best chance of obtaining three of the apples would be by taking the shapes of hawks. Thus they would have strength enough in their claws to carry the apples away, together with sufficient quickness upon the wing to hope to escape the arrows, darts, and sling-stones which would be shot and hurled at them by the warders of the garden.

They swooped down upon the orchard from above. It was done so swiftly that they carried off the three apples, unhit either by shaft or stone. But their difficulties were not yet over. The king of the country had three daughters who were well skilled in witchcraft. By sorcery they changed themselves into three ospreys, and pursued the three hawks. But the sons of Tuirenn reached the shore first, and, changing themselves into swans, dived into the sea. They came up close to their coracle, and got into it, and sailed swiftly away with the spoil.

Thus their first quest was finished, and they voyaged on to Greece, to seek the pig's-skin of King Tuis. No one could go without some excuse into a king's court, so they decided to disguise themselves as poets, and to tell the door-keeper that they were professional bards from Erin, seeking largess at the hands of kings. The porter let them into the great hall, where the poets of Greece were singing before the king.

When those had all finished, Brian rose, and asked permission to show his art. This was accorded; and he sang:

> "O Tuis, we conceal not thy fame.
> We praise thee as the oak above the kings;
> The skin of a pig, bounty without hardness!
> This is the reward which I ask for it.

> "A stormy host and raging sea
> Are a dangerous power, should one oppose
> The skin of a pig, bounty without hardness!
> This is the reward I ask, O Tuis."

"That is a good poem," said the king, "only I do not understand it."

"I will explain it," said Brian. "'*We praise thee as the oak above the kings*'; this means that, as the oak excels all other trees, so do you excel all other kings in nobility and generosity. '*The skin of a pig, bounty without hardness*'; that is a pig's-skin which you have, O Tuis, and which I should like to receive as the reward of my poem. '*A stormy host and raging sea are a dangerous power, should one oppose it*'; this means to say, that we are not used to going without anything on which we have set our hearts, O Tuis."

"I should have liked your poem better," replied the king, "if my pig's-skin had not been mentioned in it. It was not a wise thing for you to have done, O poet. But I will measure three fills of red gold out of the skin, and you shall have those."

"May all good be thine, O King!" answered Brian. "I knew that I should get a noble reward."

So the king sent for the pig's-skin to measure out the gold with. But, as soon as Brian saw it, he seized it with his left hand, and slew the man who was holding it, and Iuchar and Iucharba also hacked about them; and they cut their way down to the boat, leaving the King of Greece among the dead behind them.

"And now we will go and get King Pisear's spear," said Brian. So, leaving Greece, they sailed in their coracle to Persia.

Their plan of disguising themselves as poets had served them so well that they decided to make use of it again. So they went into the King of Persia's hall in the same way as they had entered that of the King of Greece. Brian first listened to the poets of Persia singing; then he sang his own song:

> "Small the esteem of any spear with Pisear;
>   The battles of foes are broken;
>   No oppression to Pisear;
>   Everyone whom he wounds.

> "A yew-tree, the finest of the wood,
>   It is called King without opposition.
>   May that splendid shaft drive on
>   Yon crowd into their wounds of death."

"That is a good poem, O man of Erin," said the king, "but why is my spear mentioned in it?"

"The meaning is this," replied Brian: "I should like to receive that spear as a reward for my poem,"

"You make a rash request," said the king. "If I spare your life after having heard it, it will be a sufficient reward for your poem."

Brian had one of the magic apples in his hand, and he remembered its boomerang-like quality. He hurled it full in the King of Persia's face, dashing out his brains. The Persians flew to arms, but the three sons of Tuirenn conquered them, and made them yield up the spear.

They had now to travel to Sicily, to obtain the horses and chariot of King Dobhar. But they were afraid to go as poets this time, for fear the fame of their deeds might have got abroad. They therefore decided to pretend to be mercenary soldiers from Erin, and offer the King of Sicily their service. This, they thought, would be the easiest way of finding out where the horses and the chariot were kept. So they went and stood on the green before the royal court.

When the King of Sicily heard that there had come mercenaries from Erin, seeking wages from the kings of the world, he invited them to take service with him. They agreed; but, though they stayed with him a fortnight and a month, they never saw the horses, or even found out where they were kept. So they went to the king, and announced that they wished to leave him.

"Why?" he asked, for he did not want them to go.

"We will tell you, O King!" replied Brian. "It is because we have not been honoured with your confidence, as we have been accustomed with other kings. You have two horses and a chariot, the best in the world, and we have not even been allowed to see them."

"I would have shown them to you on the first day if you had asked me," said the king; "and you shall see them at once, for I have seldom had warriors with me so good as you are, and I do not wish you to leave me."

So he sent for the steeds, and had them yoked to the chariot, and the sons of Tuirenn were witnesses of their marvellous speed, and how they could run equally well over land or water.

Brian made a sign to his brothers, and they watched their opportunity carefully, and, as the chariot passed close beside them, Brian leaped into it, hurling its driver over the side. Then, turning the horses, he struck King Dobhar with Pisear's spear, and killed him. He took his two brothers up into the chariot and they drove away.

By the time the sons of Tuirenn reached the country of Easal, King of the Pillars of Gold, rumour had gone before them. The king came down to the harbour to meet them, and asked them if it were really true that so many kings had fallen at their hands. They replied that it was true, but that they had no quarrel with any of them; only they must obtain at all costs the fine demanded by Lugh. Then Easal asked them why they had come to his land, and they told him that they needed his seven pigs to add to the tribute. So Easal thought it better to give them up, and to make friends with the three sons of Tuirenn, than to fight with such

warriors. The sons of Tuirenn were very glad at
this, for they were growing weary of battles.

It happened that the King of Ioruaidhe, who had
the hound-whelp that Lugh had demanded, was the
husband of King Easal's daughter. Therefore King
Easal did not wish that there should be fighting between him and the three sons of Tuirenn. He proposed to Brian and his brothers that he should sail
with them to Ioruaidhe, and try to persuade the king
of the country to give up the hound-whelp peacefully. They consented, and all set foot safely on
the "delightful, wonderful shores of Ioruaidhe",[1] as
the manuscript calls them. But King Easal's
son-in-law would not listen to reason. He assembled his warriors, and fought; but the sons
of Tuirenn defeated them, and compelled their
king to yield up the hound-whelp as the ransom
for his life.

All these quests had been upon the earth, but the
next was harder. No coracle, not even Manannán's
"Wave-sweeper", could penetrate to the Island of
Fianchuivé, in the depths of the sea that severs
Erin from Alba. So Brian left his brothers, and
put on his "water-dress, with his transparency of
glass upon his head"—evidently an ancient Irish
anticipation of the modern diver's dress. Thus
equipped, he explored the bottom of the sea for
fourteen days before he found the island. But
when at last he reached it, and entered the hall
of its queen, she and her sea-maidens were so
amazed at Brian's hardihood in having penetrated

---

[1] The country seems to have been identified with Norway or Iceland.

to their kingdom that they presented him with the cooking-spit, and sent him back safe.

By this time, Lugh had found out by his magic arts that the sons of Tuirenn had obtained all the treasures he had demanded as the blood-fine. He desired to get them safely into his own custody before his victims went to give their three shouts upon Miodhchaoin's Hill. He therefore wove a druidical spell round them, so that they forgot the rest of their task altogether, and sailed back to Erin. They searched for Lugh, to give him the things, but he had gone away, leaving word that they were to be handed over to Nuada, the Tuatha Dé Danann king. As soon as they were in safe-keeping, Lugh came back to Tara and found the sons of Tuirenn there. And he said to them:

"Do you not know that it is unlawful to keep back any part of a blood-fine? So have you given those three shouts upon Miodhchaoin's Hill?"

Then the magic mist of forgetfulness fell from them, and they remembered. Sorrowfully they went back to complete their task.

Miodhchaoin[1] himself was watching for them, and, when he saw them land, he came down to the beach. Brian attacked him, and they fought with the swiftness of two bears and the ferocity of two lions until Miodhchaoin fell.

Then Miodhchaoin's three sons—Corc, Conn, and Aedh—came out to avenge their father, and they drove their spears through the bodies of the three sons of Tuirenn. But the three sons of Tuirenn

[1] Pronounced *Midkēna.*

also drove their spears through the bodies of the three sons of Miodhchaoin.

The three sons of Miodhchaoin were killed, and the three sons of Tuirenn were so sorely wounded that birds might have flown through their bodies from one side to the other. Nevertheless Brian was still able to stand upright, and he held his two brothers, one in each hand, and kept them on their feet, and, all together, they gave three faint, feeble shouts.

Their coracle bore them, still living, to Erin. They sent their father Tuirenn as a suppliant to Lugh, begging him to lend them the magic pig's-skin to heal their wounds.

But Lugh would not, for he had counted upon their fight with the sons of Miodhchaoin to avenge his father Cian's death. So the children of Tuirenn resigned themselves to die, and their father made a farewell song over them and over himself, and died with them.

Thus ends that famous tale—" The Fate of the Sons of Tuirenn", known as one of the "Three Sorrowful Stories of Erin".[1]

---

[1] The other two are "The Fate of the Children of Lêr", told in chap. XI, and "The Fate of the Sons of Usnach", an episode of the Heroic Cycle, related in chap. XIII.

CHAPTER IX

THE WAR WITH THE GIANTS[1]

By this time the seven years of preparation had come to an end. A week before the Day of Samhain, the Morrígú discovered that the Fomors had landed upon Erin. She at once sent a messenger to tell the Dagda, who ordered his druids and sorcerers to go to the ford of the River Unius, in Sligo, and utter incantations against them.

The people of the goddess Danu, however, were not yet quite ready for battle. So the Dagda decided to visit the Fomorian camp as an ambassador, and, by parleying with them, to gain a little more time. The Fomors received him with apparent courtesy, and, to celebrate his coming, prepared him a feast of porridge; for it was well-known how fond he was of such food. They poured into their king's cauldron, which was as deep as five giant's fists, fourscore gallons of new milk, with meal and bacon in proportion. To this they added the whole carcasses of goats, sheep, and pigs; they boiled the mixture together, and poured it into a hole in the ground. "Now," said they, "if you do not

---

[1] This chapter is, with slight interpolations, based upon the Harleian MS. in the British Museum numbered 5280, and called the *Second Battle of Moytura*, or rather from translations made of it by Dr. Whitley Stokes, published in the *Revue Celtique*, Vol. XII, and by M. de Jubainville in his *L'Épopée Celtique en Irlande*.

eat it all, we shall put you to death, for we will not
have you go back to your own people and say that
the Fomors are inhospitable." But they did not
succeed in frightening the Dagda. He took his
spoon, which was so large that two persons of our
puny size might have reclined comfortably in the
middle of it, dipped it into the porridge, and fished
up halves of salted pork and quarters of bacon.

"If it tastes as good as it smells," he said, "it is
good fare." And so it proved; for he ate it all, and
scraped up even what remained at the bottom of the
hole. Then he went away to sleep it off, followed
by the laughter of the Fomors; for his stomach
was so swollen with food that he could hardly
walk. It was larger than the biggest cauldron in
a large house, and stood out like a sail before the
wind.

But the Fomors' little practical joke upon the
Dagda had given the Tuatha Dé Danann time to
collect their forces. It was on the eve of Samhain
that the two armies came face to face. Even then
the Fomors could not believe that the people of the
goddess Danu would offer them much resistance.

"Do you think they will really dare to give us
battle?" said Bress to Indech, the son of Domnu.
"If they do not pay their tribute, we will pound
their bones for them," he replied.

The war of gods and giants naturally mirrored
the warfare of the Gaels, in whose battles, as in those
of most semi-barbarous people, single combat figured
largely. The main armies stood still, while, every
day, duels took place between ambitious combatants.

But no great warriors either of the Tuatha Dé Danann or of the Fomors took part in them.

Sometimes a god, sometimes a giant would be the victor; but there was a difference in the net results that astonished the Fomors. If their own swords and lances were broken, they were of no more use, and if their own champions were killed, they never came back to life again; but it was quite otherwise with the people of the goddess Danu. Weapons shattered on one day re-appeared upon the next in as good condition as though they had never been used, and warriors slain on one day came back upon the morrow unhurt, and ready, if neces-sary, to be killed again.

The Fomors decided to send someone to discover the secret of these prodigies. The spy they chose was Ruadan, the son of Bress and of Brigit, daughter of the Dagda, and therefore half-giant and half-god. He disguised himself as a Tuatha Dé Danann warrior, and went to look for Goibniu. He found him at his forge, together with Luchtainé, the car-penter, and Credné, the bronze-worker. He saw how Goibniu forged lance-heads with three blows of his hammer, while Luchtainé cut shafts for them with three blows of his axe, and Credné fixed the two parts together so adroitly that his bronze nails needed no hammering in. He went back and told the Fomors, who sent him again, this time to try and kill Goibniu.

He reappeared at the forge, and asked for a javelin. Without suspicion, Goibniu gave him one, and, as soon as he got it into his hand, he thrust it

through the smith's body. But Goibniu plucked it
out, and, hurling it back at his assailant, mortally
wounded him. Ruadan went home to die, and his
father Bress and his mother Brigit mourned for him,
inventing for the purpose the Irish "keening".
Goibniu, on the other hand, took no harm. He
went to the physician Diancecht, who, with his
daughter Airmid, was always on duty at a miraculous well called the "spring of health". Whenever
one of the Tuatha Dé Danann was killed or
wounded, he was brought to the two doctors, who
plunged him into the wonder-working water, and
brought him back to life and health again.

The mystic spring was not long, however, allowed
to help the people of the goddess. A young Fomorian chief, Octriallach son of Indech, found it out.
He and a number of his companions went to it by
night, each carrying a large stone from the bed of
the River Drowes. These they dropped into the
spring, until they had filled it, dispersed the healing
water, and formed a cairn above it. Legend has
identified this place by the name of the "Cairn of
Octriallach".

This success determined the Fomors to fight a
pitched battle. They drew out their army in line.
There was not a warrior in it who had not a coat of
mail and a helmet, a stout spear, a strong buckler,
and a heavy sword. "Fighting the Fomors on that
day", says the old author, "could only be compared
to one of three things—beating one's head against a
rock, or plunging it into a fire, or putting one's hand
into a serpent's nest."

All the great fighters of the Tuatha Dé Danann were drawn out opposite to them, except Lugh. A council of the gods had decided that his varied accomplishments made his life too valuable to be risked in battle. They had, therefore, left him behind, guarded by nine warriors. But, at the last moment, Lugh escaped from his warders, and appeared in his chariot before the army. He made them a patriotic speech. "Fight bravely," he said, "that your servitude may last no longer; it is better to face death than to live in vassalage and pay tribute." With these encouraging words, he drove round the ranks, standing on tiptoe, so that all the Tuatha Dé Danann might see him.

The Fomors saw him too, and marvelled. "It seems wonderful to me,"[1] said Bress to his druids, "that the sun should rise in the west to-day and in the east every other day." "It would be better for us if it were so," replied the druids. "What else can it be, then?" asked Bress. "It is the radiance of the face of Lugh of the Long Arms," said they.

Then the two armies charged each other with a great shout. Spears and lances smote against shields, and so great was the shouting of the fighters, the shattering of shields, the clattering of swords, the rattling of quivers, and the whistling of darts and javelins that it seemed as if thunder rolled everywhere.

They fought so closely that the heads, hands, and

---

[1] I have interpolated this picturesque passage from the account of a fight between the Tuatha Dé Danann and the Fomors in the "Fate of the Children of Tuirenn". O'Curry's translation in *Atlantis*, Vol. IV.

feet of those on one side were touching the heads, hands, and feet of those on the other side; they shed so much blood on to the ground that it became hard to stand on it without slipping; and the river of Unsenn was filled with dead bodies, so hard and swift and bloody and cruel was the battle.

Many great chiefs fell on each side. Ogma, the champion of the Tuatha Dé Danann, killed Indech, the son of the goddess Domnu. But, meanwhile, Balor of the Mighty Blows raged among the gods, slaying their king, Nuada of the Silver Hand, as well as Macha, one of his warlike wives. At last he met with Lugh. The sun-god shouted a challenge to his grandfather in the Fomorian speech. Balor heard it, and prepared to use his death-dealing eye.

"Lift up my eyelid," he said to his henchmen, "that I may see this chatterer who talks to me."

The attendants lifted Balor's eye with a hook, and if the glance of the eye beneath had rested upon Lugh, he would certainly have perished. But, when it was half opened, Lugh flung a magic stone which struck Balor's eye out through the back of his head. The eye fell on the ground behind Balor, and destroyed a whole rank of thrice nine Fomors who were unlucky enough to be within sight of it.

An ancient poem has handed down the secret of this magic stone. It is there called a *tathlum*, meaning a "concrete ball" such as the ancient Irish warriors used sometimes to make out of the brains of dead enemies hardened with lime.

" A tathlum, heavy, fiery, firm,
   Which the Tuatha Dé Danann had with them,
   It was that broke the fierce Balor's eye,
   Of old, in the battle of the great armies.

" The blood of toads and furious bears,
   And the blood of the noble lion,
   The blood of vipers and of Osmuinn's trunks;—
   It was of these the tathlum was composed.

" The sand of the swift Armorian sea,
   And the sand of the teeming Red Sea;—
   All these, being first purified, were used
   In the composition of the tathlum.

" Briun, the son of Bethar, no mean warrior,
   Who on the ocean's eastern border reigned;—
   It was he that fused, and smoothly formed,
   It was he that fashioned the tathlum.

" To the hero Lugh was given
   This concrete ball,—no soft missile;—
   In Mag Tuireadh of shrieking wails,
   From his hand he threw the tathlum." [1]

This blinding of the terrible Balor turned the fortunes of the fight; for the Fomors wavered, and the
Morrígú came and encouraged the people of the
goddess Danu with a song, beginning " Kings arise
to the battle", so that they took fresh heart, and
drove the Fomors headlong back to their country
underneath the sea.

Such was the battle which is called in Irish
Mag Tuireadh na b-Fomorach, that is to say, the

---

[1] This translation was made by Eugene O'Curry from an ancient vellum MS.
formerly belonging to Mr. W. Monck Mason, but since sold by auction in London.
See his *Manners and Customs of the Ancient Irish*, Lecture XII, p. 252.

"Plain of the Towers of the Fomors", and, more
popularly, the "Battle of Moytura the Northern", to
distinguish it from the other Battle of Moytura
fought by the Tuatha Dé Danann against the Fir
Bolgs farther to the south.   More of the Fomors
were killed in it, says the ancient manuscript, than
there are stars in the sky, grains of sand on the sea-
shore, snow-flakes in winter, drops of dew upon the
meadows in spring-time, hailstones during a storm,
blades of grass trodden under horses' feet, or Manannán son of Lêr's white horses, the waves of the
sea, when a tempest breaks.   The "towers" or
pillars said to mark the graves of the combatants
still stand upon the plain of Carrowmore, near Sligo,
and form, in the opinion of Dr. Petrie, the finest collection of prehistoric monuments in the world, with
the sole exception of Carnac, in Brittany.[1]   Mega-
lithic structures of almost every kind are found
among them—stone cairns with dolmens in their
interiors, dolmens standing open and alone, dolmens
surrounded by one, two, or three circles of stones,
and circles without dolmens—to the number of over
a hundred.   Sixty-four of such prehistoric remains
stand together upon an elevated plateau not more
than a mile across, and make the battle-field of Moytura, though the least known, perhaps the most impressive of all primeval ruins.   What they really
commemorated we may never know, but, in all probability, the place was the scene of some important
and decisive early battle, the monuments marking
the graves of the chieftains who were interred as the

[1] See Fergusson: *Rude Stone Monuments*, pp. 180, &c.

result of it. Those which have been examined were found to contain burnt wood and the half-burnt bones of men and horses, as well as implements of flint and bone. The actors, therefore, were still in the Neolithic Age. Whether the horses were domesticated ones buried with their riders, or wild ones eaten at the funeral feasts, it would be hard to decide. The history of the real event must have been long lost even at the early date when its relics were pointed out as the records of a battle between the gods and the giants of Gaelic myth.

The Tuatha Dé Danann, following the routed Fomors, overtook and captured Bress. He begged Lugh to spare his life.

"What ransom will you pay for it?" asked Lugh.

"I will guarantee that the cows of Ireland shall always be in milk," promised Bress.

But, before accepting, Lugh took counsel with his druids.

"What good will that be," they decided, "if Bress does not also lengthen the lives of the cows?"

This was beyond the power of Bress to do; so he made another offer.

"Tell your people," he said to Lugh, "that, if they will spare my life, they shall have a good wheat harvest every year."

But they said: "We already have the spring to plough and sow in, the summer to ripen the crops, the autumn for reaping, and the winter in which to eat the bread; and that is all we want."

Lugh told this to Bress. But he also said: "You

shall have your life in return for a much less service to us than that."

"What is it?" asked Bress.

"Tell us when we ought to plough, when we ought to sow, and when we ought to harvest."

Bress replied: "You should plough on a Tuesday, sow on a Tuesday, and harvest on a Tuesday."

And this lying maxim (says the story) saved Bress's life.

Lugh, the Dagda, and Ogma still pursued the Fomors, who had carried off in their flight the Dagda's harp. They followed them into the submarine palace where Bress and Elathan lived, and there they saw the harp hanging on the wall. This harp of the Dagda's would not play without its owner's leave. The Dagda sang to it:

> "Come, oak of the two cries!
> Come, hand of fourfold music!
> Come, summer! Come, winter!
> Voice of harps, bellows[1], and flutes!"

For the Dagda's harp had these two names; it was called "Oak of the two cries" and "Hand of fourfold music".

It leaped down from the wall, killing nine of the Fomors as it passed, and came into the Dagda's hand. The Dagda played to the Fomors the three tunes known to all clever harpists—the weeping-tune, the laughing-tune, and the sleeping-tune. While he played the weeping-tune, they were bowed with weeping; while he played the laughing-tune,

---

1 ? Bagpipes.

they rocked with laughter; and when he played the sleeping-tune, they all fell asleep. And while they slept, Lugh, the Dagda, and Ogma got away safely.

Next, the Dagda brought the black-maned heifer which he had, by the advice of Angus son of the Young, obtained from Bress. The wisdom of Angus had been shown in this advice, for it was this very heifer that the cattle of the people of the goddess Danu were accustomed to follow, whenever it lowed. Now, when it lowed, all the cattle which the Fomors had taken away from the Tuatha Dé Danann came back again.

Yet the power of the Fomors was not wholly broken. Four of them still carried on a desultory warfare by spoiling the corn, fruit, and milk of their conquerors. But the Morrígú and Badb and Mider and Angus pursued them, and drove them out of Ireland for ever.[1]

Last of all, the Morrígú and Badb went up on to the summits of all the high mountains of Ireland, and proclaimed the victory. All the lesser gods who had not been in the battle came round and heard the news. And Badb sang a song which began:

> "Peace mounts to the heavens,
> The heavens descend to earth,
> Earth lies under the heavens,
> Everyone is strong . . .",

but the rest of it has been lost and forgotten.

Then she added a prophecy in which she foretold

[1] *Book of Fermoy.* See *Revue Celtique*, Vol. I.—"The Ancient Irish Goddess of War".

the approaching end of the divine age, and the beginning of a new one in which summers would be flowerless and cows milkless and women shameless ana men strengthless, in which there would be trees without fruit and seas without fish, when old men would give false judgments and legislators make unjust laws, when warriors would betray one another, and men would be thieves, and there would be no more virtue left in the world.

CHAPTER X

THE CONQUEST OF THE GODS BY MORTALS

Of what Badb had in mind when she uttered this prophecy we have no record. But it was true. The twilight of the Irish gods was at hand. A new race was coming across the sea to dispute the ownership of Ireland with the people of the goddess Danu. And these new-comers were not divinities like themselves, but men like ourselves, ancestors of the Gaels.

This story of the conquest of the gods by mortals —which seems such a strange one to us—is typically Celtic. The Gaelic mythology is the only one which has preserved it in any detail; but the doctrine would seem to have been common at one time to all the Celts. It was, however, of less shame to the gods than would otherwise have been; for men were of as divine descent as themselves. The dogma of the Celts was that men were descended from the god of death, and first came from the Land of the Dead to take possession of the present world.[1] Caesar tells us, in his too short account of the Gauls, that they believed themselves to be

---

[1] It may be noted that, according to Welsh legend, the ancestors of the Cymri came from Gwlâd yr Hâv, the " Land of Summer ", *i.e.* the Celtic Other World.

sprung from Dis Pater, the god of the underworld.[1]
In the Gaelic mythology Dis Pater was called Bilé,
a name which has for root the syllable *bel*, meaning
"to die". The god Beli in British mythology was
no doubt the same person, while the same idea is
expressed by the same root in the name of Balor,
the terrible Fomor whose glance was death.[2]

The post-Christian Irish chroniclers, seeking to
reconcile Christian teachings with the still vital
pagan mythology by changing the gods into ancient
kings and incorporating them into the annals of the
country, with appropriate dates, also disposed of the
genuine early doctrine by substituting Spain for
Hades, and giving a highly-fanciful account of the
origin and wanderings of their ancestors. To use
a Hibernicism, appropriate in this connection, the
first Irishman was a Scythian called Fenius Farsa.
Deprived of his own throne, he had settled in
Egypt, where his son Niul married a daughter of
the reigning Pharaoh. Her name was Scôta, and
she had a son called Goidel, whose great-grandson
was named Eber Scot, the whole genealogy being
probably invented to explain the origin of the three
names by which the Gaels called themselves—Finn,
Scot, and Goidel. Fenius and his family and clan
were turned out of Egypt for refusing to join in the
persecution of the children of Israel, and sojourned
in Africa for forty-two years. Their wanderings
took them to "the altars of the Philistines, by the

---

[1] *De Bello Gallico*, Book VI, chap. XVIII.
[2] De Jubainville: *Cycle Mythologique*, chap. X. Rhys: *Hibbert Lectures*—"The
Gaulish Pantheon".

Lake of Osiers"; then, passing between Rusicada and the hilly country of Syria, they travelled through Mauretania as far as the Pillars of Hercules; and thence landed in Spain, where they lived many years, greatly increasing and multiplying. The same route is given by the twelfth-century British historian, Geoffrey of Monmouth, as that taken by Brutus and the Trojans when they came to colonize Britain.[1] Its only connection with any kind of fact is that it corresponds fairly well with what ethnologists consider must have been the westward line of migration taken, not, curiously enough, by the Aryan Celts, but by the pre-Aryan Iberians.

It is sufficient for us to find the first men in Spain, remembering that "Spain" stood for the Celtic Hades, or Elysium. In this country Bregon, the father of two sons, Bilé and Ith, had built a watch-tower, from which, one winter's evening, Ith saw, far off over the seas, a land he had never noticed before. "It is on winter evenings, when the air is pure, that man's eyesight reaches farthest", remarks the old tract called the "Book of Invasions",[2] gravely accounting for the fact that Ith saw Ireland from Spain.

Wishing to examine it nearer, he set sail with thrice thirty warriors, and landed without mishap at the mouth of the River Scêné.[3] The country seemed to him to be uninhabited, and he marched with his

---

[1] Geoffrey of Monmouth's *Historia Britonum*, Book I, chap. II.
[2] Contained in the *Book of Leinster* and other ancient manuscripts.
[3] Now called the Kenmare River.

men towards the north. At last he reached Aileach, near the present town of Londonderry.

Here he found the three reigning kings of the people of the goddess Danu, Mac Cuill, Mac Cecht, and Mac Greiné, the sons of Ogma, and grandsons of the Dagda. These had succeeded Nuada the Silver-handed, killed in the battle with the Fomors; and had met, after burying their predecessor in a tumulus called Grianan Aileach, which still stands on the base of the Inishowen Peninsula, between Lough Swilly and Lough Foyle, to divide his king dom among them. Unable to arrive at any partition satisfactory to all, they appealed to the new-comer to arbitrate.

The advice of Ith was moral rather than practical. "Act according to the laws of justice" was all that he would say to the claimants; and then he was indiscreet enough to burst into enthusiastic praises of Ireland for its temperate climate and its richness in fruit, honey, wheat, and fish. Such sentiments from a foreigner seemed to the Tuatha Dé Danann suggestive of a desire to take the country from them. They conspired together and treacherously killed Ith at a place since called "Ith's Plain". They, however, spared his followers, who returned to "Spain", taking their dead leader's body with them. The indignation there was great, and Milé, Bilé's son and Ith's nephew, determined to go to Ireland and get revenge.

Milé therefore sailed with his eight sons and their wives. Thirty-six chiefs, each with his shipful of warriors, accompanied him. By the magic arts of their druid, Amergin of the Fair Knee, they discovered the exact place at which Ith had landed before them, and put in to shore there. Two alone failed to reach it alive. The wife of Amergin died during the voyage, and Aranon, a son of Milé, on approaching the land, climbed to the top of the mast to obtain a better view, and, falling off, was drowned. The rest disembarked safely upon the first of May.

Amergin was the first to land. Planting his right foot on Irish soil, he burst into a poem preserved in both the Book of Lecan and the Book of Ballymote.[1] It is a good example of the pantheistic philosophy of the Celtic races, and a very close parallel to it is contained in an early Welsh poem, called the "Battle of the Trees", and attributed to the famous bard Taliesin.[2] "I am the wind that blows upon the sea," sang Amergin; "I am the ocean wave; I am the murmur of the surges; I am seven battalions; I am a strong bull; I am an eagle on a rock; I am a ray of the sun; I am the most beautiful of herbs; I am a courageous wild boar; I am a salmon in the water; I am a lake upon a plain; I am a cunning artist; I am a gigantic, sword-wielding champion; I can shift my shape like a god. In what direction shall we go? Shall we hold our council in the valley or on the mountain-top? Where shall we make our home? What land is better than this island of the setting sun? Where

[1] This poem and the three following ones, all attributed to Amergin, are said to be the oldest Irish literary records.

[2] *Book of Taliesin*, poem VIII, in Skene's Four Ancient Books of Wales, Vol. I, p. 276.

shall we walk to and fro in peace and safety? Who can find you clear springs of water as I can? Who can tell you the age of the moon but I? Who can call the fish from the depths of the sea as I can? Who can cause them to come near the shore as I can? Who can change the shapes of the hills and headlands as I can? I am a bard who is called upon by seafarers to prophesy. Javelins shall be wielded to avenge our wrongs. I prophesy victory. I end my song by prophesying all other good things."[1]

The Welsh bard Taliesin sings in the same strain as the druid Amergin his unity with, and therefore his power over, all nature, animate and inanimate. "I have been in many shapes", he says, "before I attained a congenial form. I have been a narrow blade of a sword; I have been a drop in the air; I have been a shining star; I have been a word in a book; I have been a book in the beginning; I have been a light in a lantern a year and a half; I have been a bridge for passing over threescore rivers; I have journeyed as an eagle; I have been a boat on the sea; I have been a director in battle; I have been a sword in the hand; I have been a shield in fight; I have been the string of a harp; I have been enchanted for a year in the foam of water. There is nothing in which I have not been." It is strange to find Gael and Briton combining to voice almost in the same words this doctrine of the mystical Celts, who, while still in a state of semi-

---

[1] De Jubainville: *Cycle Mythologique.* See also the *Transactions of the Ossianic Society*, Vol. V.

barbarism, saw, with some of the greatest of ancient and modern philosophers, the One in the Many, and a single Essence in all the manifold forms of life.

The Milesians (for so, following the Irish annalists, it will be convenient to call the first Gaelic settlers in Ireland) began their march on Tara, which was the capital of the Tuatha Dé Danann, as it had been in earlier days the chief fortress of the Fir Bolgs, and would in later days be the dwelling of the high kings of Ireland. On their way they met with a goddess called Banba, the wife of Mac Cuill. She greeted Amergin. "If you have come to conquer Ireland," she said, "your cause is no just one." "Certainly it is to conquer it we have come," replied Amergin, without condescending to argue upon the abstract morality of the matter. "Then at least grant me one thing," she asked. "What is that?" replied Amergin. "That this island shall be called by my name." "It shall be," replied Amergin.

A little farther on, they met a second goddess, Fotla, the wife of Mac Cecht, who made the same request, and received the same answer from Amergin.

Last of all, at Uisnech, the centre of Ireland, they came upon the third of the queens, Eriu, the wife of Mac Greiné. "Welcome, warriors," she cried. "To you who have come from afar this island shall henceforth belong, and from the setting to the rising sun there is no better land. And your race will be the most perfect the world has ever seen." "These are fair words and a good prophecy," said Amergin. "It will be no thanks to you," broke in Donn, Milé's eldest son. "Whatever success we have we shall owe to our own strength." "That which I prophesy has no concern with you," retorted the goddess, "and neither you nor your descendants will live to enjoy this island." Then, turning to Amergin, she, too, asked that Ireland might be called after her. "It shall be its principal name," Amergin promised.

And so it has happened. Of the three ancient names of Ireland—Banba, Fotla, and Eriu—the last, in its genitive form of "Erinn", is the one that has survived.

The invaders came to Tara, then called Drumcain, that is, the "Beautiful Hill". Mac Cuill, Mac Cecht, and Mac Greiné met them, with all the host of the Gaelic gods. As was usual, they held a parley. The people of the goddess Danu complained that they had been taken by surprise, and the Milesians admitted that to invade a country without having first warned its inhabitants was not strictly according to the courtesies of chivalrous warfare. The Tuatha Dé Danann proposed to the invaders that they should leave the island for three days, during which they themselves would decide whether to fight for their kingdom or to surrender it; but the Milesians did not care for this, for they knew that, as soon as they were out of the island, the Tuatha Dé Danann would oppose them with druidical enchantments, so that they would not be able to make a fresh landing. In the end, Mac Cuill, Mac Cecht, and Mac Greiné offered to submit the matter to the arbitration of Amergin, the Milesians' own lawgiver, with the express stipulation that, if he gave an obviously partial judgment, he was to suffer death at their hands. Donn asked his druid if he were prepared to accept this very delicate duty. Amergin replied that he was, and at once delivered the first judgment pronounced by the Milesians in Ireland.

> " The men whom we found dwelling in the land, to them is possession due by right.
> It is therefore your duty to set out to sea over nine green waves;
> And if you shall be able to effect a landing again in spite of them,
> You are to engage them in battle, and I adjudge to you the land in which you found them living.
> I adjudge to you the land wherein you found them dwelling, by the right of battle.
> But although you may desire the land which these people possess, yet yours is the duty to show them justice.
> I forbid you from injustice to those you have found in the land, however you may desire to obtain it."[1]

This judgment was considered fair by both parties. The Milesians retired to their ships, and waited at a distance of nine waves' length from the land until the signal was given to attack, while the Tuatha Dé Danann, drawn up upon the beach, were ready with their druidical spells to oppose them.

The signal was given, and the Milesians bent to their oars. But they had hardly started before they discovered that a strong wind was blowing straight

[1] Translated by Professor Owen Connellan in Vol. V of the *Transactions of the Ossianic Society*.

towards them from the shore, so that they could
make no progress. At first they thought it might be
a natural breeze, but Donn smelt magic in it. He
sent a man to climb the mast of his ship, and see
if the wind blew as strong at that height as it did
at the level of the sea. The man returned, report-
ing that the air was quite still "up aloft". Evidently it was a druidical wind. But Amergin soon
coped with it. Lifting up his voice, he invoked
the Land of Ireland itself, a power higher than the
gods it sheltered.

> "I invoke the land of Eriu!
> The shining, shining sea!
> The fertile, fertile hill!
> The wooded vale!
> The river abundant, abundant in water!
> The fishful, fishful lake!"

In such strain runs the original incantation, one
of those magic formulas whose power was held by
ancient, and still is held by savage, races to reside
in their exact consecrated wording rather than in
their meaning. To us it sounds nonsense, and so
no doubt it did to those who put the old Irish
mythical traditions into literary shape; for a later
version expands and explains it as follows:[1]—

> "I implore that we may regain the land of Erin,
> We who have come over the lofty waves,

[1] The original versions of this and the following charm are from De Jubainville: *Cycle Mythologique Irlandais*, the later from Professor Owen Connellan's trans- lations in Vol. V of the *Transactions of the Ossianic Society*. "Some of these poems", explains the Professor, "have been glossed by writers or commentators of the Middle Ages, without which it would be almost impossible now for any Irish scholar to interpret them; and it is proper to remark that the translation accom- panying them is more in accordance with this gloss than with the original text."

This land whose mountains are great and extensive,
Whose streams are clear and numerous,
Whose woods abound with various fruit,
Its rivers and waterfalls are large and beautiful,
Its lakes are broad and widely spread,
It abounds with fountains on elevated grounds!
May we gain power and dominion over its tribes!
May we have kings of our own ruling at Tara!
May Tara be the regal residence of our many succeeding
    kings!
May the Milesians be the conquerors of its people!
May our ships anchor in its harbours!
May they trade along the coast of Erin!
May Eremon be its first ruling monarch!
May the descendants of Ir and Eber be mighty kings!
I implore that we may regain the land of Erin,
                I implore!"

The incantation proved effectual. The Land of Ireland was pleased to be propitious, and the druidical wind dropped down.

But success was not quite so easy as they had hoped. Manannán, son of the sea and lord of headlands, shook his magic mantle at them, and hurled a fresh tempest out over the deep. The galleys of the Milesians were tossed helplessly on the waves; many sank with their crews. Donn was among the lost, thus fulfilling Eriu's prophecy, and three other sons of Milé also perished. In the end, a broken remnant, after long beating about the coasts, came to shore at the mouth of the River Boyne. They landed; and Amergin, from the shore, invoked the aid of the sea as he had already done that of the land.

I

> " Sea full of fish!
> Fertile land!
> Fish swarming up!
> Fish there!
> Under-wave bird!
> Great fish!
> Crab's hole!
> Fish swarming up!
> Sea full of fish!"

which, being interpreted like the preceding charm, seems to have meant:

> " May the fishes of the sea crowd in shoals to the land for our use!
> May the waves of the sea drive forth to the shore abundance of fish!
> May the salmon swim abundantly into our nets!
> May all kinds of fish come plentifully to us from the sea!
> May its flat-fishes also come in abundance!
> This poem I compose at the sea-shore that fishes may swim in shoals to our coast."

Then, gathering their forces, they marched on the people of the goddess Danu.

Two battles were fought, the first in Glenn Faisi, a valley of the Slieve Mish Mountains, south of Tralee, and the second at Tailtiu, now called Tell-town. In both, the gods were beaten. Their three kings were killed by the three surviving sons of Milé—Mac Cuill by Eber, Mac Cecht by Eremon, and Mac Greiné by the druid Amergin. Defeated and disheartened, they gave in, and, retiring beneath the earth, left the surface of the land to their conquerors.

From this day begins the history of Ireland according to the annalists. Milé's eldest son, Donn, having perished, the kingdom fell by right to the second, Eremon. But Eber, the third son, backed by his followers, insisted upon a partition, and Ireland was divided into two equal parts. At the end of a year, however, war broke out between the brothers; Eber was killed in battle, and Eremon took the sole rule.

CHAPTER XI

THE GODS IN EXILE

But though mortals had conquered gods upon a scale unparalleled in mythology, they had by no means entirely subdued them. Beaten in battle, the people of the goddess Danu had yet not lost their divine attributes, and could use them either to help or hurt. "Great was the power of the Dagda", says a tract preserved in the Book of Leinster, "over the sons of Milé, even after the conquest of Ireland; for his subjects destroyed their corn and milk, so that they must needs make a treaty of peace with the Dagda. Not until then, and thanks to his good-will, were they able to harvest corn and drink the milk of their cows."[1] The basis of this lost treaty seems to have been that the Tuatha Dé Danann, though driven from the soil, should receive homage and offerings from their successors. We are told in the verse *dinnsenchus* of Mag Slecht, that—

> "Since the rule
> Of Eremon, the noble man of grace,
> There was worshipping of stones
> Until the coming of good Patrick of Macha".[2]

[1] De Jubainville: *Cycle Mythologique Irlandais*, p. 269.
[2] See chap. IV—"The Religion of the Ancient Britons and Druidism".

Dispossessed of upper earth, the gods had, however, to seek for new homes. A council was convened, but its members were divided between two opinions. One section of them chose to shake the dust of Ireland off its disinherited feet, and seek refuge in a paradise over-seas, situate in some unknown, and, except for favoured mortals, unknowable island of the west, the counterpart in Gaelic myth of the British

> . . . "island-valley of Avilion;
> Where falls not hail, or rain, or any snow,
> Nor ever wind blows loudly; but it lies
> Deep-meadow'd, happy, fair with orchard-lawns
> And bowery hollows crown'd with summer sea"[1]

—a land of perpetual pleasure and feasting, described variously as the "Land of Promise" (*Tir Tairngiré*), the "Plain of Happiness" (*Mag Mell*), the "Land of the Living" (*Tir-nam-beo*), the "Land of the Young" (*Tir-nan-ōg*), and "Breasal's Island" (*Hy-Breasail*). Celtic mythology is full of the beauties and wonders of this mystic country, and the tradition of it has never died out. Hy-Breasail has been set down on old maps as a reality again and again;[2] some pioneers in the Spanish seas thought they had discovered it, and called the land they found "Brazil"; and it is still said, by lovers of old lore, that a patient watcher, after long gazing westward from the westernmost shores of Ireland or Scotland,

[1] Tennyson: *Idylls of the King: The Passing of Arthur.*
[2] See Wood-Martin: *Traces of the Elder Faiths of Ireland*, Vol I, pp. 213-215.

may sometimes be lucky enough to catch a glimpse against the sunset of its—

" summer isles of Eden lying in dark-purple spheres of sea ".

Of these divine emigrants the principal was Manannán son of Lêr. But, though he had cast in his lot beyond the seas, he did not cease to visit Ireland. An old Irish king, Bran, the son of Febal, met him, according to a seventh-century poem, as Bran journeyed to, and Manannán from, the earthly paradise. Bran was in his boat, and Manannán was driving a chariot over the tops of the waves, and he sang:[1]

" Bran deems it a marvellous beauty
In his coracle across the clear sea:
While to me in my chariot from afar
It is a flowery plain on which he rides about.

" What is a clear sea
For the prowed skiff in which Bran is,
That is a happy plain with profusion of flowers
To me from the chariot of two wheels.

" Bran sees
The number of waves beating across the clear sea:
I myself see in Mag Mon[2]
Red-headed flowers without fault.

" Sea-horses glisten in summer
As far as Bran has stretched his glance:
Rivers pour forth a stream of honey
In the land of Manannán son of Lêr.

---

[1] The following verses are taken from Dr. Kuno Meyer's translation of the romance entitled *The Voyage of Bran, Son of Febal*, published in Mr. Nutt's Grimm Library, Vol. IV.　　　　　　　　　[2] The Plain of Sports.

" The sheen of the main, on which thou art,
The white hue of the sea, on which thou rowest about,
Yellow and azure are spread out,
It is land, and is not rough.

" Speckled salmon leap from the womb
Of the white sea, on which thou lookest:
They are calves, they are coloured lambs
With friendliness, without mutual slaughter.

" Though but one chariot-rider is seen
In Mag Mell[1] of many flowers,
There are many steeds on its surface,
Though them thou seest not.

. . . .

" Along the top of a wood has swum
Thy coracle across ridges,
There is a wood of beautiful fruit
Under the prow of thy little skiff.

" A wood with blossom and fruit,
On which is the vine's veritable fragrance;
A wood without decay, without defect,
On which are leaves of a golden hue."

And, after this singularly poetical enunciation of the philosophical and mystical doctrine that all things are, under their diverse forms, essentially the same, he goes on to describe to Bran the beauties and pleasures of the Celtic Elysium.

But there were others—indeed, the most part—of the gods who refused to expatriate themselves. For these residences had to be found, and the Dagda, their new king, proceeded to assign to each of those who stayed in Ireland a *sídh*. These *sídhe* were barrows, or hillocks, each being the door to an under-

[1] The Happy Plain.

ground realm of inexhaustible splendour and delight, according to the somewhat primitive ideas of the Celts. A description is given of one which the Dagda kept for himself, and out of which his son Angus cheated him, which will serve as a fair example of all. There were apple-trees there always in fruit, and one pig alive and another ready roasted, and the supply of ale never failed. One may still visit in Ireland the *sidhe* of many of the gods, for the spots are known, and the traditions have not died out. To Lêr was given *Sidh Fionnachaidh*[1], now known as the "Hill of the White Field", on the top of Slieve Fuad, near Newtown Hamilton, in County Armagh. Bodb Derg received a *sidh* called by his own name, *Sidh Bodb*[2], just to the south of Portumna, in Galway. Mider was given the *sidh* of *Bri Leith*, now called Slieve Golry, near Ardagh, in County Longford. Ogma's *sidh* was called *Airceltrai*; to Lugh was assigned *Rodrubân*; Manannán's son, Ilbhreach, received *Sidh Eas Aedha Ruaidh*[3], now the Mound of Mullachshee, near Ballyshannon, in Donegal; Fionnbharr[4] had *Sidh Meadha*, now "Knockma", about five miles west of Tuam, where, as present king of the fairies, he is said to live to-day; while the abodes of other gods of lesser fame are also recorded. For himself the Dagda retained two, both near the River Boyne, in Meath, the best of them being the famous Brugh-na-Boyne. None of the members of the Tuatha Dé Danann were left unprovided for, save one.

---

[1] Pronounced *Shee Finneha*.   [2] Pronounced *Shee Bove*.
[3] Pronounced *Shee Assaroe*.   [4] Pronounced *Finnvar*.

It was from this time that the Gaelic gods received the name by which the peasantry know them to-day—*Aes Sídhe*, the "People of the Hills", or, more shortly, the *Sídhe*. Every god, or fairy, is a *Fer-Sídhe*[1], a "Man of the Hill"; and every goddess a *Bean-Sídhe*, a "Woman of the Hill", the *banshee* of popular legend.[2]

The most famous of such fairy hills are about five miles from Drogheda.[3] They are still connected with the names of the Tuatha Dé Danann, though they are now not called their dwelling-places, but their tombs. On the northern bank of the Boyne stand seventeen barrows, three of which—Knowth, Dowth, and New Grange—are of great size. The last named, largest, and best preserved, is over 300 feet in diameter, and 70 feet high, while its top makes a platform 120 feet across. It has been explored, and Roman coins, gold torques, copper pins, and iron rings and knives have been found in it; but what else it may have once contained will never be known, for, like Knowth and Dowth, it was thoroughly ransacked by Danish spoilers in the ninth century. It is entered by a square doorway, the rims of which are elaborately ornamented with a kind of spiral pattern. This entrance leads to a stone passage, more than 60 feet long, which gradually widens and rises, until it opens into a chamber with a conical dome 20 feet high. On each side of this central chamber is a recess, with a shallow oval

---

[1] Pronounced *Far-shee*.
[2] O'Curry: *Lectures on the MS. Materials of Ancient Irish History*, Appendix p. 505.　　　[3] See Fergusson: *Rude Stone Monuments*, pp. 200-213.

stone basin in it. The huge slabs of which the
whole is built are decorated upon both the outer
and the inner faces with the same spiral pattern as
the doorway.

The origin of these astonishing prehistoric monuments is unknown, but they are generally attributed
to the race that inhabited Ireland before the Celts.
Gazing at marvellous New Grange, one might very
well echo the words of the old Irish poet Mac Nia,
in the Book of Ballymote: .

> " Behold the *Sidh* before your eyes,
> It is manifest to you that it is a king's mansion,
> Which was built by the firm Dagda,
> It was a wonder, a court, an admirable hill."[1]

It is not, however, with New Grange, or even
with Knowth or Dowth, that the Dagda's name is
now associated. It is a smaller barrow, nearer to
the Boyne, which is known as the "Tomb of the
Dagda". It has never been opened, and Dr. James
Fergusson, the author of *Rude Stone Monuments*,
who holds the Tuatha Dé Danann to have been a
real people, thinks that "the bones and armour of
the great Dagda may still be found in his honoured
grave".[2] Other Celtic scholars might not be so
sanguine, though verses as old as the eleventh
century assert that the Tuatha Dé Danann used
the brughs for burial. It was about this period that
the mythology of Ireland was being rewoven into
spurious history. The poem, which is called the
"Chronicles of the Tombs", not only mentions the

1 O'Curry: *MS. Materials*, p. 505.
2 Fergusson: *Rude Stone Monuments*, p. 209.

"Monument of the Dagda" and the "Monument of the Morrígú", but also records the last resting-places of Ogma, Etain, Cairpré, Lugh, Boann, and Angus.

We have for the present, however, to consider Angus in a far less sepulchral light. He is, indeed, very much alive in the story to be related. The "Son of the Young" was absent when the distri-bution of the *sídhe* was made. When he returned, he came to his father, the Dagda, and demanded one. The Dagda pointed out to him that they had all been given away. Angus protested, but what could be done? By fair means, evidently nothing; but by craft, a great deal. The wily Angus ap-peared to reconcile himself to fate, and only begged his father to allow him to stay at the *sídh* of Brugh-na-Boyne (New Grange) for a day and a night. The Dagda agreed to this, no doubt congratulating himself on having got out of the difficulty so easily. But when he came to Angus to remind him that the time was up, Angus refused to go. He had been granted, he claimed, day and night, and it is of days and nights that time and eternity are composed; therefore there was no limit to his tenure of the *sídh*. The logic does not seem very convincing to our modern minds, but the Dagda is said to have been satisfied with it. He abandoned the best of his two palaces to his son, who took peaceable pos-session of it. Thus it got a second name, that of the *Sídh* or *Brugh* of the "Son of the Young".[1]

The Dagda does not, after this, play much active

[1] This story is contained in the Book of Leinster.

part in the history of the people of the goddess Danu. We next hear of a council of gods to elect a fresh ruler. There were five candidates for the vacant throne—Bodb the Red, Mider, Ilbhreach[1] son of Manannán, Lêr, and Angus himself, though the last-named, we are told, had little real desire to rule, as he preferred a life of freedom to the dignities of kingship. The Tuatha Dé Danann went into consultation, and the result of their deliberation was that their choice fell upon Bodb the Red, for three reasons—firstly, for his own sake; secondly, for his father, the Dagda's sake; and thirdly, because he was the Dagda's eldest son. The other competitors approved this choice, except two. Mider refused to give hostages, as was the custom, to Bodb Derg, and fled with his followers to "a desert country round Mount Leinster", in County Carlow, while Lêr retired in great anger to Sídh Fionnachaidh, declining to recognize or obey the new king.

Why Lêr and Mider should have so taken the matter to heart is difficult to understand, unless it was because they were both among the oldest of the gods. The indifference of Angus is easier to explain. He was the Gaelic Eros, and was busy living up to his character. At this time, the object of his love was a maiden who had visited him one night in a dream, only to vanish when he put out his arms to embrace her. All the next day, we are told, Angus took no food. Upon the following night, the unsubstantial lady again appeared, and played and

[1] Pronounced *Ilbreç*.

sang to him. That following day, he also fasted. So things went on for a year, while Angus pined and wasted for love. At last the physicians of the Tuatha Dé Danann guessed his complaint, and told him how fatal it might be to him. Angus asked that his mother Boann might be sent for, and, when she came, he told her his trouble, and implored her help. She went to the Dagda and begged him, if he did not wish to see his son die of unrequited love, a disease that all Diancecht's medicine and Goibniu's magic could not heal, to find the dream-maiden. The Dagda could do nothing himself, but he sent to Bodb the Red, and the new king of the gods sent in turn to the lesser deities of Ireland, ordering all of them to search for her. For a year she could not be found, but at last the disconsolate lover received a message, charging him to come and see if he could recognize the lady of his dreams. Angus came, and knew her at once, even though she was surrounded by thrice fifty attendant nymphs. Her name was Caer, and she was the daughter of Etal Ambuel, who had a *sídh* at Uaman, in Con-naught. Bodb the Red demanded her for Angus in marriage, but her father declared that he had no control over her. She was a swan-maiden, he said; and every year, as soon as summer was over, she went with her companions to a lake called "Dragon-Mouth", and there all of them became swans. But, refusing to be thus put off, Angus waited in patience until the day of the magical change, and then went down to the shore of the lake. There, surrounded by thrice fifty swans, he saw Caer, herself a swan surpassing all the rest in beauty and whiteness. He called to her, proclaiming his passion and his name, and she promised to be his bride, if he too would become a swan. He agreed, and with a word she changed him into swan-shape, and thus they flew side by side to Angus's *sídh*, where they retook the human form, and, no doubt, lived happily as long as could be expected of such changeable immortals as pagan deities.[1]

Meanwhile, the people of the goddess Danu were justly incensed against both Lêr and Mider. Bodb the Red made a yearly war upon Mider in his *sídh*, and many of the divine race were killed on either side. But against Lêr, the new king of the gods refused to move, for there had been a great affection between them. Many times Bodb Derg tried to regain Lêr's friendship by presents and compliments, but for a long time without success.

At last Lêr's wife died, to the sea-god's great sorrow. When Bodb the Red heard the news, he sent a messenger to Lêr, offering him one of his own foster-daughters, Aebh[2], Aeife[3], and Ailbhe[4], the children of Ailioll of Arran. Lêr, touched by this, came to visit Bodb the Red at his *sídh*, and chose Aebh for his wife. "She is the eldest, so she must be the noblest of them," he said. They were married, and a great feast made; and Lêr took her back with him to Sídh Fionnachaidh.

Aebh bore four children to Lêr. The eldest was

---

[1] This story, called the *Dream of Angus*, will be found translated into English by Dr. Edward Müller in Vol. III. of the *Revue Celtique*, from an eighteenth-century MS. in the British Museum.

[2] Pronounced *Aive*.   [3] Pronounced *Aiva*.   [4] Pronounced *Alva*.

a daughter called Finola, the second was a son called Aed; the two others were twin boys called Fiachra and Conn, but in giving birth to those Aebh died.

Bodb the Red then offered Lêr another of his foster-children, and he chose the second, Aeife. Every year Lêr and Aeife and the four children used to go to Manannán's "Feast of Age", which was held at each of the *sídhe* in turn. The four children grew up to be great favourites among the people of the goddess Danu.

But Aeife was childless, and she became jealous of Lêr's children; for she feared that he would love them more than he did her. She brooded over this until she began, first to hope for, and then to plot their deaths. She tried to persuade her servants to murder them, but they would not. So she took the four children to Lake Darvra (now called Lough Derravargh in West Meath), and sent them into the water to bathe. Then she made an incantation over them, and touched them, each in turn, with a druidical wand, and changed them into swans.

But, though she had magic enough to alter their shapes, she had not the power to take away their human speech and minds. Finola turned, and threatened her with the anger of Lêr and of Bodb the Red when they came to hear of it. She, however, hardened her heart, and refused to undo what she had done. The children of Lêr, finding their case a hopeless one, asked her how long she intended to keep them in that condition.

"You would be easier in mind," she said, "if you had not asked the question; but I will tell you.

You shall be three hundred years here, on Lake Darvra; and three hundred years upon the Sea of Moyle[1], which is between Erin and Alba; and three hundred years more at Irros Domnann[2] and the Isle of Glora in Erris[3]. Yet you shall have two consolations in your troubles; you shall keep your human minds, and yet suffer no grief at knowing that you have been changed into swans, and you shall be able to sing the softest and sweetest songs that were ever heard in the world."

Then Aeife went away and left them. She returned to Lêr, and told him that the children had fallen by accident into Lake Darvra, and were drowned.

But Lêr was not satisfied that she spoke the truth, and went in haste to the lake, to see if he could find traces of them. He saw four swans close to the shore, and heard them talking to one another with human voices. As he approached, they came out of the water to meet him. They told him what Aeife had done, and begged him to change them back into their own shapes. But Lêr's magic was not so powerful as his wife's, and he could not.

Nor even could Bodb the Red—to whom Lêr went for help,—for all that he was king of the gods. What Aeife had done could not be undone. But she could be punished for it! Bodb ordered his foster-daughter to appear before him, and, when she came, he put an oath on her to tell him truly "what shape of all others, on the earth, or above the earth,

---

[1] Now called "North Channel"   [2] The Peninsula of Erris, in Mayo.
[3] A small island off Benmullet.

or beneath the earth, she most abhorred, and into which she most dreaded to be transformed". Aeife was obliged to answer that she most feared to become a demon of the air. So Bodb the Red struck her with his wand, and she fled from them, a shrieking demon.

All the Tuatha Dé Danann went to Lake Darvra to visit the four swans. The Milesians heard of it, and also went; for it was not till long after this that gods and mortals ceased to associate. The visit became a yearly feast. But, at the end of three hundred years, the children of Lêr were compelled to leave Lake Darvra, and go to the Sea of Moyle, to fulfil the second period of their exile.

They bade farewell to gods and men, and went. And, for fear lest they might be hurt by anyone, the Milesians made it law in Ireland that no man should harm a swan, from that time forth for ever.

The children of Lêr suffered much from tempest and cold on the stormy Sea of Moyle, and they were very lonely. Once only during that long three hundred years did they see any of their friends. An embassy of the Tuatha Dé Danann, led by two sons of Bodb the Red, came to look for them, and told them all that had happened in Erin during their exile.

At last that long penance came to an end, and they went to Irros Domnann and Innis Glora for their third stage. And while it was wearily dragging through, Saint Patrick came to Ireland, and put an end to the power of the gods for ever. They had been banned and banished when the children of

Lêr found themselves free to return to their old
home. Sídh Fionnechaidh was empty and deserted,
for Lêr had been killed by Caoilté, the cousin of
Finn mac Coul.[1]

So, after long, vain searching for their lost relatives,
they gave up hope, and returned to the Isle of Glora.
They had a friend there, the Lonely Crane of Inniskea[2], which has lived upon that island ever since the
beginning of the world, and will be still sitting there
on the day of judgment. They saw no one else
until, one day, a man came to the island. He told
them that he was Saint Caemhoc[3], and that he had
heard their story. He brought them to his church,
and preached the new faith to them, and they believed
on Christ, and consented to be baptised. This broke
the pagan spell, and, as soon as the holy water was
sprinkled over them, they returned to human shape.
But they were very old and bowed—three aged men
and an ancient woman. They did not live long after
this, and Saint Caemhoc, who had baptised them,
buried them all together in one grave.[4]

But, in telling this story, we have leaped nine
hundred years—a great space in the history even
of gods. We must retrace our steps, if not quite
to the days of Eremon and Eber, sons of Milé, and
first kings of Ireland, at any rate to the beginning
of the Christian era.

---

[1] See chap. XIV—"Finn and the Fenians".
[2] An island off the coast of Mayo. Its lonely crane was one of the "Wonders
of Ireland", and is still an object of folk-belief.   [3] Pronounced *Kemoc.*
[4] This famous story of the *Fate of the Children of Lêr* is not found in any MS.
earlier than the beginning of the seventeenth century. A translation of it has been
published by Eugene O'Curry in *Atlantis*, Vol. IV, from which the present abridg-
ment is made.

At this time Eochaid Airem was high king of Ireland, and reigned at Tara; while, under him, as vassal monarchs, Conchobar mac Nessa ruled over the Red Branch Champions of Ulster; Curoi son of Daire[1], was king of Munster; Mesgegra was king of Leinster; and Ailell, with his famous queen, Medb, governed Connaught.

Shortly before, among the gods, Angus Son of the Young, had stolen away Etain, the wife of Mider. He kept her imprisoned in a bower of glass, which he carried everywhere with him, never allowing her to leave it, for fear Mider might recapture her. The Gaelic Pluto, however, found out where she was, and was laying plans to rescue her, when a rival of Etain's herself decoyed Angus away from before the pleasant prison-house, and set his captive free. But, instead of returning her to Mider, she changed the luckless goddess into a fly, and threw her into the air, where she was tossed about in great wretchedness at the mercy of every wind.

At the end of seven years, a gust blew her on to the roof of the house of Etair, one of the vassals of Conchobar, who was celebrating a feast. The unhappy fly, who was Etain, was blown down the chimney into the room below, and fell, exhausted, into a golden cup full of beer, which the wife of the master of the house was just going to drink. And the woman drank Etain with the beer.

But, of course, this was not the end of her—for the gods cannot really die,—but only the beginning of a new life. Etain was reborn as the daughter of

---

[1] Pronounced *Dara*.

Etair's wife, no one knowing that she was not of mortal lineage. She grew up to be the most beautiful woman in Ireland.

When she was twenty years old, her fame reached the high king, who sent messengers to see if she was as fair as men reported. They saw her, and returned to the king full of her praises. So Eochaid himself went to pay her a visit. He chose her to be his queen, and gave her a splendid dowry.

It was not till then that Mider heard of her. He came to her in the shape of a young man, beautifully dressed, and told her who she really was, and how she had been his wife among the people of the goddess Danu. He begged her to leave the king, and come with him to his *sídh* at Bri Leith. But Etain refused with scorn.

"Do you think," she said, "that I would give up the high king of Ireland for a person whose name and kindred I do not know, except from his own lips?"

The god retired, baffled for the time. But one day, as King Eochaid sat in his hall, a stranger entered. He was dressed in a purple tunic, his hair was like gold, and his eyes shone like candles.

The king welcomed him.

"But who are you?" he asked; "for I do not know you."

"Yet I have known you a long time," returned the stranger.

"Then what is your name?"

"Not a very famous one. I am Mider of Bri Leith."

" Why have you come here?"

" To challenge you to a game of chess."

" I am a good chess-player," replied the king, who was reputed to be the best in Ireland.

" I think I can beat you," answered Mider.

" But the chess-board is in the queen's room, and she is asleep," objected Eochaid.

" It does not matter," replied Mider. " I have brought a board with me which can be in no way worse than yours."

He showed it to the king, who admitted that the boast was true. The chess-board was made of silver set in precious stones, and the pieces were of gold.

" Play!" said Mider to the king.

" I never play without a wager," replied Eochaid.

" What shall be the stake?" asked Mider.

" I do not care," replied Eochaid.

" Good!" returned Mider. " Let it be that the loser pays whatever the winner demands."

" That is a wager fit for a king," said Eochaid.

They played, and Mider lost. The stake that Eochaid claimed from him was that Mider and his subjects should make a road through Ireland. Eochaid watched the road being made, and noticed how Mider's followers yoked their oxen, not by the horns, as the Gaels did, but at the shoulders, which was better. He adopted the practice, and thus got his nickname, Airem, that is, " The Ploughman".

After a year, Mider returned and challenged the king again, the terms to be the same as before. Eochaid agreed with joy; but, this time, he lost.

"I could have beaten you before, if I had wished," said Mider, "and now the stake I demand is Etain, your queen."

The astonished king, who could not for shame go back upon his word, asked for a year's delay. Mider agreed to return upon that day year to claim Etain. Eochaid consulted with his warriors, and they decided to keep watch through the whole of the day fixed by Mider, and let no one pass in or out of the royal palace till sunset. For Eochaid held that if the fairy king could not get Etain upon that one day, his promise would be no longer binding on him.

So, when the day came, they barred the door and guarded it, but suddenly they saw Mider among them in the hall. He stood beside Etain, and sang this song to her, setting out the pleasures of the homes of the gods under the enchanted hills.

"O fair lady! will you come with me
　To a wonderful country which is mine,
　Where the people's hair is of golden hue,
　And their bodies the colour of virgin snow?

"There no grief or care is known;
　White are their teeth, black their eyelashes;
　Delight of the eye is the rank of our hosts,
　With the hue of the fox-glove on every cheek.

"Crimson are the flowers of every mead,
　Gracefully speckled as the blackbird's egg;
　Though beautiful to see be the plains of Inisfail [1]
　They are but commons compared to our great plains.

---

[1] A poetical name for Ireland.

" Though intoxicating to you be the ale-drink of Inisfail,
  More intoxicating the ales of the great country;
  The only land to praise is the land of which I speak,
  Where no one ever dies of decrepit age.

" Soft sweet streams traverse the land;
  The choicest of mead and of wine;
  Beautiful people without any blemish;
  Love without sin, without wickedness.

" We can see the people upon all sides,
  But by no one can we be seen;
  The cloud of Adam's transgression it is
  That prevents them from seeing us.

" O lady, should you come to my brave land,
  It is golden hair that will be on your head;
  Fresh pork, beer, new milk, and ale,
  You there with me shall have, O fair lady!"[1]

Then Mider greeted Eochaid, and told him that he had come to take away Etain, according to the king's wager. And, while the king and his warriors looked on helplessly, he placed one arm round the now willing woman, and they both vanished. This broke the spell that hung over everyone in the hall; they rushed to the door, but all they could see were two swans flying away.

The king would not, however, yield to the god. He sent to every part of Ireland for news of Etain, but his messengers all came back without having been able to find her. At last, a druid named Dalân learned, by means of ogams carved upon wands of yew, that she was hidden under Mider's

[1] Translated by O'Curry, *Manners and Customs of the Ancient Irish*, Lecture IX, p. 192, 193.

sídh of Bri Leith.   So Eochaid marched there with
an army, and began to dig deep into the abode of
the gods of which the "fairy hill" was the portal.
Mider, as terrified as was the Greek god Hades
when it seemed likely that the earth would be rent
open,[1] and his domains laid bare to the sight, sent
out fifty fairy maidens to Eochaid, every one of
them having the appearance of Etain.   But the
king would only be content with the real Etain, so
that Mider, to save his *sídh*, was at last obliged to
give her up.   And she lived with the King of Ireland after that until the death of both of them.

But Mider never forgave the insult.   He bided
his time for three generations, until Eochaid and
Etain had a male descendant.   For they had no
son, but only a daughter called Etain, like her
mother, and this second Etain had a daughter called
Messbuachallo, who had a son called Conairé, surnamed "the Great".   Mider and the gods wove
the web of fate round Conairé, so that he and all his
men died violent deaths.[2]

---

[1] *Iliad*, Book XX.
[2] The story of Mider's revenge and Conairé's death is told in the romance
Bruidhen Dá Derga, "The Destruction of Da Derga's Fort", translated by Dr.
Whitley Stokes, Eugene O'Curry and Professor Zimmer from the original text.

CHAPTER XII

THE IRISH ILIAD

With Eber and Eremon, sons of Milé, and conquerors of the gods, begins a fresh series of characters in Gaelic tradition—the early "Milesian" kings of Ireland. Though monkish chroniclers have striven to find history in the legends handed down concerning them, they are none the less almost as mythical as the Tuatha Dé Danann. The first of them who has the least appearance of reality is Tigernmas, who is recorded to have reigned a hundred years after the coming of the Milesians. He seems to have been what is sometimes called a "Culture-king", bearing much the same kind of relation to Ireland as Theseus bore to Athens or Minos to Crete. During his reign, nine new lakes and three new rivers broke forth from beneath the earth to give their waters to Erin. Under his auspices, gold was first smelted, ornaments of gold and silver were first made, and clothes first dyed. He is said to have perished mysteriously[1] with

---

[1] "There came
Tigernmas, the prince of Tara yonder,
On Hallowe'en with many hosts,
A cause of grief to them was the deed.

"Dead were the men
Of Banba's host, without happy strength,

three-fourths of the men of Erin while worshipping
Cromm Cruaich on the field of Mag Slecht.   In him
Mr. Nutt sees, no doubt rightly, the great mythical
king who, in almost all national histories, closes
the strictly mythological age, and inaugurates a new
era of less obviously divine, if hardly less apocryphal
characters.[1]

In spite, however, of the worship of the Tuatha
Dé Danann instituted by Eremon, we find the early
kings and heroes of Ireland walking very familiarly
with their gods.   Eochaid Airem, high king of
Ireland, was apparently reckoned a perfectly fit
suitor for the goddess Etain, and proved a far from
unsuccessful rival of Mider, the Gaelic Pluto.[2]   And
adventures of love or war were carried quite as
cheerfully among the *sídh* dwellers by Eochaid's
contemporaries — Conchobar son of Nessa, King
of Ulster, Curoi son of Daire, King of Munster,
Mesgegra, King of Leinster, and Ailell and Medb[3],
King and Queen of Connaught.

All these figures of the second Gaelic cycle (that
of the heroes of Ulster, and especially of their
great champion, Cuchulainn) lived, according to
Irish tradition, at about the beginning of the

Around Tigernmas, the destructive man in the North,
From the worship of Cromm Cruaich—'t was no luck for them.

" For I have learnt,
Except one-fourth of the keen Gaels
Not a man alive—lasting the snare!
Escaped without death in his mouth."
—Dr. Kuno Meyer's translation of the *Dinnsenchus of Mag Slecht*.

[1] Nutt: *Voyage of Bran*, p. 164.
[2] See chap. XI—"The Gods in Exile".
[3] Pronounced *Maive*.

Christian era. Conchobar, indeed, is said to have
expired in a fit of rage on hearing of the death
of Christ.[1]

But this is a very transparent monkish interpola-
tion into the original story. A quite different view
is taken by most modern scholars, who would see
gods and not men in all the legendary characters
of the Celtic heroic cycles. Upon such a subject,
however, one may legitimately take sides. Were
King Conchobar and his Ultonian champions, Finn
and his Fenians, Arthur and his Knights once living
men round whom the attributes of gods have
gathered, or were they ancient deities renamed and
stripped of some of their divinity to make them
more akin to their human worshippers? History
or mythology? A mingling, perhaps, of both.
Cuchulainn[2] may have been the name of a real
Gaelic warrior, however suspiciously he may now
resemble the sun-god, who is said to have been his
father. King Conchobar may have been the real
chief of a tribe of Irish Celts before he became an
adumbration of the Gaelic sky-god. It is the same
problem that confronts us in dealing with the heroic
legends of Greece and Rome. Were Achilles,
Agamemnon, Odysseus, Paris, Æneas gods, demi-
gods, or men? Let us call them all alike—whether
they be Greek or Trojan heroes, Red Branch
Champions, or followers of the Gaelic Finn or the
British Arthur—demi-gods. Even so, they stand

[1] The story of the *Tragical Death of King Conchobar*, translated by Eugene
O'Curry from the Book of Leinster, will be found in the appendix to his *MS.
Materials of Irish History*, and (more accessible) in Miss Hull's *Cuchullin Saga*.
[2] The name is best pronounced *Cŭhoolin* or *Cuchullin* (*ch* as in German).

definitely apart from the older gods who were greater than they were.

We are stretching no point in calling them demi-gods, for they were god-descended.[1]   Cuchulainn, the greatest hero of the Ulster cycle, was doubly so; for on his mother's side he was the grandson of the Dagda, while Lugh of the Long Hand is said to have been his father.   His mother, Dechtiré, daughter of Maga, the daughter of Angus " Son of the Young ", was half-sister to King Conchobar, and all the other principal heroes were of hardly less lofty descent.   It is small wonder that they are described in ancient manuscripts [2] as terrestrial gods and goddesses.

" Terrestrial " they may have been in form, but their acts were superhuman.   Indeed, compared with the more modest exploits of the heroes of the " Iliad ", they were those of giants.   Where Greek warriors slew their tens, these Ultonians despatched their hundreds.   They came home after such ex-ploits so heated that their cold baths boiled over. When they sat down to meat, they devoured whole oxen, and drank their mead from vats.   With one stroke of their favourite swords they beheaded hills for sport.   The gods themselves hardly did more, and it is easy to understand that in those old days not only might the sons of gods look upon the daughters of men and find them fair, but immortal

---

[1] The descent of the principal Red Branch Heroes from the Tuatha Dé Danann is given in a table in Miss Hull's Introduction to her *Cuchullin Saga.*

[2] Conchobar is called a terrestrial god of the Ultonians in the Book of the Dun Cow, and Dechtiré is termed a goddess in the Book of Leinster.

women also need not be too proud to form passing alliances with mortal men.

Some of the older deities seem to have already passed out of memory at the time of the compilation of the Ulster cycle. At any rate, they make no appearance in it. Dead Nuada rests in the *grianan* of Aileach; Ogma lies low in *sídh* Airceltrai; while the Dagda, thrust into the background by his son Angus, mixes himself very little in the affairs of Erin.[1] But the Morrígú is no less eager in encouraging human or semi-divine heroes to war than she was when she revived the fainting spirits of the folk of the goddess Danu at the Battle of Moytura. The gods who appear most often in the cycle of the Red Branch of Ulster are the same that have lived on throughout with the most persistent vitality. Lugh the Long-handed, Angus of the Brugh, Mider, Bodb the Red, and Manannán son of Lêr, are the principal deities that move in the background of the stage where the chief parts are now played by mortals. But, to make up for the loss of some of the greater divine figures, the ranks of the gods are being recruited from below. All manner of inferior divinities claim to be members of the tribe of the goddess Danu. The goblins and sprites and demons of the air who shrieked around battles are described collectively as Tuatha Dé Danann.[2]

As for the Fomors, they have lost their distinctive names, though they are still recognized as dwellers beneath the deep, who at times raid upon

[1] He is last heard of as chief cook to Conairé the Great, a mythical king of Ireland.   [2] In the Book of Leinster.

the coast, and do battle with the heroes over whom Conchobar ruled at Emain Macha.

This seat of his government, the traditionary site of which is still marked by an extensive prehistoric entrenchment called Navan Fort[1], near Armagh, was the centre of an Ulster that stretched southwards as far as the Boyne, and round its ruler gathered such a galaxy of warriors as Ireland had never seen before, or will again. They called themselves the "Champions of the Red Branch"; there was not one of them who was not a hero; but they are all dwarfed by one splendid figure—Cuchulainn, whose name means "Culann's Hound". Mr. Alfred Nutt calls him "the Irish Achilles"[2], while Professor Rhys would rather see in him a Heracles of the Gaels.[3] Like Achilles, he was the chosen hero of his people, invincible in battle, and yet "at once to early death and sorrows doomed beyond the lot of man", while, like Heracles, his life was a series of wonderful exploits and labours. It matters little enough; for the lives of all such mythical heroes must be of necessity somewhat alike.

If Achilles and Heracles were, as some think, personifications of the sun, Cuchulainn is not less so. Most of his attributes, as the old stories record them, are obviously solar symbols. He seemed generally small and insignificant, yet, when he was

[1] For a description of Navan Fort see a paper by M. de Jubainville in the *Revue Celtique*, Vol. XVI.

[2] *Cuchulainn, the Irish Achilles*. By Alfred Nutt. Popular Studies in Mythology, Romance, and Folklore, No. 8.

[3] See a series of interesting parallels between Cuchulainn and Heracles in *Studies in the Arthurian Legend*, chap. IX and X.

at his full strength, no one could look him in the
face without blinking, while the heat of his constitution melted snow for thirty feet all round him.
He turned red and hissed as he dipped his body
into its bath—the sea.   Terrible was his transformation when sorely oppressed by his enemies,
as the sun is by mist, storm, or eclipse.   At such
times "among the aërial clouds over his head were
visible the virulent pouring showers and sparks of
ruddy fire which the seething of his savage wrath
caused to mount up above him.   His hair became
tangled about his head, as it had been branches of
a red thorn-bush stuffed into a strongly-fenced gap.
. . . Taller, thicker, more rigid, longer than mast
of a great ship was the perpendicular jet of dusky
blood which out of his scalp's very central point
shot upwards and then was scattered to the four
cardinal points; whereby was formed a magic mist
of gloom resembling the smoky pall that drapes
a regal dwelling, what time a king at nightfall of a
winter's day draws near to it."[1]

So marvellous a being[2] was, of course, of marvellous birth.   His mother, Dechtiré, was on the
point of being married to an Ulster chieftain called
Sualtam, and was sitting at the wedding-feast, when
a may-fly flew into her cup of wine and was un-
wittingly swallowed by her.   That same afternoon

[1] The *Táin Bó Chuailgné.*   Translated by Standish Hayes O'Grady.
[2] The Irish romances relating to Cuchulainn and his cycle, nearly a hundred in
number, need hardly be referred to severally in this chapter.   Of many of the
tales, too, there exist several slightly-varying versions.   Many of them have been
translated by different scholars.   The reader desiring a more complete survey of
the Cuchulainn legend is referred to Miss Hull's *Cuchullin Saga* or to Lady
Gregory's *Cuchulain of Muirthemne.*

she fell into a deep sleep, and in her dream the sun-god Lugh appeared to her, and told her that it was he whom she had swallowed, and bore within her. He ordered her and her fifty attendant maidens to come with him at once, and he put upon them the shapes of birds, so that they were not seen to go. Nothing was heard of them again. But one day, months later, a flock of beautiful birds appeared before Emain Macha, and drew out its warriors in their chariots to hunt them.

They followed the birds till nightfall, when they found themselves at the Brugh on the Boyne, where the great gods had their homes. As they looked everywhere for shelter, they suddenly saw a splendid palace. A tall and handsome man, richly dressed, came out and welcomed them and led them in. Within the hall were a beautiful and noble-faced woman and fifty maidens, and on the tables were the richest meats and wines, and everything fit for the needs of warriors. So they rested there the night, and, during the night, they heard the cry of a new-born child. The next morning, the man told them who he was, and that the woman was Conchobar's half-sister Dechtiré, and he ordered them to take the child, and bring it up among the warriors of Ulster. So they brought him back, together with his mother and the maidens, and Dechtiré married Sualtam, and all the chiefs, champions, druids, poets, and lawgivers of Ulster vied with one another in bringing up the mysterious infant.

At first they called him Setanta; and this is how he came to change his name. While still a child, he was the strongest of the boys of Emain Macha, and the champion in their sports. One day he was playing hurley single-handed against all the others, and beating them, when Conchobar the King rode by with his nobles on the way to a banquet given by Culann, the chief smith of the Ultonians. Conchobar called to the boy, inviting him to go with them, and he replied that, when the game was finished, he would follow. As soon as the Ulster champions were in Culann's hall, the smith asked the king's leave to unloose his terrible watch-dog, which was as strong and fierce as a hundred hounds; and Conchobar, forgetting that the boy was to follow them, gave his permission. Immediately the hound saw Setanta coming, it rushed at him, open-mouthed. But the boy flung his playing-ball into its mouth, and then, seizing it by the hind-legs, dashed it against a rock till he had killed it.

The smith Culann was very angry at the death of his dog; for there was no other hound in the world like him for guarding a house and flocks. So Setanta promised to find and train up another one, not less good, for Culann, and, until it was trained, to guard the smith's house as though he were a dog himself. This is why he was called Cuchulainn, that is, "Culann's Hound"; and Cathbad the Druid prophesied that the time would come when the name would be in every man's mouth.

Not long after this, Cuchulainn overheard Cathbad giving druidical instruction, and one of his pupils asking him what that day would be propitious for. Cathbad replied that, if any young man first took arms on that day, his name would be greater than that of any other hero's, but his life would be short. At once, the boy went to King Conchobar, and demanded arms and a chariot. Conchobar asked him who had put such a thought into his head; and he answered that it was Cathbad the Druid. So Conchobar gave him arms and armour, and sent him out with a charioteer. That evening, Cuchulainn brought back the heads of three champions who had killed many of the warriors of Ulster. He was then only seven years old.

The women of Ulster so loved Cuchulainn after this that the warriors grew jealous, and insisted that a wife should be found for him. But Cuchulainn was very hard to please. He would have only one, Emer[1], the daughter of Forgall the Wily, the best maiden in Ireland for the six gifts—the gift of beauty, the gift of voice, the gift of sweet speech, the gift of needlework, the gift of wisdom, and the gift of chastity. So he went to woo her, but she laughed at him for a boy. Then Cuchulainn swore by the gods of his people that he would make his name known wherever the deeds of heroes were spoken of, and Emer promised to marry him if he could take her from her warlike kindred.

When Forgall, her father, came to know of this betrothal, he devised a plan to put an end to it. He went to visit King Conchobar at Emain Macha. There he pretended to have heard of Cuchulainn for the first time, and he saw him do all his feats.

[1] Pronounced *Avair.*

He said, loud enough to be overheard by all, that if so promising a youth dared to go to the Island of Scathach the Amazon, in the east of Alba,[1] and learn all her warrior-craft, no living man would be able to stand before him. It was hard to reach Scathach's Isle, and still harder to return from it, and Forgall felt certain that, if Cuchulainn went, he would get his death there.

Of course, nothing would now satisfy Cuchulainn but going. His two friends, Laegaire the Battle-winner and Conall the Victorious, said that they would go with him. But, before they had gone far, they lost heart and turned back. Cuchulainn went on alone, crossing the Plain of Ill-Luck, where men's feet stuck fast, while sharp grasses sprang up and cut them, and through the Perilous Glens, full of devouring wild beasts, until he came to the Bridge of the Cliff, which rose on end, till it stood straight up like a ship's mast, as soon as anyone put foot on it. Three times Cuchulainn tried to cross it, and thrice he failed. Then anger came into his heart, and a magic halo shone round his head, and he did his famous feat of the "hero's salmon leap", and landed, in one jump, on the middle of the bridge, and then slid down it as it rose up on end.

Scathach was in the *dún*, with her two sons. Cuchulainn went to her, and put his sword to her breast, and threatened to kill her if she would not teach him all her own skill in arms. So he became her pupil, and she taught him all her war-craft. In return, Cuchulainn helped her against a rival queen

---

[1] Usually identified, however, with the Isle of Skye.

of the Amazons, called Aoife[1]. He conquered Aoife, and compelled her to make peace with Scathach.

Then he returned to Ireland, and went in a scythed chariot to Forgall's palace. He leaped over its triple walls, and slew everyone who came near him. Forgall met his death in trying to escape Cuchulainn's rage. He found Emer, and placed her in his chariot, and drove away; and, every time that Forgall's warriors came up to them, he turned, and slew a hundred, and put the rest to flight. He reached Emain Macha in safety, and he and Emer were married there.

And so great, after this, were the fame of Cuchulainn's prowess and Emer's beauty that the men and women of Ulster yielded them precedence—him among the warriors and her among the women—in every feast and banquet at Emain Macha.

But all that Cuchulainn had done up to this time was as nothing to the deeds he did in the great war which all the rest of Ireland, headed by Ailill and Medb, King and Queen of Connaught, made upon Ulster, to get the Brown Bull of Cualgne.[2] This Bull was one of two, of fairy descent. They had originally been the swineherds of two of the gods, Bodb, King of the Sídhe of Munster, and Ochall Ochne, King of the Sídhe of Connaught. As swineherds they were in perpetual rivalry; then, the better to carry on their quarrel, they changed themselves into two ravens, and fought for a year;

---

[1] Pronounced *Eefa*.

[2] A literal translation by Miss Winifred Faraday of the *Táin Bo Chuailgné* from the Book of the Dun Cow and the Yellow Book of Lecan has been published by Mr. Nutt—Grimm Library, No. 16.

next they turned into water - monsters, which tore one another for a year in the Suir and a year in the Shannon; then they became human again and fought as champions; and ended by changing into eels. One of these eels went into the River Cruind, in Cualgne [1], in Ulster, where it was swallowed by a cow belonging to Daire of Cualgne, and the other into the spring of Uaran Garad, in Connaught, where it passed into the belly of a cow of Queen Medb's. Thus were born those two famous beasts, the Brown Bull of Ulster and the White-horned Bull of Connaught.

Now the White-horned was of such proud mind that he scorned to belong to a woman, and he went out of Medb's herds into those of her husband Ailill. So that when Ailill and Medb one day, in their idleness, counted up their possessions, to set them off one against the other, although they were equal in every other thing, in jewels and clothes and household vessels, in sheep and horses and swine and cattle, Medb had no one bull that was worthy to be set beside Ailill's White-horned. Refusing to be less in anything than her husband, the proud queen sent heralds, with gifts and compliments, to Daire, asking him to lend her the Brown Bull for a year. Daire would have done so gladly had not one of Medb's messengers been heard boasting in his cups that, if Daire had not lent the Brown Bull of his own free-will, Medb would have taken it. This was reported to Daire, who at once swore that she should never have it. Medb's messenger

1 Pronounced *Cooley*.

returned; and the Queen of Connaught, furious at his refusal, vowed that she would take it by force.

She assembled the armies of all the rest of Ireland to go against Ulster, and made Fergus son of Roy, an Ulster champion who had quarrelled with King Conchobar, its leader. They expected to have an easy victory, for the warriors of Ulster were at that time lying under a magic weakness which fell upon them for many days in each year, as the result of a curse laid upon them, long before, by a goddess who had been insulted by one of Conchobar's ancestors. Medb called up a prophetess of her people to fore-tell victory. "How do you see our hosts?" asked the queen of the seeress. "I see crimson on them; I see red," she replied. "But the warriors of Ulster are lying in their sickness. Nay, how do you see our men?" "I see them all crimson; I see them all red," she repeated. And then she added to the astonished queen, who had expected a quite different foretelling: "For I see a small man doing deeds of arms, though there are many wounds on his smooth skin; the hero-light shines round his head, and there is victory on his forehead; he is richly clothed, and young and beautiful and modest, but he is a dragon in battle. His appearance and his valour are those of Cuchulainn of Muirthemne; who that 'Culann's hound' from Muirthemne may be, I do not know; but I know this, that all our army will be reddened by him. He is setting out for battle; he will hew down your hosts; the slaughter he shall make will be long remembered; there will be many women crying over the bodies mangled by the Hound of the Forge whom I see before me now."[1] For Cuchulainn was, for some reason unknown to us, the only man in Ulster who was not subject to the magic weakness, and therefore it fell upon him to defend Ulster single-handed against the whole of Medb's army.

In spite of the injury done him by King Conchobar, Fergus still kept a love for his own country. He had not the heart to march upon the Ultonians without first secretly sending a messenger to warn them. So that, though all the other champions of the Red Branch were helpless, Cuchulainn was watching the marches when the army came.

Now begins the story of the *aristeia* of the Gaelic hero. It is, after the manner of epics, the record of a series of single combats, in each of which Cuchulainn slays his adversary. Man after man comes against him, and not one goes back. In the intervals between these duels, Cuchulainn harasses the army with his sling, slaying a hundred men a day. He kills Medb's pet dog, bird, and squirrel, and creates such terror that no one dares to stir out of the camp. Medb herself has a narrow escape; for one of her serving-women, who puts on her mistress's golden head-dress, is killed by a stone flung from Cuchulainn's sling.

The great queen determines to see with her own eyes this marvellous hero who is holding all her warriors at bay. She sends an envoy, asking him to come and parley with her. Cuchulainn agrees, and, at the meeting, Medb is amazed at his boyish

[1] This prophecy (here much abridged) is, in the original, in verse.

look.   She finds it hard to believe that it is this beardless stripling of seventeen who is killing her champions, until the whole army seems as though it were melting away.   She offers him her own friendship and great honours and possessions in Connaught if he will forsake Conchobar.   He refuses; but she offers it again and again.   At last Cuchulainn indignantly declares that the next man who comes with such a message will do so at his peril.   One bargain, however, he will make.   He is willing to fight one of the men of Ireland every day, and, while the duel lasts, the main army may march on; but, as soon as Cuchulainn has killed his man, it must halt until the next day.   Medb agrees to this, thinking it better to lose one man a day than a hundred.

Medb makes the same offer to every famous warrior, to induce him to go against Cuchulainn.   The reward for the head of the champion will be the hand of her daughter, Findabair[1].   In spite of this, not one of the aspirants to the princess can stand before Cuchulainn.   All perish; and Findabair, when she finds out how she is being promised to a fresh suitor every day, dies of shame.   But, while Cuchulainn is engaged in these combats, Medb sends men who scour Ulster for the brown bull, and find him, and drive him, with fifty heifers, into her camp.

Meanwhile the Æs Sídhe, the fairy god-clan, are watching the half-divine, half-mortal hero, amazed at his achievements.   His exploits kindle love in the fierce heart of the Morrígú, the great war-goddess.

[1] Finnavár.

Cuchulainn is awakened from sleep by a terrible shout from the north. He orders his driver, Laeg, to yoke the horses to his chariot, so that he may find out who raised it. They go in the direction from which the sound had come, and meet with a woman in a chariot drawn by a red horse. She has red eyebrows, and a red dress, and a long, red cloak, and she carries a great, gray spear. He asks her who she is, and she tells him that she is a king's daughter, and that she has fallen in love with him through hearing of his exploits. Cuchulainn says that he has other things to think of than love. She replies that she has been giving him her help in his battles, and will still do so; and Cuchulainn answers that he does not need any woman's help. "Then," says she, "if you will not have my love and help, you shall have my hatred and enmity. When you are fighting with a warrior as good as yourself, I will come against you in various shapes and hinder you, so that he shall have the advantage." Cuchulainn draws his sword, but all he sees is a hoodie crow sitting on a branch. He knows from this that the red woman in the chariot was the great queen of the gods.

The next day, a warrior named Loch went to meet Cuchulainn. At first he refused to fight one who was beardless; so Cuchulainn smeared his chin with blackberry juice, until it looked as though he had a beard. While Cuchulainn was fighting Loch, the Morrígú came against him three times—first as a heifer which tried to overthrow him, and next as an eel which got beneath his feet as he stood in running water, and then as a wolf which seized hold of his right arm. But Cuchulainn broke the heifer's leg, and trampled upon the eel, and put out one of the wolf's eyes, though, every one of these three times, Loch wounded him. In the end, Cuchulainn slew Loch with his invincible spear, the *gae bolg*[1], made of a sea-monster's bones. The Morrígú came back to Cuchulainn, disguised as an old woman, to have her wounds healed by him, for no one could cure them but he who had made them. She became his friend after this, and helped him.

But the fighting was so continuous that Cuchulainn got no sleep, except just for a while, from time to time, when he might rest a little, with his head on his hand and his hand on his spear and his spear on his knee. So that his father, Lugh the Long-handed, took pity on him and came to him in the semblance of a tall, handsome man in a green cloak and a gold-embroidered silk shirt, and carrying a black shield and a five-pronged spear. He put him into a sleep of three days and three nights, and, while he rested, he laid druidical herbs on to all his wounds, so that, in the end, he rose up again completely healed and as strong as at the very beginning of the war. While he was asleep, the boy-troop of Emain Macha, Cuchulainn's old companions, came and fought instead of him, and slew three times their own number, but were all killed.

It was at this time that Medb asked Fergus to go and fight with Cuchulainn. Fergus answered that he would never fight against his own foster-

---

[1] " Bellows-dart ", apparently a kind of harpoon. It had thirty barbs.

son. Medb asked him again and again, and at last
he went, but without his famous sword. "Fergus,
my guardian," said Cuchulainn, "it is not safe for
you to come out against me without your sword."
"If I had the sword," replied Fergus, "I would not
use it on you." Then Fergus asked Cuchulainn,
for the sake of all he had done for him in his boy-
hood, to pretend to fight with him, and then give
way before him and run away. Cuchulainn answered
that he was very loth to be seen running from any
man. But Fergus promised Cuchulainn that, if
Cuchulainn would run away from Fergus then,
Fergus would run away from Cuchulainn at some
future time, whenever Cuchulainn wished. Cuchulainn agreed to this, for he knew that it would be
for the profit of Ulster. So they fought a little,
and then Cuchulainn turned and fled in the sight
of all Medb's army. Fergus went back; and Medb
could not reproach him any more.

But she cast about to find some other way of
vanquishing Cuchulainn. The agreement made had
been that only one man a day should be sent against
him. But now Medb sent the wizard Calatin with
his twenty-seven sons and his grandson all at once,
for she said "they are really only one, for they are
all from Calatin's body". They never missed a
throw with their poisoned spears, and every man
they hit died, either on the spot or within the week.
When Fergus heard of this, he was in great grief,
and he sent a man called Fiacha, an exile, like himself, from Ulster, to watch the fight and report how
it went. Now Fiacha did not mean to join in it,

but when he saw Cuchulainn assailed by twenty-nine at a time, and overpowered, he could not restrain himself. So he drew his sword and helped Cuchulainn, and, between them, they killed Calatin and his whole family.

As a last resource, now, Medb sent for Ferdiad, who was the great champion of the Iberian "Men of Domnu", who had thrown in their lot with Medb in the war for the Brown Bull. Ferdiad had been a companion and fellow-pupil of Cuchulainn with Scathach, and he did not wish to fight with him. But Medb told him that, if he refused, her satirists should make such lampoons on him that he would die of shame, and his name would be a reproach for ever. She also offered him great rewards and honours, and bound herself in six sureties to keep her promises. At last, reluctantly, he went.

Cuchulainn saw him coming, and went out to welcome him; but Ferdiad said that he had not come as a friend, but to fight. Now Cuchulainn had been Ferdiad's junior and serving-boy in Scathach's Island, and he begged him by the memory of those old times to go back; but Ferdiad said he could not. They fought all day, and neither had gained any advantage by sunset. So they kissed one another, and each went back to his camp. Ferdiad sent half his food and drink to Cuchulainn, and Cuchulainn sent half his healing herbs and medicines to Ferdiad, and their horses were put in the same stable, and their charioteers slept by the same fire. And so it happened on the second day. But at the end of the third day they parted gloomily, knowing that on the morrow one of them must fall; and their horses were not put in the same stall that night, neither did their charioteers sleep at the same fire. On the fourth day, Cuchulainn succeeded in killing Ferdiad, by casting the *gae bolg* at him from underneath. But when he saw that he was dying, the battle-fury passed away, and he took his old companion up in his arms, and carried him across the river on whose banks they had fought, so that he might be with the men of Ulster in his death, and not with the men of Ireland. And he wept over him, and said: "It was all a game and a sport until Ferdiad came; Oh, Ferdiad! your death will hang over me like a cloud for ever. Yesterday he was greater than a mountain; to-day he is less than a shadow."

By this time, Cuchulainn was so covered with wounds that he could not bear his clothes to touch his skin, but had to hold them off with hazel-sticks, and fill the spaces in between with grass. There was not a place on him the size of a needle-point that had not a wound on it, except his left hand, which held the shield.

But Sualtam, Cuchulainn's reputed father, had learned what a sore plight his son was in. "Do I hear the heaven bursting, or the sea running away, or the earth breaking open," he cried, "or is it my son's groaning that I hear?" He came to look for him, and found him covered with wounds and blood. But Cuchulainn would not let his father either weep for him or try to avenge him. "Go, rather," he said to him, "to Emain Macha, and tell Conchobar that I can no longer defend Ulster against all the four provinces of Erin without help. Tell him that there is no part of my body on which there is not a wound, and that, if he wishes to save his kingdom, he must make no delay."

Sualtam mounted Cuchulainn's war-horse, the "Gray of Battle", and galloped to Emain Macha. Three times he shouted: "Men are being killed, women carried off, and cattle lifted in Ulster". Twice he met with no response. The third time, Cathbad the Druid roused himself from his lethargy to denounce the man who was disturbing the king's sleep. In his indignation Sualtam turned away so sharply that the gray steed reared, and struck its rider's shield against his neck with such force that he was decapitated. The startled horse then turned back into Conchobar's stronghold, and dashed through it, Sualtam's severed head continuing to cry out: "Men are being killed, women carried off, and cattle lifted in Ulster." Such a portent was enough to rouse the most drowsy. Conchobar, himself again, swore a great oath. "The heavens are over us, the earth is beneath us, and the sea circles us round, and, unless the heavens fall, with all their stars, or the earth gives way beneath us, or the sea bursts over the land, I will restore every cow to her stable, and every woman to her home."

He sent messengers to rally Ulster, and they gathered, and marched on the men of Erin. And then was fought such a battle as had never been before in Ireland. First one side, then the other, gave way and rallied again, until Cuchulainn heard the noise of the fight, and rose up, in spite of all his wounds, and came to it.

He called out to Fergus, reminding him how he had bound himself with an oath to run from him when called upon to do so. So Fergus ran before Cuchulainn, and when Medb's army saw their leader running they broke and fled like one man.

But the Brown Bull of Cualgne went with the army into Connaught, and there he met Ailill's bull, the White-horned. And he fought the White-horned, and tore him limb from limb, and carried off pieces of him on his horns, dropping the loins at Athlone and the liver at Trim. Then he went back to Cualgne, and turned mad, killing all who crossed his path, until his heart burst with bellowing, and he fell dead.

This was the end of the great war called *Táin Bó Chuailgné*, the "Driving of the Cattle of Cooley".

Yet, wondrous as it was, it was not the most marvellous of Cuchulainn's exploits. Like all the solar gods and heroes of Celtic myth, he carried his conquests into the dark region of Hades. On this occasion the mysterious realm is an island called *Dún Scaith*, that is, the "Shadowy Town", and though its king is not mentioned by name, it seems likely that he was Mider, and that Dún Scaith is another name for the Isle of Falga, or Man. The story, as a poem[1] relates it, is curiously suggestive of a raid which the powers of light, and especially the sun-gods, are represented as having made upon

[1] It is contained in the Book of the Dun Cow story called the "Phantom Chariot".

Hades in kindred British myth.[1] The same loath-
some combatants issue out of the underworld to
repel its assailants. There was a pit in the centre
of Dún Scaith, out of which swarmed a vast throng
of serpents. No sooner had Cuchulainn and the
heroes of Ulster disposed of these than "a house full
of toads" was loosed upon them—"sharp, beaked
monsters" (says the poem), which caught them by
the noses, and these were in turn replaced by fierce
dragons. Yet the heroes prevailed and carried off
the spoil—three cows of magic qualities and a
marvellous cauldron in which was always found an
inexhaustible supply of meat, with treasure of silver
and gold to boot. They started back for Ireland in
a coracle, the three cows being towed behind, with
the treasure in bags around their necks. But the
gods of Hades raised a storm which wrecked their
ship, and they had to swim home. Here Cuchulainn's
more than mortal prowess came in useful. We are
told that he floated nine men to shore on each of his
hands, and thirty on his head, while eight more,
clinging to his sides, used him as a kind of life-belt.

After this, came the tragedy of Cuchulainn's
career, the unhappy duel in which he killed his only
son, not knowing who he was. The story is one
common, apparently, to the Aryan nations, for it is
found not only in the Gaelic, but in the Teutonic
and Persian mythic traditions. It will be remembered that Cuchulainn defeated a rival of Scathach
the Amazon, named Aoife, and compelled her to
render submission. The hero had also a son by

[1] See chap. xx—"The Victories of Light over Darkness".

Aoife, and he asked that the boy should be called Conlaoch[1], and that, when he was of age to travel, he should be sent to Ireland to find his father. Aoife promised this, but, a little later, news came to her that Cuchulainn had married Emer. Mad with jealousy, she determined to make the son avenge her slight upon the father. She taught him the craft of arms until there was no more that he could learn, and sent him to Ireland. Before he started, she laid three *geasa*[2] upon him. The first was that he was not to turn back, the second that he was never to refuse a challenge, and the third that he was never to tell his name.

He arrived at Dundealgan[3], Cuchulainn's home, and the warrior Conall came down to meet him, and asked him his name and lineage. He refused to tell them, and this led to a duel, in which Conall was disarmed and humiliated. Cuchulainn next approached him, asked the same question, and received the same answer. "Yet if I was not under a command," said Conlaoch, who did not know he was speaking to his father, "there is no man in the world to whom I would sooner tell it than to yourself, for I love your face." Even this compliment could not stave off the fight, for Cuchulainn felt it his duty to punish the insolence of this stripling who refused to declare who he was. The fight was a fierce one, and the invincible Cuchulainn found himself so pressed that the "hero-light" shone round

---

[1] Pronounced *Conla*.
[2] A kind of mystic prohibition or taboo; singular, *geis*.
[3] Now called Dundalk.

him and transfigured his face.   When Conlaoch saw this, he knew who his antagonist must be, and purposely flung his spear slantways that it might not hit his father.   But before Cuchulainn understood, he had thrown the terrible *gae bolg*.   Conlaoch, dying, declared his name; and so passionate was Cuchulainn's grief that the men of Ulster were afraid that in his madness he might wreak his wrath upon them.   They, therefore, called upon Cathbad the Druid to put him under a glamour.   Cathbad turned the waves of the sea into the appearance of armed men, and Cuchulainn smote them with his sword until he fell prone from weariness.

It would take too long to relate all the other adventures and exploits of Cuchulainn.   Enough has been done if any reader of this chapter should be persuaded by it to study the wonderful saga of ancient Ireland for himself.   We must pass on quickly to its tragical close—the hero's death.

Medb, Queen of Connaught, had never forgiven him for keeping back her army from raiding Ulster, and for slaying so many of her friends and allies. So she went secretly to all those whose relations Cuchulainn had killed (and they were many), and stirred them up to revenge.

Besides this, she had sent the three daughters of Calatin the Wizard, born after their father's death at the hands of Cuchulainn, to Alba and to Babylon to learn witchcraft.   When they came back they were mistresses of every kind of sorcery, and could make the illusion of battle with an incantation.

And, lest she might fail even then, she waited

with patience until the Ultonians were again in their magic weakness, and there was no one to help Cuchulainn but himself.

Lugaid[1], son of the Curoi, King of Munster whom Cuchulainn had killed for the sake of Blathnat, Mider's daughter, gathered the Munster men; Erc, whose father had also fallen at Cuchulainn's hands, called the men of Meath; the King of Leinster brought out his army; and, with Ailill and Medb and all Connaught, they marched into Ulster again, and began to ravage it.

Conchobar called his warriors and druids into council, to see if they could find some means of putting off war until they were ready to meet it. He did not wish Cuchulainn to go out single-handed a second time against all the rest of Ireland, for he knew that, if the champion perished, the prosperity of Ulster would fall with him for ever. So, when Cuchulainn came to Emain Macha, the king set all the ladies, singers, and poets of the court to keep his thoughts from war until the men of Ulster had recovered from their weakness.

But while they sat feasting and talking in the "sunny house", the three daughters of Calatin came fluttering down on to the lawn before it, and began gathering grass and thistles and puff-balls and withered leaves, and turning them into the semblance of armies. And, by the same magic, they caused shouts and shrieks and trumpet-blasts and the clattering of arms to be heard all round the house, as though a battle were being fought.

[1] Pronounced *Lewy*.

Cuchulainn leaped up, red with shame to think that fighting should be going on without his help, and seized his sword. But Cathbad's son caught him by the arms. All the druids explained to him that what he saw was only an enchantment raised by the children of Calatin to draw him out to his death. But it was as much as all of them could do to keep him quiet while he saw the phantom armies and heard the magic sounds.

So they decided that it would be well to remove Cuchulainn from Emain Macha to *Glean-na-Bodhar*[1], the "Deaf Valley", until all the enchantments of the daughters of Calatin were spent. It was the quality of this valley that, if all the men of Ireland were to shout round it at once, no one within it would hear a sound.

But the daughters of Calatin went there too, and again they took thistles and puff-balls and withered leaves, and put on them the appearance of armed men; so that there seemed to be no place outside the whole valley that was not filled with shouting battalions. And they made the illusion of fires all around and the sound of women shrieking. Everyone who heard that outcry was frightened at it, not only the men and women, but even the dogs.

Though the women and the druids shouted back with all the strength of their voices, to drown it they could not keep Cuchulainn from hearing. "Alas!" he cried, "I hear the men of Ireland shouting as they ravage the province. My triumph is at an end; my fame is gone; Ulster lies low for ever."

[1] Pronounced *Glen na Mower*.

"Let it pass," said Cathbad; "it is only the idle magic noises made by the children of Calatin, who want to draw you out, to put an end to you. Stay here with us, and take no heed of them."

Cuchulainn obeyed; and the daughters of Calatin went on for a long time filling the air with noises of battle. But they grew tired of it at last; for they saw that the druids and women had outwitted them.

They did not succeed until one of them took the form of a leman of Cuchulainn's, and came to him, crying out that Dundealgan was burnt, and Muirthemne ruined, and the whole province of Ulster ravaged. Then, at last, he was deceived, and took his arms and armour, and, in spite of all that was said to him, he ordered Laeg to yoke his chariot.

Signs and portents now began to gather as thickly round the doomed hero as they did round the wooers in the hall of Odysseus. His famous war-horse, the Gray of Macha, refused to be bridled, and shed large tears of blood. His mother, Dechtiré, brought him a goblet full of wine, and thrice the wine turned into blood as he put it to his lips. At the first ford he crossed, he saw a maiden of the *sidhe* washing clothes and armour, and she told him that it was the clothes and arms of Cuchulainn, who was soon to be dead. He met three ancient hags cooking a hound on spits of rowan, and they invited him to partake of it. He refused, for it was taboo to him to eat the flesh of his namesake; but they shamed him into doing so by telling him that he ate at rich men's tables and refused the hospitality of the poor. The forbidden meat paralysed half his body. Then he saw his enemies coming up against him in their chariots.

Cuchulainn had three spears, of which it was prophesied that each should kill a king. Three druids were charged in turn to ask for these spears; for it was not thought lucky to refuse anything to a druid. The first one came up to where Cuchulainn was making the plain red with slaughter. "Give me one of those spears," he said, "or I will lampoon you." "Take it," replied Cuchulainn, "I have never yet been lampooned for refusing anyone a gift." And he threw the spear at the druid, and killed him. But Lugaid, son of Curoi, got the spear, and killed Laeg with it. Laeg was the king of all chariot-drivers.

"Give me one of your spears, Cuchulainn," said the second druid. "I need it myself," he replied. "I will lampoon the province of Ulster because of you, if you refuse." "I am not obliged to give more than one gift in a day," said Cuchulainn, "but Ulster shall never be lampooned because of me." He threw the spear at the druid, and it went through his head. But Erc, King of Leinster, got it, and mortally wounded the Gray of Macha, the king of all horses.

"Give me your spear," said the third druid. "I have paid all that is due from myself and Ulster," replied Cuchulainn. "I will satirize your kindred if you do not," said the druid. "I shall never go home, but I will be the cause of no lampoons there," answered Cuchulainn, and he threw the spear at the asker, and killed him. But Lugaid threw it back, and it went through Cuchulainn's body, and wounded him to the death.

Then, in his agony, he greatly desired to drink. He asked his enemies to let him go to a lake that lay close by, and quench his thirst, and then come back again. " If I cannot come back to you, come to fetch me," he said; and they let him go.

Cuchulainn drank, and bathed, and came out of the water. But he found that he could not walk; so he called to his enemies to come to him. There was a pillar-stone near; and he bound himself to it with his belt, so that he might die standing up, and not lying down. His dying horse, the Gray of Macha, came back to fight for him, and killed fifty men with his teeth and thirty with each of his hoofs. But the "hero-light" had died out of Cuchulainn's face, leaving it as pale as "a one-night's snow", and a crow came and perched upon his shoulder.

" Truly it was not upon that pillar that birds used to sit," said Erc.

Now that they were certain that Cuchulainn was dead, they all gathered round him, and Lugaid cut off his head to take it to Medb. But vengeance came quickly, for Conall the Victorious was in pursuit, and he made a terrible slaughter of Cuchulainn's enemies.

Thus perished the great hero of the Gaels in the twenty-seventh year of his age. And with him fell the prosperity of Emain Macha and of the Red Branch of Ulster.

CHAPTER XIII

SOME GAELIC LOVE-STORIES

The heroic age of Ireland was not, however, the mere orgy of battle which one might assume from the previous chapter. It had room for its Helen and its Andromache as well as for its Achilles and its Hector. Its champions could find time to make love as well as war. More than this, the legends of their courtships often have a romantic beauty found in no other early literature. The women have free scope of choice, and claim the respect of their wooers. Indeed, it has been pointed out that the mythical stories of the Celts must have created the chivalrous romances of mediæval Europe. In them, and in no other previous literature, do we find such knightly treatment of an enemy as we see in the story of Cuchulainn and Ferdiad, or such poetic delicacy towards a woman as is displayed in the wooing of Emer.[1] The talk between man and maid when Cuchulainn comes in his chariot to pay his suit to Emer at Forgall's *dún* might, save for its strangeness, almost have come out of some quite modern romance.

[1] The romance of the *Wooing of Emer*, a fragment of which is contained in the Book of the Dun Cow, has been translated by Dr. Kuno Meyer, and published by him in the *Archæological Review*, Vol. I, 1888. Miss Hull has included this translation in her *Cuchullin Saga*. Another version of it from a Bodleian MS., translated by the same scholar, will be found in the *Revue Celtique*, Vol. XI.

" Emer lifted up her lovely face and recognised Cuchulainn, and she said, ' May God make smooth the path before you!'

" 'And you,' he said, ' may you be safe from every harm.' "

She asks him whence he has come, and he tells her. Then he questions her about herself.

" I am a Tara of women," she replies, " the whitest of maidens, one who is gazed at but who gazes not back, a rush too far to be reached, an untrodden way. . . . I was brought up in ancient virtues, in lawful behaviour, in the keeping of chastity, in rank equal to a queen, in stateliness of form, so that to me is attributed every noble grace among the hosts of Erin's women." In more boastful strain Cuchulainn tells of his own birth and deeds. Not like the son of a peasant had he been reared at Conchobar's court, but among heroes and champions, jesters and druids. When he is weakest his strength is that of twenty; alone he will fight against forty; a hundred men would feel safe under his protection. One can imagine Emer's smile as she listens to these braggings. " Truly," she says, " they are goodly feats for a tender boy, but they are not yet those of chariot-chiefs." Very modern, too, is the way in which she coyly reminds her wooer that she has an elder sister as yet unwed. But, when at last he drives her to the point, she answers him with gentle, but proud decision. Not by words, but by deeds is she to be won. The man she will marry must have his name mentioned wherever the exploits of heroes are spoken of.

"Even as thou hast commanded, so shall all by me be done," said Cuchulainn.

"And by me your offer is accepted, it is taken, it is granted," replied Emer.

It seems a pity that, after so fine a wooing, Cuchulainn could not have kept faithful to the bride he won. Yet such is not the way of heroes whom goddesses as well as mortal women conspire to tempt from their loyalty. Fand, the wife of Manannán son of Lêr, deserted by the sea-god, sent her sister Liban to Cuchulainn as an ambassador of love. At first he refused to visit her, but ordered Laeg, his charioteer, to go with Liban to the "Happy Plain" to spy out the land. Laeg returned enraptured. "If all Ireland were mine," he assured his master, "with supreme rule over its fair inhabitants, I would give it up without regret to go and live in the place that I have seen."

So Cuchulainn himself went and stayed a month in the Celtic Paradise with Fand, the fairest woman of the Sídhe. Returning to the land of mortals, he made a tryst with the goddess to meet him again in his own country by the yew-tree at the head of Baile's strand.

But Emer came to hear of it, and went to the meeting-place herself, with fifty of her maidens, each armed with a knife to kill her rival. There she found Cuchulainn, Laeg, and Fand.

"What has led you, Cuchulainn," said Emer, "to shame me before the women of Erin and all honourable people? I came under your shelter, trusting in your faithfulness, and now you seek a cause of quarrel with me."

But Cuchulainn, hero-like, could not understand why his wife should not be content to take her turn with this other woman—surely no unworthy rival, for she was beautiful, and came of the lofty race of gods. We see Emer yield at last, with queenly pathos.

" I will not refuse this woman to you, if you long for her," she said, for I know that everything that is new seems fair, and everything that is common seems bitter, and everything we have not seems desirable to us, and everything we have we think little of. And yet, Cuchulainn, I was once pleasing to you, and I would wish to be so again."

Her grief touched him. " By my word," he said, "you are pleasing to me, and will be as long as I live."

" Then let me be given up," said Fand. " It is better that I should be," replied Emer. " No," said Fand; "it is I who must be given up in the end.

" It is I who will go, though I go with great sorrow. I would rather stay with Cuchulainn than live in the sunny home of the gods.

"O Emer, he is yours, and you are worthy of him! What my hand cannot have, my heart may yet wish well to.

"A sorrowful thing it is to love without return. Better to renounce than not to receive a love equal to one's own.

"It was not well of you, O fair-haired Emer, to come to kill Fand in her misery."

It was while the goddess and the human woman were contending with one another in self-sacrifice that Manannán, Son of the Sea, heard of Fand's trouble, and was sorry that he had forsaken her. So he came, invisible to all but her alone. He asked her pardon, and she herself could not forget that she had once been happy with the "horseman of the crested waves", and still might be happy with him again. The god asked her to make her choice between them, and, when she went to him, he shook his mantle between her and Cuchulainn. It was one of the magic properties of Manannán's mantle that those between whom it was shaken could never meet again. Then Fand returned with her divine husband to the country of the immortals; and the druids of Emain Macha gave Cuchulainn and Emer each a drink of oblivion, so that Cuchulainn forgot his love and Emer her jealousy.[1]

The scene of this story takes its name from another, and hardly less beautiful love-tale. The "yew-tree at the head of Baile's strand" had grown out of the grave of Baile of the Honeyed Speech, and it bore the appearance of Baile's love, Ailinn. This Gaelic Romeo and Juliet were of royal birth: Baile was heir to Ulster, and Ailinn was daughter of the King of Leinster's son. Not by any feud of Montague and Capulet were they parted, however, but by the craft of a ghostly enemy. They had appointed to meet one another at Dundealgan,

[1] This story, known as the *Sick-Bed of Cuchulainn*, translated into French by M. d'Arbois de Jubainville, will be found in his *L'Épopée Celtique en Irlande*, the fifth volume of *Cour de Littérature Celtique*. Another translation, into English, by Eugene O'Curry is in *Atlantis*, Vols. I and II.

and Baile, who arrived there first, was greeted by a stranger. "What news do you bring?" asked Baile. "None," replied the stranger, "except that Ailinn of Leinster was setting out to meet her lover, but the men of Leinster kept her back, and her heart broke then and there from grief." When Baile heard this, his own heart broke, and he fell dead on the strand, while the messenger went on the wings of the wind to the home of Ailinn, who had not yet started. "Whence come you?" she asked him. "From Ulster, by the shore of Dundealgan, where I saw men raising a stone over one who had just died, and on the stone I read the name of Baile. He had come to meet some woman he was in love with, but it was destined that they should never see one another again in life." At this news Ailinn, too, fell dead, and was buried; and we are told that an apple-tree grew out of her grave, the apples of which bore the likeness of the face of Baile, while a yew-tree sprung from Baile's grave, and took the appearance of Ailinn. This legend, which is probably a part of the common heritage of the Aryans, is found in folk-lore over an area which stretches from Ireland to India. The Gaelic version has, however, an ending unknown to the others. The two trees, it relates, were cut down, and made into wands upon which the poets of Ulster and of Leinster cut the songs of the love-tragedies of their two provinces, in *ogam*. But even these mute memorials of Baile and Ailinn were destined not to be divided. After two hundred years, Art the "Lonely", High-King of Ireland, ordered them to be brought to the hall of Tara, and, as soon as the wands found themselves under the same roof, they all sprang together, and no force or skill could part them again. So the king commanded them to be "kept, like any other jewel, in the treasury of Tara."[1]

Neither of these stories, however, has as yet attained the fame of one now to be retold.[2] To many, no doubt, Gaelic romance is summed up in the one word Deirdre. It is the legend of this Gaelic Helen that the poets of the modern Celtic school most love to elaborate, while old men still tell it round the peat-fires of Ireland and the Highlands. Scholar and peasant alike combine to preserve a tradition no one knows how many hundred years old, for it was written down in the twelfth-century Book of Leinster as one of the "prime stories" which every bard was bound to be able to recite It takes rank with the "Fate of the Sons of Tuirenn", and with the "Fate of the Children of Lêr", as one of the "Three Sorrowful Stories of Erin".

So favourite a tale has naturally been much altered and added to in its passage down the generations. But its essential story is as follows:—

King Conchobar of Ulster was holding festival in the house of one of his bards, called Fedlimid, when Fedlimid's wife gave birth to a daughter, concerning whom Cathbad the Druid uttered a prophecy. He

---

[1] For the full story of Baile and Ailinn see Dr. Kuno Meyer's translation in Vol. XIII of the *Revue Celtique.*

[2] There are not only numerous translations of this romance, but also many Gaelic versions. The oldest of the latter is in the Book of Leinster, while the fullest are in two MSS. in the Advocates' Library at Edinburgh. The version followed here is from one of these, the so-called Glenn Masáin MS., translated by Dr. Whitley Stokes, and contained in Miss Hull's *Cuchullin Saga.*

foretold that the new-born child would grow up to be the most lovely woman the world had ever seen, but that her beauty would bring death to many heroes, and much peril and sorrow to Ulster. On hearing this, the Red Branch warriors demanded that she should be killed, but Conchobar refused, and gave the infant to a trusted serving-woman, to be hidden in a secret place in the solitude of the mountains, until she was of an age to be his own wife.

So Deirdre (as Cathbad named her) was taken away to a hut so remote from the paths of men that none knew of it save Conchobar. Here she was brought up by a nurse, a fosterer, and a teacher, and saw no other living creatures save the beasts and birds of the hills. Nevertheless, woman-like, she aspired to be loved.

One day, her fosterer was killing a calf for their food, and its blood ran out upon the snowy ground, which brought a black raven swooping to the spot. "If there were a man," said Deirdre, "who had hair of the blackness of that raven, skin of the whiteness of the snow, and cheeks as red as the calf's blood, that is the man whom I would wish to marry me."

"Indeed there is such a man," replied her teacher thoughtlessly. "Naoise[1], one of the sons of Usnach[2], heroes of the same race as Conchobar the King.

The curious Deirdre prevailed upon her teacher to bring Naoise to speak with her. When they met she made good use of her time, for she offered

---

[1] Pronounced *Naisi*. [2] Pronounced *Usna*.

Naoise her love, and begged him to take her away from King Conchobar.

Naoise, bewitched by her beauty, consented. Accompanied by his two brothers, Ardan and Ainle, and their followers, he fled with Deirdre to Alba, where they made alliance with one of its kings, and wandered over the land, living by following the deer, and by helping the king in his battles.

The revengeful Conchobar bided his time. One day, as the heroes of the Red Branch feasted together at Emain Macha, he asked them if they had ever heard of a nobler company than their own. They replied that the world could not hold such another. "Yet", said the king, "we lack our full tale. The three sons of Usnach could defend the province of Ulster against any other province of Ireland by themselves, and it is a pity that they should still be exiles, for the sake of any woman in the world. Gladly would I welcome them back!"

"We ourselves", replied the Ultonians, "would have counselled this long ago had we dared, O King!"

"Then I will send one of my three best champions to fetch them," said Conchobar. "Either Conall the Victorious, or Cuchulainn, the son of Sualtam, or Fergus, the son of Roy; and I will find out which of those three loves me best."

First he called Conall to him secretly.

"What would you do, O Conall," he asked, "if you were sent to fetch the sons of Usnach, and they were killed here, in spite of your safe-conduct?"

"There is not a man in Ulster," answered Conall,

"who had hand in it that would escape his own death from me."

"I see that I am not dearest of all men to you," replied Conchobar, and, dismissing Conall, he called Cuchulainn, and put the same question to him.

"By my sworn word," replied Cuchulainn, "if such a thing happened with your consent, no bribe or blood-fine would I accept in lieu of your own head, O Conchobar."

"Truly," said the king, "it is not you I will send."

The king then asked Fergus, and he replied that, if the sons of Usnach were slain while under his protection, he would revenge the deed upon anyone who was party to it, save only the king himself.

"Then it is you who shall go," said Conchobar. "Set forth to-morrow, and rest not by the way, and when you put foot again in Ireland at the *Dún* of Borrach, whatever may happen to you yourself, send the sons of Usnach forward without delay."

The next morning, Fergus, with his two sons, Illann the Fair and Buinne the Ruthless Red, set out for Alba in their galley, and reached Loch Etive, by whose shores the sons of Usnach were then living. Naoise, Ainle, and Ardan were sitting at chess when they heard Fergus's shout.

"That is the cry of a man of Erin," said Naoise.

"Nay," replied Deirdre, who had forebodings of trouble. "Do not heed it; it is only the shout of a man of Alba." But the sons of Usnach knew better, and sent Ardan down to the sea-shore, where he found Fergus and his sons, and gave them greeting, and heard their message, and brought them back with him.

That night Fergus persuaded the sons of Usnach to return with him to Emain Macha. Deirdre, with her "second sight", implored them to remain in Alba. But the exiles were weary for the sight of their own country, and did not share their companion's fears. As they put out to sea, Deirdre uttered her beautiful "Farewell to Alba", that land she was never to behold again.

> "A lovable land is yon eastern land,
>   Alba, with its marvels.
> I would not have come hither out of it,
>   Had I not come with Naoise.
>
> "Lovable are Dún-fidga and Dún-finn,
>   Lovable the fortress over them;
> Dear to the heart Inis Draigende,
>   And very dear is Dún Suibni.
>
> "Caill Cuan!
>   Unto which Ainle would wend, alas!
> Short the time seemed to me,
>   With Naoise in the region of Alba.
>
> "Glenn Láid!
>   Often I slept there under the cliff;
> Fish and venison and the fat of the badger
>   Was my portion in Glenn Láid.
>
> "Glenn Masáin!
>   Its garlic was tall, its branches white;
> We slept a rocking sleep,
>   Over the grassy estuary of Masáin.

"Glenn Etive!
Where my first house I raised;
Beauteous its wood:—upon rising
A cattle-fold for the sun was Glenn Etive.

. . . .

"Glenn Dá-Rúad!
My love to every man who hath it as an heritage!
Sweet the cuckoos' note on bending bough,
On the peak over Glenn Dá-Rúad.

"Beloved is Draigen,
Dear the white sand beneath its waves;
I would not have come from it, from the East,
Had I not come with my beloved."

They crossed the sea, and arrived at the *Dún* of
Borrach, who bade them welcome to Ireland. Now
King Conchobar had sent Borrach a secret command, that he should offer a feast to Fergus on his
landing. Strange taboos called *geasa* are laid upon
the various heroes of ancient Ireland in the stories;
there are certain things that each one of them may
not do without forfeiting life or honour; and it was
a *geis* upon Fergus to refuse a feast.

Fergus, we are told, "reddened with anger from
crown to sole" at the invitation. Yet he could not
avoid the feast. He asked Naoise what he should
do, and Deirdre broke in with: "Do what is asked
of you if you prefer to forsake the sons of Usnach
for a feast. Yet forsaking them is a good price to
pay for it."

Fergus, however, perceived a possible compro-
mise. Though he himself could not refuse to stop
to partake of Borrach's hospitality, he could send

Deirdre and the sons of Usnach on to Emain
Macha at once, under the safeguard of his two sons,
Illann the Fair and Buinne the Ruthless Red. So
this was done, albeit to the annoyance of the sons
of Usnach and the terror of Deirdre. Visions came
to the sorrowful woman; she saw the three sons of
Usnach and Illann, the son of Fergus, without their
heads; she saw a cloud of blood always hanging
over them. She begged them to wait in some safe
place until Fergus had finished the feast. But
Naoise, Ainle, and Ardan laughed at her fears.
They arrived at Emain Macha, and Conchobar
ordered the " Red Branch" palace to be placed at
their disposal.

In the evening Conchobar called Levarcham,
Deirdre's old teacher, to him. "Go", he said, "to
the 'Red Branch', and see Deirdre, and bring me
back news of her appearance, whether she still
keeps her former beauty, or whether it has left her."

So Levarcham came to the " Red Branch", and
kissed Deirdre and the three sons of Usnach, and
warned them that Conchobar was preparing treachery. Then she went back to the king, and reported
to him that Deirdre's hard life upon the mountains
of Alba had ruined her form and face, so that she
was no longer worthy of his regard.

At this, Conchobar's jealousy was partly allayed,
and he began to doubt whether it would be wise to
attack the sons of Usnach. But later on, when he
had drunk well of wine, he sent a second messenger
to see if what Levarcham had reported about Deirdre was truth.

The messenger, this time a man, went and looked in through a window. Deirdre saw him and pointed him out to Naoise, who flung a chessman at the peering face, and put out one of its eyes. But the man went back to Conchobar, and told him that, though one of his eyes had been struck out, he would gladly have stayed looking with the other, so great was Deirdre's loveliness.

Then Conchobar, in his wrath, ordered the men of Ulster to set fire to the Red Branch House and slay all within it except Deirdre. They flung firebrands upon it, but Buinne the Ruthless Red came out and quenched them, and drove the assailants back with slaughter. But Conchobar called to him to parley, and offered him a "hundred" of land and his friendship to desert the sons of Usnach. Buinne was tempted, and fell; but the land given him turned barren that very night in indignation at being owned by such a traitor.

The other of Fergus's sons was of different make. He charged out, torch in hand, and cut down the Ultonians, so that they hesitated to come near the house again. Conchobar dared not offer him a bribe. But he armed his own son, Fiacha, with his own magic weapons, including his shield, the "Moaner", which roared when its owner was in danger, and sent him to fight Illann.

The duel was a fierce one, and Illann got the better of Fiacha, so that the son of Conchobar had to crouch down beneath his shield, which roared for help. Conall the Victorious heard the roar from far off, and thought that his king must be in peril. He came to the place, and, without asking questions, thrust his spear " Blue-green " through Illann. The dying son of Fergus explained the situation to Conall, who, by way of making some amends, at once killed Fiacha as well.

After this, the sons of Usnach held their fort till dawn against all Conchobar's host. But, with day, they saw that they must either escape or resign themselves to perish. Putting Deirdre in their centre, protected by their shields, they opened the door suddenly and fled out.

They would have broken through and escaped, had not Conchobar asked Cathbad the Druid to put a spell upon them, promising to spare their lives. So Cathbad raised the illusion of a stormy sea before and all around the sons of Usnach. Naoise lifted Deirdre upon his shoulder, but the magic waves rose higher, until they were all obliged to fling away their weapons and swim.

Then was seen the strange sight of men swimming upon dry land. And, before the glamour passed away, the sons of Usnach were seized from behind, and brought to Conchobar.

In spite of his promise to the druid, the king condemned them to death. None of the men of Ulster would, however, deal the blow. In the end, a foreigner from Norway, whose father Naoise had slain, offered to behead them. Each of the brothers begged to die first, that he might not witness the deaths of the others. But Naoise ended this noble rivalry by lending their executioner the sword called " The Retaliator ", which had been given

him by Manannán son of Lêr. They knelt down
side by side, and one blow of the sword of the god
shore off all their heads.

As for Deirdre, there are varying stories of her
death, but most of them agree that she did not
survive the sons of Usnach many hours. But,
before she died, she made an elegy over them.
That it is of a singular pathos and beauty the few
verses which there is space to give will show.[1]

> "Long the day without Usnach's children!
> It was not mournful to be in their company!
> Sons of a king by whom sojourners were entertained,
> Three lions from the Hill of the Cave.
>
> . . . .
>
> "Three darlings of the women of Britain,
> Three hawks of Slieve Gullion,
> Sons of a king whom valour served,
> To whom soldiers used to give homage!
>
> . . . .
>
> "That I should remain after Naoise
> Let no one in the world suppose:
> After Ardan and Ainle
> My time would not be long.
>
> "Ulster's over-king, my first husband,
> I forsook for Naoise's love.
> Short my life after them:
> I will perform their funeral game.
>
> "After them I shall not be alive—
> Three that would go into every conflict,

---

1 It will be found in full in Miss Hull's *Cuchullin Saga*. The version there
given was first translated into French by M. Ponsinet from the Book of Leinster.

Three who liked to endure hardships,
Three heroes who refused not combats.

. . . .

" O man, that diggest the tomb
And puttest my darling from me,
Make not the grave too narrow:
I shall be beside the noble ones."

It was a poor triumph for Conchobar. Deirdre in all her beauty had escaped him by death. His own chief followers never forgave it. Fergus, when he returned from Borrach's feast, and found out what had been done, gathered his own people, slew Conchobar's son and many of his warriors, and fled to Ulster's bitterest enemies, Ailill and Medb of Connaught. And Cathbad the Druid cursed both king and kingdom, praying that none of Conchobar's race might ever reign in Emain Macha again.

So it came to pass. The capital of Ulster was only kept from ruin by Cuchulainn's prowess. When he perished, it also fell, and soon became what it is now—a grassy hill.

CHAPTER XIV

FINN AND THE FENIANS[1]

The epoch of Emain Macha is followed in the annals of ancient Ireland by a succession of monarchs who, though doubtless as mythical as King Conchobar and his court, seem to grow gradually more human. Their line lasts for about two centuries, culminating in a dynasty with which legend has occupied itself more than with its immediate predecessors. This is the one which began, according to the annalists, in A.D. 177, with the famous Conn "the Hundred-Fighter", and, passing down to the reign of his even more famous grandson, Cormac "the Magnificent", is connected with the third Gaelic cycle—that which relates the exploits of Finn and the Fenians. All these kings had their dealings with the national gods. A story contained in a fifteenth-century Irish manuscript, and called "The Champion's Prophecy",[2] tells how Lugh appeared to Conn, enveloped him in a magic mist, led him away to an enchanted palace, and there prophesied to him the number of his descendants, the length of·their reigns,

---

[1] The translations of Fenian stories are numerous. The reader will find many of them popularly retold in Lady Gregory's *Gods and Fighting Men*. Thence he may pass on to Mr. Standish Hayes O'Grady's *Silva Gadelica*; the *Waifs and Strays of Celtic Tradition*, especially Vol. IV; Mr. J. G. Campbell's *The Fians*; as well as the volumes of the *Revue Celtique* and the *Transactions of the Ossianic Society*.

[2] See O'Curry's translation in Appendix CXXVIII to his *MS. Materials*.

and the manner of their deaths. Another tradition relates how Conn's son, Connla, was wooed by a goddess and borne away, like the British Arthur, in a boat of glass to the Earthly Paradise beyond the sea.[1] Yet another relates Conn's own marriage with Becuma of the Fair Skin, wife of that same Labraid of the Quick Hand on Sword who, in another legend, married Liban, the sister of Fand, Cuchulainn's fairy love. Becuma had been discovered in an intrigue with Gaiar, a son of Manannán, and, banished from the "Land of Promise", crossed the sea that sunders mortals and immortals to offer her hand to Conn. The Irish king wedded her, but evil came of the marriage. She grew jealous of Conn's other son, Art, and insisted upon his banishment; but they agreed to play chess to decide which should go, and Art won. Art, called "the Lonely" because he had lost his brother Connla, was king after Conn, but he is chiefly known to legend as the father of Cormac.

Many Irish stories occupy themselves with the fame of Cormac, who is pictured as a great legislator —a Gaelic Solomon. Certain traditions credit him with having been the first to believe in a purer doctrine than the Celtic polytheism, and even with having attempted to put down druidism, in revenge for which a druid called Maelcen sent an evil spirit who placed a salmon-bone crossways in the king's throat, as he sat at meat, and so compassed his death. Another class of stories, however, make him

---

[1] The story, found in the Book of the Dun Cow, appears in French in De Jubainville's *Épopée Celtique*.

an especial favourite with those same heathen deities.
Manannán son of Lêr, was so anxious for his friendship that he decoyed him into fairyland, and gave
him a magic branch. It was of silver, and bore
golden apples, and, when it was shaken, it made
such sweet music that the wounded, the sick, and
the sorrowful forgot their pains, and were lulled into
deep sleep. Cormac kept this treasure all his life;
but, at his death, it returned into the hands of the
gods.[1]

King Cormac was a contemporary of Finn mac
Coul[2], whom he appointed head of the *Fianna*[3]
Eirinn, more generally known as the "Fenians".
Around Finn and his men have gathered a cycle
of legends which were equally popular with the
Gaels of both Scotland and Ireland. We read of
their exploits in stories and poems preserved in the
earliest Irish manuscripts, while among the peasantry both of Ireland and of the West Highlands
their names and the stories connected with them are
still current lore. Upon some of these floating traditions, as preserved in folk ballads, MacPherson
founded his factitious *Ossian*, and the collection
of them from the lips of living men still affords
plenty of employment to Gaelic students.

How far Finn and his followers may have been
historical personages it is impossible to say. The
Irish people themselves have always held that the
Fenians were a kind of native militia, and that Finn

---

[1] This famous story is told in several MSS. of the fourteenth and fifteenth centuries. For translations see Dr. Whitley Stokes, *Irische Texte*, and Standish Hayes
O'Grady, *Transactions of the Ossianic Society*, Vol. III.
[2] In Gaelic spelling, Fionn mac Cumhail. [3] Pronounced *Fēna*.

was their general. The early historical writers of Ireland supported this view. The chronicler Tighernach, who died in 1088, believed in him, and the "Annals of the Four Masters", compiled between the years 1632 and 1636 from older chronicles, while they ignore King Conchobar and his Red Branch Champions as unworthy of the serious consideration of historians, treat Finn as a real person whose death took place in 283 A.D. Even so great a modern scholar as Eugene O'Curry declared in the clearest language that Finn, so far from being "a merely imaginary or mythical character", was "an undoubtedly historical personage; and that he existed about the time at which his appearance is recorded in the Annals is as certain as that Julius Caesar lived and ruled at the time stated on the authority of the Roman historians".[1]

The opinion of more recent Celtic scholars, however, is opposed to this view. Finn's pedigree, preserved in the Book of Leinster, may seem at first to give some support to the theory of his real existence, but, on more careful examination of it, his own name and that of his father equally bewray him. Finn or Fionn, meaning "fair", is the name of one of the mythical ancestors of the Gaels, while his father's name, Cumhal[2], signifies the "sky", and is the same word as *Camulus*, the Gaulish heaven-god identified by the Romans with Mars. His followers are as doubtfully human as himself. One may compare them with Cuchulainn and the rest of the heroes of Emain Macha. Their deeds are not less marvellous.

[1] O'Curry: *MS. Materials*, Lecture XIV, p. 303.   [2] Pronounced *Coul* or *Cooal*.

Like the Ultonian warriors, they move, too, on equal terms with the gods. "The Fianna of Erin", says a tract called "The Dialogue of the Elders",[1] contained in thirteenth and fourteenth century manuscripts, "had not more frequent and free intercourse with the men of settled habitation than with the Tuatha Dé Danann".[2] Angus, Mider, Lêr, Manannán, and Bodb the Red, with their countless sons and daughters, loom as large in the Fenian, or so-called "Ossianic" stories as do the Fenians themselves. They fight for them, or against them; they marry them, and are given to them in marriage.

A luminous suggestion of Professor Rhys also hints that the Fenians inherited the conduct of that ancient war formerly waged between the Tuatha Dé Danann and the Fomors. The most common antagonists of Finn and his heroes are tribes of invaders from oversea, called in the stories the *Lochlannach.* These "Men of Lochlann" are usually identified, by those who look for history in the stories of the Fenian cycle, with the invading bands of Norsemen who harried the Irish coasts in the ninth century. But the nucleus of the Fenian tales antedates these Scandinavian raids, and mortal foes have probably merely stepped into the place of those immortal enemies of the gods whose "Lochlann" was a country, not over the sea—but under it.[3]

The earlier historians of Ireland were as ready with their dates and facts regarding the Fenian band

---

[1] *Agalamh na Senórach.* Under the title *The Colloquy of the Ancients*, there is an excellent translation of it, from the Book of Lismore, in Standish Hayes O'Grady's *Silva Gadelica.*   [2] O'Grady: *Silva Gadelica.*   [3] *Hibbert Lectures*, p. 355.

as an institution as with the personality of Finn. It was said to have been first organized by a king called Fiachadh, in 300 B.C., and abolished, or rather, exterminated, by Cairbré, the son of Cormac mac Art, in 284 A.D. We are told that it consisted of three regiments modelled on the Roman legion; each of these bodies contained, on a peace footing, three thousand men, but in time of war could be indefinitely strengthened. Its object was to defend the coasts of Ireland and the country generally, throwing its weight upon the side of any prince who happend to be assailed by foreign foes. During the six months of winter, its members were quartered upon the population, but during the summer they had to forage for themselves, which they did by hunting and fishing. Thus they lived in the woods and on the open moors, hardening themselves for battle by their adventurous life. The sites of their enormous camp-fires were long pointed out under the name of the "Fenians' cooking-places".

It was not easy to become a member of this famous band. A candidate had to be not only an expert warrior, but a poet and a man of culture as well. He had practically to renounce his tribe; at any rate he made oath that he would neither avenge any of his relatives nor be avenged by them. He put himself under bonds never to refuse hospitality to anyone who asked, never to turn his back in battle, never to insult any woman, and not to accept a dowry with his wife. In addition to all this, he had to pass successfully through the most stringent physical tests. Indeed, as these have come down to us, magnified by the perfervid Celtic imagination, they are of an altogether marvellous and impossible character. An aspirant to the *Fianna Eirinn*, we are told, had first to stand up to his knees in a pit dug for him, his only arms being his shield and a hazel wand, while nine warriors, each with a spear, standing within the distance of nine ridges of land, all hurled their weapons at him at once; if he failed to ward them all off, he was rejected. Should he succeed in this first test, he was given the distance of one tree-length's start, and chased through a forest by armed men; if any of them came up to him and wounded him, he could not belong to the Fenians. If he escaped unhurt, but had unloosed a single lock of his braided hair, or had broken a single branch in his flight, or if, at the end of the run, his weapons trembled in his hands, he was refused. As, besides these tests, he was obliged to jump over a branch as high as his forehead, and stoop under one as low as his knee, while running at full speed, and to pluck a thorn out of his heel without hindrance to his flight, it is clear that even the rank and file of the Fenians must have been quite exceptional athletes.[1]

But it is time to pass on to a more detailed description of these champions.[2] They are a goodly company, not less heroic than the mighty men of Ulster. First comes Finn himself, not the strongest in body of the Fenians, but the truest, wisest, and kindest, gentle to women, generous to men, and

---

[1] See *The Enumeration of Finn's Household*, translated by O'Grady in *Silva Gadelica*. [2] For a good account, see J. G. Campbell's *The Fians*, pp. 10–80.

trusted by all.   If he could help it, he would never
let anyone be in trouble or poverty.   "If the dead
leaves of the forest had been gold, and the white
foam of the water silver, Finn would have given it
all away."

Finn had two sons, Fergus and his more famous
brother Ossian[1].   Fergus of the sweet speech was
the Fenian's bard, and, also, because of his honeyed
words, their diplomatist and ambassador.   Yet, by
the irony of fate, it is to Ossian, who is not mentioned as a poet in the earliest texts, that the poems
concerning the Fenians which are current in Scotland under the name of "Ossianic Ballads" are
attributed.   Ossian's mother was Sadb, a daughter
of Bodb the Red.   A rival goddess changed her into
a deer—which explains how Ossian got his name,
which means "fawn".   With such advantages of
birth, naturally he was speedy enough to run down
a red deer hind and catch her by the ear, though
far less swift-footed than his cousin Caoilte[2], the
"Thin Man".   Neither was he so strong as his own
son Oscar, the mightiest of all the Fenians, yet, in
his youth, so clumsy that the rest of the band refused
to take him with them on their warlike expeditions.
They changed their minds, however, when, one day,
he followed them unawares, found them giving way
before an enemy, and, rushing to their help, armed
only with a great log of wood which lay handy on
the ground, turned the fortunes of the fight.   After
this, Oscar was hailed the best warrior of all the

---

[1] In more correct spelling, *Oisin*, and pronounced *Usheen* or *Isheen*.
[2] Pronounced *K'ylta* or *Cweeltia*

Fianna; he was given command of a battalion, and its banner, called the "Terrible Broom", was regarded as the centre of every battle, for it was never known to retreat a foot. Other prominent Fenians were Goll[1], son of Morna, at first Finn's enemy but afterwards his follower, a man skilled alike in war and learning. Even though he was one-eyed, we are told that he was much loved by women, but not so much as Finn's cousin, Diarmait O'Duibhne[2], whose fatal beauty ensnared even Finn's betrothed bride, Grainne[3]. Their comic character was Conan, who is represented as an old, bald, vain, irritable man, as great a braggart as ancient Pistol and as foul-mouthed as Thersites, and yet, after he had once been shamed into activity, a true man of his hands. These are the prime Fenian heroes, the chief actors in its stories.

The Fenian epic begins, before the birth of its hero, with the struggle of two rival clans, each of whom claimed to be the real and only Fianna Eirinn. They were called the Clann Morna, of which Goll mac Morna was head, and the Clann Baoisgne[4], commanded by Finn's father, Cumhal. A battle was fought at Cnucha[5], in which Goll killed Cumhal, and the Clann Baoisgne was scattered. Cumhal's wife, however, bore a posthumous son, who was brought up among the Slieve Bloom Mountains secretly, for fear his father's enemies should find and kill him. The boy, who was at first

---

[1] Pronounced *Gaul*. [2] Pronounced *Dermat O'Dyna*. [3] Pronounced *Grania*.
[4] Pronounced *Baskin*.   [5] Now Castleknock, near Dublin.

called Deimne[1], grew up to be an expert hurler, swimmer, runner, and hunter. Later, like Cuchulainn, and indeed many modern savages, he took a second, more personal name. Those who saw him asked who was the "fair" youth. He accepted the omen, and called himself Deimne Finn.

At length, he wandered to the banks of the Boyne, where he found a soothsayer called Finn the Seer living beside a deep pool near Slane, named "Fec's Pool", in hope of catching one of the "salmons of knowledge", and, by eating it, obtaining universal wisdom. He had been there seven years without result, though success had been prophesied to one named "Finn". When the wandering son of Cumhal appeared, Finn the Seer engaged him as his servant. Shortly afterwards, he caught the coveted fish, and handed it over to our Finn to cook, warning him to eat no portion of it. "Have you eaten any of it?" he asked the boy, as he brought it up ready boiled. "No indeed," replied Finn; "but, while I was cooking it, a blister rose upon the skin, and, laying my thumb down upon the blister, I scalded it, and so I put it into my mouth to ease the pain." The man was perplexed. "You told me your name was Deimne," he said; "but have you any other name?" "Yes, I am also called Finn.' "It is enough," replied his disappointed master. "Eat the salmon yourself, for you must be the one of whom the prophecy told." Finn ate the "salmon of knowledge", and thereafter he had only to put his thumb under his tooth, as he had done when he scalded it, to receive fore-knowledge and magic counsel.[1]

Thus armed, Finn was more than a match for the Clann Morna. Curious legends tell how he dis covered himself to his father's old followers, confounded his enemies with his magic, and turned them into faithful servants.[2] Even Goll of the Blows had to submit to his sway. Gradually he welded the two opposing clans into one Fianna, over which he ruled, taking tribute from the kings of Ireland, warring against the Fomorian " Loch lannach ", destroying every kind of giant, serpent, or monster that infested the land, and at last carry ing his mythical conquests over all Europe.

Out of the numberless stories of the Fenian ex ploits it is hard to choose examples. All are heroic, romantic, wild, fantastic. In many of them the Tuatha Dé Danann play prominent parts. One such story connects itself with an earlier mythological episode already related. The reader will remember[3] how, when the Dagda gave up the kingship of the immortals, five aspirants appeared to claim it; how of these five—Angus, Mider, Lêr, Ilbhreach son of Mannanán, and Bodb the Red—the latter was chosen; how Lêr refused to acknowledge him, but was reconciled later; how Mider, equally rebellious, fled to "desert country round Mount Leinster" in County Carlow; and how a yearly war was waged upon him and his people by the rest of the gods to

---

[1] This and other "boy-exploits" of Finn mac Cumhail are contained in a little tract written upon a fragment of the ninth century Psalter of Cashel. It is trans lated in Vol. IV of the *Transactions of the Ossianic Society*.

[2] Campbell's *Fians*, p. 22.   [3] See chap. XI—" The Gods in Exile".

bring them to subjection.   This war was still raging
in the time of Finn, and Mider was not too proud to
seek his help.   One day that Finn was hunting in
Donegal, with Ossian, Oscar, Caoilte, and Diarmait,
their hounds roused a beautiful fawn, which, although
at every moment apparently nearly overtaken, led
them in full chase as far as Mount Leinster.   Here
it suddenly disappeared into a cleft in the hillside.
Heavy snow, "making the forest's branches as it
were a withe-twist", now fell, forcing the Fenians to
seek for some shelter, and they therefore explored
the place into which the fawn had vanished.   It led
to a splendid *sídh* in the hollow of the hill.   Entering it, they were greeted by a beautiful goddess-
maiden, who told them that it was she, Mider's
daughter, who had been the fawn, and that she had
taken that shape purposely to lead them there, in
the hope of getting their help against the army that
was coming to attack the *sídh*.   Finn asked who the
assailants would be, and was told that they were
Bodb the Red with his seven sons, Angus "Son
of the Young" with his seven sons, Lêr of Sídh
Fionnechaidh with his twenty-seven sons, and
Fionnbharr of Sídh Meadha with his seventeen
sons, as well as numberless gods of lesser fame
drawn from *sídhe* not only over all Ireland, but from
Scotland and the islands as well.   Finn promised
his aid, and, with the twilight of that same day, the
attacking forces appeared, and made their annual
assault.   They were beaten off, after a battle that
lasted all night, with the loss of "ten men, ten
score, and ten hundred".   Finn, Oscar, and Diarmait,

as well as most of Mider's many sons, were sorely wounded, but the leech Labhra healed all their wounds.[1]

Sooth to say, the Fenians did not always require the excuse of fairy alliance to start them making war on the race of the hills. One of the so-called "Ossianic ballads" is entitled "The Chase of the Enchanted Pigs of Angus of the Brugh[2]". This Angus is, of course, the "Son of the Young", and the Brugh that famous *sídh* beside the Boyne out of which he cheated his father, the Dagda. After the friendly manner of gods towards heroes, he invited Finn and a picked thousand of his followers to a banquet at the Brugh. They came to it in their finest clothes, "goblets went from hand to hand, and waiters were kept in motion". At last conversation fell upon the comparative merits of the pleasures of the table and of the chase, Angus stoutly contending that "the gods' life of perpetual feasting" was better than all the Fenian huntings, and Finn as stoutly denying it. Finn boasted of his hounds, and Angus said that the best of them could not kill one of his pigs. Finn angrily replied that his two hounds, Bran[3] and Sgeolan[4], would kill any pig that trod on dry land. Angus answered that he could show Finn a pig that none of his hounds or huntsmen could catch or kill. Here were the makings of a pretty quarrel among such inflammable creatures as gods and heroes, but the steward of

[1] From the *Colloquy of the Ancients* in O'Grady's *Silva Gadelica*.
[2] It is translated in Vol. VI of the *Transactions of the Ossianic Society.*
[3] Pronounced *Brán*, not *Brän*.   [4] Pronounced *Shólaun* or *Scolaing.*

the feast interposed and sent everyone to bed. The next morning, Finn left the Brugh, for he did not want to fight all Angus's fairies with his handful of a thousand men. A year passed before he heard more of it; then came a messenger from Angus, reminding Finn of his promise to pit his men and hounds against Angus's pigs. The Fenians seated themselves on the tops of the hills, each with his favourite hound in leash, and they had not been there long before there appeared on the eastern plain a hundred and one such pigs as no Fenian had ever seen before. Each was as tall as a deer, and blacker than a smith's coals, having hair like a thicket and bristles like ships' masts. Yet such was the prowess of the Fenians that they killed them all, though each of the pigs slew ten men and many hounds. Then Angus complained that the Fenians had murdered his son and many others of the Tuatha Dé Danann, who, indeed, were none other than the pigs whose forms they had taken. There were mighty recriminations on both sides, and, in the end, the enraged Fenians prepared to attack the Brugh on the Boyne. Then only did Angus begin to yield, and, by the advice of Ossian, Finn made peace with him and his fairy folk.

Such are specimens of the tales which go to make up the Fenian cycle of sagas. Hunting is the most prominent feature of them, for the Fenians were essentially a race of mighty hunters. But the creatures of their chase were not always flesh and blood. Enchanters who wished the Fenians ill could always lure them into danger by taking the shape of boar or deer, and many a story begins with an innocent chase and ends with a murderous battle. But out of such struggles the Fenians always emerge successfully, as Ossian is represented proudly boasting, "through truthfulness and the might of their hands".

The most famous chase of all is, however, not that of deer or boar, but of a woman and a man, Finn's betrothed wife and his nephew Diarmait.[1] Ever fortunate in war, the Fenian leader found disaster in his love. Wishing for a wife in his old age, he sent to seek Grainne, the daughter of Cormac, the High-King of Ireland. Both King Cormac and his daughter consented, and Finn's ambassadors returned with an invitation to the suitor to come in a fortnight's time to claim his bride. He arrived with his picked band, and was received in state in the great banqueting-hall of Tara. There they feasted, and there Grainne, the king's daughter, casting her eyes over the assembled Fenian heroes, saw Diarmait O'Duibhne.

This Fenian Adonis had a beauty-spot upon his cheek which no woman could see without falling instantly in love with him. Grainne, for all her royal birth, was no exception to this rule. She asked a druid to point her out the principal guests. The druid told her all their names and exploits. Then she called for a jewelled drinking-horn, and, filling it with a drugged wine, sent it round to each in turn, except to Diarmait. None could be so

---

[1] A fine translation of the *Pursuit of Diarmait and Grainne* has been published by S. H. O'Grady in Vol. III of the *Transactions of the Ossianic Society*

discourteous as to refuse wine from the hand of a princess.   All drank, and fell into deep sleep.

Then, rising, she came to Diarmait, told him her passion for him, and asked for its return.   " I will not love the betrothed of my chief," he replied, "and, even if I wished, I dare not."   And he praised Finn's virtues, and decried his own fame. But Grainne merely answered that she put him under *geasa* (bonds which no hero could refuse to redeem) to flee with her; and at once went back to her chair before the rest of the company awoke from their slumber.

After the feast, Diarmait went round to his comrades, one by one, and told them of Grainne's love for him, and of the *geasa* she had placed upon him to take her from Tara.   He asked each of them what he ought to do.   All answered that no hero could break a *geis* put upon him by a woman.   He even asked Finn, concealing Grainne's name, and Finn gave him the same counsel as the others. That night, the lovers fled from Tara to the ford of the Shannon at Athlone, crossed it, and came to a place called the "Wood of the Two Tents", where Diarmait wove a hut of branches for Grainne to shelter in.

Meanwhile Finn had discovered their flight, and his rage knew no bounds.   He sent his trackers, the Clann Neamhuain[1], to follow them.   They tracked them to the wood, and one of them climbed a tree, and, looking down, saw the hut, with a strong seven-doored fence built round it, and Diarmait and

---

[1] Pronounced *Navin* or *Nowin*.

Grainne inside. When the news came to the Fenians, they were sorry, for their sympathies were with Diarmait and not with Finn. They tried to warn him, but he took no heed; for he had determined to fight and not to flee. Indeed, when Finn himself came to the fence, and called over it to Diarmait, asking if he and Grainne were within, he replied that they were, but that none should enter unless he gave permission.

So Diarmait, like Cuchulainn in the war of Ulster against Ireland, found himself matched single-handed against a host. But, also like Cuchulainn, he had a divine helper. The favourite of the Tuatha Dé Danann, he had been the pupil of Manannán son of Lêr in the "Land of Promise", and had been fostered by Angus of the Brugh. Manannán had given him his two spears, the "Red Javelin" and the "Yellow Javelin", and his two swords, the "Great Fury" and the "Little Fury". And now Angus came to look for his foster-son, and brought with him the magic mantle of invisibility used by the gods. He advised Diarmait and Grainne to come out wrapped in the cloak, and thus rendered invisible. Diarmait still refused to flee, but asked Angus to protect Grainne. Wrapping the magic mantle round her, the god led the princess away unseen by any of the Fenians.

By this time, Finn had posted men outside all the seven doors in the fence. Diarmait went to each of them in turn. At the first, were Ossian and Oscar with the Clann Baoisgne. They offered him their protection. At the second, were Caoilte and the

Clann Ronan, who said they would fight to the death for him. At the third, were Conan and the Clann Morna, also his friends. At the fourth, stood Cuan with the Fenians of Munster, Diarmait's native province. At the fifth, were the Ulster Fenians, who also promised him protection against Finn. But at the sixth, were the Clann Neamhuain, who hated him; and at the seventh, was Finn himself.

" It is by your door that I will pass out, O Finn," cried Diarmait. Finn charged his men to surround Diarmait as he came out, and kill him. But he leaped the fence, passing clean over their heads, and fled away so swiftly that they could not follow him. He never halted till he reached the place to which he knew Angus had taken Grainne. The friendly god left them with a little sage advice: never to hide in a tree with only one trunk; never to rest in a cave with only one entrance; never to land on an island with only one channel of approach; not to eat their supper where they had cooked it, nor to sleep where they had supped, and, where they had slept once, never to sleep again. With these Red-Indian-like tactics, it was some time before Finn discovered them.

However, he found out at last where they were, and sent champions with venomous hounds to take or kill them. But Diarmait conquered all who were sent against him.

Yet still Finn pursued, until Diarmait, as a last hope of escape, took refuge under a magic quicken-tree[1], which bore scarlet fruit, the ambrosia of the

---

[1] The mountain-ash, or rowan.

gods. It had grown from a single berry dropped by one of the Tuatha Dé Danann, who, when they found that they had carelessly endowed mortals with celestial and immortal food, had sent a huge, one-eyed Fomor called Sharvan the Surly to guard it, so that no man might eat of its fruit. All day, this Fomor sat at the foot of the tree, and, all night, he slept among its branches, and so terrible was his appearance that neither the Fenians nor any other people dared to come within several miles of him.

But Diarmait was willing to brave the Fomor in the hope of getting a safe hiding-place for Grainne. He came boldly up to him, and asked leave to camp and hunt in his neighbourhood. The Fomor told him surlily that he might camp and hunt where he pleased, so long as he refrained from taking any of the scarlet berries. So Diarmait built a hut near a spring; and he and Grainne lived there, killing the wild animals for food.

But, unhappily, Grainne conceived so strong a desire to eat the quicken berries that she felt that she must die unless her wish could be gratified. At first she tried to hide this longing, but in the end she was forced to tell her companion. Diarmait had no desire to quarrel with the Fomor; so he went to him and told the plight that Grainne was in, and asked for a handful of the berries as a gift.

But the Fomor merely answered: " I swear to you that if nothing would save the princess and her unborn child except my berries, and if she were the last woman upon the earth, she should not have any of them." Whereupon Diarmait fought the Fomor, and, after much trouble, killed him.

It was reported to Finn that the guardian of the magic quicken-tree lived no longer, and he guessed that Diarmait must have killed him; so he came down to the place with seven battalions of the Fenians to look for him. By this time, Diarmait had abandoned his own hut and taken possession of that built by the Fomor among the branches of the magic quicken. He was sitting in it with Grainne when Finn and his men came and camped at the foot of the tree, to wait till the heat of noon had passed before beginning their search.

To beguile the time, Finn called for his chess-board and challenged his son Ossian to a game. They played until Ossian had only one more move.

"One move would make you a winner," said Finn to him, "but I challenge you and all the Fenians to guess it."

Only Diarmait, who had been looking down through the branches upon the players, knew the move. He could not resist dropping a berry on to the board, so deftly that it hit the very chess-man which Ossian ought to move in order to win. Ossian took the hint, moved it, and won. A second and a third game were played; and in each case the same thing happened. Then Finn felt sure that the berries that had prompted Ossian must have been thrown by Diarmait.

He called out, asking Diarmait if he were there, and the Fenian hero, who never spoke an untruth, answered that he was. So the quicken-tree was surrounded by armed men, just as the fenced hut in the woods had been. But, again, things happened in the same way; for Angus of the Brugh took away Grainne wrapped in the invisible magic cloak, while Diarmait, walking to the end of a thick branch, cleared the circle of Fenians at a bound, and escaped untouched.

This was the end of the famous "Pursuit"; for Angus came as ambassador to Finn, urging him to become reconciled to the fugitives, and all the best of the Fenians begged Finn to consent. So Diarmait and Grainne were allowed to return in peace.

But Finn never really forgave, and, soon after, he urged Diarmait to go out to the chase of the wild boar of Benn Gulban[1]. Diarmait killed the boar without getting any hurt; for, like · the Greek Achilles, he was invulnerable, save in his heel alone. Finn, who knew this, told him to measure out the length of the skin with his bare feet. Diarmait did so. Then Finn, declaring that he had measured it wrongly, ordered him to tread it again in the opposite direction. This was against the lie of the bristles; and one of them pierced Diarmait's heel, and inflicted a poisoned and mortal wound.

This "Pursuit of Diarmait and Grainne", which has been told at such length, marks in some degree the climax of the Fenian power, after which it began to decline towards its end. The friends of Diarmait never forgave the treachery with which Finn had

[1] Now called Benbulben. It is near Sligo.

compassed his death.   The ever-slumbering rivalry
between Goll and his Clann Morna and Finn and
his Clann Baoisgne began to show itself as open
enmity.   Quarrels arose, too, between the Fenians
and the High-Kings of Ireland, which culminated
at last in the annihilation of the Fianna at the battle
of Gabhra[1].

This is said to have been fought in A.D. 284.
Finn himself had perished a year before it, in a
skirmish with rebellious Fenians at the Ford of
Brea on the Boyne.   King Cormac the Magnificent,
Grainne's father, was also dead.   It was between
Finn's grandson Oscar and Cormac's son Cairbré
that war broke out.   This mythical battle was as
fiercely waged as that of Arthur's last fight at
Camlan.   Oscar slew Cairbré, and was slain by him.
Almost all the Fenians fell, as well as all Cairbré's
forces.

Only two of the greater Fenian figures survived.
One was Caoilte, whose swiftness of foot saved
him at the end when all was lost.   The famous
story, called the " Dialogue of the Elders", represents
him discoursing to St. Patrick, centuries after, of
the Fenians' wonderful deeds.   Having lost his
friends of the heroic age, he is said to have cast
in his lot with the Tuatha Dé Danann.   He fought
in a battle, with Ilbhreach son of Manannán, against
Lêr himself, and killed the ancient sea-god with his
own hand.[2]   The tale represents him taking possession of Lêr's fairy palace of Sídh Fionnechaidh,
after which we know no more of him, except that

---

[1] Pronounced *Gavra*.   [2] See O'Grady's *Silva Gadelica.*

he has taken rank in the minds of the Irish peasantry as one of, and a ruler among, the Sídhe.

The other was Ossian, who did not fight at Gabhra, for, long before, he had taken the great journey which most heroes of mythology take, tc that bourne from which no ordinary mortal ever returns. Like Cuchulainn, it was upon the invitation of a goddess that he went. The Fenians were hunting near Lake Killarney when a lady of more than human beauty came to them, and told them that her name was Niamh[1], daughter of the Son of the Sea. The Gaelic poet, Michael Comyn, who, in the eighteenth century, rewove the ancient story into his own words,[2] describes her in just the same way as one of the old bards would have done:

" A royal crown was on her head;
  And a brown mantle of precious silk,
  Spangled with stars of red gold,
  Covering her shoes down to the grass.

" A gold ring was hanging down
  From each yellow curl of her golden hair;
  Her eyes, blue, clear, and cloudless,
  Like a dew-drop on the top of the grass.

" Redder were her cheeks than the rose,
  Fairer was her visage than the swan upon the wave,
  And more sweet was the taste of her balsam lips
  Than honey mingled thro' red wine.

[1] Pronounced *Nee-av*.
[2] *The Lay of Oisin in the Land of Youth*, translated by Brian O'Looney foi the Ossianic Society—*Transactions*, Vol. IV. A fine modern poem on the same subject is W. B. Yeats' *Wanderings of Oisin*.

" A garment, wide, long, and smooth
  Covered the white steed,
  There was a comely saddle of red gold,
  And her right hand held a bridle with a golden bit.

" Four shoes well-shaped were under him,
  Of the yellow gold of the purest quality;
  A silver wreath was on the back of his head,
  And there was not in the world a steed better."

Such was Niamh of the Golden Hair, Manannán's
daughter; and it is small wonder that, when she
chose Ossian from among the sons of men to be her
lover, all Finn's supplications could not keep him.
He mounted behind her on her fairy horse, and
they rode across the land to the sea-shore, and then
over the tops of the waves. As they went, she
described the country of the gods to him in just the
same terms as Manannán himself had pictured it
to Brân, son of Febal, as Mider had painted it to
Etain, and as everyone that went there limned it
to those that stayed at home on earth.

" It is.the most delightful country to be found
  Of greatest repute under the sun;
  Trees drooping with fruit and blossom,
  And foliage growing on the tops of boughs.

" Abundant, there, are honey and wine,
  And everything that eye has beheld,
  There will not come decline on thee with lapse of time.
  Death or decay thou wilt not see."

As they went they saw wonders. Fairy palaces with

bright sun-bowers and lime-white walls appeared on
the surface of the sea. At one of these they halted,
and Ossian, at Niamh's request, attacked a fierce
Fomor who lived there, and set free a damsel of
the Tuatha Dé Danann whom he kept imprisoned.
He saw a hornless fawn leap from wave to wave,
chased by one of those strange hounds of Celtic
myth which are pure white, with red ears. At last
they reached the "Land of the Young", and there
Ossian dwelt with Niamh for three hundred years
before he remembered Erin and the Fenians. Then
a great wish came upon him to see his own country
and his own people again, and Niamh gave him
leave to go, and mounted him upon a fairy steed
for the journey. One thing alone she made him
swear—not to let his feet touch earthly soil. Ossian
promised, and reached Ireland on the wings of the
wind. But, like the children of Lêr at the end of
their penance, he found all changed. He asked
for Finn and the Fenians, and was told that they
were the names of people who had lived long ago,
and whose deeds were written of in old books. The
Battle of Gabhra had been fought, and St. Patrick
had come to Ireland, and made all things new. The
very forms of men had altered; they seemed dwarfs
compared with the giants of his day. Seeing three
hundred of them trying in vain to raise a marble
slab, he rode up to them in contemptuous kindness,
and lifted it with one hand. But, as he did so, the
golden saddle-girth broke with the strain, and he
touched the earth with his feet. The fairy horse
vanished, and Ossian rose from the ground, no

longer divinely young and fair and strong, but a blind, gray-haired, withered old man.

A number of spirited ballads[1] tell how Ossian, stranded in his old age upon earthly soil, unable to help himself or find his own food, is taken by St. Patrick into his house to be converted. The saint paints to him in the brightest colours the heaven which may be his own if he will but repent, and in the darkest the hell in which he tells him his old comrades now lie in anguish. Ossian replies to the saint's arguments, entreaties, and threats in language which is extraordinarily frank. He will not believe that heaven could be closed to the Fenians if they wished to enter it, or that God himself would not be proud to claim friendship with Finn. And if it be not so, what is the use to him of eternal life where there is no hunting, or wooing fair women, or listening to the songs and tales of bards? No, he will go to the Fenians, whether they sit at the feast or in the fire; and so he dies as he had lived.

---

[1] See the *Transactions of the Ossianic Society.* They are generally called the *Dialogues of Oisin and Patrick.*

CHAPTER XV

THE DECLINE AND FALL OF THE GODS

In spite, however, of the wide-spread popularity of the ballads that took the form of dialogues between Ossian and Patrick, certain traditions say that the saint succeeded in converting the hero. Caoilté, the other great surviving Fenian, was also represented as having gladly exchanged his pagan lore for the faith and salvation offered him. We may see the same influence on foot in the later legends concerning the Red Branch Champions. It was the policy of the first Christianizers of Ireland to describe the loved heroes of their still half-heathen flocks as having handed in their submission to the new creed. The tales about Conchobar and Cuchulainn were amended, to prove that those very pagan personages had been miraculously brought to accept the gospel at the last. An entirely new story told how the latter hero was raised from the dead by Saint Patrick that he might bear witness of the truth of Christianity to Laogaire the Second, King of Ireland, which he did with such fervour and eloquence that the sceptical monarch was convinced.[1]

[1] The story, contained in the Book of the Dun Cow, is called *The Phantom Chariot*. It has been translated by Mr. O'Beirne Crowe, and is included in Miss Hull's *Cuchulinn Saga*.

Daring attempts were also made to change the Tuatha Dé Danann from pagan gods into Christian saints, but these were by no means so profitable as the policy pursued towards the more human-seeming heroes. With one of them alone, was success immediate and brilliant. Brigit, the goddess of fire, poetry, and the hearth, is famous to-day as Saint Bridget, or Bride. Most popular of all the Irish saints, she can still be easily recognized as the daughter of the Dagda. Her Christian attributes, almost all connected with fire, attest her pagan origin.[1]   She was born at sunrise; a house in which she dwelt blazed into a flame which reached to heaven; a pillar of fire rose from her head when she took the veil; and her breath gave new life to the dead. As with the British goddess Sul, worshipped at Bath, who—the first century Latin writer Solinus[2] tells us—"ruled over the boiling springs, and at her altar there flamed a perpetual fire which never whitened into ashes, but hardened into a stony mass", the sacred flame on her shrine at Kildare was never allowed to go out. It was extinguished once, in the thirteenth century, but was relighted, and burnt with undying glow until the suppression of the monasteries by Henry the Eighth. This sacred fire might not be breathed on by the impure human breath. For nineteen nights it was tended by her nuns, but on the twentieth night it was left untouched, and kept itself alight miraculously. With so little of her essential character

---

[1] See Elton, *Origins of English History*, pp. 269-271.
[2] Caius Julius Solinus, known as Polyhistor, chap. XXIV.

and ritual changed, it is small wonder that the half-pagan, half-Christian Irish gladly accepted the new saint in the stead of the old goddess.

Doubtless a careful examination of Irish hagiology would result in the discovery of many other saints whose names and attributes might render them suspect of previous careers as pagan gods. But their acceptation was not sufficiently general to do away with the need of other means of counteracting the still living influence of the Gaelic Pantheon. Therefore a fresh school of euhemerists arose to prove that the gods were never even saints, but merely worldly men who had once lived and ruled in Erin. Learned monks worked hard to construct a history of Ireland from the Flood downwards. Mr. Eugene O'Curry has compiled from the various pedigrees they elaborated, and inserted into the books of Ballymote, Lecan, and Leinster an amazing genealogy which shows how, not merely the Tuatha Dé Danann, but also the Fir Bolgs, the Fomors, the Milesians, and the races of Partholon and Nemed were descended from Noah. Japhet, the patriarch's son, was the father of Magog, from whom came two lines, the first being the Milesians, while the second branched out into all the other races.[1]

Having once worked the gods, first into universal history, and then into the history of Ireland, it was an easy matter to supply them with dates of birth and death, local habitations, and places of burial.

---

[1] It is appended to his translation of the tale of the *Exile of the Children of Usnach* in *Atlantis*, Vol. III.

We are told with precision exactly how long Nuada, the Dagda, Lugh, and the others reigned at Tara. The barrows by the Boyne provided them with comfortable tombs. Their enemies, the Fomors, became real invaders who were beaten in real battles. Thus it was thought to make plain prose of their divinities.

It is only fair, however, to these early euhemerists to say that they have their modern disciples. There are many writers, of recognized authority upon their subjects, who, in dealing with the history of Ireland or the composition of the British race, claim to find real peoples in the tribes mentioned in Gaelic myth. Unfortunately, the only point they agree upon is the accepted one—that the "Milesians" were Aryan Celts. They are divided upon the question of the "Fir Bolgs", in whom some see the pre-Aryan tribes, while others, led astray by the name, regard them as Belgic Gauls; and over the really mythological races they run wild. In the Tuatha Dé Danann are variously found Gaels, Picts, Danes, Scandinavians, Ligurians, and Finns, while the Fomors rest under the suspicion of having been Iberians, Moors, Romans, Finns, Goths, or Teutons. As for the people of Partholon and Nemed, they have even been explained as men of the Palæolithic Age. This chaos of opinion was fortunately avoided by the native annalists, who had no particular views upon the question of race, except that everybody came from "Spain".

Of course there were dissenters from this prevailing mania for euhemerization. As late as the tenth century, a poet called Eochaid O'Flynn, writing of the Tuatha Dé Danann, at first seems to hesitate whether to ascribe humanity or divinity to them, and at last frankly avows their godhead. In his poem, preserved in the Book of Ballymote,[1] he says:—

> "Though they came to learned Erinn
> Without buoyant, adventurous ships,
> No man in creation knew
> Whether they were of the earth or of the sky.

> "If they were diabolical demons,
> They came from that woeful expulsion;[2]
> If they were of a race of tribes and nations,
> If they were human, they were of the race of Beothach."

Then he enumerates them in due succession, and ends by declaring:—

> "Though I have treated of these deities in their order,
> Yet I have not adored them".

One may surmise with probability that the common people agreed rather with the poet than with the monk. Pious men in monasteries might write what they liked, but mere laymen would not be easily persuaded that their cherished gods had never been anything more than men like themselves. Probably they said little, but acted in secret according to their inherited ideas. Let it be granted, for the sake of peace, that Goibniu was only a man; none the less, his name was known to be uncommonly effective in an incantation. This

---

[1] See Cusack's *History of Ireland*, pp. 160–162.   [2] *I.e.* from Heaven.

applied equally to Diancecht, and invocations to both of them are contained in some verses which an eighth-century Irish monk wrote on the margin of a manuscript still preserved at St. Gall, in Switzerland. Some prescriptions of Diancecht's have come down to us, but it must be admitted that they hardly differ from those current among ordinary mediæval physicians. Perhaps, after that unfortunate spilling of the herbs that grew out of Miach's body, he had to fall back upon empirical research. He invented a porridge for "the relief of ailments of the body, as cold, phlegm, throat cats, and the presence of living things in the body, as worms"; it was compounded of hazel buds, dandelion, chickweed, sorrel, and oatmeal; and was to be taken every morning and evening. He also prescribed against the effects of witchcraft and the fourteen diseases of the stomach.

Goibniu, in addition to his original character as the divine smith and sorcerer, gained a third reputation among the Irish as a great builder and bridge-maker. As such he is known as the Gobhan Saer, that is, Goibniu the Architect, and marvellous tales, current all over Ireland attest his prowess.

> "Men call'd him Gobhan Saer, and many a tale
>   Yet lingers in the by-ways of the land
> Of how he cleft the rock, or down the vale
>   Led the bright river, child-like, in his hand:
> Of how on giant ships he spread great sail,
>   And many marvels else by him first plann'd",

writes a poet of modern Ireland.[1] Especially were

---

[1] Thomas D'Arcy M'Gee: *Poems*, p. 78, "The Gobhan Saer".

the "round towers" attributed to him, and the Christian clerics appropriated his popularity by describing him as having been the designer of their churches. He used, according to legend, to wander over the country, clad, like the Greek Hephaestus, whom he resembles, in working dress, seeking commissions and adventures. His works remain in the cathedrals and churches of Ireland; and, with regard to his adventures, many strange legends are still, or were until very recently, current upon the lips of old people in remote parts of Ireland.

Some of these are, as might have been expected, nothing more than half-understood recollections of the ancient mythology. In them appear as characters others of the old, yet not quite forgotten gods —Lugh, Manannán, and Balor—names still remembered as those of long-past druids, heroes, and kings of Ireland in the misty olden time.

One or two of them are worth re-telling. Mr. William Larminie, collecting folk-tales in Achill Island, took one from the lips of an aged peasant which tells in its confused way what might almost be called the central incident of Gaelic mythology, the mysterious birth of the sun-god from demoniac parentage, and his eventual slaying of his grandfather when he came to full age.[1]

Gobhan the Architect and his son, young Gobhan, runs the tale, were sent for by Balor of the Blows to build him a palace. They built it so well that Balor decided never to let them leave his kingdom alive, for fear they should build another one

[1] Larminie: *West Irish Folk-Tales*, pp. 1-9.

equally good for someone else.   He therefore had
all the scaffolding removed from round the palace
while they were still on the top, with the intention
of leaving them up there to die of hunger.   But,
when they discovered this, they began to destroy
the roof, so that Balor was obliged to let them come
down.

He, none the less, refused to allow them to return
to Ireland.   The crafty Gobhan, however, had his
plan ready.   He told Balor that the injury that had
been done to the palace roof could not be repaired
without special tools, which he had left behind him
at home.   Balor declined to let either old Gobhan
or young Gobhan go back to fetch them; but he
offered to send his own son.   Gobhan gave Balor's
son directions for the journey.   He was to travel
until he came to a house with a stack of corn at
the door.   Entering it, he would find a woman with
one hand and a child with one eye.

Balor's son found the house, and asked the woman
for the tools.   She expected him; for it had been
arranged between Gobhan and his wife what should
be done, if Balor refused to let him return.   She
took Balor's son to a huge chest, and told him that
the tools were at the bottom of it, so far down that
she could not reach them, and that he must get into
the chest, and pick them up himself.   But, as soon
as he was safely inside, she shut the lid on him,
telling him that he would have to stay there until
his father allowed old Gobhan and young Gobhan
to come home with their pay.   And she sent the
same message to Balor himself.

There was an exchange of prisoners, Balor giving the two Gobhans their pay and a ship to take them home, and Gobhan's wife releasing Balor's son. But, before the two builders went, Balor asked them whom he should now employ to repair his palace. Old Gobhan told him that, next to himself, there was no workman in Ireland better than one Gavidjeen Go.

When Gobhan got back to Ireland, he sent Gavidjeen Go to Balor. But he gave him a piece of advice—to accept as pay only one thing: Balor's gray cow, which would fill twenty barrels at one milking. Balor agreed to this, but, when he gave the cow to Gavidjeen Go to take back with him to Ireland, he omitted to include her byre-rope, which was the only thing that would keep her from returning to her original owner.

The gray cow gave so much trouble to Gavidjeen Go by her straying, that he was obliged to hire military champions to watch her during the day and bring her safely home at night. The bargain made was that Gavidjeen Go should forge the champion a sword for his pay, but that, if he lost the cow, his life was to be forfeited.

At last, a certain warrior called Cian was unlucky enough to let the cow escape. He followed her tracks down to the sea-shore and right to the edge of the waves, and there he lost them altogether. He was tearing his hair in his perplexity, when he saw a man rowing a coracle. The man, who was no other than Manannán son of Lêr, came in close to the shore, and asked what was the matter.

Cian told him.

"What would you give to anyone who would take you to the place where the gray cow is?" asked Manannán.

"I have nothing to give," replied Cian.

"All I ask," said Manannán, "is half of whatever you gain before you come back."

Cian agreed to that willingly enough, and Manannán told him to get into the coracle. In the wink of an eye, he had landed him in Balor's kingdom, the realm of the cold, where they roast no meat, but eat their food raw. Cian was not used to this diet, so he lit himself a fire, and began to cook some food. Balor saw the fire, and came down to it, and he was so pleased that he appointed Cian to be his fire-maker and cook.

Now Balor had a daughter, of whom a druid had prophesied that she would, some day, bear a son who would kill his grandfather. Therefore, like Acrisius, in Greek legend, he shut her up in a tower, guarded by women, and allowed her to see no man but himself. One day, Cian saw Balor go to the tower. He waited until he had come back, and then went to explore. He had the gift of opening locked doors and shutting them again after him. When he got inside, he lit a fire, and this novelty so delighted Balor's daughter that she invited him to visit her again. After this—in the Achill islander's quaint phrase—"he was ever coming there, until a child happened to her." Balor's daughter gave the baby to Cian to take away. She also gave him the byre-rope which belonged to the gray cow.

Cian was in great danger now, for Balor had found out about the child. He led the gray cow away with the rope to the sea-shore, and waited for Manannán. The Son of Lêr had told Cian that, when he was in any difficulty, he was to think of him, and he would at once appear. Cian thought of him now, and, in a moment, Manannán appeared with his coracle. Cian got into the boat, with the baby and the gray cow, just as Balor, in hot pursuit, came down to the beach.

Balor, by his incantations, raised a great storm to drown them; but Manannán, whose druidism was greater, stilled it. Then Balor turned the sea into fire, to burn them; but Manannán put it out with a stone.

When they were safe back in Ireland, Manannán asked Cian for his promised reward.

"I have gained nothing but the boy, and I cannot cut him in two, so I will give him to you whole," he replied.

"That is what I was wanting all the time," said Manannán; "when he grows up, there will be no champion equal to him."

So Manannán baptized the boy, calling him "the Dul-Dauna". This name, meaning "Blind-Stubborn", is certainly a curious corruption of the original *Ioldanach*[1] "Master of all Knowledge". When the boy had grown up, he went one day to the sea-shore. A ship came past, in which was a man. The traditions of Donnybrook Fair are evidently prehistoric, for the boy, without troubling to ask who

[1] Pronounced *Ildāna*.

the stranger was, took a dart "out of his pocket", hurled it, and hit him. The man in the boat happened to be Balor. Thus, in accordance with the prophecy, he was slain by his grandson, who, though the folk-tale does not name him, was obviously Lugh.

Another version of the same legend, collected by the Irish scholar O'Donovan on the coast of Donegal, opposite Balor's favourite haunt, Tory Island, is interesting as completing the one just narrated.[1] In this folk-tale, Goibniu is called Gavida, and is made one of three brothers, the other two being called Mac Kineely and Mac Samthainn. They were chiefs of Donegal, smiths and farmers, while Balor was a robber who harassed the mainland from his stronghold on Tory Island. The gray cow belonged to Mac Kineely, and Balor stole it. Its owner determined to be revenged, and, knowing the prediction concerning Balor's death at the hands of an as yet unborn grandson, he persuaded a kindly fairy to spirit him in female disguise to Tor Mor, where Balor's daughter, who was called Ethnea, was kept imprisoned. The result of this expedition was not merely the one son necessary to fulfil the prophecy, but three. This apparent superfluity was fortunate; for Balor drowned two of them, the other being picked out of the sea by the same fairy who had been incidentally responsible for his birth, and handed over to his father, Mac Kineely, to be brought up. Shortly after this, Balor managed to capure Mac Kineely, and, in retaliation for the wrong done him, chopped off his head upon a large white

1 It is told in Rhys's *Hibbert Lectures*, pp. 314-317.

stone, still known locally as the "Stone of Kineely".
Satisfied with this, and quite unaware that one of
his daughter's children had been saved from death,
and was now being brought up as a smith by Gavida,
Balor went on with his career of robbery, varying it
by visits to the forge to purchase arms. One day,
being there during Gavida's absence, he began boasting to the young assistant of how he had compassed
Mac Kineely's death. He never finished the story,
for Lugh—which was the boy's name—snatched a
red-hot iron from the fire, and thrust it into Balor's
eye, and through his head.

Thus, in these two folk-tales,[1] gathered in different parts of Ireland, at different times, by
different persons, survives quite a mass of mythological detail only to be found otherwise in
ancient manuscripts containing still more ancient
matter. Crystallized in them may be found the
names of six members of the old Gaelic Pantheon,
each filling the same part as of old. Goibniu has
not lost his mastery of smithcraft; Balor is still the
Fomorian king of the cold regions of the sea; his
daughter Ethniu becomes, by Cian, the mother of
the sun-god; Lugh, who still bears his old title of
Iolaanach, though it is strangely corrupted into a
name meaning almost the exact opposite, is still
fostered by Manannán, Son of the Sea, and in the
end grows up to destroy his grandfather by a blow
in the one vulnerable place, his death-dealing eye.
Perhaps, too, we may claim to see a genuine, though

[1] For still other folk-tale versions of this same myth see Curtin's *Hero Tales of Ireland*.

jumbled tradition, in the Fomor-like deformities of
Gobhan's wife and child, and in the story of the
gray cow and her byre-rope, which recalls that of
the Dagda's black-maned heifer, Ocean.

The memories of the peasantry still hold many
stories of Lugh, as well as of Angus, and others of
the old gods. But, next to the Gobhan Saer, the
one whose fame is still greatest is that ever-potent
and ever-popular figure, the great Manannán.

The last, perhaps, to receive open adoration, he is
represented by kindly tradition as having been still
content to help and watch over the people who had
rejected and ceased to worship him. Up to the
time of St. Columba, he was the special guardian
of Irishmen in foreign parts, assisting them in their
dangers and bringing them home safe. For the
peasantry, too, he caused favourable weather and
good crops. His fairy subjects tilled the ground while
men slept. But this is said to have come to an end
at last. Saint Columba, having broken his golden
chalice, gave it to a servant to get repaired. On
his way, the servant was met by a stranger, who
asked him where he was going. The man told
him, and showed him the chalice. The stranger
breathed upon it, and, at once, the broken parts re-
united. Then he begged him to return to his master,
give him the chalice, and tell him that Manannán
son of Lêr, who had mended it, desired to know in
very truth whether he would ever attain paradise.
" Alas," said the ungrateful saint, " there is no forgiveness for a man who does such works as this!"
The servant went back with the answer, and Man-

annán, when he heard it, broke out into indignant lament. "Woe is me, Manannán mac Lêr! for years I've helped the Catholics of Ireland, but I'll do it no more, till they're as weak as water. I'll go to the gray waves in the Highlands of Scotland."[1]

And there he remained. For, unless the charming stories of Miss Fiona Macleod are mere beautiful imaginings and nothing more, he is not unknown even to-day among the solitary shepherds and fishers of "the farthest Hebrides". In the *Contemporary Review* for October, 1902,[2] she tells how an old man of four-score years would often be visited in his shieling by a tall, beautiful stranger, with a crest on his head, "like white canna blowing in the wind, but with a blueness in it", and "a bright, cold, curling flame under the soles of his feet". The man told him many things, and prophesied to him the time of his death. Generally, the stranger's hands were hidden in the folds of the white cloak he wore, but, once, he moved to touch the shepherd, who saw then that his flesh was like water, with sea-weed floating among the bones. So that Murdo MacIan knew that he could be speaking with none other than the Son of the Sea.

Nor is he yet quite forgotten in his own Island of Man, of which local tradition says he was the first inhabitant. He is also described as its king, who kept it from invasion by his magic. He would cause mists to rise at any moment and conceal the island,

[1] A Donegal story, collected by Mr. David Fitzgerald and published in the *Revue Celtique*, Vol. IV, p. 177.

[2] The paper is called "Sea-Magic and Running Water".

and by the same glamour he could make one man seem like a hundred, and little chips of wood which he threw into the water to appear like ships of war. It is no wonder that he held his kingdom against all-comers, until his sway was ended, like that of the other Gaelic gods, by the arrival of Saint Patrick. After this, he seems to have declined into a traditionary giant who used to leap from Peel Castle to Contrary Head for exercise, or hurl huge rocks, upon which the mark of his hand can still be seen. It is said that he took no tribute from his subjects, or worshippers except bundles of green rushes, which were placed every Midsummer Eve upon two mountain peaks, one called Warre-field in olden days, but now South Barrule, and the other called Man, and not now to be identified. His grave, which is thirty yards long, is pointed out, close to Peel Castle. The most curious legend connected with him, however, tells us that he had three legs, on which he used to travel at a great pace. How this was done may be seen from the arms of the island, on which are pictured his three limbs, joined together, and spread out like the spokes of a wheel.[1]

An Irish tradition tells us that, when Manannán left Ireland for Scotland, the vacant kingship of the gods or fairies was taken by one Mac Moineanta, to the great grief of those who had known Man-annán.[2] Perhaps this great grief led to Mac Moine-anta's being deposed, for the present king of the

[1] Moore: *Folklore of the Isle of Man.*
[2] See an article in the *Dublin University Magazine* for June, 1864

Irish fairies is Finvarra, the same Fionnbharr to whom the Dagda allotted the *sídh* of Meadha after the conquest of the Tuatha Dé Danann by the Milesians, and who takes a prominent part in the Fenian stories. So great is the persistence of tradition in Ireland that this hill of Meadha, now spelt Knockma, is still considered to be the abode of him and his queen, Onagh. Numberless stories are told about Finvarra, including, of course, that very favourite Celtic tale of the stolen bride, and her recapture from the fairies by the siege and digging up of the *sídh* in which she was held prisoner. Finvarra, like Mider of Bri Leith, carried away a human Etain—the wife, not of a high king, but of an Irish lord. The modern Eochaid Airem, having heard an invisible voice tell him where he was to look for his lost bride, gathered all his workmen and labourers and proceeded to demolish Knockma. Every day they almost dug it up, but every night the breach was found to have been repaired by fairy workmen of Finvarra's. This went on for three days, when the Irish lord thought of the well-known device of sanctifying the work of excavation by sprinkling the turned-up earth with salt. Needless to say, it succeeded. Finvarra gave back the bride, still in the trance into which he had thrown her; and the deep cut into the fairy hill still remains to furnish proof to the incredulous.[1]

Finvarra does not always appear, however, in

[1] The story is among those told by Lady Wilde in her *Ancient Legends of Ireland*, Vol. I, pp. 77–82.

such unfriendly guise. He was popularly reputed to have under his special care the family of the Kirwans of Castle Hacket, on the northern slope of Knockma. Owing to his benevolent influence, the castle cellars never went dry, nor did the quality of the wine deteriorate. Besides the wine-cellar, Finvarra looked after the stables, and it was owing to the exercise that he and his fairy followers gave the horses by night that Mr. John Kirwan's racers were so often successful on the Curragh. That such stories could have passed current as fact, which they undoubtedly did, is excellent proof of how late and how completely a mythology may survive among the uncultured.[1]

Finvarra rules to-day over a wide realm of fairy folk. Many of these, again, have their own vassal chieftains, forming a tribal hierarchy such as must have existed in the Celtic days of Ireland. Finvarra and Onagh are high king and queen, but, under them, Cliodna[2] is tributary queen of Munster, and rules from a *sídh* near Mallow in County Cork, while, under her again, are Aoibhinn[3], queen of the fairies of North Munster, and Ainé, queen of the fairies of South Munster. These names form but a single instance. A map of fairy Ireland could without much difficulty be drawn, showing, with almost political exactness, the various kingdoms of the Sídhe.

Far less easy, however, would be the task of ascertaining the origin and lineage of these fabled

[1] *Dublin University Magazine*, June, 1864.
[2] Pronounced *Cleena*.   [3] Pronounced *Evin*.

beings.   Some of them can still be traced as older gods and goddesses.   In the eastern parts of Ireland, Badb and her sisters have become "banshees" who wail over deaths not necessarily found in battle. Aynia, deemed the most powerful fairy in Ulster, and Ainé, queen of South Munster, are perhaps the same person, the mysterious and awful goddess once adored as Anu, or Danu.   Of the two, it is Ainé who especially seems to carry on the traditions of the older Anu, worshipped, according to the "Choice of Names", in Munster as a goddess of prosperity and abundance.   Within living memory, she was propitiated by a magical ritual upon every Saint John's Eve, to ensure fertility during the coming year.   The villagers round her *sídh* of Cnoc Ainé (Knockainy) carried burning bunches of hay or straw upon poles to the top of the hill, and thence dispersed among the fields, waving these torches over the crops and cattle.   This fairy, or goddess was held to be friendly, and, indeed, more than friendly, to men.   Whether or not she were the mother of the gods, she is claimed as first ancestress by half a dozen famous Irish families.

Among her children was the famous Earl Gerald, offspring of her alliance with the fourth Earl of Desmond, known as "The Magician".   As in the well-known story of the Swan-maidens, the magician-earl is said to have stolen Ainé's cloak while she was bathing, and refused to return it unless she became his bride.   But, in the end, he lost her. Ainé had warned her husband never to show surprise at anything done by their son; but a wonderful

feat which he performed made the earl break this
condition, and Ainé was obliged, by fairy law, to
leave him.   But, though she had lost her husband,
she was not separated from her son, who was received into the fairy world after his death, and now
lives under the surface of Lough Gur, in County
Limerick, waiting, like the British Arthur, for the
hour to strike in which he shall lead forth his warriors to drive the foreigners from Ireland.   But this
will not be until, by riding round the lake once in
every seventh year, he shall have worn his horse's
silver shoes as thin as a cat's ear.[1]

Not only the tribe of Danu, but heroes of the
other mythical cycles swell the fairy host to-day.
Donn, son of Milé, who was drowned before ever
he set foot on Irish soil, lives at " Donn's House",
a line of sand-hills in the Dingle Peninsula of Kerry,
and, as late as the eighteenth century, we find him
invoked by a local poet, half in jest, no doubt, but
still, perhaps also a little in earnest.[2]   The heroes of
Ulster have no part in fairyland; but their enemy,
Medb, is credited with queenly rule among the
Sídhe, and is held by some to have been the original
of "Queen Mab".   Caoilté, last of the Fenians,
was, in spite of his leanings towards Christianity,
enrolled among the Tuatha Dé Danann, but none
of his kin are known there, neither Ossian, nor
Oscar, nor even Finn himself.   Yet not even to
merely historical mortals are the gates of the gods
necessarily closed.   The Barry, chief of the barony

---

[1] See Fitzgerald, *Popular Tales of Ireland*, in Vol. IV of the *Revue Celtique*.
[2] *Dublin University Magazine*, June, 1864.

of Barrymore, is said to inhabit an enchanted palace in Knockthierna, one of the Nagles Hills. The not less traditionally famous O'Donaghue, whose domain was near Killarney, now dwells beneath the waters of that lake, and may still be seen, it is said, upon May Day.[1]

But besides these figures, which can be traced in mythology or history, and others who, though all written record of them has perished, are obviously of the same character, there are numerous beings who suggest a different origin from that of the Aryan-seeming fairies. They correspond to the elves and trolls of Scandinavian, or the silenoi and satyrs of Greek myth. Such is the Leprechaun, who makes shoes for the fairies, and knows where hidden treasures are; the Gan Ceanach, or "love-talker", who fills the ears of idle girls with pleasant fancies when, to merely mortal ideas, they should be busy with their work; the Pooka, who leads travellers astray, or, taking the shape of an ass or mule, beguiles them to mount upon his back to their discomfiture; the Dulachan, who rides without a head; and other friendly or malicious sprites. Whence come they? A possible answer suggests itself. Preceding the Aryans, and surviving the Aryan conquest all over Europe, was a large non-Aryan population, which must have had its own gods, who would retain their worship, be revered by successive generations, and remain rooted to the soil. May not these uncouth and half-developed

[1] For stories of these two Norman-Irish heroes, see Crofton Croker's *Fairy Legends and Traditions of the South of Ireland.*

Irish Leprechauns, Pookas, and Dulachans, together with the Scotch Cluricanes, Brownies, and their kin, be no " creations of popular fancy ", but the dwindling figures of those darker gods of " the dark Iberians "?

THE BRITISH GODS AND THEIR STORIES

CHAPTER XVI

THE GODS OF THE BRITONS

The descriptions and the stories of the British gods have hardly come down to us in so ample or so compact a form as those of the deities of the Gaels, as they are preserved in the Irish and Scottish manuscripts. They have also suffered far more from the sophistications of the euhemerist. Only in the "Four Branches of the Mabinogi" do the gods of the Britons appear in anything like their real character of supernatural beings, masters of magic, and untrammelled by the limitations which hedge in mortals. Apart from those four fragments of mythology, and from a very few scattered references in the early Welsh poems, one must search for them under strange disguises. Some masquerade as kings in Geoffrey of Monmouth's more than apocryphal *Historia Britonum*. Others have received an undeserved canonization, which must be stripped from them before they can be seen in their true colours. Others, again, were adopted by the Norman-French romancers, and turned into the champions of chivalry now known as Arthur's Knights of the Round Table. But, however disguised, their real nature can still be discerned. The Gaels and the Britons were but two branches of one race—the Celtic. In many of the gods of the Britons we shall recognize, with names alike and attributes the same, the familiar features of the Gaelic Tuatha Dé Danann.

The British gods are sometimes described as divided into three families—the "Children of Dôn", the "Children of Nudd", and the "Children of Llyr". But these three families are really only two; for Nudd, or Lludd, as he is variously called, is himself described as a son of Beli, who was the husband of the goddess Dôn. There can be no doubt that Dôn herself is the same divine personage as Danu, the mother of the Tuatha Dé Danann, and that Beli is the British equivalent of the Gaelic Bilé, the universal Dis Pater who sent out the first Gaels from Hades to take possession of Ireland. With the other family, the "Children of Llyr", we are equally on familiar ground; for the British Llyr can be none other than the Gaelic sea-god Lêr. These two families or tribes are usually regarded as in opposition, and their struggles seem to symbolize in British myth that same conflict between the powers of heaven, light, and life and of the sea, darkness, and death which are shadowed in Gaelic mythology in the battles between the Tuatha Dé Danann and the Fomors.

For the children of Dôn were certainly gods of the sky. Their names are writ large in heaven. The glittering W which we call "Cassiopeia's Chair" was to our British ancestors *Llys Dôn*, or "Dôn's Court"; our "Northern Crown" was *Caer Arianrod*, the "Castle of Arianrod", Dôn's daughter;

while the "Milky Way" was the "Castle of Gwydion", Dôn's son.[1]   More than this, the greatest of her children, the Nudd or Lludd whom some make the head of a dynasty of his own, was the Zeus alike of the Britons and of the Gaels.   His epithet of *Llaw Ereint*, that is, "of the Hand of Silver", proves him the same personage as Nuada the "Silver-Handed".   The legend which must have existed to explain this peculiarity has been lost on British ground, but it was doubtless the same as that told of the Irish god.   With it, and, no doubt, much else, has disappeared any direct account of battles fought by him as sky-god against Fomor-like enemies. But, under the faint disguise of a king of Britain, an ancient Welsh tale[2] records how he put an end to three supernatural "plagues" which oppressed his country.   In addition to this, we find him under his name of Nudd described in a Welsh Triad as one of "the three generous heroes of the Isle of Britain", while another makes him the owner of twenty-one thousand milch cows — an expression which must, to the primitive mind, have implied inexhaustible wealth.   Both help us to the conception of a god of heaven and battle, triumphant, and therefore rich and liberal.[3]

More tangible evidence is, however, not lacking to prove the wide-spread nature of his worship.   A temple dedicated to him in Roman times under the name of Nodens, or Nudens, has been discovered at

---

[1] Lady Guest's *Mabinogion*, a note to *Math, the Son of Mathonwy*.
[2] *The Story of Lludd and Llevelys*.   See chap. XXIV—"The Decline and Fall of the Gods".   [3] Rhys: *Hibbert Lectures*, p. 128.

Lydney, on the banks of the Severn. The god is pictured on a plaque of bronze as a youthful deity, haloed like the sun, and driving a four-horsed chariot. Flying spirits, typifying the winds, accompany him; while his power over the sea is symbolized by attendant Tritons.[1] This was in the west of Britain, while, in the east, there is good reason to believe that he had a shrine overlooking the Thames. Tradition declares that St. Paul's Cathedral occupies the site of an ancient pagan temple; while the spot on which it stands was called, we know from Geoffrey of Monmouth, "Parth Lludd" by the Britons, and "Ludes Geat" by the Saxons.[2]

Great, however, as he probably was, Lludd, or Nudd occupies less space in Welsh story, as we have it now, than his son. Gwyn ap Nudd has outlived in tradition almost all his supernatural kin. Professor Rhys is tempted to see in him the British equivalent of the Gaelic Finn mac Cumhail.[3] The name of both alike means "white"; both are sons of the heaven-god; both are famed as hunters. Gwyn, however, is more than that; for his game is man. In the early Welsh poems, he is a god of battle and of the dead, and, as such, fills the part of a *psychopompos*, conducting the slain into Hades, and there ruling over them. In later, semi-Christianized story he is described as "Gwyn, son of Nudd, whom God has placed over the brood of devils in Annwn, lest they should destroy the pre-

[1] See a monograph by the Right Hon. Charles Bathurst: *Roman Antiquities in Lydney Park, Gloucestershire.*
[2] See chap. XXIV—"The Decline and Fall of the Gods".
[3] *Hibbert Lectures*, pp. 178, 179.

sent race[1]". Later again, as paganism still further degenerated, he came to be considered as king of the *Tylwyth Teg*, the Welsh fairies,[2] and his name as such has hardly yet died out of his last haunt, the romantic vale of Neath. He is the wild huntsman of Wales and the West of England, and it is his pack which is sometimes heard at chase in waste places by night.

In his earliest guise, as a god of war and death, he is the subject of a poem in dialogue contained in the Black Book of Caermarthen.[3] Obscure, like most of the ancient Welsh poems,[4] it is yet a spirited production, and may be quoted here as a favourable specimen of the poetry of the early Cymri. In it we shall see mirrored perhaps the clearest figure of the British Pantheon, the "mighty hunter", not of deer, but of men's souls, riding his demon horse, and cheering on his demon hound to the fearful chase. He knows when and where all the great warriors fell, for he gathered their souls upon the field of battle, and now rules over them in Hades, or upon some "misty mountain-top".[5] It describes a mythical prince, named Gwyddneu Garanhir, known to Welsh legend as the ruler of a lost country now covered by the waters of Cardigan Bay, asking protection of the god, who

---

[1] So translated by Lady Guest. Professor Rhys, however, renders it, "in whom God has put the instinct of the demons of Annwn". *Arthurian Legend*, p. 341.

[2] Lady Guest's *Mabinogion*. Note to "Kulhwch and Olwen".

[3] Black Book of Caermarthen, poem XXXIII. Vol. I, p. 293, of Skene's *Four Ancient Books*.

[4] I have taken the liberty of omitting a few lines whose connection with their context is not very apparent.

[5] Gwyn was said to specially frequent the summits of hills.

accords it, and then relates the story of his exploits:

Gwyddneu.

A bull of conflict was he, active in dispersing an arrayed
 army,
The ruler of hosts, indisposed to anger,
Blameless and pure his conduct in protecting life.

Gwyn.

Against a hero stout was his advance,
The ruler of hosts, disposer of wrath,
There will be protection for thee since thou askest it.

Gwyddneu.

For thou hast given me protection
How warmly wert thou welcomed!
The hero of hosts, from what region thou comest?

Gwyn.

I come from battle and conflict
With a shield in my hand;
Broken is the helmet by the pushing of spears.

Gwyddneu.

I will address thee, exalted man,
With his shield in distress.
Brave man, what is thy descent?

Gwyn.

Round-hoofed is my horse, the torment of battle,
Fairy am I called, Gwyn the son of Nudd,[1]
The lover of Creurdilad, the daughter of Lludd.

---

[1] This line is Professor Rhys's. Skene translates it: "Whilst I am called Gwyn the son of Nudd".

Gwyddneu.

Since it is thou, Gwyn, an upright man,
From thee there is no concealing:
I am Gwyddneu Garanhir.

Gwyn.

Hasten to my ridge, the Tawë abode;
Not the nearest Tawë name I to thee,
But that Tawë which is the farthest.[1]

Polished is my ring, golden my saddle and bright:
To my sadness
I saw a conflict before Caer Vandwy.[2]

Before Caer Vandwy a host I saw,
Shields were shattered and ribs broken;
Renowned and splendid was he who made the assault.

Gwyddneu.

Gwyn, son of Nudd, the hope of armies,
Quicker would legions fall before the hoofs
Of thy horse than broken rushes to the ground.

Gwyn.

Handsome my dog, and round-bodied,
And truly the best of dogs;
Dormarth[3] was he, which belonged to Maelgwyn.

Gwyddneu.

Dormarth with the ruddy nose! what a gazer
Thou art upon me because I notice
Thy wanderings on Gwibir Vynyd.[4]

[1] I have here preferred Rhys's rendering: *Arthurian Legend*, p. 364.
[2] A name for Hades, of unknown meaning.
[3] Dormarth means "Death's Door". Rhys: *Arthurian Legend*, pp. 156-158.
[4] Rhys has it:
> "Dormarth, red-nosed, ground-grazing—
> On him we perceived the speed
> Of thy wandering on Cloud Mount."
> —*Arthurian Legend*, p. 156.

Gwyn.

I have been in the place where was killed Gwendoleu,
The son of Ceidaw, the pillar of songs,
When the ravens screamed over blood.

I have been in the place where Brân was killed,
The son of Iweridd, of far extending fame,
When the ravens of the battle-field screamed.

I have been where Llacheu was slain,
The son of Arthur, extolled in songs,
When the ravens screamed over blood.

I have been where Meurig was killed,
The son of Carreian, of honourable fame,
When the ravens screamed over flesh.

I have been where Gwallawg was killed,
The son of Goholeth, the accomplished,
The resister of Lloegyr, the son of Lleynawg.

I have been where the soldiers of Britain were slain,
From the east to the north:
I am the escort of the grave.[1]

I have been where the soldiers of Britain were slain,
From the east to the south:
I am alive, they in death!

A line in this poem allows us to see Gwyn in another and less sinister rôle. "The lover of Creurdilad, the daughter of Lludd," he calls himself; and an episode in the mythical romance of "Kulhwch and Olwen", preserved in the Red Book of Hergest, gives the details of his courtship. Gwyn had as rival a deity called Gwyrthur ap Greidawl,

[1] Rhys: *Arthurian Legend*, p. 383. Skene translates: " I am alive, they in their graves!"

that is "Victor, son of Scorcher".[1] These two waged perpetual war for Creurdilad, or Creudylad, each in turn stealing her from the other, until the matter was referred to Arthur, who decided that Creudylad should be sent back to her father, and that Gwyn and Gwyrthur "should fight for her every first of May, from henceforth until the day of doom, and that whichever of them should then be conqueror should have the maiden". What satisfaction this would be to the survivor of what might be somewhat flippantly described as, in two senses, the longest engagement on record, is not very clear; but its mythological interpretation appears fairly obvious. In Gwyn, god of death and the underworld, and in the solar deity, Gwyrthur, we may see the powers of darkness and sunshine, of winter and summer, in contest,[2] each alternately winning and losing a bride who would seem to represent the spring with its grain and flowers. Creudylad, whom the story of "Kulhwch and Olwen" calls "the most splendid maiden in the three islands of the mighty and in the three islands adjacent", is, in fact, the British Persephoné. As the daughter of Lludd, she is child of the shining sky. But a different tradition must have made her a daughter of Llyr, the sea-god; for her name as such passed, through Geoffrey of Monmouth, to Shakespeare, in whose hands she became that pathetic figure, Cordelia in "King Lear". It may not be altogether unworthy of notice, though perhaps it is only a coincidence, that in some myths

[1] Rhys: *Hibbert Lectures*, p. 561. [2] Rhys: *Hibbert Lectures*, pp. 561–563.

the Greek Persephoné is made a daughter of Zeus and in others of Poseidon.[1]

Turning from the sky-god and his son, we find others of Dôn's children to have been the exponents of those arts of life which early races held to have been taught directly by the gods to men. Dôn herself had a brother, Mâth, son of a mysterious Mâthonwy, and recognizable as a benevolent ruler of the underworld akin to Beli, or perhaps that god himself under another title, for the name Mâth, which means "coin, money, treasure",[2] recalls that of Plouton, the Greek god of Hades, in his guise of possessor and giver of metals. It was a belief common to the Aryan races that wisdom, as well as wealth, came originally from the underworld; and we find Mâth represented, in the Mabinogi bearing his name, as handing on his magical lore to his nephew and pupil Gwydion, who, there is good reason to believe, was the same divine personage whom the Teutonic tribes worshipped as "Woden" and "Odin". Thus equipped, Gwydion son of Dôn became the druid of the gods, the "master of illusion and phantasy", and, not only that, but

---

[1] Dyer: *Studies of the Gods in Greece*, p. 48.

Gwyn, son of Nudd, had a brother, Edeyrn, of whom so little has come down to us that he finds his most suitable place in a foot-note. Unmentioned in the earliest Welsh legends, he first appears as a knight of Arthur's court in the *Red Book* stories of "Kulhwch and Olwen", the "Dream of Rhonabwy", and "Geraint, the Son of Erbin". He accompanied Arthur on his expedition to Rome, and is said also to have slain "three most atrocious giants" at Brentenol (Brent Knoll), near Glastonbury. His name occurs in a catalogue of Welsh saints, where he is described as a bard, and the chapel of Bodedyrn, near Holyhead, still stands to his honour. Modern readers will know him from Tennyson's Idyll of "Geraint and Enid", which follows very closely the Welsh romance of "Geraint, the Son of Erbin".

[2] Rhys—who calls him "a Cambrian Pluto": *Lectures on Welsh Philology*, p. 414.

the teacher of all that is useful and good, the friend and helper of mankind, and the perpetual fighter against niggardly underworld powers for the good gifts which they refused to allow out of their keeping. Shoulder to shoulder with him in this "holy war" of culture against ignorance, and light against darkness, stood his brothers Amaethon, god of agriculture, and Govannan, a god of smithcraft identical with the Gaelic Giobniu. He had also a sister called Arianrod, or "Silver Circle", who, as is common in mythologies, was not only his sister, but also his wife. So Zeus wedded Heré; and, indeed, it is difficult to say where otherwise the partners of gods are to come from. Of this connection two sons were born at one birth—Dylan and Lleu, who are considered as representing the twin powers of darkness and light. With darkness the sea was inseparably connected by the Celts, and, as soon as the dark twin was born and named, he plunged headlong into his native element. "And immediately when he was in the sea," says the Mabinogi of Mâth, son of Mâthonwy, "he took its nature, and swam as well as the best fish that was therein. And for that reason was he called Dylan, the Son of the Wave. Beneath him no wave ever broke." He was killed with a spear at last by his uncle, Govannan, and, according to the bard Taliesin, the waves of Britain, Ireland, Scotland, and the Isle of Man wept for him.[1] Beautiful legends grew up around his death. The clamour of the waves dash-

---

[1] *Book of Taliesin*, XLIII. The *Death-song of Dylan, Son of the Wave*, Vol. I, p 288 of Skene.

ing upon the beach is the expression of their longing to avenge their son.   The sound of the sea rushing up the mouth of the River Conway is still known as "Dylan's death-groan"[1].   A small promontory on the Carnarvonshire side of the Menai Straits, called *Pwynt Maen Tylen*, or *Pwynt Maen Dulan*, preserves his name.[2]

The other child of Gwydion and Arianrod grew up to become the British sun-god, Lleu Llaw Gyffes, the exact counterpart of the Gaelic Lugh Lamh-fada, "Light the Long-handed".   Like all solar deities, his growth was rapid.   When he was a year old, he seemed to be two years; at the age of two, he travelled by himself; and when he was four years old, he was as tall as a boy of eight, and was his father's constant companion.

One day, Gwydion took him to the castle of Arianrod—not her castle in the sky, but her abode on earth, the still-remembered site of which is marked by a patch of rocks in the Menai Straits, accessible without a boat only during the lowest spring and autumn tides.   Arianrod had disowned her son, and did not recognize him when she saw him with Gwydion.   She asked who he was, and was much displeased when told.   She demanded to know his name, and, when Gwydion replied that he had as yet received none, she "laid a destiny upon" him, after the fashion of the Celts, that he should be without a name until she chose to bestow one on him herself.

[1] Rhys: *Hibbert Lectures*, p. 387.   [2] Rhys: *Celtic Folklore*, p. 210.

To be without a name was a very serious thing to the ancient Britons, who seem to have held the primitive theory that the name and the soul are the same. So Gwydion cast about to think by what craft he might extort from Arianrod some remark from which he could name their son. The next day, he went down to the sea-shore with the boy, both of them disguised as cordwainers. He made a boat out of sea-weed by magic, and some beautifully-coloured leather out of some dry sticks and sedges. Then they sailed the boat to the port of Arianrod's castle, and, anchoring it where it could be seen, began ostentatiously to stitch away at the leather. Naturally, they were soon noticed, and Arianrod sent someone out to see who they were and what they were doing. When she found that they were shoemakers, she remembered that she wanted some shoes. Gwydion, though he had her measure, purposely made them, first too large, and then too small. This brought Arianrod herself down to the boat to be fitted.

While Gwydion was measuring Arianrod's foot for the shoes, a wren came and stood upon the deck. The boy took his bow and arrow, and hit the wren in the leg—a favourite shot of Celtic "crack" archers, at any rate in romance. The goddess was pleased to be amiable and complimentary. "Truly," said she, "the lion aimed at it with a steady hand." It is from such incidents that primitive people take their names, all the world over. The boy had got his. "It is no thanks to you," said Gwydion to Arianrod, "but now he has a name. And a good name it is. He shall be called Llew Llaw Gyffes[1]."

This name of the sun-god is a good example of how obsolete the ancient pagan tradition had become before it was put into writing. The old word *Lleu*, meaning "light", had passed out of use, and the scribe substituted for a name that was unintelligible to him one like it which he knew, namely *Llew*, meaning "lion". The word *Gyffes* seems also to have suffered change, and to have meant originally not "steady", but "long"[2].

At any rate, Arianrod was defeated in her design to keep her son nameless. Neither did she even get her shoes; for, as soon as he had gained his object, Gwydion allowed the boat to change back into sea-weed, and the leather to return to sedge and sticks. So, in her anger, she put a fresh destiny on the boy, that he should not take arms till she herself gave them him.

Gwydion, however, took Lleu to Dinas Dinllev, his castle, which still stands at the edge of the Menai Straits, and brought him up as a warrior. As soon as he thought him old enough to have arms, he took him with him again to Caer Arianrod. This time, they were disguised as bards. Arianrod received them gladly, heard Gwydion's songs and tales, feasted them, and prepared a room for them to sleep in.

The next morning, Gwydion got up very early, and prepared his most powerful incantations. By his druidical arts he made it seem as if the whole

---

[1] *i.e.* The Lion with the Steady Hand.
[2] See Rhys: *Hibbert Lectures*, note 10 p. 237.

country rang with the shouts and trumpets of an army, and he put a glamour over everyone, so that they saw the bay filled with ships. Arianrod came to him in terror, asking what could be done to protect the castle. "Give us arms," he replied, "and we will do the best we can." So Arianrod's maidens armed Gwydion, while Arianrod herself put arms on Lleu. By the time she had finished, all the noises had ceased, and the ships had vanished. "Let us take our arms off again," said Gwydion; "we shall not need them now." "But the army is all round the castle!" cried Arianrod. "There was no army," answered Gwydion; "it was only an illusion of mine to cause you to break your prophecy and give our son arms. And now he has got them, without thanks to you." "Then I will lay a worse destiny on him," cried the infuriated goddess. "He shall never have a wife of the people of this earth." "He shall have a wife in spite of you," said Gwydion.

So Gwydion went to Mâth, his uncle and tutor in magic, and between them they made a woman out of flowers by charms and illusion. "They took the blossoms of the oak, and the blossoms of the broom, and the blossoms of the meadow-sweet, and produced from them a maiden, the fairest and most graceful that man ever saw." They called her Blodeuwedd (Flower-face), and gave her to Lleu as his wife. And they gave Lleu a palace called Mur y Castell, near Bala Lake.

All went well until, one day, Gronw Pebyr, one of the gods of darkness, came by, hunting, and

killed the stag at nightfall near Lleu's castle. The
sun-god was away upon a visit to Mâth, but Blodeuwedd asked the stranger to take shelter with her.
That night they fell in love with one another, and
conspired together how Lleu might be put away.
When Lleu came back from Mâth's court, Blodeuwedd, like a Celtic Dalilah, wormed out of him the
secret of how his life was preserved. He told her
that he could only die in one way; he could not be
killed either inside or outside a house, either on
horseback or on foot, but that if a spear that had
been a year in the making, and which was never
worked upon except during the sacrifice on Sunday,
were to be cast at him as he stood beneath a roof of
thatch, after having just bathed, with one foot upon
the edge of the bath and the other upon a buck
goat's back, it would cause his death. Blodeuwedd
piously thanked Heaven that he was so well protected, and sent a messenger to her paramour, telling
him what she had learned. Gronw set to work on
the spear; and in a year it was ready. When she
knew this, Blodeuwedd asked Lleu to show her
exactly how it was he could be killed.

Lleu agreed; and Blodeuwedd prepared the bath
under the thatched roof, and tethered the goat by it.
Lleu bathed, and then stood with one foot upon the
edge of the bath, and the other upon the goat's back.
At this moment, Gronw, from an ambush, flung the
spear, and hit Lleu, who, with a terrible cry, changed
into an eagle, and flew away. He never came back;
and Gronw took possession of both his wife and his
palace.

But Gwydion set out to search everywhere for his son. At last, one day, he came to a house in North Wales where the man was in great anxiety about his sow; for as soon as the sty was opened, every morning, she rushed out, and did not return again till late in the evening. Gwydion offered to follow her, and, at dawn, the man took him to the sty, and opened the door. The sow leaped forth, and ran, and Gwydion ran after her. He tracked her to a brook between Snowdon and the sea, still called Nant y Llew, and saw her feeding underneath an oak. Upon the top of the tree there was an eagle, and, every time it shook itself, there fell off it lumps of putrid meat, which the sow ate greedily. Gwydion suspected that the eagle must be Lleu. So he sang this verse:

"Oak that grows between the two banks;
  Darkened is the sky and hill!
  Shall I not tell him by his wounds,
  That this is Lleu?"

The eagle, on hearing this, came half-way down the tree. So Gwydion sang:

"Oak that grows in upland ground,
  Is it not wetted by the rain? Has it not been drenched
  By nine score tempests?
  It bears in its branches Lleu Llaw Gyffes."

The eagle came slowly down until it was on the lowest branch. Gwydion sang:

"Oak that grows beneath the steep;
  Stately and majestic is its aspect!
  Shall I not speak it?
  That Lleu will come to my lap?"

Then the eagle came down, and sat on Gwydion's knee.   Gwydion struck it with his magic wand, and it became Lleu again, wasted to skin and bone by the poison on the spear.

Gwydion took him to Mâth to be healed, and left him there, while he went to Mur y Castell, where Blodeuwedd was.   When she heard that he was coming, she fled.   But Gwydion overtook her, and changed her into an owl, the bird that hates the day.   A still older form of this probably extremely ancient myth of the sun-god—the savage and repulsive details of which speak of a hoary antiquity— makes the chase of Blodeuwedd by Gwydion to have taken place in the sky, the stars scattered over the Milky Way being the traces of it.[1]   As for her accomplice, Lleu would accept no satisfaction short of Gronw's submitting to stand exactly where Lleu had stood, to be shot at in his turn.   To this he was obliged to agree; and Lleu killed him.[2]

There are two other sons of Beli and Dôn of whom so little is recorded that it would hardly be worth while mentioning them, were it not for the wild poetry of the legend connected with them. The tale, put into writing at a time when all the gods were being transfigured into simple mortals, tells us that they were two kings of Britain, brothers. One starlight night they were walking together. "See," said Nynniaw to Peibaw, "what a fine, wide-spreading field I have."   "Where is it?" asked

<hr />

[1] Rhys: *Hibbert Lectures*, p. 240.
[2] Retold from the Mabinogi of *Math, Son of Mathonwy*, in Lady Guest's *Mabinogion*.

Peibaw. "There," replied Nynniaw; "the whole stretch of the sky, as far as the eye reaches." "Look then," returned Peibaw, "what a number of cattle I have grazing on your field." "Where are they?" asked Nynniaw. "All the stars that you can see," replied Peibaw, "every one of them of fiery-coloured gold, with the moon for a shepherd over them." "They shall not feed on my field," cried Nynniaw. "They shall," exclaimed Peibaw. "They shall not," cried Nynniaw, "They shall," said Peibaw. "They shall not," Nynniaw answered; and so they went on, from contradiction to quarrel, and from private quarrel to civil war, until the armies of both of them were destroyed, and the two authors of the evil were turned by God into oxen for their sins.[1]

Last of the children of Dôn, we find a goddess called Penardun, of whom little is known except that she was married to the sea-god Llyr. This incident is curious, as forming a parallel to the Gaelic story which tells of intermarriage between the Tuatha Dé Danann and the Fomors.[2] Brigit, the Dagda's daughter, was married to Bress, son of Elathan, while Cian, the son of Diancecht, wedded Ethniu, the daughter of Balor. So, in this kindred mythology, a slender tie of relationship binds the gods of the sky to the gods of the sea.

The name *Llyr* is supposed, like its Irish equivalent Lêr, to have meant "the Sea".[3] The British sea-god is undoubtedly the same as the Gaelic; in-

---

[1] The Iolo Manuscripts: collected by Edward Williams, the bard, at about the beginning of the nineteenth century—*The Tale of Rhitta Gawr*.
[2] See Chapter VII—"The Rise of the Sun-God".
[3] Rhys: *Studies in the Arthurian Legend*, p. 130.

deed, the two facts that he is described in Welsh
literature as Llyr Llediath, that is, "Llyr of the
Foreign Dialect", and is given a wife called Iweridd
(Ireland)[1], suggest that he may have been borrowed
by the Britons from the Gaels later than any myth-
ology common to both. As a British god, he was
the far-off original of Shakespeare's "King Lear".
The chief city of his worship is still called after him,
Leicester, that is, Llyr-cestre, in still earlier days,
Caer Llyr.

Llyr, we have noticed, married two wives, Penardun and Iweridd. By the daughter of Dôn he
had a son called Manawyddan, who is identical
with the Gaelic Manannán mac Lir.[2] We know
less of his character and attributes than we do of the
Irish god; but we find him equally a ruler in that
Hades or Elysium which the Celtic mind ever connected with the sea. Like all the inhabitants of
that other world, he is at once a master of magic
and of the useful arts, which he taught willingly to
his friends. To his enemies, however, he could
show a different side of his character. A triad tells
us that—

"The achievement of Manawyddan the Wise,
  After lamentation and fiery wrath,
  Was the constructing of the bone-fortress of Oeth and
    Anoeth",[3]

which is described as a prison made, in the shape of

[1] Rhys: *Arthurian Legend*, p. 130.
[2] The old Irish tract called *Coir Anmann* (the *Choice of Names*) says: "Man-
annan mac Lir . . . the Britons and the men of Erin deemed that he was the god
of the sea".
[3] *Iolo MSS.*, stanza 18 of *The Stanzas of the Achievements*, composed bv the
Azure Bard of the Chair.

a bee-hive, entirely of human bones mortared together, and divided into innumerable cells, forming a
kind of labyrinth. In this ghastly place he immured
those whom he found trespassing in Hades; and
among his captives was no less a person than the
famous Arthur.[1]

"Ireland" bore two children to Llyr: a daughter
called Branwen and a son called Brân. The little
we know of Branwen of the "Fair Bosom" shows
her as a goddess of love—child, like the Greek
Aphrodité, of the sea. Brân, on the other hand,
is, even more clearly than Manawyddan, a dark
deity of Hades. He is represented as of colossal
size, so huge, in fact, that no house or ship was big
enough to hold him.[2] He delighted in battle and
carnage, like the hoodie-crow or raven from which
he probably took his name,[3] but he was also the
especial patron of bards, minstrels, and musicians,
and we find him in one of the poems ascribed to
Taliesin claiming to be himself a bard, a harper,
a player on the crowth, and seven - score other
musicians all at once.[4] His son was called Caradawc the Strong-armed, who, as the British mythology crumbled, became confounded with the historical Caratacus, known popularly as "Caractacus".

Both Brân and Manawyddan were especially connected with the Swansea peninsula. The bone-
fortress of Oeth and Anoeth was placed by tradition in

---

[1] See note to chap. XXII—"The Treasures of Britain".
[2] Mabinogi of *Branwen, Daughter of Llyr*.
[3] Rhys: *Hibbert Lectures*, p. 245.
[4] *Book of Taliesin*, poem XLVIII, in Skene's *Four Ancient Books of Wales*. Vol I.
p. 297.

Gower.[1] That Brân was equally at home there may
be proved from the Morte Darthur, in which storehouse of forgotten and misunderstood mythology
Brân of Gower survives as "King Brandegore".[2]

Such identification of a mere mortal country with
the other world seems strange enough to us, but to
our Celtic ancestors it was a quite natural thought.
All islands—and peninsulas, which, viewed from an
opposite coast, probably seemed to them islands—
were deemed to be pre-eminently homes of the dark
Powers of Hades. Difficult of access, protected by
the turbulent and dangerous sea, sometimes rendered
quite invisible by fogs and mists and, at other times,
looming up ghostlily on the horizon, often held by
the remnant of a hostile lower race, they gained a
mystery and a sanctity from the law of the human
mind which has always held the unknown to be the
terrible. The Cornish Britons, gazing from the
shore, saw Gower and Lundy, and deemed them
outposts of the over-sea Other World. To the
Britons of Wales, Ireland was no human realm, a
view reciprocated by the Gaels, who saw Hades
in Britain, while the Isle of Man was a little Hades
common to them both. Nor even was the sea
always necessary to sunder the world of ghosts
from that of "shadow-casting men". Glastonbury
Tor, surrounded by almost impassable swamps, was
one of the especial haunts of Gwyn ap Nudd. The
Britons of the north held that beyond the Roman

---

[1] The *Verses of the Graves of the Warriors*, in the Black Book of Caermarthen.
See also Rhys: *Arthurian Legend*, p. 347.
[2] Rhys: *Studies in the Arthurian Legend*, p. 160.

wall and the vast Caledonian wood lived ghosts and not men. Even the Roman province of De-metia—called by the Welsh Dyfed, and correspond-ing, roughly, to the modern County of Pembroke-shire—was, as a last stronghold of the aborigines, identified with the mythic underworld.

As such, Dyfed was ruled by a local tribe of gods, whose greatest figures were Pwyll, "Head of Annwn" (the Welsh name for Hades), with his wife Rhiannon, and their son Pryderi. These beings are described as hostile to the children of Dôn, but friendly to the race of Llyr. After Pwyll's death or disappearance, his widow Rhiannon becomes the wife of Manawyddan.[1]   In a poem of Taliesin's we find Manawyddan and Pryderi joint-rulers of Hades, and warders of that magic cauldron of inspiration [2] which the gods of light attempted to steal or capture, and which became famous after-wards as the "Holy Grail". Another of their treasures were the "Three Birds of Rhiannon", which, we are told in an ancient book, could sing the dead to life and the living into the sleep of death. Fortunately they sang seldom. "There are three things," says a Welsh triad, "which are not often heard: the song of the birds of Rhiannon, a song of wisdom from the mouth of a Saxon, and an invitation to a feast from a miser."

Nor is the list of British gods complete with-out mention of Arthur, though most readers will be surprised to find him in such company. The

---

[1] Mabinogi of *Manawyddan, Son of Llyr*.
[2] *Book of Taliesin*, poem xiv, Vol. I, p. 276, of Skene.

genius of Tennyson, who drew his materials mostly from the Norman-French romances, has stereotyped the popular conception of Arthur as a king of early Britain who fought for his fatherland and the Christian faith against invading Saxons. Possibly there may, indeed, have been a powerful British chieftain bearing that typically Celtic name, which is found in Irish legend as Artur, one of the sons of Nemed who fought against the Fomors, and on the Continent as Artaius, a Gaulish deity whom the Romans identified with Mercury, and who seems to have been a patron of agriculture.[1] But the original Arthur stands upon the same ground as Cuchulainn and Finn. His deeds are mythical, because superhuman. His companions can be shown to have been divine. Some we know were worshipped in Gaul. Others are children of Dôn, of Llyr, and of Pwyll, dynasties of older gods to whose head Arthur seems to have risen, as his cult waxed and theirs waned. Stripped of their godhead, and strangely transformed, they fill the pages of romance as Knights of the Table Round.

These deities were the native gods of Britain. Many others are, however, mentioned upon inscriptions found in our island, but these were almost all exotic and imported. Imperial Rome brought men of diverse races among her legions, and these men brought their gods. Scattered over Britain, but especially in the north, near the Wall, we find evidence that deities of many nations—from Germany to Africa, and from Gaul to Persia—were

[1] Rhys: *Studies in the Arthurian Legend*, p. 48 and note.

sporadically worshipped.[1] Most of these foreign
gods were Roman, but a temple at Eboracum (now
York) was dedicated to Serapis, and Mithras, the
Persian sun-god, was also adored there; while at
Corbridge, in Northumberland (the ancient Corspitium), there have been found altars to the Tyrian
Hercules and to Astarte. The war-god was also
invoked under many strange names—as " Cocidius "
by a colony of Dacians in Cumberland; as Toutates,
Camulus, Coritiacus, Belatucador, Alator, Loucetius,
Condates, and Rigisamos by men of different countries. A goddess of war was worshipped at Bath
under the name of Nemetona. The hot springs
of the same town were under the patronage of a
divinity called Sul, identified by the Romans with
Minerva, and she was helped by a god of medicine
described on a dedicatory tablet as " Sol Apollo
Anicetus ". Few of these "strange gods", however,
seem to have taken hold of the imagination of the
native Britons. Their worshippers did not prose-
lytize, and their general influence was probably
about equal to that of an Evangelical Church in
a Turkish town. The sole exceptions to this rule
are where the foreign gods are Gaulish; but in
several instances it can be proved that they were
not so much of Roman, as of original Celtic
importation. The warlike heaven - god Camulus
appears in Gaelic heroic myth as Cumhal, the
father of Finn, and in British mythical history as
Coel, a duke of Caer Coelvin (known earlier as

[1] See a paper in the *Edinburgh Review* for July, 1851—"The Romans in
Britain ".

Camulodunum, and now as Colchester), who seized the crown of Britain, and spent his short reign in a series of battles.[1]   The name of the sun-god Maponos is found alike upon altars in Gaul and Britain, and in Welsh literature as Mabon, a follower of Arthur; while another Gaulish sun-god, Belinus, who had a splendid temple at Bajocassos (the modern Bayeux), though not mentioned in the earliest British mythology, as its scattered records have come down to us, must have been connected with Brân, for we find in Geoffrey of Monmouth's History "King Belinus" as brother of "King Brennius",[2] and in the Morte Darthur "Balin" as brother of "Balan".[3]   A second-century Greek writer gives an account of a god of eloquence worshipped in Gaul under the name of Ogmios, and represented as equipped like Heracles, a description which exactly corresponds to the conception of the Gaelic Ogma, at once patron of literature and writing and professional strong man of the Tuatha Dé Danann.   Nemetona, the war-goddess worshipped at Bath, was probably the same as Nemon, one of Nuada's Valkyr-wives, while a broken inscription to *athubodva*, which probably stood, when intact, for *Cathubodva*, may well have been addressed to the Gaulish equivalent of Badb Catha, the "War-fury".   Lugh, or Lleu, was also widely known on the Continent as Lugus.   Three important towns—

---

[1] It is said that the "Old King Cole" of the popular ballad, who "was a merry old soul", represents the last faint tradition of the Celtic god.

[2] *Geoffrey of Monmouth*, Book III, chap. I.

[3] *Morte Darthur*, Book I, chap. XVI.

Laon, Leyden, and Lyons—were all anciently called after him *Lugu-dunum* (Lugus' town), and at the last and greatest of these a festival was still held in Roman times upon the sun-god's day—the first of August—which corresponded to the *Lugnassad* (Lugh's commemoration) held in ancient Ireland. Brigit, the Gaelic Minerva, is also found in Britain as Brigantia, tutelary goddess of the Brigantes, a Northern tribe, and in Eastern France as Brigindo, to whom Iccavos, son of Oppianos, made a dedicatory offering of which there is still record.[1]

Other, less striking agreements between the mythical divine names of the Insular and Continental Celts might be cited. These recorded should, however, prove sufficiently that Gaul, Gael, and Briton shared in a common heritage of mythological names and ideas, which they separately developed into three superficially different, but essentially similar cults.

[1] For full account of Gaulish gods, and their Gaelic and British affinities, see Rhys: *Hibbert Lectures*, I and II—"The Gaulish Pantheon".

CHAPTER XVII

THE ADVENTURES OF THE GODS OF HADES

It is with the family of Pwyll, deities connected with the south-west corner of Wales, called by the Romans Demetia, and by the Britons Dyfed, and, roughly speaking, identical with the modern county of Pembrokeshire, that the earliest consecutive accounts of the British gods begin. The first of the Four Branches of the Mabinogi tell us how "Pwyll, Prince of Dyfed", gained the right to be called *Pen Annwn*, the "Head of Hades". Indeed, it almost seems as if it had been deliberately written to explain how the same person could be at once a mere mortal prince, however legendary, and a ruler in the mystic Other World, and so to reconcile two conflicting traditions.[1] But to an earlier age than that in which the legend was put into a literary shape, such forced reconciliation would not have been needed; for the two legends would not have been considered to conflict. When Pwyll, head of Annwn, was a mythic person whose tradition was still alive, the unexplored, rugged, and savage country of Dyfed, populated by the aboriginal Iberians whom the Celt had driven into such remote districts, appeared to those who dwelt upon the

[1] Rhys. *Studies in the Arthurian Legend*, p. 282.

eastern side of its dividing river, the Tawë, at least a dependency of Annwn, if not that weird realm itself. But, as men grew bolder, the frontier was crossed, and Dyfed entered and traversed, and found to be not so unlike other countries. Its inhabitants, if not of Celtic race, were yet of flesh and blood. So that, though the province still continued to bear to a late date the names of the " Land of Illusion" and the " Realm of Glamour ",[1] it was no longer deemed to be Hades itself. That fitful and shadowy country had folded its tents, and departed over or under seas.

The story of " Pwyll, Prince of Dyfed",[2] tells us how there was war in Annwn between its two kings —or between two, perhaps, of its many chieftains. Arawn ("Silver-Tongue") and Havgan ("Summer-White") each coveted the dominions of the other. In the continual contests between them, Arawn was worsted, and in despair he visited the upper earth to seek for a mortal ally.

At this time Pwyll, Prince of Dyfed, held his court at Narberth. He had, however, left his capital upon a hunting expedition to Glyn Cûch, known to-day as a valley upon the borders of the two counties of Pembroke and Carmarthen. Like so many kings of European and Oriental romance, when an adventure is at hand, he became separated from his party, and was, in modern parlance, "thrown out ". He could, however, still hear the music of his hounds, and was listening to them, when he also

---

[1] It is constantly so-called by the fourteenth-century Welsh poet, Dafydd ab Gwilym, so much admired by George Borrow.

[2] This chapter is retold from Lady Guest's translation of the Mabinogi of *Pwyll. Prince of Dyfed.*

distinguished the cry of another pack coming towards him. As he watched and listened, a stag came into view; and the strange hounds pulled it down almost at his feet. At first Pwyll hardly looked at the stag, he was so taken up with gazing at the hounds, for "of all the hounds that he had seen in the world, he had never seen any that were like unto these. For their hair was of a brilliant shining white, and their ears were red; and as the whiteness of their bodies shone, so did the redness of their ears glisten." They were, indeed, though Pwyll does not seem to have known it, of the true Hades breed—the snow-white, red-eared hounds we meet in Gaelic legends, and which are still said to be sometimes heard and seen scouring the hills of Wales by night. Seeing no rider with the hounds, Pwyll drove them away from the dead stag, and called up his own pack to it.

While he was doing this, a man "upon a large, light-gray steed, with a hunting-horn round his neck, and clad in garments of gray woollen in the fashion of a hunting garb" appeared, and rated Pwyll for his unsportsmanlike conduct. "Greater discourtesy," said he, "I never saw than your driving away my dogs after they had killed the stag, and calling your own to it. And though I may not be revenged upon you for this, I swear that I will do you more damage than the value of a hundred stags."

Pwyll expressed his contrition, and, asking the new-comer's name and rank, offered to atone for his fault. The stranger told his name—Arawn, a king of Annwn—and said that Pwyll could gain his forgiveness only in one way, by going to Annwn instead of him, and fighting for him with Havgan. Pwyll agreed to do this, and the King of Hades put his own semblance upon the mortal prince, so that not a person in Annwn—not even Arawn's own wife —would know that he was not that king. He led him by a secret path into Annwn, and left him before his castle, charging him to return to the place where they had first met, at the end of a year from that day. On the other hand, Arawn took on Pwyll's shape, and went to Narberth.

No one in Annwn suspected Pwyll of being anyone else than their king. He spent the year in ruling the realm, in hunting, minstrelsy, and feasting. Both by day and night, he had the company of Arawn's wife, the most beautiful woman he had ever yet seen, but he refrained from taking advantage of the trust placed in him. At last the day came when he was to meet Havgan in single combat. One blow settled it; for Pwyll, Havgan's destined conqueror, thrust his antagonist an arm's and a spear's length over the crupper of his horse, breaking his shield and armour, and mortally wounding him. Havgan was carried away to die, and Pwyll, in the guise of Arawn, received the submission of the dead king's subjects, and annexed his realm. Then he went back to Glyn Cûch, to keep his tryst with Arawn.

They retook their own shapes, and each returned to his own kingdom. Pwyll learned that Dyfed had never been ruled so well, or been so prosperous, as during the year just passed. As for the King of Hades, he found his enemy gone, and his domains extended. And when he caressed his wife, she asked him why he did so now, after the lapse of a whole year. So he told her the truth, and they both agreed that they had indeed got a true friend in Pwyll.

After this, the kings of Annwn and Dyfed made their friendship strong between them. From that time forward, says the story, Pwyll was no longer called Prince of Dyfed, but *Pen Annwn*, "the Head of Hades".

The second mythological incident in the Mabinogi of Pwyll, Prince of Dyfed, tells how the Head of Hades won his wife, Rhiannon, thought by Professor Rhys to have been a goddess either of the dawn or of the moon.[1] There was a mound outside Pwyll's palace at Narberth which had a magical quality. To anyone who sat upon it there happened one of two things: either he received wounds and blows, or else he saw a wonder. One day, it occurred to Pwyll that he would like to try the experience of the mound. So he went and sat upon it.

No unseen blows assailed Pwyll, but he had not been sitting long upon the mound before he saw, coming towards him, "a lady on a pure-white horse of large size, with a garment of shining gold around her", riding very quietly. He sent a man on foot to ask her who she was, but, though she seemed to be moving so slowly, the man could not come up to her. He failed utterly to overtake her, and she passed on out of sight.

The next day, Pwyll went again to the mound.

[1] Rhys: *Hibbert Lectures*, p. 678.

The lady appeared, and, this time, Pwyll sent a horseman. At first, the horseman only ambled along at about the same pace at which the lady seemed to be going; then, failing to get near her, he urged his horse into a gallop. But, whether he rode slow or fast, he could come no closer to the lady than before, although she seemed to the eyes of those who watched to have been going only at a foot's pace.

The day after that, Pwyll determined to accost the lady himself. She came at the same gentle walk, and Pwyll at first rode easily, and then at his horse's topmost speed, but with the same result, or lack of it. At last, in despair, he called to the mysterious damsel to stop. "I will stop gladly," said she, "and it would have been better for your horse if you had asked me before." She told him that her name was Rhiannon, daughter of Heveydd the Ancient. The nobles of her realm had determined to give her in marriage against her will, so she had come to seek out Pwyll, who was the man of her choice. Pwyll was delighted to hear this, for he thought that she was the most beautiful lady he had ever seen. Before they parted, they had plighted troth, and Pwyll had promised to appear on that day twelvemonth at the palace of her father, Heveydd. Then she vanished, and Pwyll returned to Narberth.

At the appointed time, Pwyll went to visit Heveydd the Ancient, with a hundred followers. He was received with much welcome, and the disposition of the feast put under his command, as the Celts seem to have done to especially honoured guests. As they sat at meat, with Pwyll between Rhiannon and her father, a tall auburn-haired youth came into the hall, greeted Pwyll, and asked a boon of him. "Whatever boon you may ask of me," said Pwyll thoughtlessly, "if it is in my power, you shall have it." Then the suitor threw off all disguise, called the guests to witness Pwyll's promise, and claimed Rhiannon as his bride. Pwyll was dumb. "Be silent as long as you will," said the masterful Rhiannon; "never did a man make worse use of his wits than you have done." "Lady," replied the amazed Pwyll, "I knew not who he was." "He is the man to whom they would have given me against my will," she answered, "Gwawl, the son of Clûd. You must bestow me upon him now, lest shame befall you." "Never will I do that," said Pwyll. "Bestow me upon him," she insisted, "and I will cause that I shall never be his." So Pwyll promised Gwawl that he would make a feast that day year, at which he would resign Rhiannon to him.

The next year, the feast was made, and Rhiannon sat by the side of her unwelcome bridegroom. But Pwyll was waiting outside the palace, with a hundred men in ambush. When the banquet was at its height, he came into the hall, dressed in coarse, ragged garments, shod with clumsy old shoes, and carrying a leather bag. But the bag was a magic one, which Rhiannon had given to her lover, with directions as to its use. Its quality was that, however much was put into it, it could never be filled. "I crave a boon," he said to Gwawl. "What is it?" Gwawl replied. "I am a poor man, and all I ask is to have this bag filled with meat." Gwawl granted what he said was "a request within reason", and ordered his followers to fill the bag. But the more they put into it, the more room in it there seemed to be. Gwawl was astonished, and asked why this was. Pwyll replied that it was a bag that could never be filled until someone possessed of lands and riches should tread the food down with both his feet. "Do this for the man," said Rhiannon to Gwawl. "Gladly I will," replied he, and put both his feet into the bag. But no sooner had he done so than Pwyll slipped the bag over Gwawl's head, and tied it up at the mouth. He blew his horn, and all his followers came in. "What have you got in the bag?" asked each one in turn. "A badger," replied Pwyll. Then each, as he received Pwyll's answer, kicked the bag, or hit it with a stick. "Then," says the story, "was the game of 'Badger in the Bag' first played."

Gwawl, however, fared better than we suspect that the badger usually did; for Heveydd the Ancient interceded for him. Pwyll willingly released him, on condition that he promised to give up all claim to Rhiannon, and renounced all projects of revenge. Gwawl consented, and gave sureties, and went away to his own country to have his bruises healed.

This country of Gwawl's was, no doubt, the sky; for he was evidently a sun-god. His name bewrays him; for the meaning of "Gwawl" is "light".[1] It

---

[1] Rhys: *Hibbert Lectures*, p. 123 and note. Clûd was probably the goddess of the River Clyde. See Rhys: *Arthurian Legend*, p. 294.

was one of the hours of victory for the dark powers, such as were celebrated in the Celtic calendar by the Feast of Samhain, or Summer End.

There was no hindrance now to the marriage of Pwyll and Rhiannon. She became his bride, and returned with him to Dyfed.

For three years, they were without an heir, and the nobles of Dyfed became discontented. They petitioned Pwyll to take another wife instead of Rhiannon. He asked for a year's delay. This was granted, and, before the end of the year, a son was born. But, on the night of his birth, the six women set to keep watch over Rhiannon all fell asleep at once; and when they woke up, the boy had vanished. Fearful lest their lives should be forfeited for their neglect, they agreed to swear that Rhiannon had eaten her child. They killed a litter of puppies, and smeared some of the blood on Rhiannon's face and hands, and put some of the bones by her side. Then they awoke her with a great outcry, and accused her. She swore that she knew nothing of the death of her son, but the women persisted that they had seen her devour him, and had been unable to prevent it. The druids of that day were not sufficiently practical anatomists to be able to tell the bones of a child from those of a dog, so they condemned Rhiannon upon the evidence of the women. But, even now, Pwyll would not put her away; so she was assigned a penance. For seven years, she was to sit by a horse-block outside the gate, and offer to carry visitors into the palace upon her back. "But it rarely happened," says the Mabinogi, "that any would permit her to do so."

Exactly what had become of Rhiannon's child seems to have been a mystery even to the writer of the Mabinogi. It was, at any rate, in some way connected with the equally mysterious disappearance on every night of the first of May—Beltaine, the Celtic sun-festival—of the colts foaled by a beautiful mare belonging to Teirnyon Twryv Vliant, one of Pwyll's vassals. Every May-day night, the mare foaled, but no one knew what became of the colt. Teirnyon decided to find out. He caused the mare to be taken into a house, and there he watched it, fully armed. Early in the night, the colt was born. Then there was a great noise, and an arm with claws came through the window, and gripped the colt's mane. Teirnyon hacked at the arm with his sword, and cut it off. Then he heard wailing, and opened the door, and found a baby in swaddling clothes, wrapped in a satin mantle. He took it up and brought it to his wife, and they decided to adopt it. They called the boy Gwri Wallt Euryn, that is "Gwri of the Golden Hair".

The older the boy grew, the more it seemed to Teirnyon that he became like Pwyll. Then he remembered that he had found him upon the very night that Rhiannon lost her child. So he consulted with his wife, and they both agreed that the baby they had so mysteriously found must be the same that Rhiannon had so mysteriously lost. And they decided that it would not be right for them to keep the son of another, while so good a lady as Rhiannon was being punished wrongfully.

So, the very next day, Teirnyon set out for Narberth, taking the boy with him. They found Rhiannon sitting, as usual, by the gate, but they would not allow her to carry them into the palace on her back. Pwyll welcomed them; and that evening, as they sat at supper, Teirnyon told his hosts the story from beginning to end. And he presented her son to Rhiannon.

As soon as everyone in the palace saw the boy, they admitted that he must be Pwyll's son. So they adopted him with delight; and Pendaran Dyfed, the head druid of the kingdom, gave him a new name. He called him " Pryderi[1]", meaning "trouble", from the first word that his mother had uttered when he was restored to her. For she had said: " *Trouble* is, indeed, at an end for me, if this be true".

[1] Pronounced *Pridairy*.

CHAPTER XVIII

THE WOOING OF BRANWEN AND THE BEHEADING OF BRÂN[1]

In the second of the "Four Branches", Pryderi, come to man's estate, and married to a wife called Kicva, appears as a guest or vassal at the court of a greater god of Hades than himself—Brân, the son of the sea-god Llyr. The children of Llyr—Brân, with his sister Branwen of the "Fair Bosom" and his half-brother Manawyddan, as well as two sons of Manawyddan's mother, Penardun, by an earlier marriage, were holding court at *Twr Branwen,* "Branwen's Tower", now called Harlech. As they sat on a cliff, looking over the sea, they saw thirteen ships coming from Ireland. The fleet sailed close under the land, and Brân sent messengers to ask who they were, and why they had come. It was replied that they were the vessels of Matholwch, King of Ireland, and that he had come to ask Brân for his sister Branwen in marriage. Brân consented, and they fixed upon Aberffraw, in Anglesey, as the place at which to hold the wedding feast. Matholwch and his fleet went there by sea, and Brân and his host by land. When they arrived, and met, they set up pavilions; for "no house could ever hold the

---

[1] Retold from Lady Guest's translation of the Mabinogi of *Branwer., the Daughter of Llyr.*

blessed Brân". And there Branwen became the
King of Ireland's bride.[1]

These relations were not long, however, allowed
to be friendly. Of the two other sons of Llyr's wife,
Penardun, the mother of Manawyddan, one was
called Nissyen, and the other, Evnissyen. Nissyen
was a lover of peace, and would always "cause his
family to be friends when their wrath was at the
highest", but Evnissyen "would cause strife between
his two brothers when they were most at peace".
Now Evnissyen was enraged because his consent
had not been asked to Branwen's marriage. Out of
spite at this, he cut off the lips, ears, eyebrows, and
tails of all Matholwch's horses.

When the King of Ireland found this out, he was
very indignant at the insult. But Brân sent an
embassy to him twice, explaining that it had not
been done by his consent or with his knowledge.
He appeased Matholwch by giving him a sound
horse in place of every one that Evnissyen had
mutilated, as well as a staff of silver as large and tall
as Matholwch himself, and a plate of gold as broad
as Matholwch's face. To these gifts he also added a
magic cauldron brought from Ireland. Its property
was that any slain man who was put into it was
brought to life again, except that he lost the use of
speech. The King of Ireland accepted this recompense for the insult done him, renewed his friendship
with the children of Llyr, and sailed away with
Branwen to Ireland.

[1] Rhys—*Lectures on Welsh Philology*—compares Matholwch with Mâth, and the
story, generally, with the Greek myth of Persephoné.

Before a year was over, Branwen bore a son. They called him Gwern, and put him out to be foster-nursed among the best men of Ireland. But, during the second year, news came to Ireland of the insult that Matholwch had received in Britain. The King of Ireland's foster-brothers and near relations insisted that he should revenge himself upon Branwen. So the queen was compelled to serve in the kitchen, and, every day, the butcher gave her a box upon the ear. That this should not become known to Brân, all traffic was forbidden between Ireland and Britain. This went on for three years.

But, in the meantime, Branwen had reared a tame starling, and she taught it to speak, and tied a letter of complaint to the root of its wing, and sent it off to Britain. At last it found Brân, whom its mistress had described to it, and settled upon his shoulder, ruffling its wings. This exposed the letter, and Brân read it. He sent messengers to one hundred and forty-four countries, to raise an army to go to Ireland. Leaving his son Caradawc, with seven others, in charge of Britain, he started—himself wading through the sea, while his men went by ship.

No one in Ireland knew that they were coming until the royal swineherds, tending their pigs near the sea-shore, beheld a marvel. They saw a forest on the surface of the sea—a place where certainly no forest had been before—and, near it, a mountain with a lofty ridge on its top, and a lake on each side of the ridge. Both the forest and the mountain were swiftly moving towards Ireland. They informed

Matholwch, who could not understand it, and sent messengers to ask Branwen what she thought it might be. "It is the men of the Island of the Mighty[1]," said she, "who are coming here because they have heard of my ill-treatment. The forest that is seen on the sea is made of the masts of ships. The mountain is my brother Brân, wading into shoal water; the lofty ridge is his nose, and the two lakes, one on each side of it, are his eyes."

The men of Ireland were terrified. They fled beyond the Shannon, and broke down the bridge over it. But Brân lay down across the river, and his army walked over him to the opposite side.

Matholwch now sent messengers suing for peace. He offered to resign the throne of Ireland to Gwern, Branwen's son and Brân's nephew. "Shall I not have the kingdom myself?" said Brân, and would not hear of anything else. So the counsellors of Matholwch advised him to conciliate Brân by building him a house so large that it would be the first house that had ever held him, and, in it, to hand over the kingdom to his will. Brân consented to accept this, and the vast house was built.

It concealed treachery. Upon each side of the hundred pillars of the house was hung a bag, and in the bag was an armed man, who was to cut himself out at a given signal. But Evnissyen came into the house, and seeing the bags there, suspected the plot. "What is in this bag?" he said to one of the Irish, as he came up to the first one. "Meal,"

---

[1] A bardic name for Britain

replied the Irishman. Then Evnissyen kneaded the bag in his hands, as though it really contained meal, until he had killed the man inside; and he treated all of them in turn in the same way.

A little later, the two hosts met in the house. The men of Ireland came in on one side, and the men of Britain on the other, and met at the hearth in the middle, and sat down. The Irish court did homage to Brân, and they crowned Gwern, Branwen's son, King of Ireland in place of Matholwch. When the ceremonies were over, the boy went from one to another of his uncles, to make acquaintance with them. Brân fondled and caressed him, and so did Manawyddan, and Nissyen. But when he came to Evnissyen, the wicked son of Penardun seized the child by the feet, and dropped him head first into the great fire.

When Branwen saw her son killed, she tried to leap into the flames after him, but Brân held her back. Then every man armed himself, and such a tumult was never heard in one house before. Day after day they fought; but the Irish had the advantage, for they had only to plunge their dead men into the magic cauldron to bring them back to life. When Evnissyen knew this, he saw a way of atoning for the misfortunes his evil nature had brought upon Britain. He disguised himself as an Irishman, and lay upon the floor as if dead, until they put him into the cauldron. Then he stretched himself, and, with one desperate effort, burst both the cauldron and his own heart.

Thus things were made equal again, and in the

next battle the men of Britain killed all the Irish. But of themselves there were only seven left unhurt—Pryderi; Manawyddan; Gluneu, the son of Taran[1]; Taliesin the Bard; Ynawc; Grudyen, the son of Muryel; and Heilyn, the son of Gwynn the Ancient.

Brân himself was wounded in the foot with a poisoned dart, and was in agony. So he ordered his seven surviving followers to cut off his head, and to take it to the White Mount in London[2], and bury it there, with the face towards France. He prophesied how they would perform the journey. At Harlech they would be feasting seven years, the birds of Rhiannon singing to them all the time, and Brân's own head conversing with them as agreeably as when it was on his body. Then they would be fourscore years at Gwales[3]. All this while, Brân's head would remain uncorrupted, and would talk so pleasantly that they would forget the flight of time. But, at the destined hour, someone would open a door which looked towards Cornwall, and, after that, they could stay no longer, but must hurry to London to bury the head.

So the seven beheaded Brân, and set off, taking Branwen also with them. They landed at the mouth of the River Alaw, in Anglesey. Branwen first looked back towards Ireland, and then forward towards Britain. "Alas," she cried, "that I was

---

[1] This personage may have been the same as the Gaulish god Taranis. Mention, too, is made in an ancient Irish glossary of "Etirun, an idol of the Britons".

[2] This spot, called by a twelfth-century Welsh poet "The White Eminence of London, a place of splendid fame", was probably the hill on which the Tower of London now stands.   [3] The island of Gresholm, off the coast of Pembrokeshire.

ever born! two islands have been destroyed because of me." Her heart broke with sorrow, and she died. An old Welsh poem says, with a touch of real pathos:

> "Softened were the voices in the brakes
> Of the wondering birds
> On seeing the fair body.
> Will there not be relating again
> Of that which befel the paragon
> At the stream of Amlwch?"[1]

"They made her a four-sided grave," says the Mabinogi, "and buried her upon the banks of the Alaw." The traditionary spot has always borne the name of *Ynys Branwen*, and, curiously enough, an urn was found there, in 1813, full of ashes and half-burnt bones, which certain enthusiastic local antiquaries saw "every reason to suppose" were those of the fair British Aphrodité herself.[2]

The seven went on towards Harlech, and, as they journeyed, they met men and women who gave them the latest news. Caswallawn, a son of Beli, the husband of Dôn, had destroyed the ministers left behind by Brân to take care of Britain. He had made himself invisible by the help of a magic veil, and thus had killed all of them except Pendaran Dyfed, foster-father of Pryderi, who had escaped into the woods, and Caradawc son of Brân, whose heart had broken from grief. Thus he had made himself king of the whole island in place of

---

[1] *The Gododin* of Aneurin, as translated by T. Stephens. Branwen is there called "the lady Bradwen".
[2] See note to *Branwen, the Daughter of Llyr* in Lady Guest's *Mabinogion*.

Manawyddan, its rightful heir now that Brân was dead.

However, the destiny was upon the seven that they should go on with their leader's head. They went to Harlech and feasted for seven years, the three birds of Rhiannon singing them songs compared with which all other songs seemed unmelodious. Then they spent fourscore years in the Isle of Gwales, eating and drinking, and listening to the pleasant conversation of Brân's head. The "Entertaining of the Noble Head" this eighty years' feast was called. Brân's head, indeed, is almost more notable in British mythology than Brân before he was decapitated. Taliesin and the other bards invoke it repeatedly as *Urddawl Ben* (the "Venerable Head") and *Uther Ben* (the "Wonderful Head").

But all pleasure came to an end when Heilyn, the son of Gwynn, opened the forbidden door, like Bluebeard's wife, "to know if that was true which was said concerning it". As soon as they looked towards Cornwall, the glamour that had kept them merry for eighty-seven years failed, and left them as grieved about the death of their lord as though it had happened that very day. They could not rest for sorrow, but went at once to London, and laid the now dumb and corrupting head in its grave on Tower Hill, with its face turned towards France, to watch that no foe came from foreign lands to Britain. There it reposed until, ages afterwards, Arthur, in his pride of heart, dug it up, "as he thought it beneath his dignity to hold the island

otherwise than by valour ".   Disaster, in the shape
of

> " the godless hosts
> Of heathen swarming o'er the Northern sea ",[1]

came of this disinterment; and therefore it is called,
in a triad, one of the " Three Wicked Uncoverings
of Britain ".

[1] Tennyson: *Idylls of the King*—" Guinevere ".

CHAPTER XIX

THE WAR OF ENCHANTMENTS [1]

Manawyddan was now the sole survivor of the family of Llyr. He was homeless and landless. But Pryderi offered to give him a realm in Dyfed, and his mother, Rhiannon, for a wife. The lady, her son explained, was still not uncomely, and her conversation was pleasing. Manawyddan seems to have found her attractive, while Rhiannon was not less taken with the son of Llyr. They were wedded, and so great became the friendship of Pryderi and Kicva, Manawyddan and Rhiannon, that the four were seldom apart.

One day, after holding a feast at Narberth, they went up to the same magic mound where Rhiannon had first met Pwyll. As they sat there, thunder pealed, and immediately a thick mist sprang up, so that not one of them could see the other. When it cleared, they found themselves alone in an uninhabited country. Except for their own castle, the land was desert and untilled, without sign of dwelling, man, or beast. One touch of some unknown magic had utterly changed the face of Dyfed from a rich realm to a wilderness.

Manawyddan and Pryderi, Rhiannon and Kicva

---

[1] Retold from Lady Guest's translation of the Mabinogi of *Manawyddan, the Son of Llyr.*

traversed the country on all sides, but found nothing
except desolation and wild beasts. For two years
they lived in the open upon game and honey.

During the third year, they grew weary of this
wild life, and decided to go into Lloegyr[1], and support themselves by some handicraft. Manawyddan
could make saddles, and he made them so well that
soon no one in Hereford, where they had settled,
would buy from any saddler but himself. This
aroused the enmity of all the other saddlers, and
they conspired to kill the strangers. So the four
went to another city.

Here they made shields, and soon no one would
purchase a shield unless it had been made by
Manawyddan and Pryderi. The shield-makers
became jealous, and again a move had to be made.

But they fared no better at the next town, where
they practised the craft of cordwainers, Manawyddan
shaping the shoes and Pryderi stitching them. So
they went back to Dyfed again, and occupied themselves in hunting.

One day, the hounds of Manawyddan and Pryderi
roused a white wild boar. They chased it till they
came to a castle at a place where both the huntsmen were certain that no castle had been before.
Into this castle went the boar, and the hounds
after it. For some time, Manawyddan and Pryderi
waited in vain for their return. Pryderi then proposed that he should go into the castle, and see what
had become of them. Manawyddan tried to dis-
suade him, declaring that whoever their enemy was

[1] Saxon Britain—England.

who had laid Dyfed waste had also caused the appearance of this castle. But Pryderi insisted upon entering.

In the castle, he found neither the boar nor his hounds, nor any trace of man or beast. There was nothing but a fountain in the centre of the castle floor, and, on the brink of the fountain, a beautiful golden bowl fastened to a marble slab by chains.

Pryderi was so pleased with the beauty of the bowl that he put out his hands and took hold of it. Whereupon his hands stuck to the bowl, so that he could not move from where he stood.

Manawyddan waited for him till the evening, and then returned to the palace, and told Rhiannon. She, more daring than her husband, rebuked him for cowardice, and went straight to the magic castle. In the court she found Pryderi, his hands still glued to the bowl and his feet to the slab. She tried to free him, but became fixed, herself, and, with a clap of thunder and a fall of mist, the castle vanished with its two prisoners.

Manawyddan was now left alone with Kicva, Pryderi's wife. He calmed her fears, and assured her of his protection. But they had lost their dogs, and could not hunt any more, so they set out together to Lloegyr, to practise again Manawyddan's old trade of cordwainer. A second time, the envious cordwainers conspired to kill them, so they were obliged to return to Dyfed.

But Manawyddan took back a burden of wheat with him to Narberth, and sowed three crofts, all of which sprang up abundantly.

When harvest time came, he went to look at his first croft, and found it ripe. "I will reap this to-morrow," he said. But in the morning he found nothing but the bare straw. Every ear had been taken away.

So he went to the next croft, which was also ripe. But, when he came to cut it, he found it had been stripped like the first. Then he knew that whoever had wasted Dyfed, and carried off Rhiannon and Pryderi, was also at work upon his wheat.

The third croft was also ripe, and over this one he determined to keep watch. In the evening he armed himself and waited. At midnight he heard a great tumult, and, looking out, saw a host of mice coming. Each mouse bit off an ear of wheat and ran off with it. He rushed among them, but could only catch one, which was more sluggish than the rest. This one he put into his glove, and took it back; and showed it to Kicva.

"To-morrow I will hang it," he said. "It is not a fit thing for a man of your dignity to hang a mouse," she replied. "Nevertheless will I do so," said he. "Do so then," said Kicva.

The next morning, Manawyddan went to the magic mound, and set up two forks on it, to make a gallows. He had just finished, when a man dressed like a poor scholar came towards him, and greeted him.

"What are you doing, Lord?" he said.

"I am going to hang a thief," replied Manaw-yddan.

"What sort of a thief? I see an animal like a

mouse in your hand, but a man of rank like yours should not touch so mean a creature. Let it go free."

"I caught it robbing me," replied Manawyddan, "and it shall die a thief's death."

"I do not care to see a man like you doing such a thing," said the scholar. "I will give you a pound to let it go."

"I will not let it go," replied Manawyddan, "nor will I sell it."

"As you will, Lord. It is nothing to me," returned the scholar. And he went away.

Manawyddan laid a cross-bar along the forks. As he did so, another man came by, a priest riding on a horse. He asked Manawyddan what he was doing, and was told. "My lord," he said, "such a reptile is worth nothing to buy, but rather than see you degrade yourself by touching it, I will give you three pounds to let it go."

"I will take no money for it," replied Manawyddan. "It shall be hanged."

"Let it be hanged," said the priest, and went his way.

Manawyddan put the noose round the mouse's neck, and was just going to draw it up, when he saw a bishop coming, with his whole retinue.

"Thy blessing, Lord Bishop," he said.

"Heaven's blessing upon you," said the bishop. "What are you doing?"

"I am hanging a thief," replied Manawyddan. "This mouse has robbed me."

"Since I happen to have come at its doom, I

will ransom it," said the bishop. " Here are seven pounds. Take them, and let it go."

" I will not let it go," replied Manawyddan.

" I will give you twenty-four pounds of ready money if you will let it go," said the bishop.

" I would not, for as much again," replied Manawyddan.

" If you will not free it for that," said the bishop, " I will give you all my horses and their baggage to let it go."

" I will not," replied Manawyddan.

" Then name your own price," said the bishop.

" That offer I accept," replied Manawyddan. " My price is that Rhiannon and Pryderi be set free."

" They shall be set free," replied the bishop.

" Still I will not let the mouse go," said Manawyddan.

" What more do you ask?" exclaimed the bishop.

" That the charm be removed from Dyfed," replied Manawyddan.

" It shall be removed," promised the bishop. "So set the mouse free."

" I will not," said Manawyddan, "till I know who the mouse is."

" She is my wife," replied the bishop, "and I am called Llwyd, the son of Kilcoed, and I cast the charm over Dyfed, and upon Rhiannon and Pryderi, to avenge Gwawl son of Clûd for the game of 'badger in the bag' which was played on him by Pwyll, Head of Annwn. It was my household that came in the guise of mice and took away your corn

But since my wife has been caught, I will restore Rhiannon and Pryderi and take the charm off Dyfed if you will let her go."

"I will not let her go," said Manawyddan, "until you have promised that there shall be no charm put upon Dyfed again."

"I will promise that also," replied Llwyd. "So let her go."

"I will not let her go," said Manawyddan, "unless you swear to take no revenge for this hereafter."

"You have done wisely to claim that," replied Llwyd. "Much trouble would else have come upon your head because of this. Now I swear it. So set my wife free."

"I will not," said Manawyddan, "until I see Rhiannon and Pryderi."

Then he saw them coming towards him; and they greeted one another.

"Now set my wife free," said the bishop.

"I will, gladly," replied Manawyddan. So he released the mouse, and Llwyd struck her with a wand, and turned her into "a young woman, the fairest ever seen".

And when Manawyddan looked round him, he saw Dyfed tilled and cultivated again, as it had formerly been.

The powers of light had, this time, the victory. Little by little, they increased their mastery over the dominion of darkness, until we find the survivors of the families of Llyr and Pwyll mere vassals of Arthur.

CHAPTER XX

THE VICTORIES OF LIGHT OVER DARKNESS

The powers of light were, however, by no means invariably successful in their struggles with the powers of darkness. Even Gwydion son of Dôn had to serve his apprenticeship to misfortune. Assailing Caer Sidi—Hades[1] under one of its many titles,—he was caught by Pwyll and Pryderi, and endured a long imprisonment.[2] The sufferings he underwent made him a bard—an ancient Celtic idea which one can still see surviving in the popular tradition that whoever dares to spend a night alone either upon the chair of the Giant Idris (the summit of Cader Idris, in Merionethshire), or under the haunted Black Stone of Arddu, upon the Llanberis side of Snowdon, will be found in the morning either inspired or mad.[3] How he escaped we are not told; but the episode does not seem to have quenched his ardour against the natural enemies of his kind.

Helped by his brother, Amaethon, god of agriculture, and his son, Lleu, he fought the Battle of Godeu, or "the Trees", an exploit which is not the least curious of Celtic myths. It is known also as the Battle of Achren, or Ochren, a name for Hades

---

1 Or the Celtic Elysium, "a mythical country beneath the waves of the sea".
2 See the *Spoiling of Annwn*, quoted in chap. XXI—"The Mythological 'Coming of Arthur'".   3 Rhys: *Hibbert Lectures*, pp. 250–251.

of unknown meaning, but appearing again in the remarkable Welsh poem which describes the "Spoiling of Annwn" by Arthur. The King of Achren was Arawn; and he was helped by Brân, who apparently had not then made his fatal journey to Ireland. The war was made to secure three boons for man—the dog, the deer, and the lapwing, all of them creatures for some reason sacred to the gods of the nether world.

Gwydion was this time not alone, as he apparently was when he made his first unfortunate reconnaissance of Hades. Besides his brother and his son, he had an army which he raised for the purpose. For a leader of Gwydion's magical attainments there was no need of standing troops. He could call battalions into being with a charm, and dismiss them when they were no longer needed. The name of the battle shows what he did on this occasion; and the bard Taliesin adds his testimony:

"I have been in the battle of Godeu, with Lleu and Gwydion,
They changed the forms of the elementary trees and sedges".

In a poem devoted to it[1] he describes in detail what happened. The trees and grasses, he tells us, hurried to the fight: the alders led the van, but the willows and the quickens came late, and the birch, though courageous, took long in arraying himself;

---

[1] *Book of Taliesin VIII*, Vol. I, p. 276, of Skene. I have followed Skene's translation, with the especial exception of the curious line referring to the bean, so translated in D. W. Nash's *Taliesin*. If a correct rendering of the Welsh original, it offers an interesting parallel to certain superstitions of the Greeks concerning this vegetable.

the elm stood firm in the centre of the battle,
and would not yield a foot; heaven and earth
trembled before the advance of the oak-tree, that
stout door-keeper against an enemy; the heroic
holly and the hawthorn defended themselves with
their spikes; the heather kept off the enemy on
every side, and the broom was well to the front,
but the fern was plundered, and the furze did not
do well; the stout, lofty pine, the intruding pear-
tree, the gloomy ash, the bashful chestnut-tree, the
prosperous beech, the long-enduring poplar, the
scarce plum-tree, the shelter-seeking privet and
woodbine, the wild, foreign laburnum; "the bean,
bearing in its shade an army of phantoms"; rose-
bush, raspberry, ivy, cherry-tree, and medlar—all
took their parts.

In the ranks of Hades there were equally strange
fighters. We are told of a hundred-headed beast,
carrying a formidable battalion under the root of its
tongue and another in the back of its head; there
was a gaping black toad with a hundred claws; and
a crested snake of many colours, within whose flesh
a hundred souls were tormented for their sins—in
fact, it would need a Doré or a Dante to do justice
to this weird battle between the arrayed magics of
heaven and hell.

It was magic that decided its fate. There was
a fighter in the ranks of Hades who could not be
overcome unless his antagonist guessed his name—
a peculiarity of the terrene gods, remarks Professor
Rhys,[1] which has been preserved in our popular

[1] Rhys: *Hibbert Lectures*, note to p. 245.

fairy tales. Gwydion guessed the name, and sang
these two verses:—

> "Sure-hoofed is my steed impelled by the spur;
> The high sprigs of alder are on thy shield;
> *Brân* art thou called, of the glittering branches!

> "Sure-hoofed is my steed in the day of battle:
> The high sprigs of alder are on thy hand:
> *Brân* . . . by the branch thou bearest
> Has Amaethon the Good prevailed!"[1]

Thus the power of the dark gods was broken,
and the sons of Dôn retained for the use of men
the deer, the dog, and the lapwing, stolen from that
underworld, whence all good gifts came.

It was always to obtain some practical benefit
that the gods of light fought against the gods of
darkness.   The last and greatest of Gwydion's raids
upon Hades was undertaken to procure—pork![2]

Gwydion had heard that there had come to Dyfed
some strange beasts, such as had never been seen
before.   They were called "pigs" or "swine", and
Arawn, King of Annwn, had sent them as a gift to
Pryderi son of Pwyll.   They were small animals,
and their flesh was said to be better than the flesh
of oxen.   He thought it would be a good thing to
get them, either by force or fraud, from the dark
powers.   Mâth son of Mâthonwy, who ruled the
children of Dôn from his Olympus of Caer Dathyl[3],
gave his consent, and Gwydion set off, with eleven

---

[1] Lady Guest's translation in her notes to *Kulhwch and Olwen*.
[2] The following episode is retold from Lady Guest's translation of the Mabinogi of *Mâth, Son of Mathonwy*.
[3] Now called Pen y Gaer.   It is on the summit of a hill half-way between Llanrwst and Conway, and about a mile from the station of Llanbedr.

others, to Pryderi's palace[1]. They disguised themselves as bards, so as to be received by Pryderi,
and Gwydion, who was "the best teller of tales in
the world", entertained the Prince of Dyfed and
his court more than they had ever been entertained
by any story-teller before. Then he asked Pryderi
to grant him a boon—the animals which had come
from Annwn. But Pryderi had pledged his word
to Arawn that he would neither sell nor give away
any of the new creatures until they had increased
to double their number, and he told the disguised
Gwydion so.

"Lord," said Gwydion, "I can set you free from
your promise. Neither give me the swine at once,
nor yet refuse them to me altogether, and to-morrow
I will show you how."

He went to the lodging Pryderi had assigned him,
and began to work his charms and illusions. Out
of fungus he made twelve gilded shields, and twelve
horses with gold harness, and twelve black greyhounds with white breasts, each wearing a golden
collar and leash. And these he showed to Pryderi.

"Lord," said he, "there is a release from the
word you spoke last evening concerning the swine
—that you may neither give them nor sell them.
You may exchange them for something which is
better. I will give you these twelve horses with
their gold harness, and these twelve greyhounds
with their gold collars and leashes, and these twelve
gilded shields for them."

[1] Said to have been at Rhuddlan Teivi, which is, perhaps, Glan Teivy, near
Cardigan Bridge.

Pryderi took counsel with his men, and agreed to the bargain. So Gwydion and his followers took the swine and went away with them, hurrying as fast as they could, for Gwydion knew that the illusion would not last longer than a day. The memory of their journey was long kept up; every place where they rested between Dyfed and Caer Dathyl is remembered by a name connecting it with pigs. There is a Mochdrev ("Swine's Town") in each of the three counties of Cardiganshire, Montgomeryshire, and Denbighshire, and a Castell y Moch ("Swine's Castle") near Mochnant ("Swine's Brook"), which runs through part of the two latter counties. They shut up the pigs in safety, and then assembled all Mâth's army; for the horses and hounds and shields had returned to fungus, and Pryderi, who guessed Gwydion's part in it, was coming northward in hot haste.

There were two battles—one at Maenor Penardd, near Conway, and the other at Maenor Alun, now called Coed Helen, near Caernarvon. Beaten in both, Pryderi fell back upon Nant Call, about nine miles from Caernarvon. Here he was again defeated with great slaughter, and sent hostages, asking for peace and a safe retreat.

This was granted by Mâth; but, none the less, the army of the sons of Dôn insisted on following the retreating host, and harassing it. So Pryderi sent a complaint to Mâth, demanding that, if there must still be war, Gwydion, who had caused all the trouble, should fight with him in single combat.

Gwydion agreed, and the champions of light and

darkness met face to face. But Pryderi was the waning power, and he fell before the strength and magic of Gwydion. " And at Maen Tyriawc, above Melenryd, was he buried, and there is his grave", says the Mabinogi, though the ancient Welsh poem, called the " Verses of the Graves of the Warriors"[1], assigns him a different resting-place.[2]

This decisive victory over Hades and its kings was the end of the struggle, until it was renewed, with still more complete success, by one greater than Gwydion—the invincible Arthur.

[1] Poem XIX in the *Black Book of Caermarthen*, Vol. I, p. 309, of Skene.
[2] " In Aber Gwenoli is the grave of Pryderi,
       Where the waves beat against the land."

CHAPTER XXI

THE MYTHOLOGICAL "COMING OF ARTHUR"

The "Coming of Arthur", his sudden rise into prominence, is one of the many problems of the Celtic mythology. He is not mentioned in any of the Four Branches of the Mabinogi, which deal with the races of British gods equivalent to the Gaelic Tuatha Dé Danann. The earliest references to him in Welsh literature seem to treat him as merely a warrior-chieftain, no better, if no worse, than several others, such as "Geraint, a tributary prince of Devon", immortalized both by the bards[1] and by Tennyson. Then, following upon this, we find him lifted to the extraordinary position of a king of gods, to whom the old divine families of Dôn, of Llyr, and of Pwyll pay unquestioned homage. Triads tell us that Lludd—the Zeus of the older Pantheon—was one of Arthur's "Three Chief War-Knights", and Arawn, King of Hades, one of his "Three Chief Counselling Knights". In the story called the "Dream of Rhonabwy", in the Red Book of Hergest, he is shown as a leader to whom are subject those we know to have been of

---

[1] A poem in praise of Geraint, "the brave man from the region of Dyvnaint (Devon) . . . the enemy of tyranny and oppression", is contained in both the Black Book of Caermarthen and the Red Book of Hergest. "When Geraint was born, open were the gates of heaven", begins its last verse. It is translated in Vol. I of Skene, p. 267.

divine race—sons of Nudd, of Llyr, of Brân, of Govannan, and of Arianrod. In another "Red Book" tale, that of "Kulhwch and Olwen", even greater gods are his vassals. Amaethon son of Dôn, ploughs for him, and Govannan son of Dôn, rids the iron, while two other sons of Beli, Nynniaw and Peibaw, "turned into oxen on account of their sins", toil at the yoke, that a mountain may be cleared and tilled and the harvest reaped in one day. He assembles his champions to seek the "treasures of Britain"; and Manawyddan son of Llyr, Gwyn son of Nudd, and Pryderi son of Pwyll rally round him at his call.

The most probable, and only adequate explanation, is given by Professor Rhys, who considers that the fames of two separate Arthurs have been accidentally confused, to the exceeding renown of a composite, half-real, half-mythical personage into whom the two blended.[1] One of these was a divine Arthur, a god more or less widely worshipped in the Celtic world—the same, no doubt, whom an *ex voto* inscription found in south-eastern France calls *Mercurius Artaius*.[2] The other was a human Arthur, who held among the Britons the post which, under Roman domination, had been called *Comes Britanniæ*. This "Count of Britain" was the supreme military authority; he had a roving commission to defend the country against foreign invasion; and under his orders were two slightly subordinate officers, the *Dux Britanniarum* (Duke of the Britains), who had charge of the northern

---

[1] Rhys: *Arthurian Legend*, p. 8.   [2] Rhys: *Hibbert Lectures*, pp. 40–41.

wall, and the *Comes Littoris Saxonici* (Count of the Saxon Shore), who guarded the south-eastern coasts. The Britons, after the departure of the Romans, long kept intact the organization their conquerors had built up; and it seems reasonable to believe that this post of leader in war was the same which early Welsh literature describes as that of "emperor", a title given to Arthur alone among the British heroes.[1] The fame of Arthur the Emperor blended with that of Arthur the God, so that it became conterminous with the area over which we have traced Brythonic settlement in Great Britain.[2] Hence the many disputes, ably, if unprofitably, conducted, over "Arthurian localities" and the sites of such cities as Camelot, and of Arthur's twelve great battles. Historical elements doubtless coloured the tales of Arthur and his companions, but they are none the less as essentially mythic as those told of their Gaelic analogues—the Red Branch Heroes of Ulster and the Fenians.

Of those two cycles, it is with the latter that the Arthurian legend shows most affinity.[3] Arthur's position as supreme war-leader of Britain curiously parallels that of Finn's as general of a "native Irish militia". His "Round Table" of warriors also reminds one of Finn's Fenians sworn to adventure. Both alike battle with human and superhuman foes.

---

[1] Rhys: *Arthurian Legend*, p. 7.

[2] "It is worthy of remark that the fame of Arthur is widely spread; he is claimed alike as a prince in Brittany, Cornwall, Wales, Cumberland, and the Lowlands of Scotland; that is to say, his fame is conterminous with the Brythonic race, and does not extend to the Gaels".—*Chambers's Encyclopædia*.

[3] For Arthurian and Fenian parallels see Campbell's *Popular Tales of the West Highlands*.

Both alike harry Europe, even to the walls of Rome. The love-story of Arthur, his wife Gwynhwyvar (Guinevere), and his nephew Medrawt (Mordred), resembles in several ways that of Finn, his wife Grainne, and his nephew Diarmait. In the stories of the last battles of Arthur and of the Fenians, the essence of the kindred myth still subsists, though the actual exponents of it slightly differ. At the fight of Camlan, it was Arthur and Medrawt themselves who fought the final duel. But in the last stand of the Fenians at Gabhra, the original protagonists have given place to their descendants and representatives. Both Finn and Cormac were already dead. It is Oscar, Finn's grandson, and Cairbré, Cormac's son, who fight and slay each other. And again, just as Arthur was thought by many not to have really died, but to have passed to "the island valley of Avilion", so a Scottish legend tells us how, ages after the Fenians, a man, landing by chance upon a mysterious western island, met and spoke with Finn mac Coul. Even the alternative legend, which makes Arthur and his warriors wait under the earth in a magic sleep for the return of their triumph, is also told of the Fenians.

But these parallels, though they illustrate Arthur's pre-eminence, do not show his real place among the gods. To determine this, we must examine the ranks of the older dynasties carefully, to see if any are missing whose attributes this new-comer may have inherited. We find Lludd and Gwyn, Arawn, Pryderi, and Manawyddan side by side with him

under their own names.   Among the children of
Dôn are Amaethon and Govannan.   But here the
list stops, with a notable omission.   There is no
mention, in later myth, of Gwydion.   That greatest
of the sons of Dôn has fallen out, and vanished
without a sign.

Singularly enough, too, the same stories that were
once told of Gwydion are now attached to the
name of Arthur.   So that we may assume, with
Professor Rhys, that Arthur, the prominent god of
a new Pantheon, has taken the place of Gwydion
in the old.[1]   A comparison of Gwydion-myths and
Arthur-myths shows an almost exact correspondence
in everything but name.

Like Gwydion, Arthur is the exponent of culture
and of arts.   Therefore we see him carrying on the
same war against the underworld for wealth and
wisdom that Gwydion and the sons of Dôn waged
against the sons of Llyr, the Sea, and of Pwyll, the
Head of Hades.

Like Gwydion, too, Arthur suffered early reverses.
He failed, indeed, even where his prototype had
succeeded.   Gwydion, we know from the Mabinogi
of Mâth, successfully stole Pryderi's pigs, but Arthur
was utterly baffled in his attempt to capture the
swine of a similar prince of the underworld, called
March son of Meirchion.[2]   Also as with Gwydion,
his earliest reconnaissance of Hades was disastrous,

---

[1] See chap. 1 of Rhys's *Arthurian Legend*—" Arthur, Historical and Mythical ".

[2] A triad in the Hengwrt MS. 536, translated by Skene.   It was Trystan who was
watching the swine for his uncle, while the swineherd went with a message to
Essylt (Iseult), " and Arthur desired one pig by deceit or by theft, and could not
get it "

and led to his capture and imprisonment. Manawyddan son of Llyr, confined him in the mysterious
and gruesome bone-fortress of Oeth and Anoeth,
and there he languished for three days and three
nights before a rescuer came in the person of Goreu,
his cousin.[1] But, in the end, he triumphed. A
Welsh poem, ascribed to the bard Taliesin, relates,
under the title "The Spoiling of Annwn",[2] an expedition of Arthur and his followers into the very
heart of that country, from which he appears to
have returned (for the verses are somewhat obscure)
with the loss of almost all his men, but in possession
of the object of his quest—the magic cauldron of
inspiration and poetry.

Taliesin tells the story as an eye-witness. He
may well have done so; for it was his boast that
from the creation of the world he had allowed himself to miss no event of importance. He was in
Heaven, he tells us,[3] when Lucifer fell, and in the
Court of Dôn before Gwydion was born; he had
been among the constellations both with Mary
Magdalene and with the pagan goddess Arianrod;
he carried a banner before Alexander, and was chief
director of the building of the Tower of Babel; he
saw the fall of Troy and the founding of Rome; he
was with Noah in the Ark, and he witnessed the
destruction of Sodom and Gomorrah; and he was
present both at the Manger of Bethlehem and at
the Cross of Calvary. But, unfortunately, Taliesin,

---

[1] See note to chap. XXII—"The Treasures of Britain".

[2] *Book of Taliesin*, poem XXX, Skene, Vol. I, p. 256.

[3] In a probably very ancient poem embedded in the sixteenth-century Welsh
romance called *Taliesin*, included by Lady Guest in her *Mabinogion*.

as a credible personage, rests under exactly the same disabilities as Arthur himself. It is not denied by scholars that there was a real Taliesin, a sixth-century bard to whom were attributed, and who may have actually composed, some of the poems in the Book of Taliesin.[1] But there was also another Taliesin, whom, as a mythical poet of the British Celts, Professor Rhys is inclined to equate with the Gaelic Ossian.[2] The traditions of the two mingled, endowing the historic Taliesin with the god-like attributes of his predecessor, and clothing the mythical Taliesin with some of the actuality of his successor.[3]

It is regrettable that our bard did not at times sing a little less incoherently, for his poem contains the fullest description that has come down to us of the other world as the Britons conceived it. Apparently the numerous names, all different and some now untranslatable, refer to the same place, and they must be collated to form a right idea of what Annwn was like. With the exception of an obviously spurious last verse, here omitted, the poem is magnificently pagan, and quite a storehouse of British mythology[4].

[1] " The existence of a sixth-century bard of this name, a contemporary of the heroic stage of British resistance to the Germanic invaders, is well attested. A number of poems are found in mediæval Welsh MSS., chief among them the so-called *Book of Taliesin*, ascribed to this sixth-century poet. Some of these are almost as old as any remains of Welsh poetry, and may go back to the early tenth or the ninth century; others are productions of the eleventh, twelfth, and even thirteenth centuries."—Nutt: Notes to his (1902) edition of Lady Guest's *Mabinogion.*

[2] Rhys: *Hibbert Lectures,* p. 551.

[3] " There can be little doubt but that the sixth-century bard succeeded to the form and attributes of a far older, a prehistoric, a mythic singer."—Nutt: Notes to *Mabinogion.*

[4] I have been obliged to collate four different translators to obtain an acceptable version of what Mr. T. Stephens, in his *Literature of the Kymri,* calls " one of the

" I will praise the Sovereign, supreme Lord of the land,
Who hath extended his dominion over the shore of the
world.
Stout was the prison of Gweir[1], in Caer Sidi,
Through the spite of Pwyll and Pryderi:
No one before him went into it.
The heavy blue chain firmly held the youth,
And before the spoils of Annwn woefully he sang,
And thenceforth till doom he shall remain a bard.
Thrice enough to fill Prydwen[2] we went into it;
Except seven, none returned from Caer Sidi[3].

" Am I not a candidate for fame, to be heard in song
In Caer Pedryvan[4], four times revolving?
The first word from the cauldron, when was it spoken?
By the breath of nine maidens it was gently warmed.
Is it not the cauldron of the chief of Annwn? What is
its fashion?
A rim of pearls is round its edge.
It will not cook the food of a coward or one forsworn.
A sword flashing bright will be raised to him,
And left in the hand of Lleminawg.
And before the door of the gate of Uffern[5] the lamp was
burning.
When we went with Arthur—a splendid labour!—
Except seven, none returned from Caer Vedwyd[6].

" Am I not a candidate for fame, to be heard in song
In Caer Pedryvan, in the Isle of the Strong Door,
Where twilight and pitchy darkness meet together,
And bright wine is the drink of the host?
Thrice enough to fill Prydwen we went on the sea.
Except seven, none returned from Caer Rigor[7].

least intelligible of the mythological poems". My authorities have been Skene,
Stephens, Nash, and Rhys.
                                [1] A form of the name Gwydion.
     [2] The name of Arthur's ship.   [3] Revolving Castle.
     [4] Four-cornered Castle.   [5] The Cold Place.
     [6] Castle of Revelry.   [7] Kingly Castle.

" I will not allow much praise to the leaders of literature.
  Beyond Caer Wydyr[1] they saw not the prowess of
    Arthur;
  Three-score hundreds stood on the walls;
  It was hard to converse with their watchman.
  Thrice enough to fill Prydwen we went with Arthur;
  Except seven, none returned from Caer Golud[2].

" I will not allow much praise to the spiritless.
  They know not on what day, or who caused it,
  Or in what hour of the serene day Cwy was born,
  Or who caused that he should not go to the dales of
    Devwy.
  They know not the brindled ox with the broad head-
    band,
  Whose yoke is seven-score handbreadths.
  When we went with Arthur, of mournful memory,
  Except seven, none returned from Caer Vandwy[3].

" I will not allow much praise to those of drooping courage.
  They know not on what day the chief arose,
  Nor in what hour of the serene day the owner was born,
  Nor what animal they keep, with its head of silver.
  When we went with Arthur, of anxious striving,
  Except seven, none returned from Caer Ochren[4]".

Many of the allusions of this poem will perhaps
never be explained. We know no better than the
" leaders of literature" whom the vainglorious Taliesin taunted with their ignorance and lack of spirit
in what hour Cwy was born, or even who he was,
much less who prevented him from going to the
dales of Devwy, wherever they may have been.
We are in the dark as much as they were with

---

[1] Glass Castle.   [2] Castle of Riches.
[3] Meaning is unknown. See chap. XVI—"The Gods of the Britons".
[4] Meaning is unknown. See chap. XX—"The Victories of Light over Darkness".

regard to the significance of the brindled ox with the broad head-band, and of the other animal with the silver head.[1] But the earlier portion of the poem is, fortunately, clearer, and it gives glimpses of a grandeur of savage imagination. The strong-doored, foursquare fortress of glass, manned by its dumb, ghostly sentinels, spun round in never-ceasing revolution, so that few could find its entrance; it was pitch-dark save for the twilight made by the lamp burning before its circling gate; feasting went on there, and revelry, and in its centre, choicest of its many riches, was the pearl-rimmed cauldron of poetry and inspiration, kept bubbling by the breaths of nine British pythonesses, so that it might give forth its oracles. To this scanty information we may add a few lines, also by Taliesin, and contained in a poem called " A Song Concerning the Sons of Llyr ab Brochwel Powys ":—

" Perfect is my chair in Caer Sidi:
  Plague and age hurt not him who 's in it—
  They know, Manawyddan and Pryderi.
  Three organs round a fire sing before it,
  And about its points are ocean's streams
  And the abundant well above it—
  Sweeter than white wine the drink in it."[2]

Little is, however, added by it to our knowledge. It reminds us that Annwn was surrounded by the sea—" the heavy blue chain" which held Gweir so firmly;—it informs us that the " bright wine" which

---

[1] Unless they should be " the yellow and the brindled bull" mentioned in the story of *Kulhwch and Olwen*.

[2] *Book of Taliesin*, poem XIV.   The translation is by Rhys: *Arthurian Legend*. p. 301.

was "the drink of the host" was kept in a well; it adds to the revelry the singing of the three organs; it makes a point that its inhabitants were freed from age and death; and, last of all, it shows us, as we might have expected, the ubiquitous Taliesin as a privileged resident of this delightful region. We have two clues as to where the country may have been situated. Lundy Island, off the coast of Devonshire, was anciently called *Ynys Wair*, the "Island of Gweir", or Gwydion. The Welsh translation of the *Seint Greal*, an Anglo-Norman romance embodying much of the old mythology, locates its "Turning Castle"—evidently the same as Caer Sidi —in the district around and comprising Puffin Island off the coast of Anglesey.[1] But these are slender threads by which to tether to firm ground a realm of the imagination.

With Gwydion, too, have disappeared the whole of the characters connected with him in that portion of the Mabinogi of Mâth, Son of Mathonwy, which recounts the myth of the birth of the sun-god. Neither Mâth himself, nor Lleu Llaw Gyffes, nor Dylan, nor their mother, Arianrod, play any more part; they have vanished as completely as Gwydion. But the essence of the myth of which they were the figures remains intact. Gwydion was the father by his sister Arianrod, wife of a waning heaven-god called Nwyvre (Space), of twin sons, Lleu, a god of light, and Dylan, a god of darkness; and we find this same story woven into the very innermost texture of the legend of Arthur.[2] The new Arianrod,

---

[1] Rhys: *Arthurian Legend*, p. 325.   [2] Rhys: *ibid.*, chap. 1.

though called "Morgawse" by Sir Thomas Malory[1], and "Anna" by Geoffrey of Monmouth[2], is known to earlier Welsh myth as "Gwyar"[3]. She was the sister of Arthur and the wife of the sky-god, Lludd, and her name, which means "shed blood" or "gore", reminds us of the relationship of the Morrígú, the war-goddess of the Gaels, to the heaven-god Nuada[4]. The new Lleu Llaw Gyffes is called Gwalchmei, that is, the "Falcon of May"[5], and the new Dylan is Medrawt, at once Arthur's son and Gwalchmei's brother, and the bitterest enemy of both[6].

Besides these "old friends with new faces", Arthur brings with him into prominence a fresh Pantheon, most of whom also replace the older gods of the heavens and earth and the regions under the earth. The Zeus of Arthur's cycle is called Myrddin, who passed into the Norman-French romances as "Merlin". All the myths told of him bear witness to his high estate. The first name of Britain, before it was inhabited, was, we learn from a triad, *Clas Myrddin*, that is, "Myrddin's Enclosure".[7] He is given a wife whose attributes recall those of the consorts of Nuada and Lludd. She is described as the only daughter of Coel—the British name of the Gaulish *Camulus*, a god of war and the sky—and was called Elen Lwyddawg, that is, "Elen, Leader of Hosts". Her memory is still preserved in Wales in connection with ancient roadways; such names

[1] Malory's *Morte Darthur*, Book II, chap. 11.
[2] *Historia Britonum*, Book VIII, chap. xx.
[3] Rhys: *Arthurian Legend*, p. 169.
[4] Rhys: *ibid.*, p 169.
[5] Rhys: *Arthurian Legend*, p. 13.
[6] Rhys: *ibid.*, pp. 19-23.
[7] Rhys: *Hibbert Lectures*, p. 168.

as *Ffordd Elen* ("Elen's Road") and *Sarn Elen* ("Elen's Causeway") seem to show that the paths on which armies marched were ascribed or dedicated to her.[1] As Myrddin's wife, she is credited with having founded the town of Carmarthen (*Caer Myrddin*), as well as the "highest fortress in Arvon", which must have been the site near Beddgelert still called *Dinas Emrys*, the "Town of Emrys", one of Myrddin's epithets or names.[2]

Professor Rhys is inclined to credit Myrddin, or, rather, the British Zeus under whatever name, with having been the god especially worshipped at Stonehenge.[3] Certainly this impressive temple, ever unroofed and open to the sun and wind and rain of heaven, would seem peculiarly appropriate to a British supreme god of light and sky. Neither are we quite without documentary evidence which will allow us to connect it with him. Geoffrey of Monmouth[4], whose historical fictions usually conceal mythological facts, relates that the stones which compose it were erected by Merlin. Before that, they had stood in Ireland, upon a hill which Geoffrey calls "Mount Killaraus", and which can be identified as the same spot known to Irish legend as the "Hill of Uisnech", and, still earlier, connected with Balor. According to British tradition, the primeval giants who first colonized Ireland had brought them from their original home on "the farthest coast of Africa",

---

[1] Rhys: *Hibbert Lectures*, p. 167.

[2] See Rhys's exposition of the mythological meaning of the *Red Book* romance of the *Dream of Maxen Wledig*, in his *Hibbert Lectures*, pp. 160–175.

[3] Rhys: *Hibbert Lectures*, pp. 192–195.

[4] *Historia Britonum*, Book VIII, chaps. IX–XII.

on account of their miraculous virtues; for any water in which they were bathed became a sovereign remedy either for sickness or for wounds. By the order of Aurelius, a half-real, half-mythical king of Britain, Merlin brought them thence to England, to be set up on Salisbury Plain as a monument to the British chieftains treacherously slain by Hengist and his Saxons. With this scrap of native information about Stonehenge we may compare the only other piece we have—the account of the classic Diodorus, who called it a temple of Apollo.[1] At first, these two statements seem to conflict. But it is far from unlikely that the earlier Celtic settlers in Britain made little or no religious distinction between sky and sun. The sun-god, as a separate personage, seems to have been the conception of a comparatively late age. Celtic mythology allows us to be present, as it were, at the births both of the Gaelic Lugh Lamhfada and the British Lleu Llaw Gyffes.

Even the well-known story of Myrddin's, or Merlin's final imprisonment in a tomb of airy enchantment—"a tour withouten walles, or withoute eny closure"—reads marvellously like a myth of the sun "with all his fires and travelling glories round him".[2] Encircled, shielded, and made splendid by his atmosphere of living light, the Lord of Heaven moves slowly towards the west, to disappear at last into the sea (as one local version of the myth puts it), or on to a far-off island (as another says), or into a dark forest (the choice of a third).[3] When the

---

[1] See chap. IV and Rhys: *Hibbert Lectures*, p. 194.
[2] Rhys: *Hibbert Lectures*, pp. 158, 159.   [3] *Ibid.*, p. 155.

myth became finally fixed, it was Bardsey Island, off the extreme westernmost point of Caernarvonshire, that was selected as his last abode. Into it he went with nine attendant bards, taking with him the "Thirteen Treasures of Britain", thenceforth lost to men. Bardsey Island no doubt derives its name from this story; and what is probably an allusion to it is found in a first-century Greek writer called Plutarch, who describes a grammarian called Demetrius as having visited Britain, and brought home an account of his travels. He mentioned several uninhabited and sacred islands off our coasts which he said were named after gods and heroes, but there was one especially in which Cronos was imprisoned with his attendant deities, and Briareus keeping watch over him as he slept; "for sleep was the bond forged for him".[1] Doubtless this disinherited deity, whom the Greek, after his fashion, called "Cronos", was the British heaven- and sun-god, after he had descended into the prison of the west.

Among other new-comers is Kai, who, as Sir Kay the Seneschal, fills so large a part in the later romances. Purged of his worst offences, and reduced to a surly butler to Arthur, he is but a shadow of the earlier Kai who murdered Arthur's son Llacheu[2], and can only be acquitted, through the obscurity of the poem that relates the incident, of having also carried off, or having tried to carry off, Arthur's wife, Gwynhwyvar.[3] He is thought

[1] Plutarch: *De Defectu Oraculorum.*
[2] The *Seint Greal*, quoted by Rhys: *Arthurian Legend*, pp. 61–62.
[3] Rhys: *Arthurian Legend*, p. 59.

to have been a personification of fire,[1] upon the strength of a description given of him in the mythical romance of "Kulhwch and Olwen". "Very subtle", it says, "was Kai. When it pleased him he could render himself as tall as the highest tree in the forest. And he had another peculiarity—so great was the heat of his nature, that, when it rained hardest, whatever he carried remained dry for a handbreadth above and a handbreadth below his hand; and when his companions were coldest, it was to them as fuel with which to light their fire."

Another personage who owes his prominence in the Arthurian story to his importance in Celtic myth was March son of Meirchion, whose swine Arthur attempted to steal, as Gwydion had done those of Pryderi. In the romances, he has become the cowardly and treacherous Mark, king, according to some stories, of Cornwall, but according to others, of the whole of Britain, and known to all as the husband of the Fair Isoult, and the uncle of Sir Tristrem. But as a deformed deity of the underworld[2] he can be found in Gaelic as well as in British myth. He cannot be considered as originally different from Morc, a king of the Fomors at the time when from their Glass Castle they so fatally oppressed the Children of Nemed.[3] The Fomors were distinguished by their animal features, and March had the same peculiarity.[4] When Sir

---

[1] Elton: *Origins of English History*, p. 269.
[2] Rhys: *Arthurian Legend*, p. 12.   [3] *Ibid.*, p. 70.
[4] The name March means "horse".

Thomas Malory relates how, to please Arthur and Sir Launcelot, Sir Dinadan made a song about Mark, "which was the worst lay that ever harper sang with harp or any other instruments",[1] he does not tell us wherein the sting of the lampoon lay. It no doubt reminded King Mark of the unpleasant fact that he had—not like his Phrygian counterpart, ass's but—horse's ears. He was, in fact, a Celtic Midas, a distinction which he shared with one of the mythical kings of early Ireland.[2]

Neither can we pass over Urien, a deity of the underworld akin to, or perhaps the same as, Brân.[3] Like that son of Llyr, he was at once a god of battle and of minstrelsy;[4] he was adored by the bards as their patron;[5] his badge was the raven (*bran*, in Welsh);[6] while, to make his identification complete, there is an extant poem which tells how Urien, wounded, ordered his own head to be cut off by his attendants.[7] His wife was Modron,[8] known as the mother of Mabon, the sun-god to whom inscriptions exist as *Maponos*. Another of the children of Urien and Modron is Owain, which was perhaps only another name for Mabon.[9] Taliesin calls him "chief of the glittering west",[10] and he is as certainly a sun-god as his father Urien, "lord of the evening",[11] was a ruler of the dark underworld.

---

[1] *Morte Darthur.* Book X, chap. xxvii.   [2] Called Labraid Longsech.
[3] Rhys: *Arthurian Legend.* See chap. xi—"Urien and his Congeners".
[4] *Ibid.*, p. 260.   [5] *Ibid.*, p. 261.   [6] *Ibid.*, p. 256.
[7] Red Book of Hergest, XII.   Rhys: *Arthurian Legend*, pp. 253–256.
[8] Rhys: *Arthurian Legend*, p. 247.   [9] *Ibid.*
[10] *The Death-song of Owain.*   Taliesin, xliv, Skene, Vol. I, p. 366.
[11] Book of Taliesin, xxxii.   Skene, however, translates the word rendered "evening" by Rhys as "cultivated plain".

It is by reason of the pre-eminence of Arthur that we find gathered round him so many gods, all probably various tribal personifications of the same few mythological ideas. The Celts, both of the Gaelic and the British branches, were split up into numerous petty tribes, each with its own local deities embodying the same essential conceptions under different names. There was the god of the underworld, gigantic in figure, patron alike of warrior and minstrel, teacher of the arts of eloquence and literature, and owner of boundless wealth, whom some of the British tribes worshipped as Brân, others as Urien, others as Pwyll, or March, or Mâth, or Arawn, or Ogyrvran. There was the lord of an elysium—Hades in its aspect of a paradise of the departed rather than of the primeval subterranean realm where all things originated—whom the Britons of Wales called Gwyn, or Gwynwas; the Britons of Cornwall, Melwas; and the Britons of Somerset, Avallon, or Avallach. Under this last title, his realm is called *Ynys Avallon*, "Avallon's Island", or, as we know the word, Avilion. It was said to be in the "Land of Summer", which, in the earliest myth, signified Hades; and it was only in later days that the mystic Isle of Avilion became fixed to earth as Glastonbury, and the Elysian "Land of Summer" as Somerset.[1] There was a mighty ruler of heaven, a "god of battles", worshipped on high places, in whose hands was "the stern arbitrament of war"; some knew him as Lludd, others as Myrddin, or as Emrys.

---

[1] Rhys: *Arthurian Legend*, p. 345.

There was a gentler deity, friendly to man, to help whom he fought or cajoled the powers of the underworld; Gwydion he was called, and Arthur. Last, perhaps, to be imagined in concrete shape, there was a long-armed, sharp-speared sun-god who aided the culture-god in his work, and was known as Lleu, or Gwalchmei, or Mabon, or Owain, or Peredur, and no doubt by many another name; and with him is usually found a brother representing not light, but darkness. This expression of a single idea by different names may be also observed in Gaelic myth, though not quite so clearly. In the hurtling of clan against clan, many such divinities perished altogether out of memory, or survived only as names, to make up, in Ireland, the vast, shadowy population claiming to be Tuatha Dé Danann, and, in Britain, the long list of Arthur's followers. Others—gods of stronger communities—would increase their fame as their worshippers increased their territory, until, as happened in Greece, the chief deities of many tribes came together to form a national Pantheon.

We have already tried to explain the "Coming of Arthur" historically. Mythologically, he came, as, according to Celtic ideas, all things came originally, from the underworld. His father is called Uther Pendragon.[1] But Uther Pendragon is (for the word "dragon" is not part of the name, but a title signifying "war-leader") *Uther Ben*, that is, Brân, under his name of the "Wonderful Head",[2] so that, in spite of the legend which describes

---

[1] Both by Malory and Geoffrey of Monmouth.
[2] Rhys: *Arthurian Legend*, p. 256.

Arthur as having disinterred Brân's head on Tower Hill, where it watched against invasion, because he thought it beneath his dignity to keep Britain in any other way than by valour,[1] we must recognize the King of Hades as his father. This being so, it would only be natural that he should take a wife from the same eternal country, and we need not be surprised to find in Gwynhwyvar's father, Ogyrvran, a personage corresponding in all respects to the Celtic conception of the ruler of the underworld. He was of gigantic size;[2] he was the owner of a cauldron out of which three Muses had been born;[3] and he was the patron of the bards,[4] who deemed him to have been the originator of their art. More than this, his very name, analysed into its original *ocur vran*, means the evil *bran*, or raven, the bird of death.[5]

But Welsh tradition credits Arthur with three wives, each of them called Gwynhwyvar. This peculiar arrangement is probably due to the Celtic love of triads; and one may compare them with the three Etains who pass through the mythico-heroic story of Eochaid Airem, Etain, and Mider. Of these three Gwynhwyvars,[6] besides the Gwynhwyvar, daughter of Ogyrvran, one was the daughter of Gwyrd Gwent, of whom we know nothing but the name, and the other of Gwyrthur ap Greidawl,

---

[1] See chap. XVIII—"The Wooing of Branwen and the Beheading of Brân".
[2] He is called Ogyrvran the Giant.   [3] Rhys: *Arthurian Legend*, p. 326.
[4] Rhys: *Hibbert Lectures*, pp. 268–269.
[5] Rhys: *Lectures on Welsh Philology*, p. 306. But the derivation is only tentative, and an interesting alternative one is given, which equates him with the Persian Ahriman.
[6] The enumeration of Arthur's three Gwynhwyvars forms one of the Welsh triads.

the same "Victor son of Scorcher" with whom Gwyn son of Nudd, fought, in earlier myth, perpetual battle for the possession of Creudylad, daughter of the sky-god Lludd. This same eternal strife between the powers of light and darkness for the possession of a symbolical damsel is waged again in the Arthurian cycle; but it is no longer for Creudylad that Gwyn contends, but for Gwynhwyvar, and no longer with Gwyrthur, but with Arthur. It would seem to have been a Cornish form of the myth; for the dark god is called "Melwas", and not "Gwynwas", or "Gwyn", his name in Welsh.[1] Melwas lay in ambush for a whole year, and finally succeeded in carrying off Gwynhwyvar to his palace in Avilion. But Arthur pursued, and besieged that stronghold, just as Eochaid Airem had, in the Gaelic version of the universal story, mined and sapped at Mider's *sídh* of Bri Leith.[2] Mythology, as well as history, repeats itself; and Melwas was obliged to restore Gwynhwyvar to her rightful lord.

It is not Melwas, however, that in the best-known versions of the story contends with Arthur for the love of Gwynhwyvar. The most widespread early tradition makes Arthur's rival his nephew Medrawt. Here Professor Rhys traces a striking parallel between the British legend of Arthur, Gwynhwyvar, and Medrawt, and the Gaelic story of Airem, Etain, and Mider.[3] The two myths are practically counterparts; for the names of all

---

[1] Rhys: *Arthurian Legend*, p. 342. [2] See chap. XI—"The Gods in Exile".
[3] Rhys: *Arthurian Legend*, chap. II—"Arthur and Airem".

the three pairs agree in their essential meaning. "Airem", like "Arthur", signifies the "Plough-man", the divine institutor of agriculture; "Etain", the "Shining One", is a fit parallel to "Gwynhwy-var", the "White Apparition"; while "Mider" and "Medrawt" both come from the same root, a word meaning "to hit", either literally, or else metaphori-cally, with the mind, in the sense of coming to a decision. To attempt to explain this myth is to raise the vexed question of the meaning of myth-ology. Is it day and dark that strive for dawn, or summer and winter for the lovely spring, or does it shadow forth the rescue of the grain that makes man's life from the devouring underworld by the farmer's wit? When this can be finally resolved, a multitude of Celtic myths will be explained. Every-where arise the same combatants for the stolen bride; one has the attributes of light, the other is a champion of darkness.

Even in Sir Thomas Malory's version of the Arthurian story, taken by him from French ro-mances far removed from the original tradition, we find the myth subsisting. Medrawt's original place as the lover of Arthur's queen had been taken in the romances by Sir Launcelot, who, if he was not some now undiscoverable Celtic god,[1] must have been an invention of the Norman adapters. But the story which makes Medrawt Arthur's rival

---

[1] In the mysterious Lancelot, not found in Arthurian story before the Norman adaptations of it, Professor Rhys is inclined to see a British sun-god, or solar hero. A number of interesting comparisons are drawn between him and the Peredur and Owain of the later "Mabinogion" tales, as well as with the Gaelic Cuchulainn. See *Studies in the Arthurian Legend.*

has been preserved in the account of how Sir
Mordred would have wedded Guinevere by force,
as part of the rebellion which he made against his
king and uncle.[1]   This strife was Celtic myth long
before it became part of the pseudo-history of early
Britain.   The triads[2] tell us how Arthur and Medrawt raided each other's courts during the owner's
absence.   Medrawt went to Kelli Wic, in Cornwall,
ate and drank everything he could find there, and
insulted Queen Gwynhwyvar, in revenge for which
Arthur went to Medrawt's court and killed man
and beast.   Their struggle only ended with the
Battle of Camlan; and that mythical combat, which
chroniclers have striven to make historical, is full
of legendary detail.   Tradition tells how Arthur
and his antagonist shared their forces three times
during the fight, which caused it to be known as
one of the "Three Frivolous Battles of Britain",
the idea of doing so being one of "Britain's Three
Criminal Resolutions".   Four alone survived the
fray: one, because he was so ugly that all shrank
from him, believing him to be a devil; another,
whom no one touched because he was so beautiful
that they took him for an angel; a third, whose
great strength no one could resist; and Arthur
himself, who, after revenging the death of Gwalchmei upon Medrawt, went to the island of Avilion
to heal him of his grievous wounds.

And thence—from the Elysium of the Celts—

---

[1] *Morte Darthur*, Book XXI, chap. I.
[2] The fullest list of translated triads is contained in the appendix to Probert's
Ancient Laws of Cambria, 1823.   Many are also given as an appendix in Skene's
Four Ancient Books of Wales.

popular belief has always been that he will some day return. But just as the gods of the Gaels are said to dwell sometimes in the "Land of the Living", beyond the western wave, and sometimes in the palace of a hollow hill, so Arthur is sometimes thought to be in Avilion, and sometimes to be sitting with his champions in a charmed sleep in some secret place, waiting for the trumpet to be blown that shall call him forth to reconquer Britain. The legend is found in the Eildon Hills; in the Snowdon district; at Cadbury, in Somerset, the best authenticated Camelot; in the Vale of Neath, in South Wales; as well as in other places. He slumbers, but he has not died. The ancient Welsh poem called "The Verses of the Graves of the Warriors"[1] enumerates the last resting-places of most of the British gods and demi-gods. "The grave of Gwydion is in the marsh of Dinlleu", the grave of Lleu Llaw Gyffes is "under the protection of the sea with which he was familiar", and "where the wave makes a sullen sound is the grave of Dylan"; we know the graves of Pryderi, of Gwalchmei, of March, of Mabon, even of the great Beli, but

"Not wise the thought—a grave for Arthur".[2]

---

[1] *Black Book of Caermarthen XIX*, Vol. I, pp. 309–318 in Skene.

[2] This is Professor Rhys's translation of the Welsh line, no doubt more strictly correct than the famous rendering: "Unknown is the grave of Arthur".

CHAPTER XXII

THE TREASURES OF BRITAIN

It is in keeping with the mythological character of Arthur that the early Welsh tales recorded of him are of a different nature from those which swell the pseudo-histories of Nennius[1] and of Geoffrey of Monmouth. We hear nothing of that subjugation of the countries of Western Europe which fills so large a part in the two books of the *Historia Britonum* which Geoffrey has devoted to him.[2] Conqueror he is, but his conquests are not in any land known to geographers. It is against Hades, and not against Rome, that he achieves his highest triumphs. This is the true history of King Arthur, and we may read more fragments and snatches of it in two prose-tales preserved in the Red Book of Hergest. Both these tales date, in the actual form in which they have come down to us, from the twelfth century. But, in each of them, the writer seems to be stretching out his hands to gather in the dying traditions of a very remote past.

When a Welsh man-at-arms named Rhonabwy lay down, one night, to sleep upon a yellow calf-skin, the only furniture in a noisome hut, in which he had taken shelter, that was comparatively free from vermin, he had the vision which is related in the tale

[1] "History of the Britons", § 50.
[2] Geoffrey of Monmouth. Books IX and X, and chaps. I and II of XI.

called "The Dream of Rhonabwy".[1] He thought that he was travelling with his companions towards the Severn, when they heard a rushing noise behind them, and, looking back, saw a gigantic rider upon a monstrous horse. So terrible was the horseman's appearance that they all started to run from him. But their running was of no avail, for every time the horse drew in its breath, it sucked them back to its very chest, only, however, to fling them forward as it breathed out again. In despair they fell down and besought their pursuer's mercy. He granted it, asked their names, and told them, in return, his own. He was known as Iddawc the Agitator of Britain; for it was he who, in his love of war, had purposely precipitated the Battle of Camlan. Arthur had sent him to reason with Medrawt; but though Arthur had charged him with the fairest sayings he could think of, Iddawc translated them into the harshest he could devise. But he had done seven years' penance, and had been forgiven, and was now riding to Arthur's camp. Thither he insisted upon taking Rhonabwy and his companions.

Arthur's army was encamped for a mile around the ford of Rhyd y Groes, upon both sides of the road; and on a small flat island in the middle of the river was the Emperor himself, in converse with Bedwini the Bishop and Gwarthegyd, the son of Kaw. Like Ossian, when he came back to Ireland after his three hundred years' sojourn in the "Land of Promise",[2] Arthur marvelled at the puny size of

---

[1] Translated by Lady Guest in her *Mabinogion*.
[2] See chap. XIV—"Finn and the Fenians".

the people whom Iddawc had brought for him to look at. "And where, Iddawc, didst thou find these little men?" "I found them, Lord, up yonder on the road." Then the Emperor smiled. "Lord," said Iddawc, "wherefore dost thou laugh?" "Iddawc," replied Arthur, "I laugh not; but it pitieth me that men of such stature as these should have this island in their keeping, after the men that guarded it of yore." Then he turned away, and Iddawc told Rhonabwy and his companions to keep silent, and they would see what they would see.

The scope of such a book as this allows no space to describe the persons and equipments of the warriors who came riding down with their companies to join Arthur, as he made his great march to fight the Battle of Badon, thought by some to be historical, and located at Bath. The reader who turns to the tale itself will see what Rhonabwy saw. Many of Arthur's warriors he will know by name: Caradawc the Strong-armed, who is here called a son, not of Brân, but of Llyr; March son of Meirchion, the underworld king; Kai, described as "the fairest horseman in all Arthur's court"; Gwalchmei, the son of Gwyar and of Arthur himself; Mabon, the son of Modron; Trystan son of Tallwch, the lover of "The Fair Isoult"; Goreu, Arthur's cousin and his rescuer from Manawyddan's bone-prison; these, and many more, will pass before him, as they passed before Rhonabwy during the three days and three nights that he slept and dreamed upon the calf-skin.

This story of the "Dream of Rhonabwy", elaborate

as it is in all its details, is yet, in substance, little more than a catalogue. The intention of its un-known author seems to have been to draw a series of pictures of what he considered to be the principal among Arthur's followers. The other story—that of "Kulhwch and Olwen"—also takes this catalogue form, but the matters enumerated are of a different kind. It is not so much a record of men as of things. Not the heroes of Britain, but the treasures of Britain are its subject. One might compare it with the Gaelic story of the adventures of the three sons of Tuirenn.[1]

The "Thirteen Treasures of Britain" were famous in early legend. They belonged to gods and heroes, and were current in our island till the end of the divine age, when Merlin, fading out of the world, took them with him into his airy tomb, never to be seen by mortal eyes again. According to tradition,[2] they consisted of a sword, a basket, a drinking-horn, a chariot, a halter, a knife, a cauldron, a whetstone, a garment, a pan, a platter, a chess-board, and a mantle, all possessed of not less marvellous qualities than the apples, the pig-skin, the spear, the horses and chariot, the pigs, the hound-whelp, and the cooking-spit which the sons of Tuirenn obtained for Lugh.[3] It is these same legendary treasures that reappear, no doubt, in the story of "Kulhwch and Olwen". The number tallies, for there are thirteen of them. Some are certainly, and others

---

[1] Chap. VIII—"The Gaelic Argonauts".
[2] The list will be found, translated from an old Welsh MS., in the notes to *Kulhwch and Olwen*, in Lady Guest's *Mabinogion*.
[3] Chap. VIII—"The Gaelic Argonauts".

probably, identical with those of the other tradition. That there should be discrepancies need cause no surprise, for it is not unlikely that there were several different versions of their legend. Everyone had heard of the Thirteen Treasures of Britain. Many, no doubt, disputed as to what they were. Others might ask whence they came. The story of "Kulhwch and Olwen" was composed to tell them. They were won by Arthur and his mighty men.

Kulhwch[1] is the hero of the story and Olwen is its heroine, but only, as it were, by courtesy. The pair provide a love-interest which, as in the tales of all primitive people, is kept in the background. The woman, in such romances, takes the place of the gold and gems in a modern "treasure-hunt" story; she is won by overcoming external obstacles, and not by any difficulty in obtaining her own consent. In this romance[2], Kulhwch was the son of a king who afterwards married a widow with a grown-up daughter, whom his stepmother urged Kulhwch to marry. On his modestly replying that he was not yet of an age to wed, she laid the destiny on him that he should never have a wife at all, unless he could win Olwen, the daughter of a terrible father called "Hawthorn, Chief of Giants".[3]

The "Chief of Giants" was as hostile to suitors as he was monstrous in shape; and no wonder! for he knew that on his daughter's marriage his own life would come to an end. Both in this peculiarity

---

[1] Pronounced *Keelhookh.*
[2] The following pages sketch out the main incidents of the story as translated by Lady Guest in her *Mabinogion.*   [3] In Welsh, *Yspaddaden Penkawr.*

and in the description of his ponderous eyebrows, which fell so heavily over his eyes that he could not see until they had been lifted up with forks, he re-minds one of the Fomor, Balor. Of his daughter, on the other hand, the Welsh tale gives a description as beautiful as Olwen was, herself. "More yellow was her head than the flower of the broom, and her skin was whiter than the foam of the wave, and fairer were her hands and her fingers than the blossoms of the wood anemone amidst the spray of the meadow-fountain. The eye of the trained hawk, the glance of the three-mewed falcon was not brighter than hers. Her bosom was more snowy than the breast of the white swan, her cheek was redder than the reddest roses. Whoso beheld her was filled with her love. Four white trefoils sprung up wherever she trod. And there-fore was she called Olwen."[1]

Kulhwch had no need to see her to fall in love with her. He blushed at her very name, and asked his father how he could obtain her in marriage. His father reminded him that he was Arthur's cousin, and advised him to claim Olwen from him as a boon.

So Kulhwch "pricked forth upon a steed with head dappled grey, of four winters old, firm of limb, with shell-formed hoofs, having a bridle of linked gold on his head, and upon him a saddle of costly gold. And in the youth's hand were two spears of silver, sharp, well-tempered, headed with steel,

---

[1] *I.e.* She of the White Track. The beauty of Olwen was proverbial in mediæval Welsh poetry.

three ells in length, of an edge to wound the wind,
and cause blood to flow, and swifter than the fall of
the dewdrop from the blade of reed-grass upon the
earth when the dew of June is at the heaviest. A
gold-hilted sword was upon his thigh, the blade of
which was of gold, bearing a cross of inlaid gold of
the hue of the lightning of heaven; his war-horn
was of ivory. Before him were two brindled white-
breasted greyhounds, having strong collars of rubies
about their necks, reaching from the shoulder to the
ear. And the one that was on the left side bounded
across to the right side, and the one on the right to
the left, and like two sea-swallows sported around
him. And his courser cast up four sods with his
four hoofs, like four swallows in the air, about his
head, now above, now below. About him was a
four-cornered cloth of purple, and an apple of gold
was at each corner, and every one of the apples was
of the value of an hundred kine. And there was
precious gold of the value of three hundred kine
upon his shoes, and upon his stirrups, from his knee
to the tip of his toe. And the blade of grass bent
not beneath him, so light was his courser's tread as
he journeyed towards the gate of Arthur's palace."

Nor did this bold suitor stand greatly upon ceremony. He arrived after the portal of the palace
had been closed for the night, and, contrary to all
precedent, sent to Arthur demanding instant entry.
Although, too, it was the custom for visitors to dis-
mount at the horse-block at the gate, he did not do
so, but rode his charger into the hall. After greet-
ings had passed between him and Arthur, and he

had announced his name, he demanded Olwen for his bride at the hands of the Emperor and his warriors.

Neither Arthur nor any of his court had ever heard of Olwen. However, he promised his cousin either to find her for him, or to prove that there was no such person. He ordered his most skilful warriors to accompany Kulhwch; Kai, with his companion Bedwyr, the swiftest of men; Kynddelig, who was as good a guide in a strange country as in his own; Gwrhyr, who knew all the languages of men, as well as of all other creatures; Gwalchmei, who never left an adventure unachieved; and Menw, who could render himself and his companions invisible at will.

They travelled until they came to a castle on an open plain. Feeding on the plain was a countless herd of sheep, and, on a mound close by, a monstrous shepherd with a monstrous dog. Menw cast a spell over the dog, and they approached the shepherd. He was called Custennin, a brother of Hawthorn, while his wife was a sister of Kulhwch's own mother. The evil chief of giants had reduced his brother to servitude, and murdered all his twenty-four sons save one, who was kept hidden in a stone chest. Therefore he welcomed Kulhwch and the embassy from Arthur, and promised to help them secretly, the more readily since Kai offered to take the one surviving son under his protection. Custennin's wife procured Kulhwch a secret meeting with Olwen, and the damsel did not altogether discourage her wooer's suit.

The party started for Hawthorn's castle. Without raising any alarm, they slew the nine porters and the nine watch-dogs, and came unhindered into the hall. They greeted the ponderous giant, and announced the reason of their coming. " Where are my pages and my servants?" he said. " Raise up the forks beneath my two eyebrows which have fallen over my eyes, so that I may see the fashion of my son-in-law." He glared at them, and told them to come again upon the next day.

They turned to go, and, as they did so, Hawthorn seized a poisoned dart, and threw it after them. But Bedwyr caught it, and cast it back, wounding the giant's knee. They left him grumbling, slept at the house of Custennin, and returned, the next morning.

Again they demanded Olwen from her father, threatening him with death if he refused. " Her four great-grandmothers, and her four great-grand-sires are yet alive," replied Hawthorn; "it is needful that I take counsel of them." So they turned away, and, as they went, he flung a second dart, which Menw caught, and hurled back, piercing the giant's body.

The next time they came, Hawthorn warned them not to shoot at him again, unless they desired death. Then he ordered his eyebrows to be lifted up, and, as soon as he could see, he flung a poisoned dart straight at Kulhwch. But the suitor himself caught it, and flung it back, so that it pierced Hawthorn's eyeball and came out through the back of his head. Here again we are reminded of the myth of Lugh and Balor. Hawthorn, however, was not killed, though he was very much discomforted. "A cursed ungentle son-in-law, truly!" he complained. "As long as I remain alive, my eyesight will be the worse. Whenever I go against the wind, my eyes will water; and peradventure my head will burn, and I shall have a giddiness every new moon. Cursed be the fire in which it was forged! Like the bite of a mad dog is the stroke of this poisoned iron."

It was now the turn of Kulhwch and his party to warn the giant that there must be no more dart-throwing. He appeared, indeed, more amenable to reason, and allowed himself to be placed opposite to Kulhwch, in a chair, to discuss the amount of his daughter's bride-price.

Its terms, as he gradually unfolded them, were terrific. The blood-fine paid for Cian to Lugh seems, indeed, a trifle beside it. To obtain grain, for food and liquor at his daughter's wedding, a vast hill which he showed to Kulhwch must be rooted up, levelled, ploughed, sown, and harvested in one day. No one could do this except Amaethon son of Dôn, the divine husbandman, and Govannan son of Dôn, the divine smith, and they must have the service of three pairs of magic oxen. He must also have returned to him the same nine bushels of flax which he had sown in his youth, and which had never come up; for only out of this very flax should be made the white wimple for Olwen's head. For mead, too, he must have honey "nine times sweeter than the honey of the virgin swarm".

Then followed the enumeration of the thirteen treasures to be paid to him as dowry. Such a list of wedding presents was surely never known! No pot could hold such honey as he demanded but the magic vessel of Llwyr, the son of Llwyryon. There would not be enough food for all the wedding-guests, unless he had the basket of Gwyddneu Garanhir, from which all the men in the world could be fed, thrice nine at a time. No cauldron could cook the meat, except that of Diwrnach the Gael. The mystic drinking-horn of Gwlgawd Gododin must be there, to give them drink. The harp of Teirtu, which, like the Dagda's, played of itself, must make music for them. The giant father-in-law's hair could only be shorn with one instrument—the tusk of White-tooth, King of the Boars, and not even by that unless it was plucked alive out of its owner's mouth. Also, before the hair could be cut, it must be spread out, and this could not be done until it had been first softened with the blood of the perfectly black sorceress, daughter of the perfectly white sorceress, from the Source of the Stream of Sorrow, on the borders of hell. Nor could the sorceress's blood be kept warm enough unless it was placed in the bottles of Gwyddolwyn Gorr, which preserved the heat of any liquor put into them, though it was carried from the east of the world to the west. Another set of bottles he must also have to keep milk for his guests in— those bottles of Rhinnon Rhin Barnawd in which no drink ever turned sour. For himself, he required the sword of Gwrnach the Giant, which that personage would never allow out of his own keeping, because it was destined that he himself should fall by it. Last of all, he must be given the comb, the razor, and the scissors which lay between the ears of Twrch Trwyth, a king changed into the most terrible of wild boars.

It is the chase of this boar which gives the story of "Kulhwch and Olwen" its alternative title—"The Twrch Trwyth". The task was one worthy of gods and demi-gods. Its contemplation might well have appalled Kulhwch, who, however, was not so easily frightened. To every fresh demand, every new obstacle put in his way, he gave the same answer:

"It will be easy for me to compass this, although thou mayest think that it will not be easy".

Whether it was easy or not will be seen from the conditions under which alone the hunt could be brought to a successful end. No ordinary hounds or huntsmen would avail. The chief of the pack must be Drudwyn, the whelp of Greid the son of Eri, led in the one leash that would hold him, fastened, by the one chain strong enough, to the one collar that would contain his neck. No hunts-man could hunt with this dog except Mabon son of Modron; and he had, ages before, been taken from between his mother and the wall when he was three nights old, and it was not known where he was, or even whether he were living or dead. There was only one steed that could carry Mabon, namely Gwynn Mygdwn, the horse of Gweddw. Two other marvellous hounds, the cubs of Gast Rhymhi, must also be obtained; they must be held in the only leash they would not break, for it would be made out of the beard of the giant Dissull, plucked from him while he was still alive.   Even with this, no huntsman could lead them except Kynedyr Wyllt, who was himself nine times more wild than the wildest beast upon the mountains.   All Arthur's mighty men must come to help, even Gwyn son of Nudd, upon his black horse; and how could he be spared from his terrible duty of restraining the devils in hell from breaking loose and destroying the world?

Here is material for romance indeed!   But, un-happily, we shall never know the full story of how all these magic treasures were obtained, all these magic hounds captured and compelled to hunt, all these magic huntsmen brought to help.   The story—which Mr. Nutt[1] considers to be, " saving the finest tales of the ' Arabian Nights', the greatest romantic fairy tale the world has ever known"—is not, as we have it now, complete.   It reads fully enough; but, on casting backwards and forwards, between the list of feats to be performed and the body of the tale which is supposed to relate them all, we find many of them wanting.   "The host of Arthur", we are told, "dispersed themselves into parties of one and two", each party intent upon some separate quest. The adventures of some of them have come down, but those of others have not.   We are told how Kai slew Gwrnach the Giant with his own sword; how Gwyrthur son of Greidawl, Gwyn's rival for the love of Creudylad, saved an anthill from fire, and how the grateful ants searched for and found

[1] In his notes to his edition of Lady Guest's *Mabinogion*.   Published 1902.

the very flax-seeds sown by Hawthorn in his youth;
how Arthur's host surrounded and took Gast
Rhymhi's cubs, and how Kai and Bedwyr overcame
Dissull, and plucked out his beard with wooden
tweezers, to make a leash for them. We learn how
Arthur went to Ireland, and brought back the cauldron of Diwrnach the Gael, full of Irish money; how
White-tusk the Boar-king was chased and killed;
and how Arthur condescended to slay the perfectly
black sorceress with his own hand. That others of
the treasures were acquired is hinted rather than
said. Most important of all (for so much depended
on him), we find out where the stolen Mabon was,
and learn how he was rescued.

So many ages had elapsed since Mabon had disappeared that there seemed little hope of ever finding news of him. Nevertheless Gwrhyr, who spoke
the languages of all creatures, went to enquire of that
ancient bird, the Ousel of Cilgwri. But the Ousel,
though in her time she had pecked a smith's anvil
down to the size of a nut, was yet too young to have
heard of Mabon. She sent Gwrhyr to a creature
formed before her, the Stag of Redynvre. But
though the Stag had lived to see an oak-sapling
slowly grow to be a tree with a thousand branches,
and as slowly decay again till it was a withered
stump, he had never heard of Mabon.

Therefore he sent him on to a creature still older
than himself—the Owl of Cwm Cawlwyd. The
wood she lived in had been thrice rooted up, and
had thrice re-sown itself, and yet, in all that immense
time, she had never heard of Mabon. There was

but one who might have, she told Gwrhyr, and he was the Eagle of Gwern Abwy.

Here, at last, they struck Mabon's trail. "The Eagle said: 'I have been here for a great space of time, and when I first came hither there was a rock here, from the top of which I pecked at the stars every evening; and now it is not so much as a span high. From that day to this I have been here, and I have never heard of the man for whom you inquire, except once when I went in search of food as far as Llyn Llyw. And when I came there, I struck my talons into a salmon, thinking he would serve me as food for a long time. But he drew me into the deep, and I was scarcely able to escape from him. After that I went with my whole kindred to attack him, and to try to destroy him, but he sent messengers, and made peace with me; and came and besought me to take fifty fish spears out of his back. Unless he know something of him whom you seek, I cannot tell who may. However, I will guide you to the place where he is.'"

It happened that the Salmon did know. With every tide he went up the Severn as far as the walls of Gloucester, and there, he said, he had found such wrong as he had never found anywhere else. So he took Kai and Gwrhyr upon his shoulders and carried them to the wall of the prison where a captive was heard lamenting. This was Mabon son of Modron, who was suffering such imprisonment as not even Lludd of the Silver Hand or Greid, the son of Eri,[1]

---

[1] So says the text. But a triad quoted by Lady Guest in her notes gives the "Three Paramount Prisoners of Britain" differently. "The three supreme prisoners

the other two of the "Three Paramount Prisoners of Britain", had endured before him. But it came to an end now; for Kai sent to Arthur, and he and his warriors stormed Gloucester, and brought Mabon away.

All was at last ready for the final achievement— the hunting of Twrch Trwyth, who was now, with his seven young pigs, in Ireland. Before he was roused, it was thought wise to send the wizard Menw to find out by ocular inspection whether the comb, the scissors, and the razor were still between his ears. Menw took the form of a bird, and settled upon the Boar's head. He saw the coveted treasures, and tried to take one of them, but Twrch Trwyth shook himself so violently that some of the venom from his bristles spurted over Menw, who was never quite well again from that day.

Then the hunt was up, the men surrounded him, and the dogs were loosed at him from every side. On the first day, the Irish attacked him. On the second day, Arthur's household encountered him and were worsted. Then Arthur himself fought with him for nine days and nine nights without even killing one of the little pigs.

A truce was now called, so that Gwrhyr, who spoke all languages, might go and parley with him. Gwrhyr begged him to give up in peace the comb, the scissors, and the razor, which were all that

of the Island of Britain, Llyr Llediath in the prison of Euroswydd Wledig, and Madoc, or Mabon, and Gweir, son of Gweiryoth; and one more exalted than the three, and that was Arthur, who was for three nights in the Castle of Oeth and Anoeth, and three nights in the prison of Wen Pendragon, and three nights in the dark prison under the stone. And one youth released him from these three prisons; that youth was Goreu the son of Custennin, his cousin."

Arthur wanted. But the Boar Trwyth, indignant
of having been so annoyed, would not. On the
contrary, he promised to go on the morrow into
Arthur's country, and do all the harm he could
there.

So Twrch Trwyth with his seven pigs crossed
the sea into Wales, and Arthur followed with his
warriors in the ship "Prydwen". Here the story
becomes wonderfully realistic and circumstantial.
We are told of every place they passed through on
the long chase through South Wales, and can trace
the course of the hunt over the map.[1] We know of
every check the huntsmen had, and what happened
every time the boars turned to bay. The "casualty-
list" of Arthur's men is completely given; and we
can also follow the shrinking of Twrch Trwyth's
herd, as his little pigs fell one by one. None were
left but Trwyth himself by the time the Severn
estuary was reached, at the mouth of the Wye.

Here the hunt came up with him, and drove him
into the water, and in this unfamiliar element he
was outmatched. Osla Big-Knife[2], Manawyddan
son of Llyr, Kacmwri, the servant of Arthur, and
Gwyngelli caught him by his four feet and plunged
his head under water, while the two chief huntsmen,
Mabon son of Modron, and Kyledyr Willt, came,
one on each side of him, and took the scissors and
the razor. Before they could get the comb, how-

---

[1] See Rhys: *Celtic Folklore*, chap. x—"Place-name Stories".
[2] The "big knife" was, we are told in the story, "a short broad dagger.
When Arthur and his hosts came before a torrent, they would seek for a narrow
place where they might pass the water, and would lay the sheathed dagger across
the torrent, and it would form a bridge sufficient for the armies of the three islands
of Britain, and of the three islands adjacent, with their spoil."

ever, he shook himself free, and struck out for Cornwall, leaving Osla and Kacmwri half-drowned in the Severn.

And all this trouble, we are told, was mere play compared with the trouble they had with him in Cornwall before they could get the comb. But, at last, they secured it, and drove the boar out over the deep sea. He passed out of sight, with two of the magic hounds in pursuit of him, and none of them have ever been heard of since.

The sight of these treasures, paraded before Hawthorn, chief of giants, was, of course, his death-warrant. All who wished him ill came to gloat over his downfall. But they should have been put to shame by the giant, whose end had, at least, a certain dignity. "My daughter", he said to Kulhwch, "is yours, but you need not thank me for it, but Arthur, who has accomplished all this. By my free will you should never have had her, for with her I lose my life."

Thereupon they cut off his head, and put it upon a pole; and that night the undutiful Olwen became Kulhwch's bride.

CHAPTER XXIII

THE GODS AS KING ARTHUR'S KNIGHTS

It is not, however, by such fragments of legend that Arthur is best known to English readers. Not Arthur the god, but Arthur the "blameless king", who founded the Table Round, from which he sent forth his knights "to ride abroad redressing human wrongs",[1] is the figure which the name conjures up. Nor is it even from Sir Thomas Malory's Morte Darthur that this conception comes to most of us, but from Tennyson's *Idylls of the King*. But Tennyson has so modernized the ancient tradition that it retains little of the old Arthur but the name. He tells us himself that his poem had but very slight relation to—

> . . . "that gray king, whose name, a ghost,
> Streams like a cloud, man-shaped, from mountain-peak,
> And cleaves to cairn and cromlech still; or him
> Of Geoffrey's book, or him of Malleor's . . . ";[2]

but that he merely used the legend to give a substantial form to his ideal figure of the perfect English gentleman—a title to which the original Arthur could scarcely have laid claim. Still less does there remain in it the least trace of anything that could suggest mythology.

As much as this, however, might be said of

---

[1] Tennyson's *Idylls of the King; Guinevere.*   [2] *Ibid.* To the Queen.

Malory's book.   We may be fairly certain that the good Sir Thomas had no idea that the personages of whom he wrote had ever been anything different from the Christian knights which they had become in the late French romances from which he compiled his own fifteenth-century work.   The old gods had been, from time to time, very completely euhemerized.   The characters of the " Four Branches of the Mabinogi" are still recognizable as divine beings. In the later Welsh stories, however, their divinity merely hangs about them in shreds and tatters, and the first Norman adapters of these stories made them still more definitely human.   By the time Malory came to build up his Morte Darthur from the foreign romances, they had altered so much that the shapes and deeds of gods could only be recognized under their mediæval knightly disguises by those who had known them in their ancient forms.

We have chosen Malory's Morte Darthur, as almost the sole representative of Arthurian literature later than the Welsh poems and prose stories, for three reasons.   Firstly, because it is the English Arthurian romance *par excellence* from which all later English authors, including Tennyson, have drawn their material.   Secondly, because the mass of foreign literature dealing with the subject of Arthur is in itself a life-study, and could not by any possibility be compressed within the limits of a chapter. Thirdly, because Malory's fine judgment caused him to choose the best and most typical foreign tales to weave into his own romance; and hence it is that we find most of our old British gods—both those of the earlier cycle and those of the system connected with Arthur—striding disguised through his pages.

Curiously enough, Sir Edward Strachey, in his preface to the "Globe" edition of Caxton's Morte Darthur, uses almost the same image to describe Malory's prose-poem that Matthew Arnold handled with such effect, in his *Study of Celtic Literature*, to point out the real nature of the Mabinogion. "Malory", he says, "has built a great, rambling, mediæval castle, the walls of which enclose rude and even ruinous work of earlier times." How rude and how ruinous these relics were Malory doubtless had not the least idea, for he has completely jumbled the ancient mythology. Not only do gods of the older and newer order appear together, but the same deities, under very often only slightly varying names, come up again and again as totally different characters.

Take, for example, the ancient deity of death and Hades. As King Brandegore, or Brandegoris (Brân of Gower), he brings five thousand mounted men to oppose King Arthur;[1] but, as Sir Brandel, or Brandiles (Brân of Gwales[2]), he is a valiant Knight of the Round Table, who dies fighting in Arthur's service.[3] Again, under his name of Uther Pendragon (Uther Ben), he is Arthur's father;[4] though as King Ban of Benwyk (the "Square Enclosure", doubtless the same as Taliesin's *Caer Pedryvan* and

---

[1] *Morte Darthur*, Book I, chap. x.
[2] Gresholm Island, the scene of "The Entertaining of the Noble Head".
[3] *Morte Darthur*, Book XX, chap. VIII. [4] *Ibid.*, Book I, chap. III.

Malory's *Carbonek*), he is a foreign monarch, who is Arthur's ally.[1] Yet again, as the father of Guinevere, Ogyrvran has become Leodegrance.[2] As King Uriens, or Urience, of Gore (Gower), he marries one of Arthur's sisters,[3] fights against him, but finally tenders his submission, and is enrolled among his knights.[4] Urien may also be identified in the Morte Darthur as King Rience, or Ryons, of North Wales,[5] and as King Nentres of Garloth;[6] while, to crown the varied disguises of this Proteus of British gods, he appears in an isolated episode as Balan, who fights with his brother Balin until they kill one another.[7]

One may generally tell the divinities of the underworld in these romances by their connection, not with the settled and civilized parts of England, but with the wild and remote north and west, and the still wilder and remoter islands. Just as Brân and Urien are kings of Gower, so Arawn, under the corruptions of his name into "Anguish" and "Anguissance", is made King of Scotland or Ireland, both countries having been probably confounded, as the same land of the Scotti, or Gaels.[8] Pwyll, Head of Annwn, we likewise discover under two disguises. As Pelles, "King of the Foreign Country"[9] and Keeper of the Holy Grail, he is a personage of great mythological significance, albeit the real nature of him and his surroundings has been overlaid with a Christian veneer as foreign to the

[1] *Morte Darthur*, Book I, chap. VIII.
[2] *Ibid.*, Book I, chap. XVI.
[3] *Ibid.*, Book I, chap. II.
[4] *Ibid.*, Book IV, chap. IV.
[5] *Ibid.*, Book I, chap. XXIV.
[6] *Ibid.*, Book I, chap. II.
[7] *Ibid.*, Book II, chap. XVIII.
[8] *Ibid.*, Book V, chap. II; Book VIII, chap. IV; Book XIX chap. XI.
[9] *Ibid.*, Book XI, chap. II.

original of Pelles as his own kingdom was to Arthur's knights. The Chief of Hades figures as a "cousin nigh unto Joseph of Arimathie",[1] who, "while he might ride supported much Christendom, and holy church".[2] He is represented as the father of Elayne (Elen[3]), whom he gives in marriage to Sir Launcelot, bestowing upon the couple a residence called "Castle Bliant",[4] the name of which, there is good evidence to show, is connected with that of Pwyll's vassal called Teirnyon Twryf Vliant in the first of the Mabinogi.[5] Under his other name of "Sir Pelleas"— the hero of Tennyson's Idyll of *Pelleas and Ettarre*—the primitive myth of Pwyll is touched at a different point. After his unfortunate love-passage with Ettarre (or Ettard, as Malory calls her), Pelleas is represented as marrying Nimue,[6] whose original name, which was Rhiannon, reached this form, as well as that of "Vivien", through a series of miscopyings of successive scribes.[7]

With Pelles, or Pelleas, is associated a King Pellean, or Pellam, his son, and, equally with him, the Keeper of the Grail, who can be no other than Pryderi.[8] Like that deity in the Mabinogi of Mâth, he is defeated by one of the gods of light. The dealer of the blow, however, is not Arthur, as successor to Gwydion, but Balin, the Gallo-British sun-god Belinus.[9]

[1] *Morte Darthur*, Book XI, chap. II.   [2] *Ibid.*, Book XVII, chap. v.
[3] *Ibid.*, Book XI, chap. II.   [4] *Ibid.*, Book XII, chap. v.
[5] Rhys: *Arthurian Legend*, p. 283.   [6] *Morte Darthur*, Book IV, chap. XXIII.
[7] Rhys: *Arthurian Legend*, p. 284 and note.
[8] The subject is treated at length by Professor Rhys in his *Arthurian Legend* chap. XII—"Pwyll and Pelles".   [9] *Morte Darthur*, Book II, chap. xv.

Another dark deity, Gwyn son of Nudd, we discover under all of his three titles. Called variously
"Sir Gwinas",[1] "Sir Guynas",[2] and "Sir Gwenbaus "[3] by Malory, the Welsh Gwynwas (or Gwyn)
is altogether on Arthur's side. The Cornish Melwas, split into two different knights, divides his
allegiance. As Sir Melias,[4] or Meleaus,[5] de Lile
("of the Isle"), he is a Knight of the Round
Table, though, on the quarrel between Arthur and
Launcelot, he sides with the knight against the
king. But as Sir Meliagraunce, or Meliagaunce,
it is he who, as in the older myth, captures Queen
Guinevere and carries her off to his castle.[6] Under
his Somerset name of Avallon, or Avallach, he is
connected with the episode of the Grail. King
Evelake[7] is a Saracen ruler who was converted by
Joseph of Arimathea, and brought by him to Britain.
In his convert's enthusiasm, he attempted the quest
of the holy vessel, but was not allowed to succeed.[8]
As a consolation, however, it was divinely promised
him that he should not die until he had seen a
knight of his blood in the ninth degree who should
achieve it. This was done by Sir Percivale, King
Evelake being then three hundred years old.[9]

Turning from deities of darkness to deities of
light, we find the sky-god figuring largely in the
Morte Darthur. The Lludd of the earlier mythology is Malory's King Loth, or Lot, of Orkney,[10]

[1] *Morte Darthur*, Book I, chap. XII.   [2] *Ibid.*, Book I, chap. XV.
[3] *Ibid.*, Book I, chap. IX.   [4] *Ibid.*, Book XIII, chap. XII.
[5] *Ibid.*, Book XIX, chap. XI.   [6] *Ibid.*, Book XIX, chap. II.
[7] *Ibid.*, Book XIII, chap. X.   [8] *Ibid.*, Book XIV, chap. IV.
[9] *Morte Darthur*, Book XIV, chap. IV.   [10] Rhys: *Arthurian Legend*, p. II.

through an intrigue with whose wife Arthur becomes the father of Sir Mordred. Lot's wife was
the mother also of Sir Gawain, whose birth Malory
does not, however, attribute to Arthur, though such
must have been the original form of the myth.[1]   Sir
Gawain, of the Arthurian legend, is the Gwalchmei
of the Welsh stories, the successor of the still earlier
Lleu Llaw Gyffes, just as Sir Mordred—the Welsh
Medrawt—corresponds to Lleu's brother Dylan.
As Sir Mordred retains the dark character of
Medrawt, so Sir Gawain, even in Malory,[2] shows
the attributes of a solar deity.   We are told that
his strength increased gradually from dawn till high
noon, and then as gradually decreased again—a piece
of pagan symbolism which forms a good example of
the appositeness of Sir Edward Strachey's figure;
for it stands out of the mediæval narrative like an
ancient brick in some more modern building.

The Zeus of the later cycle, Emrys or Myrddin,
appears in the Morte Darthur under both his names.
The word "Emrys" becomes "Bors", and King
Bors of Gaul is made a brother of King Ban of
Benwyck[3]—that is, Brân of the Square Enclosure,
the ubiquitous underworld god.   Myrddin we meet
under no such disguise.   The ever-popular Merlin
still retains intact the attributes of the sky-god.
He remains above, and apart from all the knights,
higher even in some respects than King Arthur,
to whom he stands in much the same position as
Mâth does to Gwydion in the Mabinogi.[4]   Like

---

[1] *Op. cit.*, pp. 21-22.   [2] *Morte Darthur*, Book IV, chap. XVIII.
[3] *Ibid.*, Book I, chap. VIII.   [4] Rhys: *Arthurian Legend*, p. 23.

Mâth, he is an enchanter, and, like Mâth, too, who could hear everything said in the world, in however low a tone, if only the wind met it, he is practically omniscient. The account of his final disappearance, as told in the Morte Darthur, is only a re-embellishment of the original story, the nature-myth giving place to what novelists call "a feminine interest". Everyone knows how the great magician fell into a dotage upon the "lady of the lake" whom Malory calls "Nimue", and Tennyson "Vivien"— both names being that of "Rhiannon" in disguise. "Merlin would let her have no rest, but always he would be with her . . . and she was ever passing weary of him, and fain would have been delivered of him, for she was afeard of him because he was a devil's son, and she could not put him away by no means. And so on a time it happed that Merlin showed to her in a rock whereas was a great wonder, and wrought by enchantment, that went under a great stone. So, by her subtle working, she made Merlin to go under that stone to let her wit of the marvels there, but she wrought so there for him that he never came out for all the craft that he could do. And so she departed and left Merlin."[1]

Merlin's living grave is still to be seen at the end of the *Val des Fées*, in the forest of Brécilien, in Brittany. The tomb of stone is certainly but a prosaic equivalent for the tower of woven air in which the heaven-god went to his rest. Still, it is not quite so unpoetic as the leather sack in which

[1] *Morte Darthur*, Book IV, chap. I.

Rhiannon, the original of Nimue, caught and imprisoned Gwawl, the earlier Merlin, like a badger in a bag.[1]

Elen, Myrddin's consort, appears in Malory as five different "Elaines". Two of them are wives of the dark god, under his names of "King Ban"[2] and "King Nentres".[3] A third is called the daughter of King Pellinore, a character of uncertain origin.[4] But the two most famous are the ladies who loved Sir Launcelot—"Elaine the Fair, Elaine the lovable, Elaine the lily maid of Astolat",[5] and the luckier and less scrupulous Elaine, daughter of King Pelles, and mother of Sir Launcelot's son, Galahad.[6]

But it is time, now that the most important figures of British mythology have been shown under their knightly disguises, and their place in Arthurian legend indicated, to pass on to some account of the real subject-matter of Sir Thomas Malory's romance. Externally, it is the history of an Arthur, King of Britain, whom most people of Malory's time considered as eminently a historical character. Around this central narrative of Arthur's reign and deeds are grouped, in the form of episodes, the personal exploits of the knights believed to have supported him by forming a kind of household guard. But, with the exception of a little magnified and distorted legendary history, the whole cycle of romance may

---

[1] See chap. XVII—"The Adventures of the Gods of Hades".
[2] *Morte Darthur*, Book IV, chap. I.   [3] *Ibid.*, Book I, chap. II.
[4] *Ibid.*, Book III, chap. XV.
[5] Whose story is told by Tennyson in the *Idylls*, and by Malory in Book XVIII of the *Morte Darthur*.   [6] *Morte Darthur*, Book XI, chaps. II and III.

be ultimately resolved into a few myths, not only retold, but recombined in several forms by their various tellers. The Norman adapters of the *Matière de Bretagne* found the British mythology already in process of transformation, some of the gods having dwindled into human warriors, and others into hardly less human druids and magicians. Under their hands the British warriors became Norman knights, who did their deeds of prowess in the tilt-yard, and found their inspiration in the fantastic chivalry popularized by the Trouveres, while the druids put off their still somewhat barbaric druidism for the more conventional magic of the Latin races. More than this, as soon as the real sequence and *raison d'être* of the tales had been lost sight of, their adapters used a free hand in reweaving them. Most of the romancers had their favourite characters whom they made the central figure in their stories. Sir Gawain, Sir Percival, Sir Tristrem, and Sir Owain (all of them probably once local British sun-gods) appear as the most important personages of the romances called after their names, stories of the doughty deeds of christened knights who had little left about them either of Briton or of pagan.

It is only the labours of the modern scholar that can bring back to us, at this late date, things long forgotten when Malory's book was issued from Caxton's press. But oblivion is not annihilation, and Professor Rhys points out to us the old myths lying embedded in their later setting with almost the same certainty with which the geologist can show us the fossils in the rock.[1]   Thus treated, they resolve themselves into three principal *motifs*, prominent everywhere in Celtic mythology: the birth of the sun-god; the struggle between light and darkness; and the raiding of the underworld by friendly gods for the good of man.

The first has been already dealt with.[2]   It is the retelling of the story of the origin of the sun-god in the Mabinogi of Mâth, son of Mâthonwy.   For Gwydion we now have Arthur; instead of Arianrod, the wife of the superannuated sky-god Nwyvre, we find the wife of King Lot, the superannuated sky-god Lludd; Lleu Llaw Gyffes rises again as Sir Gawain (Gwalchmei), and Dylan as Sir Mordred (Medrawt); while the wise Merlin, the Jupiter of the new system, takes the place of his wise prototype, Mâth.   Connected with this first myth is the second—the struggle between light and darkness, of which there are several versions in the Morte Darthur.   The leading one is the rebellion of the evilly-disposed Sir Mordred against Arthur and Sir Gawain; while, on other stages, Balan—the dark god Brân—fights with Balin—the sun-god Belinus; and the same Balin, or Belinus, gives an almost mortal stroke to Pellam, the Pryderi of the older mythology.

The same myth has also a wider form, in which the battle is waged for possession of a maiden. Thus (to seek no other instances) Gwynhwyvar was contended for by Arthur and Medrawt, or, in an

---

[1] See his *Studies in the Arthurian Legend.*
[2] See chap. xxi—" The Mythological ' Coming of Arthur ' ".

earlier form of the myth, by Arthur and Gwyn.   In
the Morte Darthur, Gwyn, under the corruption of
his Cornish name Melwas into " Sir Meliagraunce ",
still captures Guinevere, but it is no longer Arthur
who rescues her.   That task, or privilege, has fallen
to a new champion.   It is Sir Launcelot who follows
Sir Meliagraunce, defeats and slays him, and rescues
the fair captive.[1]   But Sir Launcelot, it must be
stated—probably to the surprise of those to whom
the Arthurian story without Launcelot and Queen
Guinevere must seem almost like the play of
" Hamlet with Hamlet left out ",—is unknown to
the original tradition.   Welsh song and story are
silent with regard to him, and he is not improbably
a creation of some Norman romancer who calmly
appropriated to his hero's credit deeds earlier told
of other "knights".

But the romantic treatment of these two myths
by the adapters of the *Matière de Bretagne* are of
smaller interest to us at the present day than that
of the third.   The attraction of the Arthurian story
lies less in the battles of Arthur or the loves of
Guinevere than in the legend that has given it its
lasting popularity—the Christian romance of the
Quest of the Holy Grail.   So great and various
has been the inspiration of this legend to noble
works both of art and literature that it seems almost
a kind of sacrilege to trace it back, like all the rest
of Arthur's story, to a paganism which could not
have even understood, much less created, its mystical beauty.   None the less is the whole story

[1] *Morte Darthur*, Book XIX, chaps. I-IX.

directly evolved from primitive pagan myths concerning a miraculous cauldron of fertility and inspiration.

In the later romances, the Holy Grail is a Christian relic of marvellous potency. It had held the Paschal lamb eaten at the Last Supper;[1] and, after the death of Christ, Joseph of Arimathea had filled it with the Saviour's blood.[2] But before it received this colouring, it had been the magic cauldron of all the Celtic mythologies—the Dagda's "Undry" which fed all who came to it, and from which none went away unsatisfied;[3] Brân's cauldron of Renovation, which brought the dead back to life;[4] the cauldron of Ogyrvran the Giant, from which the Muses ascended;[5] the cauldrons captured by Cuchulainn from the King of the Shadowy City,[6] and by Arthur from the chief of Hades;[7] as well as several other mythic vessels of less note.

In its transition from pagan to Christian form, hardly one of the features of the ancient myth has been really obscured. We may recount the chief attributes, as Taliesin tells them in his " Spoiling of Annwn", of the cauldron captured by Arthur. It was the property of Pwyll, and of his son Pryderi, who lived in a kingdom of the other world called, among other titles, the " Revolving Castle ", the " Four-cornered Castle ", the " Castle of Revelry ", the

---

[1] *Morte Darthur*, Book XVII, chap. xx.
[2] *Ibid.*, Book II, chap. xvi; Book XI, chap. xiv.
[3] See chap. v—"The Gods of the Gaels ".
[4] See chap. xviii—" The Wooing of Branwen and the Beheading of Brân "
[5] See chap. xxi—" The Mythological ' Coming of Arthur ' ".
[6] See chap. xii—" The Irish Iliad ".
[7] Chap xxi—" The Mythological ' Coming of Arthur ' ".

"Kingly Castle", the "Glass Castle", and the "Castle of Riches". This place was surrounded by the sea, and in other ways made difficult of access; there was no lack of wine there, and its happy inhabitants spent with music and feasting an existence which neither disease nor old age could assail. As for the cauldron, it had a rim of pearls around its edge; the fire beneath it was kept fanned by the breaths of nine maidens; it spoke, doubtless in words of prophetic wisdom; and it would not cook the food of a perjurer or coward.[1] Here we have considerable data on which to base a parallel between the pagan cauldron and the Christian Grail.

Nor have we far to go in search of correspondences, for they are nearly all preserved in Malory's romance. The mystic vessel was kept by King Pelles, who is Pwyll, in a castle called "Carbonek", a name which resolves itself, in the hands of the philologist, into *Caer bannawg*, the "square" or "four - cornered castle"—in other words, the *Caer Pedryvan* of Taliesin's poem.[2] Of the character of the place as a "Castle of Riches" and a "Castle of Revelry", where "bright wine was the drink of the host", we have more than a hint in the account, twice given,[3] of how, upon the appearance of the Grail—borne, it should be noticed, by a maiden or angel—the hall was filled with good odours, and every knight found on the table all the kinds of meat and drink he could imagine as most

---

[1] Chap. xxi—"The Mythological 'Coming of Arthur'".
[2] Rhys: *Arthurian Legend*, p. 305.
[3] *Morte Darthur*, Book XI, chaps. ii and iv.

desirable.   It could not be seen by sinners,[1] a
Christian refinement of the savage idea of a pot
that would not cook a coward's food; but the sight
of it alone would cure of wounds and sickness those
who approached it faithfully and humbly,[2] and in its
presence neither old age nor sickness could oppress
them.[3]   And, though in Malory we find no reference either to the spot having been surrounded by
water, or to the castle as a "revolving" one, we
have only to turn from the Morte Darthur to the
romance entitled the *Seint Greal* to discover both.
Gwalchmei, going to the castle of King Peleur
(Pryderi), finds it encircled by a great water, while
Peredur, approaching the same place, sees it turning
with greater speed than the swiftest wind.   Moreover, archers on the walls shoot so vigorously that
no armour can resist their shafts, which explains
how it happened that, of those that went with
Arthur, "except seven, none returned from Caer
Sidi".[4]

It is noticeable that Arthur himself never attempts the quest of the Grail, though it was he
who had achieved its pagan original.   We find in
Malory four competitors for the mantle of Arthur
—Sir Pelleas,[5] Sir Bors, Sir Percivale, and Sir
Galahad.[6]   The first of these may be put out of
court at once, Sir Pelleas, who, being himself Pelles,

---

[1] *Morte Darthur*, Book XVI, chap. v.
[2] *Ibid.*, Book XI, chap. XIV; Book XII, chap. IV; Book XIII, chap. XVIII.
[3] Not mentioned by Malory, but stated in the romance called *Seint Greal*.
[4] Rhys: *Arthurian Legend*, pp. 276-277; 302.
[5] *Morte Darthur*, Book IV, chap. XXIX.
[6] *Ibid.*, Book XVII, chap. XX, in which Sir Bors, Sir Percivale, and Sir Galahad are all fed from the Sangreal.

or Pwyll, the keeper of it, could have had no reason for such exertions. At the second we may look doubtfully; for Sir Bors is no other than Emrys, or Myrddin,[1] and, casting back to the earlier British mythology, we do not find the sky-god personally active in securing boons by force or craft from the underworld. The other two have better claims — Sir Percivale and Sir Galahad. "Sir Percivale" is the Norman-French name for Peredur,[2] the hero of a story in the Red Book of Hergest[3] which gives the oldest form of a Grail quest we have. It is anterior to the Norman romances, and forms almost a connecting-link between tales of mythology and of chivalry. Peredur, or Sir Percivale, therefore, is the oldest, most primitive, of Grail seekers. On the other hand, Sir Galahad is the latest and youngest. But there is reason to believe that Galahad, in Welsh "Gwalchaved", the "Falcon of Summer", is the same solar hero as Gawain, in Welsh "Gwalchmei", the "Falcon of May".[4] Both are made, in the story of "Kulhwch and Olwen", sons of the same mother, Gwyar. Sir Gawain himself is, in one Arthurian romance, the achiever of the Grail.[5] It is needless to attempt to choose between these two. Both have the attributes of sun-gods. Gwalchmei, the successor of Lleu Llaw Gyffes, and Peredur Paladr-hir, that is to say, the "Spearman with the Long

[1] Rhys: *Arthurian Legend*, p. 162.   [2] *Ibid.*, p. 133.
[3] Translated by Lady Guest in her *Mabinogion*, under the title of *Peredur, the Son of Evrawc*.
[4] Rhys: *Arthurian Legend*, p. 169.   But see whole of chap. VIII—"Galahad and Gwalchaved".
[5] The German romance *Diu Krône*, by Heinrich von dem Türlin.

Shaft ",[1] may be allowed to claim equal honours. What is important is that the quest of the Grail, once the chief treasure of Hades, is still accomplished by one who takes in later legend the place of Lleu Llaw Gyffes and Lugh Lamhfada in the earlier British and Gaelic myths as a long-armed solar deity victorious in his strife against the Powers of Darkness.

[1] Rhys: *Arthurian Legend*, p. 71.

CHAPTER XXIV

THE DECLINE AND FALL OF THE GODS

If there be love of fame in celestial minds, those gods might count themselves fortunate who shared in the transformation of Arthur. Their divinity had fallen from them, but in their new rôles, as heroes of romance, they entered upon vivid reincarnations. The names of Arthur's Knights might almost be described as "household words", while the gods who had no portion in the Table Round are known only to those who busy themselves with antiquarian lore. It is true that a few folk-tales still survive in the remoter parts of Wales, in which the names of such ancient British deities as Gwydion, Gwyn, Arianrod, and Dylan appear, but it is in such a chaos of jumbled and distorted legend that one finds it hard to pick out even the slenderest thread of story. They have none of the definite coherence of the contemporary Gaelic folk-tales quoted in a previous chapter as still preserving the myths about Goibniu, Lugh, Cian, Manannán, Ethniu, and Balor. Indeed, they have reached such a stage of disintegration that they can hardly now survive another generation.[1]

There have been, however, other paths by which the fame of a god might descend to a posterity

[1] See, for example, a folk-tale, pp. 117-123 in Rhys's *Celtic Folklore*.

which would no longer credit his divinity. The rolls of early British history were open to welcome any number of mythical personages, provided that their legends were attractive. Geoffrey of Monmouth's famous *Historia Britonum* is, under its grave pretence of exact history, as mythological as the Morte Darthur, or even the Mabinogion. The annals of early British saintship were not less accommodating. A god whose tradition was too potent to be ignored or extinguished was canonized, as a matter of course, by clerics who held as an axiom that "the toleration of the cromlech facilitated the reception of the Gospel.[1]" Only the most irreconcilable escaped them—such a one as Gwyn son of Nudd, who, found almost useless by Geoffrey and intractable by the monkish writers, remains the last survivor of the old gods—dwindled to the proportions of a fairy, but unsubdued.

This part of resistance is perhaps the most dignified; for deities can be sadly changed by the caprices of their euhemerizers. Dôn, whom we knew as the mother of the heaven gods, seems strangely described as a *king* of Lochlin and Dublin, who led the Irish into north Wales in A.D. 267.[2] More recognizable is *his* son Gwydion, who introduced the knowledge of letters into the country of his adoption. The dynasty of "King" Dôn, according to a manuscript in the collection of Mr. Edward Williams—better known under his bardic name of Iolo Morganwg—held north Wales for a hundred and twenty-nine

---

[1] Stephens's Preliminary Dissertation to his translation of Aneurin's *Gododin*.
[2] *Iolo MSS.*, p. 471.

years, when the North British king, Cunedda, invaded the country, defeated the Irish in a great battle, and drove them across sea to the Isle of Man. This battle is historical, and, putting Dôn and Gwydion out of the question, probably represented the last stand of the Gael, in the extreme west of Britain, against the second and stronger wave of Celtic invasion. In the same collection of *Iolo Manuscripts* is found a curious, and even comic, euhemeristic version of the strange myth of the Bone Prison of Oeth and Anoeth which Manawyddan son of Llyr, built in Gower. The new reading makes that ghastly abode a real building, constructed out of the bones of the "Caesarians" (Romans) killed in battle with the Cymri. It consisted of numerous chambers, some of large bones and some of small, some above ground and some under. Prisoners of war were placed in the more comfortable cells, the underground dungeons being kept for traitors to their country. Several times the "Caesarians" demolished the prison, but, each time, the Cymri rebuilt it stronger than before. At last, however, the bones decayed, and, being spread upon the ground, made an excellent manure! "From that time forth" the people of the neighbourhood "had astonishing crops of wheat and barley and of every other grain for many years".[1]

It is not, however, in these, so to speak, unauthorized narratives that we can best refind our British deities, but in the compact, coherent, and at times almost convincing *Historia Britonum* of Geoffrey of Monmouth, published in the first half of

[1] *Iolo MSS.*, pp. 597–600.

the twelfth century, and for hundreds of years gravely quoted as the leading authority on the early history of our islands. The modern critical spirit has, of course, relegated it to the region of fable. We can no longer accept the pleasant tradition of the descent of the Britons from the survivors of Troy, led westward in search of a new home by Brutus, the great-grandson of the pious Æneas. Nor indeed does any portion of the "History", from Æneas to Athelstan, quite persuade the latter-day reader. Its kings succeed one another in plausible sequence, but they themselves are too obviously the heroes of popular legend.

A large part of Geoffrey's chronicle—two books[1] out of twelve—is, of course, devoted to Arthur. In it he tells the story of that paladin's conquests, not only in his own country, against the Saxons, the Irish, the Scots, and the Picts, but over all western Europe. We see the British champion, after annexing Ireland, Iceland, Gothland, and the Orkneys, following up these minor victories by subduing Norway, Dacia (by which Denmark seems to have been meant), Aquitaine, and Gaul. After such triumphs there was clearly nothing left for him but the overthrow of the Roman empire; and this he had practically achieved when the rebellion of Mordred brought him home to his death, or rather (for even Geoffrey does not quite lose hold of the belief in the undying Arthur) to be carried to the island of Avallon to be healed of his wounds, the crown of Britain falling to "his kinsman Constantine, the son

---

[1] *Historia Britonum.* Books IX, X, and chaps. I and II of XI.

of Cador, Duke of Cornwall, in the five hundred and forty-second year of our Lord's incarnation".[1] Upon the more personal incidents connected with Arthur, Geoffrey openly professes to keep silence, possibly regarding them as not falling within the province of his history, but we are told shortly how Mordred took advantage of Arthur's absence on the Continent to seize the throne, marry Guanhamara (Guinevere), and ally himself with the Saxons, only to be defeated at that fatal battle called by Geoffrey "Cambula", in which Mordred, Arthur, and Walgan —the "Sir Gawain" of Malory and the Gwalchmei of the earlier legends—all met their dooms.

We find the gods of the older generation standing in the same position with regard to Arthur in Geoffrey's "History" as they do in the later Welsh triads and tales. Though rulers, they are yet his vassals. In "three brothers of royal blood", called Lot, Urian, and Augusel, who are represented as having been chiefs in the north, we may discern Lludd, Urien, and Arawn. To these three Arthur restored "the rights of their ancestors", handing over the semi-sovereignty of Scotland to Augusel, giving Urian the government of Murief (Moray), and re-establishing Lot "in the consulship of Loudonesia (Lothian), and the other provinces belonging to him".[2] Two other rulers subject to him are Gunvasius, King of the Orkneys, and Malvasius, King of Iceland,[3] in whom we recognize Gwyn,

---

[1] *Historia Britonum*, Book XI, chap. II.   [2] *Ibid.*, Book IX, chap. IX.
[3] *Ibid.*, Book IX, chap. XII. They appear also as Guanius, King of the Huns, and Melga, King of the Picts, in Book V, chap. XVI.

under Latinized forms of his Welsh name Gwynwas and his Cornish name Melwas. But it is characteristic of Geoffrey of Monmouth's loose hold upon his materials that, not content with having connected several of these gods with Arthur's period, he further endows them with reigns of their own. "Urien" was Arthur's vassal, but "Urianus" was himself King of Britain centuries before Arthur was born.[1] Lud (that is, Lludd) succeeded his father Beli.[2] We hear nothing of his silver hand, but we learn that he was "famous for the building of cities, and for rebuilding the walls of Trinovantum[3], which he also surrounded with innumerable towers . . . and though he had many other cities, yet he loved this above them all, and resided in it the greater part of the year; for which reason it was afterwards called Kaerlud, and by the corruption of the word, Caerlondon; and again by change of languages, in process of time, London; as also by foreigners who arrived here, and reduced this country under their subjection, it was called Londres. At last, when he was dead, his body was buried by the gate which to this time is called in the British tongue after his name Parthlud, and in the Saxon, Ludesgata." He was succeeded by his brother, Cassibellawn (Cassivelaunus), during whose reign Julius Caesar first invaded Britain.

Lludd, however, is not entirely dependent upon Geoffrey of Monmouth for his reputation as a king

[1] *Historia Britonum*, Book III, chap. XIX.   [2] *Ibid.*, Book III, chap. XX.
[3] *I.e.* London, under its traditionary earlier name, Troja Nova, given it by Brutus.

of Britain. One of the old Welsh romances,[1] translated by Lady Charlotte Guest in her Mabinogion, relates the rebuilding of London by Lludd in almost the same words as Geoffrey. The story which these pseudo-historical details introduce is, however, an obviously mythological one. It tells us how, in the days of Lludd, Britain was oppressed by three plagues. The first was the arrival of a strange race of sorcerers called the "Coranians",[2] who had three qualities which made them unpopular; they paid their way in "fairy money", which, though apparently real, returned afterwards —like the shields, horses, and hounds made by Gwydion son of Dôn, to deceive Pryderi—into the fungus out of which it had been charmed by magic; they could hear everything that was said over the whole of Britain, in however low a tone, provided only that the wind met it; and they could not be injured by any weapon. The second was "a shriek that came on every May eve, over every hearth in the Island of Britain, and went through people's hearts and so scared them that the men lost their hue and their strength, and the women their children, and the young men and the maidens their senses, and all the animals and trees and the earth and the waters were left barren". The third was a disappearance of the food hoarded in the king's palace, which was so complete that a year's provisions vanished in a single night, and so mysterious that no one could ever find out its cause.

---

[1] *The Story of Lludd and Llevelys.*
[2] The name means "dwarfs". Rhys: *Hibbert Lectures*, p. 606.

By the advice of his nobles, Lludd went to France to obtain the help of its king, his brother Llevelys, who was "a man great of counsel and wisdom". In order to be able to consult with his brother without being overheard by the Coranians, Llevelys caused a long tube of brass to be made, through which they talked to one another. The sorcerer tribe, however, got to know of it, and, though they could not hear what was being said inside the speaking-tube, they sent a demon into it, who whispered insulting messages up and down it, as though from one brother to the other. But Lludd and Llevelys knew one another too well to be deceived by this, and they drove the demon out of the tube by flooding it with wine. Then Llevelys told Lludd to take certain insects, which he would give him, and pound them in water. When the water was sufficiently permeated with their essence, he was to call both his own people and the Coranians together, as though for a conference, and, in the midst of the meeting, to cast it over all of them alike. The water, though harmless to his own people, would nevertheless prove a deadly poison to the Coranians.

As for the shriek, Llevelys explained it to be raised by a dragon. This monster was the Red Dragon of Britain, and it raised the shriek because it was being attacked by the White Dragon of the Saxons, which was trying to overcome and destroy it. The French king told his brother to measure the length and breadth of Britain, and, when he had found the exact centre of the island, to cause a pit to be dug there. In this pit was to be placed a vessel containing the best mead that could be made, with a covering of satin over it to hide it. Lludd was then to watch from some safe place. The dragons would appear and fight in the air until they were exhausted, then they would fall together on to the top of the satin cloth, and so draw it down with them into the vessel full of mead. Naturally they would drink the mead, and, equally naturally, they would then sleep. As soon as Lludd was sure that they were helpless, he was to go to the pit, wrap the satin cloth round both of them, and bury them together in a stone coffin in the strongest place in Britain. If this were safely done, there would be no more heard of the shriek.

And the disappearance of the food was caused by "a mighty man of magic", who put everyone to sleep by charms before he removed the king's provisions. Lludd was to watch for him, sitting by the side of a cauldron full of cold water. As often as he felt the approach of drowsiness, he was to plunge into the cauldron. Thus he would be able to keep awake and frustrate the thief.

So Lludd came back to Britain. He pounded the insects in the water, and then summoned both the men of Britain and the Coranians to a meeting. In the midst of it, he sprinkled the water over everyone alike. The natives took no harm from this mythological "beetle powder", but the Coranians died.

Lludd was then ready to deal with the dragons. His careful measurements proved that the centre of the island of Britain was at Oxford, and there he caused the pit to be dug, with the vessel of mead in it, hidden by the satin covering. Having made everything ready, he watched, and soon saw the dragons appear. For a long time they fought desperately in the air; then they fell down together on to the satin cloth, and, drawing it after them, subsided into the mead. Lludd waited till they were quite silent, and then pulled them out, folded them carefully in the wrapping, and took them to the district of Snowdon, where he buried them in the strong fortress whose remains, near Beddgelert, are still called "Dinas Emrys". After this the terrible shriek was not heard again until Merlin had them dug up, five hundred years later, when they recommenced fighting, and the red dragon drove the white one out of Britain.

Last of all, Lludd prepared a great banquet in his hall, and watched over it, armed, with the cauldron of water near him. In the middle of the night, he heard soft, drowsy music, such as nearly put him to sleep; but he kept awake by repeatedly dipping himself in the cold water. Just before dawn a huge man, clad in armour, came into the hall, carrying a basket, which he began to load with the viands on the table. Like the bag in which Pwyll captured Gwawl, its holding capacity seemed endless. However, the man filled it at last, and was carrying it out, when Lludd stopped him. They fought, and Lludd conquered the man of magic, and made him his vassal. Thus the "Three Plagues of Britain" came to an end.

Lludd, in changing from god to king, seems to

have lost most of his old mythological attributes. Even his daughter Creudylad is taken from him and given to another of the ancient British deities. Why Lludd, the sky-god, should have been confounded with Llyr, the sea-god, is not very apparent, but it is certain that "Creudylad" of the early Welsh legends and poems is the same as Geoffrey's "Cordeilla" and Shakespeare's "Cordelia". The great dramatist was ultimately indebted to the Celtic mythology for the groundwork of the legend which he wove into the tragic story of *King Lear*. " Leir ", as Geoffrey calls him,[1] was the son of Bladud, who built Caer Badus (Bath), and perished, like Icarus, as the result of an accident with a flying-machine of his own invention. Having no sons, but three daughters, Gonorilla, Regan, and Cordeilla, he thought in his old age of dividing his kingdom among them. But, first of all, he decided to make trial of their affection for him, with the idea of giving the best portions of his realm to the most worthy. Gonorilla, the eldest, replied to his question of how much she loved him, "that she called heaven to witness, she loved him more than her own soul ". Regan answered "with an oath, 'that she could not otherwise express her thoughts, but that she loved him above all creatures'". But when it came to Cordeilla's turn, the youngest daughter, disgusted with her sisters' hypocrisy, spoke after a quite different fashion. "'My father,' said she, 'is there any daughter that can love her father more than duty requires? In my opinion, whoever pretends to it, must disguise her real sentiments

[1] *Historia Britonum*, Book II, chap. X-XIV.

under the veil of flattery. I have always loved you as a father, nor do I yet depart from my purposed duty; and if you insist to have something more extorted from me, hear now the greatness of my affection, which I always bear you, and take this for a short answer to all your questions; look how much you have, so much is your value, and so much do I love you.'" Her enraged father immediately bestowed his kingdom upon his two other daughters, marrying them to the two highest of his nobility, Gonorilla to Maglaunus, Duke of Albania[1], and Regan to Henuinus, Duke of Cornwall. To Cordeilla he not only refused a share in his realm, but even a dowry. Aganippus, King of the Franks, married her, however, for her beauty alone.

Once in possession, Leir's two sons-in-law rebelled against him, and deprived him of all regal authority. The sole recompense for his lost power was an agreement by Maglaunus to allow him maintenance, with a body-guard of sixty soldiers. But, after two years, the Duke of Albania, at his wife Gonorilla's instigation, reduced them to thirty. Resenting this, Leir left Maglaunus, and went to Henuinus, the husband of Regan. The Duke of Cornwall at first received him honourably, but, before a year was out, compelled him to discharge all his attendants except five. This sent him back in a rage to his eldest daughter, who, this time, swore that he should not stay with her, unless he would be satisfied with one serving-man only. In despair, Leir resolved to throw himself upon the mercy of Cordeilla, and, full

1 Alba, or North Britain.

of contrition for the way he had treated her, and of misgivings as to how he might be received, took ship for Gaul.

Arriving at Karitia[1], he sent a messenger to his daughter, telling her of his plight and asking for her help. Cordeilla sent him money, robes, and a retinue of forty men, and, as soon as he was fully equipped with the state suitable to a king, he was received in pomp by Aganippus and his ministers, who gave the government of Gaul into his hands until his own kingdom could be restored to him. This the king of the Franks did by raising an army and invading Britain. Maglaunus and Henuinus were routed, and Leir replaced on the throne, after which he lived three years. Cordeilla, succeeding to the government of Britain, "buried her father in a certain vault, which she ordered to be made for him under the River Sore, in Leicester ("Llyr-cestre"), and which had been built originally under the ground to the honour of the god Janus. And here all the workmen of the city, upon the anniversary solemnity of that festival, used to begin their yearly labours."

Exactly what myth is retold in this history of Leir and his three daughters we are hardly likely ever to discover. But its mythological nature is clear enough in the light of the description of the underground temple dedicated to Llyr, at once the god of the subaqueous, and therefore subterranean, world and a British Dis Pater, connected with the origin of things, like the Roman god Janus, with whom he was apparently identified.[2]

---

[1] Now Calais.   [2] Rhys: *Arthurian Legend*, pp. 131-132

Ten kings or so after this (for any more exact way of measuring the flight of time is absent from Geoffrey's *History*) we recognize two other British gods upon the scene. Brennius (that is, Brân) disputes the kingdom with his brother Belinus. Clearly this is a version of the ancient myth of the twin brothers, Darkness and Light, which we have seen expressed in so many ways in Celtic mythology. Brân, the god of death and the underworld, is opposed to Belinus, god of the sun and health. In the original, lost myth, probably they alternately conquered and were conquered—a symbol of the alternation of night and day and of winter and summer. In Geoffrey's *History*[1], they divided Britain, Belinus taking "the crown of the island with the dominions of Loegria, Kambria, and Cornwall, because, according to the Trojan constitution, the right of inheritance would come to him as the elder", while Brennius, as the younger, had "Northumberland, which extended from the River Humber to Caithness". But flatterers persuaded Brennius to ally himself with the King of the Norwegians, and attack Belinus. A battle was fought, in which Belinus was conqueror, and Brennius escaped to Gaul, where he married the daughter of the Duke of the Allobroges, and on that ruler's death was declared successor to the throne. Thus firmly established with an army, he invaded Britain again. Belinus marched with the whole strength of the kingdom to meet him, and the armies were already drawn

---

[1] *Historia Britonum*, Book III, chaps. I-X.

out opposite to one another in battle array when Conwenna, the mother of the two kings, succeeded in reconciling them. Not having one another to fight with, the brothers now agreed upon a joint expedition with their armies into Gaul. The Britons and the Allobroges conquered all the other kings of the Franks, and then entered Italy, destroying villages and cities as they marched to Rome. Gabius and Porsena, the Roman consuls, bought them off with large presents of gold and silver and the promise of a yearly tribute, whereupon Brennius and Belinus withdrew their army into Germany and began to devastate it. But the Romans, now no longer taken by surprise and unprepared, came to the help of the Germans. This brought Brennius and Belinus back to Rome, which, after a long siege, they succeeded in taking. Brennius remained in Italy, "where he exercised unheard-of tyranny over the people"; and one may take the whole of this veracious history to be due to a patriotic desire to make out the Brennus of "Vae Victis" fame—who actually did sack Rome, in B.C. 390—a Briton. Belinus, the other brother, returned to England. " He made a gate of wonderful structure in Trinovantum, upon the bank of the Thames, which the citizens call after his name Billingsgate to this day. Over it he built a prodigiously large tower, and under it a haven or quay for ships. . . . At last, when he had finished his days, his body was burned, and the ashes put up in a golden urn, which they placed at Trinovantum, with wonderful art, on the top of the tower above mentioned." He was succeeded by Gurgiunt Brabtruc,[1] who, as he was returning by way of the Orkneys from a raid on the Danes, met the ships of Partholon and his people as they came from Spain to settle in Ireland.[2]

Llyr and his children, large as they bulk in mythical history, were hardly less illustrious as saints. The family of Llyr Llediath is always described by the early Welsh hagiologists as the first of the "Three chief Holy Families of the Isle of Britain". The glory of Llyr himself, however, is but a reflected one; for it was his son Brân "the Blesséd" who actually introduced Christianity into Britain. Legend tells us that he was taken captive to Rome with his son Caradawc (who was identified for the purpose with the historical Caratacus), and the rest of his family, and remained there seven years, during which time he became converted to the Gospel, and spread it enthusiastically on his return. Neither his son Caradawc nor his half-brother Manawyddan exactly followed in his footsteps, but their descendants did. Caradawc's sons were all saintly, while his daughter Eigen, who married a chief called Sarrlog, lord of Caer Sarrlog (Old Sarum), was the first female saint in Britain. Manawyddan's side of the family was less adaptable. His son and his grandson were both pagans, but his great-grandson obtained Christian fame as St. Dyfan, who was sent as a bishop to Wales by Pope Eleutherius, and was martyred at Merthyr Dyvan. After this, the saintly line of Llyr increases and flourishes.

---

[1] The same fabulous personage, perhaps, as the original of Rabelais' Gargantua a popular Celtic god.   [2] *Historia Britonum*, Book III, Chaps. XI–XII.

Singularly inappropriate persons are found in it—Mabon, the Gallo-British Apollo, as well as Geraint and others of King Arthur's court.[1]

It is so quaint a conceit that Christianity should have been, like all other things, the gift of the Celtic Hades, that it seems almost a pity to cast doubt on it. The witness of the classical historians sums up, however, dead in its disfavour. Tacitus carefully enumerates the family of Caratacus, and describes how he and his wife, daughter, and brother were separately interviewed by the Emperor Claudius, but makes no mention at all of the chieftain's supposed father Brân. Moreover, Dio Cassius gives the name of Caratacus's father as Cunobelinus—Shakespeare's "Cymbeline"—who, he adds, had died before the Romans first invaded Britain. The evidence is wholly against Brân as a Christian pioneer. He remains the grim old god of war and death, "blesséd" only to his pagan votaries, and especially to the bards, who probably first called him *Bendigeid Vran*, and whose stubborn adherence must have been the cause of the not less stubborn efforts of their enemies, the Christian clerics, to bring him over to their own side by canonization.[2]

They had an easier task with Brân's sister, Branwen of the " Fair Bosom". Goddesses, indeed, seem to have stood the process better than gods—witness "Saint" Brigit, the "Mary of the Gael". The

---

[1] See the *Iolo MSS.* The genealogies and families of the saints of the island of Britain. Copied by Iolo Morganwg in 1783 from the *Long Book of Thomas Truman of Pantlliwydd* in the parish of Llansanor in Glamorgan, p. 515, &c. Also see *An Essay on the Welsh Saints* by the Rev. Rice Rees, Sections IV and V.

[2] Rhys: *Arthurian Legend*, pp. 261–262.

British Aphrodité became, under the name of Bryn-
wyn, or Dwynwen, a patron saint of lovers.   As
late as the fourteenth century, her shrine at Llandwynwyn, in Anglesey, was the favourite resort of
the disappointed of both sexes, who came to pray
to her image for either success or forgetfulness.   To
make the result the more certain, the monks of the
church sold Lethean draughts from her sacred well.
The legend told of her is that, having vowed herself
to perpetual celibacy, she fell in love with a young
chief called Maelon.   One night, as she was praying
for guidance in her difficulty, she had a vision in
which she was offered a goblet of delicious liquor as
a draught of oblivion, and she also saw the same
sweet medicine given to Maelon, whom it at once
froze into a block of ice.   She was then, for her
faith, offered the granting of three boons.   The first
she chose was that Maelon might be allowed to re-
sume his natural form and temperature; the second,
that she should no longer desire to be married; and
the third, that her intercessions might be granted
for all true-hearted lovers, so that they should either
wed the objects of their affection or be cured of
their passion.[1]   From this cause came the virtues of
her shrine and fountain.   But the modern generation
no longer flocks there, and the efficacious well is
choked with sand.   None the less, she whom the
Welsh bards called the " Saint of Love "[2] still
has her occasional votaries.   Country girls of the

---

[1] *Iolo MSS*, p. 474.

[2] "The Welsh bards call Dwynwen the goddess, or saint of love and affection,
as the poets designate Venus." *Iolo MSS.*

neighbourhood seek her help when all else fails.
The water nearest to the church is thought to be
the best substitute for the now dry and ruined
original well.[1]

A striking contrast to this easy victory over
paganism is the stubborn resistance to Christian
adoption of Gwyn son of Nudd. It is true that he
was once enrolled by some monk in the train of the
"Blesséd Brân",[2] but it was done in so half-hearted
a way that, even now, one can discern that the
writer felt almost ashamed of himself. His fame
as at least a powerful fairy was too vital to be
thus tampered with. Even Spenser, though, in his
Faerie Queene, he calls him "the good Sir Guyon
. . . in whom great rule of Temp'raunce goodly doth
appeare",[3] does not attempt to conceal his real
nature. It is no man, but

"an Elfin born, of noble state
And mickle worship in his native land",[4]

who sets forth the beauties of that virtue for which
the original Celtic paradise, with its unfailing ale
and rivers of mead and wine, would hardly seem
to have been the best possible school. Save for
Spenser, all authorities agree in making Gwyn the
determined opponent of things Christian. A curious
and picturesque legend[5] is told of him in connection
with St. Collen, who was himself the great-grandson
of Brân's son, Caradawc. The saint, desirous of

[1] Wirt Sikes: *British Goblins*, p. 350.   [2] *Iolo MSS*, p. 523.
[3] *The Faerie Queene*, Prologue to Book II.   [4] *Ibid.*, Book II, canto 1, verse 6.
[5] Published in *Y Greal* (London, 1805), and is to be found quoted in Rhys:
Arthurian Legend, pp. 338, 339; also in Sikes: *British Goblins*, pp. 7-8.

still further retirement from the world, had made himself a cell beneath a rock near Glastonbury Tor, in Gwyn's own "island of Avilion". It was close to a road, and one day he heard two men pass by talking about Gwyn son of Nudd, and declaring him to be King of Annwn and the fairies. St. Collen put his head out of the cell, and told them to hold their tongues, and that Gwyn and his fairies were only demons. The two men retorted by warning the saint that he would soon have to meet the dark ruler face to face. They passed on, and not long afterwards St. Collen heard someone knocking at his door. On asking who was there, he got the answer: "I am here, the messenger of Gwyn ap Nudd, King of Hades, to bid thee come by the middle of the day to speak with him on the top of the hill." The saint did not go; and the messenger came a second time with the same message. On the third visit, he added a threat that, if St. Collen did not come now, it would be the worse for him. So, a little disquieted, he went, but not unarmed. He consecrated some water, and took it with him.

On other days the top of Glastonbury Tor had always been bare, but on this occasion the saint found it crowned by a splendid castle. Men and maidens, beautifully dressed, were going in and out. A page received him and told him that the king was waiting for him to be his guest at dinner. St. Collen found Gwyn sitting on a golden chair in front of a table covered with the rarest dainties and wines. He invited him to share them, adding that if there was anything he especially liked, it should be brought to him with all honour. "I do not eat the leaves of trees," replied the saint, who knew what fairy meats and drinks were made of. Not taken aback by this discourteous answer, the King of Annwn genially asked the saint if he did not admire his servants' livery, which was a motley costume, red on one side and blue on the other. "Their dress is good enough for its kind," said St. Collen. "What kind is that?" asked Gwyn. "The red shows which side is being scorched, and the blue shows which side is being frozen," replied the saint, and, splashing his holy water all round him, he saw castle, serving-men, and king vanish, leaving him alone on the bare, windy hill-top.

Gwyn, last of the gods of Annwn, has evidently by this time taken over the functions of all the others. He has the hounds which Arawn once had—the *Cwn Annwn*, "dogs of hell", with the white bodies and the red ears. We hear more of them in folk-lore than we do of their master, though even their tradition is dying out with the spread of newspapers and railways. We are not likely to find another Reverend Edmund Jones[1] to insist upon belief in them, lest, by closing our minds to such manifest witnesses of the supernatural world, we should become infidels. Still, we may even now find peasants ready to swear that they have heard them sweeping along the hill-sides upon stormy nights, as they pursued the flying souls of unshriven men or

[1] *A Relation of Apparitions of Spirits in the County of Monmouth and the Principality of Wales.* Published at Newport, 1813.

unbaptized babes. The tales told of them agree curiously. Their cry is like that of a pack of fox-hounds, but softer in tone. The nearer they are to a man, the less loud their voices seem, and the farther off they are, the louder. But they are less often seen than heard, and it has been suggested that the sounds were the cries of migrating bean-geese, which are not unlike those of hounds in chase. The superstition is widely spread. The *Cwn Annwn* of Wales are called in North Devon the "Yeth" (Heath or Heathen), or "Yell" Hounds, and on Dartmoor, the "Wish" Hounds. In Durham and Yorkshire they are called "Gabriel" Hounds, and they are known by various names in Norfolk, Gloucestershire, and Cornwall. In Scotland it is Arthur who leads the Wild Hunt, and the tradition is found over almost the whole of western Europe.

Not many folk - tales have been preserved in which Gwyn is mentioned by name. His memory has lingered longest and latest in the fairy-haunted Vale of Neath, so close to his " ridge, the Tawë abode . . . not the nearest Tawë . . . but that Tawë which is the farthest ". But it may be understood whenever the king of the fairies is mentioned. As the last of the greater gods of the old mythology, he has been endowed by popular fancy with the rule of all the varied fairy population of Britain, so far, at least, as it is of Celtic or pre-Celtic origin. For some of the fairies most famous in English literature are Teutonic. King Oberon derives his name, through the French *fabliaux*, from Elberich, the dwarf king of the *Niebelungenlied*,[1] though his queen, Titania, was probably named out of Ovid's *Metamorphoses*.[2] Puck, another of Shakespeare's fays, is merely the personification of his race, the "pwccas" of Wales, "pookas" of Ireland, "poakes" of Worcestershire, and "pixies" of the West of England.[3] It is Wales that at the present time preserves the most numerous and diverse collection of fairies. Some of them are beautiful, some hideous; some kindly, some malevolent. There are the gentle damsels of the lakes and streams called Gwragedd Annwn, and the fierce and cruel mountain fairies known as the Gwyllion. There are the household sprites called Bwbachod, like the Scotch and English "brownies"; the Coblynau, or gnomes of the mines (called "knockers" in Cornwall); and the Ellyllon, or elves, of whom the pwccas are a branch.[4] In the North of England the spirits belong more wholly to the lower type. The bogles, brownies, killmoulis, redcaps, and their like seem little akin to the higher, Aryan-seeming fairies. The Welsh bwbach, too, is described as brown and hairy, and the coblynau as black or copper-faced. We shall hardly do wrong in regarding such spectres as the degraded gods of a pre-Aryan race, like the Irish leprechauns and pookas, who have nothing in common with the still beautiful, still noble figures of the Tuatha Dé Danann.

Of these numberless and nameless subjects of Gwyn, some dwell beneath the earth or under the

---

[1] Thistleton Dyer: *Folklore of Shakespeare*, p. 3.   [2] *Ibid.*, p. 4.
[3] *Ibid.*, p. 5.   [4] Wirt Sikes: *British Goblins*, p. 12.

surface of lakes—which seem to take, in Wales, the
place of the Gaelic "fairy hills"—and others in
Avilion, a mysterious western isle of all delights
lying on or just beneath the sea. Pembrokeshire—
the ancient Dyfed—has kept the tradition most
completely. The story goes that there is a certain
square yard in the hundred of Cemmes in that county
which holds the secret of the fairy realm. If a man
happens to set his feet on it by chance, his eyes are
opened, and he can see that which is hidden from
other men—the fairy country and commonwealth,—
but, the moment he moves from the enchanted spot,
he loses the vision, and he can never find the same
place again.[1] That country is upon the sea, and
not far from shore; like the Irish paradise of which
it is the counterpart, it may sometimes be sighted
by sailors. The "Green Meadows of Enchantment" are still an article of faith among Pembrokeshire and Caermarthenshire sailors, and evidently
not without some reason. In 1896 a correspondent
of the *Pembroke County Guardian* sent in a report
made to him by a certain Captain John Evans to
the effect that, one summer morning, while trending
up the Channel, and passing Gresholm Island (the
scene of the entertaining of Brân's head), in what
he had always known as deep water, he was surprised to see to windward of him a large tract of
land covered with a beautiful green meadow. It
was not, however, above water, but two or three
feet below it, so that the grass waved or swam about
as the ripple floated over it, in a way that made one

[1] The *Brython*, Vol. I, p. 130.

who watched it feel drowsy. Captain Evans had often heard of the tradition of the fairy island from old people, but admitted that he had never hoped to see it with his own eyes.[1] As with the " Hounds of Annwn " one may suspect a quite natural explanation. Mirage is at once common enough and rare enough on our coasts to give rise to such a legend, and it must have been some such phenomenon as the " Fata Morgana " of Sicily which has made sober men swear so confidently to ocular evidence of the Celtic Paradise, whether seen from the farthest western coasts of Gaelic Ireland or Scotland, or of British Wales.

[1] Rhys: *Celtic Folklore*, pp. 171-172.

SURVIVALS OF THE CELTIC
PAGANISM

CHAPTER XXV

SURVIVALS OF THE CELTIC PAGANISM INTO MODERN TIMES

The fall of the Celtic state worship began earlier in Britain than in her sister island. Neither was it Christianity that struck the first blow, but the rough humanity and stern justice of the Romans. That people was more tolerant, perhaps, than any the world has ever known towards the religions of others, and gladly welcomed the Celtic gods—as gods—into its own diverse Pantheon. A friendly Gaulish or British divinity might at any time be granted the so-to-speak divine Roman citizenship, and be assimilated to Jupiter, to Mars, to Apollo, or to any other properly accredited deity whom the Romans deemed him to resemble. It was not against the god, but against his worship at the hands of his priests, that Roman law struck. The colossal human sacrifices of the druids horrified even a people who were far from squeamish about a little bloodshed. They themselves had abolished such practices by a decree of the senate before Caesar first invaded Britain,[1] and could not therefore permit within their empire a cult which slaughtered men in order to draw omens from their death-agonies.[2] Druidism was first required to be renounced by

---

[1] In the year 55 B.C.   [2] *Strabo*, Book IV, chap. IV.

those who claimed Roman citizenship; then it was
vigorously put down among the less civilized tribes.
Tacitus tells us how the Island of Mona (Anglesey)
—the great stronghold of druidism—was attacked,
its sacred groves cut down, its altars laid level, and
its priests put to the sword.[1]   Pliny, recording how
the Emperor Tiberius had "suppressed the druids",
congratulates his fellow-countrymen on having put
an end, wherever their dominion extended, to the
monstrous customs inspired by the doctrine that the
gods could take pleasure in murder and cannibalism.[2]
The practice of druidism, with its attendant barbari-
ties, abolished in Britain wherever the long Roman
arm could reach to strike, took refuge beyond the
Northern Wall, among the savage Caledonian
tribes who had not yet submitted to the invader's
yoke.   Naturally, too, it remained untouched in
Ireland.   But before the Romans left Britain, it had
been extirpated everywhere, except among "the
Picts and Scots".

Christianity, following the Roman rule, completed
the ruin of paganism in Britain, so far, at least, as
its public manifestations were concerned.   In the
sixth century of our era, the monkish writer, Gildas,
is able to refer complacently to the ancient British
religion as a dead faith.   "I shall not", he says,
"enumerate those diabolical idols of my country,
which almost surpassed in number those of Egypt,
and of which we still see some mouldering away
within or without the deserted temples, with stiff
and deformed features as was customary.   Nor will

[1] *Annals*, Book XIV, chap. XXX.   [2] *Natural History*, Book XXX.

I cry out upon the mountains, fountains, or hills, or
upon the rivers, which now are subservient to the
use of men, but once were an abomination and
destruction to them, and to which the blind people
paid divine honour."[1]   And with the idols fell the
priests.   The very word "druid" became obsolete,
and is scarcely mentioned in the earliest British
literature, though druids are prominent characters
in the Irish writings of the same period.

The secular arm had no power in Scotland and
in Ireland, consequently the battle between Paganism
and Christianity was fought upon more equal terms,
and lasted longer.   In the first country, Saint Columba, and in the second, Saint Patrick are the
personages who, at any rate according to tradition,
beat down the druids and their gods.   Adamnan,
Abbot of Iona, who wrote his *Vita Columbæ* in the
last decade of the seventh century, describes how,
a century earlier, that saint had carried the Gospel
to the Picts.   Their king, Brude, received him con-
temptuously, and the royal druids left no heathen
spell unuttered to thwart and annoy him.   But, as
the power of Moses was greater than the power of
the magicians of Egypt, so Saint Columba's prayers
caused miracles more wonderful and more convincing than any wrought by his adversaries.   Such
stories belong to the atmosphere of myth which has
always enveloped heroic men; the essential fact is
that the Picts abandoned the old religion for the
new.

A similar legend sums up the life-work of Saint

[1] Gildas.   See *Six Old English Chronicles*—Bohn's Libraries.
(B 219)   2 O

Patrick in Ireland. Before he came, Cromm Cruaich had received from time immemorial his yearly toll of human lives. But Saint Patrick faced the gruesome idol; as he raised his crozier, we are told, the demon fell shrieking from his image, which, deprived of its soul, bowed forward to the ground.

It is far easier, however, to overthrow the more public manifestations of a creed than to destroy its inner vital force. Cromm Cruaich's idol might fall, but his spirit would survive—a very Proteus. The sacred places of the ancient Celtic religion might be invaded, the idols and altars of the gods thrown down, the priests slain, scattered, or banished, and the cult officially declared to be extinct; but, driven from the important centres, it would yet survive outside and around them. The more civilized Gaels and Britons would no doubt accept the purer gospel, and abandon the gods they had once adored, but the peasantry—the bulk of the population—would still cling to the familiar rites and names. A nobler belief and a higher civilization come, after all, only as surface waves upon the great ocean of human life; beneath their agitations lies a vast slumbering abyss of half-conscious faith and thought to which culture penetrates with difficulty and in which changes come very slowly.

We have already shown how long and how faithfully the Gaelic and Welsh peasants clung to their old gods, in spite of all the efforts of the clerics to explain them as ancient kings, to transform them into wonder-working saints, or to ban them as demons of hell. This conservative religious instinct of the agricultural populations is not confined to the inhabitants of the British Islands. The modern Greeks still believe in nereids, in lamias, in sirens, and in Charon, the dark ferryman of Hades.[1] The descendants of the Romans and Etruscans hold that the old Etruscan gods and the Roman deities of the woods and fields still live in the world as spirits.[2] The high altars of the " Lord of the Mound " and his terrible kin were levelled, and their golden images and great temples left to moulder in abandonment; but the rude rustic shrine to the rude rustic god still received its offerings. It is this shifting of the care of the pagan cult from chief to peasant, from court to hovel, and, perhaps, to some extent from higher to lower race, that serves to explain how the more primitive and uncouth gods have tended so largely to supplant those of higher, more graceful mien. Aboriginal deities, thrust into obscurity by the invasion of higher foreign types, came back to their own again.

For it seems plain that we must divide the spiritual population of the British Islands into two classes. There is little in common between the "fairy", strictly so-called, and the unsightly elf who appears under various names and guises, as pooka, leprechaun, brownie, knocker, or bogle. The one belongs to such divine tribes as the Tuatha Dé Danann of Gaelic myth or their kin, the British gods of the Mabinogion. The other owes his origin

[1] Rennell Rodd: *Customs and Lore of Modern Greece*. Stuart Glennie: *Greek Folk Songs*.
[2] Charles Godfrey Leland: *Etruscan Roman Remains in Popular Tradition*

to a quite different, and much lower, kind of imagination. One might fancy that neolithic man made him in his own image.

None the less has immemorial tradition wonderfully preserved the essential features of the Celtic nature-gods. The fairy belief of the present day hardly differs at all from the conception which the Celts had of their deities. The description of the Tuatha Dé Danann in the "Dialogue of the Elders" as "sprites or fairies with corporeal or material forms but indued with immortality" would stand as an account of prevailing ideas as to the "good people" to-day. Nor do the Irish and Welsh fairies of popular belief differ from one another. Both alike live among the hills, though in Wales a lake often takes the place of the "fairy mound"; both, though they war and marry among themselves, are semi-immortal; both covet the children of men, and will steal them from the cradle, leaving one of their own uncanny brood in the mortal baby's stead; both can lay men and women under spells; both delight in music and the dance, and live lives of unreal and fantastic splendour and luxury. Another point in which they resemble one another is in their tiny size. But this would seem to be the result of the literary convention originated by Shakespeare; in genuine folktales, both Gaelic and British, the fairies are pictured as of at least mortal stature.[1]

But, Aryan or Iberian, beautiful or hideous, they

[1] Rhys: *Celtic Folklore*, p. 670; Curtin: *Tales of the Fairies and of the Ghost World*; and Mr. Leland Duncan's *Fairy Beliefs from County Leitrim* in *Folklore*, June, 1896.

are fast vanishing from belief. Every year, the secluded valleys in which men and women might still live in the old way, and dream the old dreams, tend more and more to be thrown open to the modern world of rapid movement and rapid thought. The last ten years have perhaps done more in this direction than the preceding ten generations. What lone shepherd or fisherman will ever see again the vision of the great Manannán? Have the stable-boys of to-day still any faith left in Finvarra? Is Gwyn ap Nudd often thought of in his own valleys of the Tawë and the Nedd? It would be hard, perhaps, to find a whole-hearted believer even in his local pooka or parish bogle.

It is the ritual observances of the old Celtic faith which have better weathered, and will longer survive, the disintegrating influences of time. There are no hard names to be remembered. Things may still be done for "luck" which were once done for religion. Customary observances die very slowly, held up by an only half acknowledged fear that, unless they are fulfilled, "something may happen". We shall get, therefore, more satisfactory evidence of the nature of the Celtic paganism by examining such customs than in any other way.

We find three forms of the survival of the ancient religion into quite recent times. The first is the celebration of the old solar or agricultural festivals of the spring and autumn equinoxes and of the summer and winter solstices. The second is the practice of a symbolic human sacrifice by those who have forgotten its meaning, and only know that they are keeping up an old custom, joined with late instances of the actual sacrifices of animals to avert cattle-plagues or to change bad luck. The third consists of many still - living relics of the once universal worship of sacred waters, trees, stones, and animals.

Whatever may have been the exact meaning of the Celtic state worship, there seems to be no doubt that it centred around the four great days in the year which chronicle the rise, progress, and decline of the sun, and, therefore, of the fruits of the earth. These were: Beltaine, which fell at the beginning of May; Midsummer Day, marking the triumph of sunshine and vegetation; the Feast of Lugh, when, in August, the turning-point of the sun's course had been reached; and the sad Samhain, when he bade farewell to power, and fell again for half a year under the sway of the evil forces of winter and darkness.

Of these great solar periods, the first and the last were, naturally, the most important. The whole Celtic mythology seems to revolve upon them, as upon pivots. It was on the day of Beltaine that Partholon and his people, the discoverers, and, indeed, the makers of Ireland, arrived there from the other world, and it was on the same day, three hundred years later, that they returned whence they came. It was on Beltaine-day that the Gaelic gods, the Tuatha Dé Danann, and, after them, the Gaelic men, first set foot on Irish soil. It was on the day of Samhain that the Fomors oppressed the people of Nemed with their terrible tax; and it was again at Samhain that a later race of gods of light and life finally conquered those demons at the Battle of Moytura.   Only one important mythological incident—and that was one added at a later time! —happened upon any other than one of those two days; it was upon Midsummer Day, one of the lesser solar points, that the people of the goddess Danu took Ireland from its inhabitants, the Fir Bolgs.

The mythology of Britain preserves the same root-idea as that of Ireland.   If anything uncanny took place, it was sure to be on May-day.   It was on "the night of the first of May" that Rhiannon lost, and Teirnyon Twryf Vliant found, the infant Pryderi, as told in the first of the Mabinogion.[1]   It was "on every May-eve" that the two dragons fought and shrieked in the reign of "King" Lludd.[2] It is on "every first of May" till the day of doom that Gwyn son of Nudd, fights with Gwyrthur son of Greidawl, for Lludd's fair daughter, Creudylad.[3] And it was when she was "a-maying" in the woods and fields near Westminster that the same Gwyn, or Melwas, under his romance-name of Sir Melia-graunce, captured Arthur's queen, Guinevere.[4]

The nature of the rites performed upon these days can be surmised from their pale survivals. They are still celebrated by the descendants of the Celts, though it is probable that few of them know —or would even care to know—why May Day, St. John's Day, Lammas, and Hallowe'en are times

[1] The Mabinogi of *Pwyll, Prince of Dyfed.*   [2] The story of Lludd and Llevelys.
[4] *Kulhwch and Olwen.*   [3] *Morte Darthur*, Book XIX, chaps. 1 and 11.

of ceremony. The first—called "Beltaine" in Ireland, "Bealtiunn" in Scotland, "Shenn da Boaldyn"
in the Isle of Man, and "Galan-Mai" (the Calends
of May) in Wales—celebrates the waking of the
earth from her winter sleep, and the renewal of
warmth, life, and vegetation. This is the meaning
of the May-pole, now rarely seen in our streets,
though Shakespeare tells us that in his time the
festival was so eagerly anticipated that no one could
sleep upon its eve.[1]   At midnight the people rose,
and, going to the nearest woods, tore down branches
of trees, with which the sun, when he rose, would
find doors and windows decked for him.   They
spent the day in dancing round the May-pole, with
rude, rustic mirth, man joining with nature to celebrate the coming of summer.   The opposite to it
was the day called "Samhain" in Ireland and Scotland, "Sauin" in Man, and "Nos Galan-gaeof"
(the Night of the Winter Calends) in Wales.   This
festival was a sad one: summer was over, and
winter, with its short, sunless days and long, dreary
nights, was at hand.   It was the beginning, too, of
the ancient Celtic year,[2] and omens for the future
might be extorted from dark powers by uncanny
rites.   It was the holiday of the dead and of all the
more evil supernatural beings.   "On November-
eve", says a North Cardiganshire proverb, "there
is a bogy on every stile."   The Scotch have even
invented a special bogy—the *Samhanach* or goblin
which comes out at Samhain.[3]

---

[1] *Henry VIII*, act v, scene 3.   [2] Rhys: *Hibbert Lectures*, p. 514.
[3] *Ibid.*, p. 516.

The sun-god himself is said to have instituted the August festival called "Lugnassad" (Lugh's commemoration) in Ireland, "Lla Lluanys" in Man, and "Gwyl Awst" (August Feast) in Wales; and it was once of hardly less importance than Beltaine or Samhain.   It is noteworthy, too, that the first of August was a great day at Lyons—formerly called Lugudunum, the *dún* (town) of Lugus.   The midsummer festival, on the other hand, has largely merged its mythological significance in the Christian Feast of St. John.

The characteristic features of these festivals give certain proof of the original nature of the great pagan ceremonials of which they are the survivals and travesties.[1]   In all of them, bonfires are lighted on the highest hills, and the hearth fires solemnly rekindled.   They form the excuse for much sport and jollity.   But there is yet something sinister in the air; the "fairies" are active and abroad, and one must be careful to omit no prescribed rite, if one would avoid kindling their anger or falling into their power.   To some of these still-half-believed-in nature-gods offerings were made down to a comparatively late period.   When Pennant wrote, in the eighteenth century, it was the custom on Beltaine-day in many Highland villages to offer libations and cakes not only to the "spirits" who were believed to be beneficial to the flocks and herds, but also to creatures like the fox, the eagle, and the

---

[1] A good account of the Irish festivals is given by Lady Wilde in her *Ancient Legends of Ireland*, pp. 193–221.

hoodie-crow which so often molested them.[1]   At
Hallowe'en (the Celtic Samhain) the natives of the
Hebrides used to pour libations of ale to a marine
god called Shony, imploring him to send sea-weed
to the shore.[2]   In honour, also, of such beings,
curious rites were performed.   Maidens washed
their faces in morning dew, with prayers for beauty.
They carried sprigs of the rowan, that mystic tree
whose scarlet berries were the ambrosial food of the
Tuatha Dé Danann.

In their original form, these now harmless rural
holidays were undoubtedly religious festivals of an
orgiastic nature-worship such as became so popular
in Greece in connection with the cult of Dionysus.
The great "lords of life" and of the powers of nature
that made and ruled life were propitiated by madden-
ing invocations, by riotous dances, and by human
sacrifice.

The bonfires which fill so large a part in the
modern festivals have been casually mentioned.
Originally they were no mere *feux de joie*, but had
a terrible meaning, which the customs connected
with them preserve.   At the Highland Beltaine,
a cake was divided by lot, and whoever drew the
" burnt piece" was obliged to leap three times over
the flames.   At the midsummer bonfires in Ireland
all passed through the fire; the men when the flames
were highest, the women when they were lower,
and the cattle when there was nothing left but
smoke.   In Wales, upon the last day of October,

[1] Pennant : *A Tour in Scotland and Voyage to the Hebrides,* 1772.
[2] Martin: *Description of the Western Islands of Scotland,* 1695.

the old Samhain, there was a slightly different, and still more suggestive rite. The hill-top bonfires were watched until they were announced to be extinct. Then all would race headlong down the hill, shouting a formula to the effect that the devil would get the hindmost. The devil of a new belief is the god of the one it has supplanted; in all three instances, the custom was no mere meaningless horse-play, but a symbolical human sacrifice.

A similar observance, but of a more cruel kind, was kept up in France upon St. John's Day, until forbidden by law in the reign of Louis the Fourteenth. Baskets containing living wolves, foxes, and cats were burned upon the bonfires, under the auspices and in the presence of the sheriffs or the mayor of the town.[1] Caesar noted the custom among the druids of constructing huge wicker-work images, which they filled with living men, and set on fire, and it can hardly be doubted that the wretched wolves, foxes, and cats were ceremonial substitutes for human beings.

An ingenious theory was invented, after the introduction of Christianity, with the purpose of allowing such ancient rites to continue, with a changed meaning. The passing of persons and cattle through flame or smoke was explained as a practice which interposed a magic protection between them and the powers of evil. This homœopathic device of using the evil power's own sacred fire as a means of protection against himself somewhat suggests that seething of the kid in its mother's milk which was repro-

---

[1] Gaidoz: *Esquisse de la Réligion des Gaulois*, p. 21.

bated by the Levitical law; but, no doubt, pagan
"demons" were considered fair game. The explanation, of course, is an obviously and clumsily forced
one; it was the grim druidical philosophy that—to
quote Caesar—"unless the life of man was repaid
for the life of man, the will of the immortal gods
could not be appeased" that dictated both the
national and the private human sacrifices of the
Celts, the shadows of which remain in the leaping
through the bonfires, and in the numerous recorded
sacrifices of cattle within quite recent times.

Mr. Laurence Gomme, in his *Ethnology in Folklore*, has collected many modern instances of the
sacrifices of cattle not only in Ireland and Scotland,
but also in Wales, Yorkshire, Northamptonshire,
Cornwall, and the Isle of Man.[1] "Within twenty miles
of the metropolis of Scotland a relative of Professor
Simpson offered up a live cow as a sacrifice to the
spirit of the murrain."[2] In Wales, when cattle-
sickness broke out, a bullock was immolated by
being thrown down from the top of a high rock.
Generally, however, the wretched victims were
burned alive. In 1859 an Isle of Man farmer
offered a heifer as a burnt offering near Tynwald
Hill, to avert the anger of the ghostly occupant of
a barrow which had been desecrated by opening.
Sometimes, even, these burnt oblations were offered
to an alleged Christian saint. The registers of the
Presbytery of Dingwall for the years 1656 and 1678
contain records of the sacrifices of cattle upon the

[1] Gomme: *Ethnology in Folklore*, pp. 136–139.
[2] *Ibid.*, p. 137.

site of an ancient temple in honour of a being whom
some called " St. Mourie", and others, perhaps knowing his doubtful character, "ane god Mourie".[1]   At
Kirkcudbright, it was St. Cuthbert, and at Clynnog,
in Wales, it was St. Beuno, who was thought to
delight in the blood of bulls.[2]

Such sacrifices of cattle appear mainly to have
been offered to stay plague among cattle.   Man for
man and beast for beast, was, perhaps, the old rule.
But among all nations, human sacrifices have been
gradually commuted for those of animals.   The
family of the O'Herlebys in Ballyvorney, County
Cork, used in olden days to keep an idol, "an image
of wood about two feet high, carved and painted like
a woman".[3]   She was the goddess of smallpox, and
to her a sheep was immolated on behalf of anyone
seized with that disease.

The third form of Celtic pagan survival is found
in numerous instances of the adoration of water,
trees, stones, and animals.   Like the other "Aryan"
nations, the Celts worshipped their rivers.   The
Dee received divine honours as a war-goddess with
the title of Aerfon, while the Ribble, under its name
of Belisama, was identified by the Romans with
Minerva.[4]   Myths were told of them, as of the
sacred streams of Greece.   The Dee gave oracles
as to the results of the perpetual wars between the
Welsh and the English; as its stream encroached

---

[1] Mitchell : *The Past in the Present*, pp. 271, 275.
[2] Elton : *Origins of English History*, p. 284.
[3] Gomme : *Ethnology in Folklore*, p. 140.
[4] The word Dee probably meant "divinity". The river was also called Dyfridwy,
i.e. "water of the divinity". See Rhys: *Lectures on Welsh Philology*, p. 307.

either upon the Welsh or the English side, so one
nation or the other would be victorious.[1]   The
Tweed, like many of the Greek rivers, was credited
with human descendants.[2]   That the rivers of Great
Britain received human sacrifices is clear from the
folklore concerning many of them.   Deprived of
their expected offerings, they are believed to snatch
by stealth the human lives for which they crave.
" River of Dart, River of Dart, every year thou
claimest a heart," runs the Devonshire folk-song.
The Spey, too, requires a life yearly,[3] but the Spirit
of the Ribble is satisfied with one victim at the end
of every seven years.[4]

Evidence, however, of the worship of rivers is
scanty compared with that of the adoration of wells.
" In the case of well-worship," says Mr. Gomme, " it
may be asserted with some confidence that it prevails
in every county of the three kingdoms."[5]   He finds
it most vital in the Gaelic counties, somewhat less
so in the British, and almost entirely wanting in the
Teutonic south-east.   So numerous, indeed, are "holy
wells" that several monographs have been written
solely upon them.[6]   In some cases these wells were
resorted to for the cure of diseases; in others, to
obtain change of weather, or "good luck".   Offerings were made to them, to propitiate their guardian
gods or nymphs.   Pennant tells us that in olden

---

[1] Rhys: *Celtic Britain*, p. 68,
[2] Rogers: *Social Life in Scotland*, chap. III, p. 336.
[3] *Folklore*, chap. III, p. 72.
[4] Henderson: *Folklore of Northern Counties*, p. 265.
[5] Gomme: *Ethnology in Folklore*. p. 78.
[6] Hope: *Holy Wells of England*; Harvey: *Holy Wells of Ireland*.

times the rich would sacrifice one of their horses at
a well near Abergeleu, to secure a blessing upon the
rest.[1] Fowls were offered at St Tegla's Well, near
Wrexham, by epileptic patients.[2] But of late years
the well-spirits have had to be content with much
smaller tributes—such trifles as pins, rags, coloured
pebbles, and small coins.

With sacred wells were often connected sacred
trees, to whose branches rags and small pieces of
garments were suspended by their humble votaries.
Sometimes, where the ground near the well was
bare of vegetation, bushes were artificially placed
beside the water. The same people who venerated
wells and trees would pay equal adoration to sacred
stones. Lord Roden, describing, in 1851, the Island
of Inniskea, off the coast of Mayo, asserts that a
sacred well called "Derrivla" and a sacred stone
called "Neevougi", which was kept carefully wrapped
up in flannel and brought out at certain periods to
be publicly adored, seemed to be the only deities
known to that lone Atlantic island's three hundred
inhabitants.[3] It sounds incredible; but there is
ample evidence of the worship of fetish stones by
quite modern inhabitants of our islands. The Clan
Chattan kept such a stone in the Isle of Arran; it
was believed, like the stone of Inniskea, to be able
to cure diseases, and was kept carefully "wrapped
up in fair linen cloth, and about that there was a
piece of woollen cloth".[4] Similarly, too, the worship

[1] Sikes: *British Goblins*, p. 351.   [2] *Ibid.*, p. 329.
[3] Roden: *Progress of the Reformation in Ireland*, pp. 51-54.
[4] Martin: *Description of the Western Islands*, pp. 166-226.

of wells was connected with the worship of animals. At a well in the "Devil's Causeway", between Ruckley and Acton, in Shropshire, lived, and perhaps still live, four frogs who were, and perhaps still are, believed to be "the devil and his imps"—that is to say, gods or demons of a proscribed idolatry.[1] In Ireland such guardian spirits are usually fish—trout, eels, or salmon thought to be endowed with eternal life.[2] The genius of a well in Banffshire took the form of a fly, which was also said to be undying, but to transmigrate from body to body. Its function was to deliver oracles; according as it seemed active or lethargic, its votaries drew their omens.[3] It is needless to multiply instances of a still surviving cult of water, trees, stones, and animals. Enough to say that it would be easy. What concerns us is that we are face to face in Britain with living forms of the oldest, lowest, most primitive religion in the world—one which would seem to have been once universal, and which, crouching close to the earth, lets other creeds blow over it without effacing it, and outlives one and all of them.

It underlies the three great world-religions, and still forms the real belief of perhaps the majority of their titular adherents. It is characteristic of the wisdom of the Christian Church that, knowing its power, she sought rather to sanctify than to extirpate it. What once were the Celtic equivalents of the Greek "fountains of the nymphs" were consecrated as "holy wells". The process of so adopting

1 Burne: *Shropshire Folklore*, p. 416.
2 Gomme: *Ethnology in Folklore*, pp. 92-93.   3 *Ibid.*, p. 102.

them began early. St. Columba, when he went in
the sixth century to convert the Picts, found a
spring which they worshipped as a god; he blessed
it, and "from that day the demon separated from
the water ".[1] Indeed, he so sanctified no less than
three hundred such springs.[2] Sacred stones were
equally taken under the ægis of Christianity. Some
were placed on the altars of cathedrals, others built
into consecrated walls. The animal gods either
found themselves the heroes of Christian legends,
or where, for some reason, such adoption was hopeless, were proclaimed "witches' animals", and dealt
with accordingly. Such happened to the hare, a
creature sacred to the ancient Britons,[3] but now in
bad odour among the superstitious. The wren, too,
is hunted to death upon St. Stephen's Day in Ireland. Its crime is said to be that it has "a drop of
the de'il's blood in it", but the real reason is probably to be found in the fact that the Irish druids
used to draw auguries from its chirpings.

We have made in this volume some attempt to
draw a picture of the ancient religion of our earliest
ancestors, the Gaelic and the British Celts. We
have shown what can be gathered of the broken
remnants of a mythology as splendid in conception
and as brilliant in colour as that of the Greeks.
We have tried to paint its divine figures, and to
retell their heroic stories. We have seen them

---

[1] Adamnan's *Vita Columbæ*.
[2] Dr. Whitley Stokes: *Three Middle Irish Homilies*.
[3] Caesar: *De Bello Gallico*, Book V, chap. XII.

fall from their shrines, and yet, rising again, take on new lives as kings, or saints, or knights of romance, and we have caught fading glimpses of them surviving to-day as the "fairies", their rites still cherished by worshippers who hardly know who or why they worship. Of necessity this survey has been brief and incomplete. Whether the great edifice of the Celtic mythology will ever be wholly restored one can at present only speculate. Its colossal fragments are perhaps too deeply buried and too widely scattered. But, even as it stands ruined, it is a mighty quarry from which poets yet unborn will hew spiritual marble for houses not made with hands.

APPENDIX

A FEW BOOKS UPON CELTIC MYTHOLOGY AND LITERATURE

The object of this short list is merely to supplement the marginal notes by pointing out to a reader desirous of going deeper into the subject the most recent and accessible works upon it. That they should be accessible is, in its intention, the most important thing; and therefore only books easily and cheaply obtainable will be mentioned.

INTRODUCTORY

Matthew Arnold.—THE STUDY OF CELTIC LITERATURE. Popular Edition. London, 1891.

Ernest Renan.—THE POETRY OF THE CELTIC RACES (and other studies). Translated by William G. Hutchinson. London, 1896.
Two eloquent appreciations of Celtic literature.

Magnus Maclean, M.A., D.C.L. — THE LITERATURE OF THE CELTS. Its History and Romance. London, 1902.
A handy exposition of all the branches of Celtic literature.

Elizabeth A. Sharp (editor).—LYRA CELTICA. An Anthology of Representative Celtic Poetry. Ancient Irish, Alban, Gaelic, Breton, Cymric, and Modern Scottish and Irish Celtic Poetry. With introduction and notes by William Sharp. Edinburgh, 1896.

Alfred Nutt.—CELTIC AND MEDIÆVAL ROMANCE. No. 1 of Mr. Nutt's "Popular Studies in Mythology, Romance, and Folklore". London, 1899.
A pamphlet briefly tracing the indebtedness of mediæval European literature to pre-mediæval Celtic sources.

HISTORICAL

H. d'Arbois de Jubainville.—LA CIVILISATION DES CELTES ET CELLE DE L'ÉPOPÉE HOMÉRIQUE. Paris, 1899.
   Vol. VI of the author's monumental " Cours de Littérature celtique ."

Patrick Weston Joyce.—A SOCIAL HISTORY OF ANCIENT IRELAND, treating of the Government, Military System, and Law; Religion, Learning, and Art; Trades, Industries, and Commerce; Manners, Customs, and Domestic Life of the Ancient Irish People. 2 vols. London, 1903.

Charles I. Elton, F.S.A. — ORIGINS OF ENGLISH HISTORY. Second edition, revised. London, 1890.

John Rhys.—CELTIC BRITAIN. "Early Britain" Series. London, 1882.

H. d'Arbois de Jubainville.—INTRODUCTION A L'ÉTUDE DE LA LITTÉRATURE CELTIQUE. Vol. I of the " Cours de Littérature celtique ". Paris, 1883.
   Contains, among other information, the fullest and most authentic account of the druids and druidism.

GAELIC MYTHOLOGY

H. d'Arbois de Jubainville.—LE CYCLE MYTHOLOGIQUE IRLAN-DAIS ET LA MYTHOLOGIE CELTIQUE. Vol. II of the "Cours de Littérature celtique". Paris, 1884. Translated into English as
THE IRISH MYTHOLOGICAL CYCLE AND CELTIC MYTHOLOGY. With notes by R. I. Best. Dublin, 1903.
   An account of Irish mythical history and of some of the greater Gaelic gods. With chapters on some of the more striking phases of Celtic belief.

Alfred Nutt.—THE VOYAGE OF BRAN, SON OF FEBAL. An Irish Historic Legend of the eighth century. Edited by Kuno Meyer. With essays upon the Happy Otherworld in Irish Myth and upon the Celtic Doctrine of Rebirth. Vol. I—The Happy Otherworld. Vol. II—The Celtic Doctrine of Rebirth. Grimm Library, Vols. IV and VI. London, 1895-1897.

Contains, among other notable contributions to the study of Celtic mythology, an enquiry into the nature of the Tuatha Dé Danann, a subject briefly treated in the same author's

THE FAIRY MYTHOLOGY OF SHAKESPEARE. No. 6 of "Popular Studies in Mythology, Romance, and Folklore". London, 1900.

Patrick Weston Joyce.—OLD CELTIC ROMANCES. Translated from the Gaelic. London, 1894.

A retelling in popular modern style of some of the more important mythological and Fenian stories.

Lady Gregory.—GODS AND FIGHTING MEN. The story of the Tuatha Dé Danaan and of the Fianna of Erin. Arranged and put into English by Lady Gregory. With a Preface by W. B. Yeats. London, 1904.

Covers much the same ground as Mr. Joyce's book, but in more literary manner.

Alfred Nutt.—OSSIAN AND THE OSSIANIC LITERATURE. No. 3 of "Popular Studies in Mythology, Romance, and Folklore". London, 1899.

A short survey of the literature connected with the Fenians.

John Gregorson Campbell, Minister of Tiree. — THE FIANS. Stories, poems, and traditions of Fionn and his Warrior Band, collected entirely from oral sources. With introduction and bibliographical notes by Alfred Nutt. Vol. IV of "Waifs and Strays of Celtic Tradition". London, 1891.

An account of the Fenians from the Scottish-Gaelic side.

Alfred Nutt.—CUCHULAINN THE IRISH ACHILLES. No. 8 of "Popular Studies in Mythology, Romance, and Folklore". London, 1900.

A brief but excellent introduction to the Cuchulainn cycle.

Lady Gregory.—CUCHULAIN OF MUIRTHEMNE. The story of the Men of the Red Branch of Ulster. Arranged and put into English by Lady Gregory. With a Preface by W. B. Yeats. London, 1902.

A retelling in poetic prose of the tales connected with Cuchulainn.

Eleanor Hull.—THE CUCHULLIN SAGA IN IRISH LITERATURE. Being a collection of stories relating to the Hero Cuchullin, translated from the Irish by various scholars. Compiled and

edited with introduction and notes by Eleanor Hull. With
Map of Ancient Ireland. Grimm Library, Vol. VIII.
London, 1898.

*A series of Cuchulainn stories from the ancient Irish manu-
scripts. More literal than Lady Gregory's adaptation.*

H. d'Arbois de Jubainville.—L'ÉPOPÉE CELTIQUE EN IRLANDE.
Vol. V of the "Cours de Littérature celtique". Paris, 1892.

*A collection, translated into French, of some of the principal
stories of the Cuchulainn cycle, with various appendices upon
Gaelic mythological subjects.*

L. Winifred Faraday, M.A.—THE CATTLE RAID OF CUALGNE
(Tain Bo Cuailgne). An old Irish prose-epic translated for
the first time from the Leabhar na h-Uidhri and the Yellow
Book of Lecan. Grimm Library, Vol. XVI. London,
1904.

*A strictly literal rendering of the central episode of the
Cuchulainn cycle.*

BRITISH MYTHOLOGY

Ivor B. John.—THE MABINOGION. No. 11 of "Popular Studies
in Mythology, Romance, and Folklore". London, 1901.

A pamphlet introduction to the Mabinogion literature.

Lady Charlotte Guest.—THE MABINOGION. From the Welsh of
the LLYFR COCH O HERGEST (the Red Book of Hergest)
in the library of Jesus College, Oxford. Translated, with
notes, by Lady Charlotte Guest.

First edition.   Text, translation, and notes, 3 vols., 1849.
Translation and notes only, 1 vol., 1877.
The Boys' Mabinogion, 1881.

*Cheap editions of this classic have been lately issued. One
may obtain it in Mr. Nutt's handsome little volume; as one of
Dent's " Temple Classics"; or in the " Welsh Library".*

J. Loth.—LES MABINOGION, traduits en entier pour la première
fois en français avec un commentaire explicatif et des notes
critiques. 2 vols. Vols. III and IV of De Jubainville's
"Cours de Littérature celtique". Paris, 1889.

*A more exact translation than that of Lady Guest, with
notes embodying more recent scholarship.*

J. A. Giles, D.C.I..—OLD ENGLISH CHRONICLES, including . . . Geoffrey of Monmouth's British History, Gildas, Nennius . . . Edited, with illustrative notes, by J. A. Giles, D.C.L. "Bohn's Antiquarian Library". London, 1901.

> *The most accessible edition of Geoffrey of Monmouth.*

Sir Thomas Malory.—THE MORTE DARTHUR. Edited by Dr. H. Oskar Sommer. Vol. I—the Text. Vol. II—Glossary, Index, &c. Vol. III—Study on the Sources. London, 1889–1891.

> *Vol. I of this, the best text of the Morte Darthur, can be obtained separately.*

Jessie L. Weston.—KING ARTHUR AND HIS KNIGHTS. A survey of Arthurian romance. No. 4 of "Popular Studies in Mythology, Romance, and Folklore". London, 1899.

Alfred Nutt.—THE LEGENDS OF THE HOLY GRAIL. No. 14 of "Popular Studies in Mythology, Romance, and Folklore". London, 1902.

> *Useful introductions to a more special study of Arthurian literature.*

COMPARATIVE STUDY OF CELTIC MYTHOLOGY

John Rhys.—LECTURES ON THE ORIGIN AND GROWTH OF RELIGION AS ILLUSTRATED BY CELTIC HEATHENDOM. "The Hibbert Lectures for 1886." London, 1898.

John Rhys.—STUDIES IN THE ARTHURIAN LEGEND. Oxford, 1901.

> *These two volumes are the most important attempts yet made towards a scientific and comprehensive study of the Celtic mythology.*

CELTIC FAIRY AND FOLK LORE

GAELIC

T. Crofton Croker.—FAIRY LEGENDS AND TRADITIONS OF THE SOUTH OF IRELAND.

> *This book is one of the earliest, and, if not the most scientific, perhaps the most attractive of the many collections of Irish fairy-lore. Later compilations are Mr. William Larminie's*

"*West Irish Folktales and Romances*", and Mr. *Jeremiah Curtin's* "*Hero Tales of Ireland*", "*Myths and Folklore of Ireland*", and "*Tales of the Fairies, collected in South Munster*". *On the Scotch side, notice should be particularly taken of Campbell's* "*Popular Tales of the West Highlands*" *and the volumes entitled* "*Waifs and Strays of Celtic Tradition*". *All these books are either recent or recently republished, and are merely selected out of a large list of works, valuable and otherwise, upon this lighter side of Celtic mythology.*

BRITISH

John Rhys.—CELTIC FOLKLORE, WELSH AND MANX. 2 vols. Oxford, 1901.

Wirt Sikes.—BRITISH GOBLINS: Welsh Folklore, Fairy Mythology, Legends, and Traditions. By Wirt Sikes, United States Consul for Wales. London, 1880.

FOLKLORE COMPARATIVELY TREATED

George Laurence Gomme. — ETHNOLOGY IN FOLKLORE. "Modern Science" Series. London, 1892.
An attempt to assign apparently non-Aryan beliefs and customs in the British islands to pre-Aryan inhabitants.

INDEX

Aberffraw, marriage of Branwen at, 289.

Abergeleu, sacred well at, 415.

Achill Island, folk-tales preserved at, 233.

Achilles, the Irish, 158.

Achren, battle of, 305, 306; castle of, 320.

Acrisius, 236.

Adamnan's *Life of Saint Columba*, 401, 417.

Advocates' Library at Edinburgh, 11, 190.

Aebh, wife of Lêr, 142.

Aed, son of Lêr, 143.

Aedh, son of Miodhchaoin, 105.

Aeife, wife of Lêr, 142, 143, 144.

Aerfon, a title of the river Dee, 413.

Æs Sídhe, the "folk of the mounds", the gods or fairies, 137, 168.

Africa, 19, 120, 274, 324.

Aganippus, king of the Franks, 382, 383.

Agriculture god of, British, 261; a Gaulish, 274.

Ailbhe, foster-daughter of Bodb the Red, 142.

Aileach, grave of Nuada at, 122, 157.

Ailill, king of Connaught, 147, 154, 164, 165, 175, 179, 200.

Ailinn, love-story of, 188, 189.

Ailioll of Arran, 142.

Ainé, queen of the fairies of South Munster, 244-246.

Ainle, one of the sons of Usnach, 192, 193, 196.

Airceltrai, the *sídh* of Ogma, 136, 157.

Airem, Eochaid, high king of Ireland, 147, 148, 149, 150, 151, 152, 331, 332.

Airem, meaning of the word, 149, 333.

Airmid, daughter of Diancecht, 80, 81, 82, 110.

Alator, a war-god worshipped in Britain, 275.

Alaw, river in Anglesey, 294, 295.

Alba, 97, 104, 163, 178, 192, 193, 196, 382; Deirdre's farewell to, 194-195.

Albania, a name for Alba, 382.

Ale of Goibniu, 61.

Allobroges, 384, 385.

Amaethon, son of Dôn, British god of Agriculture, 261, 305, 308, 313, 316, 345; fights against Brân in the battle of Achren, 305-308; assists Kulhwch to win Olwen, 345.

Amergin, druid of the Milesians, 123-130.

Amesbury, "castle" of, 29.

Amlwch, stream of, 295.

Ana, see Anu.

Ancient Britons, who were the, 18-23.

Aneurin, a sixth-century British bard, 11, 295, 372.

Aneurin, the Book of, 11.

Anglesey, island of, 289, 294, 322, 388, 400.

Anglo-Saxon, our descent not entirely, 3.

Anguish, Anguissance, king of Ireland, 357.

Angus, Gaelic god of love and beauty, 56, 79, 80, 117, 136, 139-142, 147, 156, 157, 205, 211-214, 217, 218, 221, 240; his attributes, 56; his wooing of Caer, 140-142; cheats his father, the Dagda, 139; steals Etain from Mider, 147; helps Diarmait and Grainne, 217, 218, 221; matches his pigs against the Fenians, 213-214.

Anicetus, Sol Apollo, a Romano-Britisn god, 275.

Animals, sacred, 406, 416, 417; sacrifices of, 406, 411, 412, 413.

Anna, sister of Arthur, 323.

Annals of the Four Masters, 204.

Annwn, the British Otherworld, 254

273, 278-282, 303, 308, 309, 318, 319, 321, 390, 391.

Annwn, the Spoiling of, a poem by Taliesin, 305, 306, 317, 366.

Anu, or Ana, a Gaelic goddess of prosperity and abundance, 50; the "Paps of Ana", 50; still living in folklore as Aynia and Ainé, 245.

Aoibhinn, queen of the fairies of North Munster, 244.

Aoife, an Amazon defeated by Cuchulainn, 164, 176, 177.

Aphrodité, the British, 271, 388.

Apollo, the Gaelic, 62; the British, 262; a temple of, in Britain, 42, 325.

Apples, of the Garden of the Hesperides, 98, 99, 102; in the Celtic Elysium, 98, 136.

Apple-tree of Ailenn, 189.

Aquitani, 22.

Aranon, son of Milé, 123.

Arawn, king of Annwn, 279, 280, 281, 306, 308, 309, 312, 315, 329, 357, 375.

Ardan, a son of Usnach, 192, 193, 196.

Ard Chein, 93.

Arddu, Black Stone of, 305.

Arês, 52.

Argetlâm, 49, 78.

Arianrod, a British goddess, 261-265, 313, 317, 322, 364, 371; her place in later legend taken by Arthur's sister, 364.

Armagh, 136, 158.

Arnold, Matthew, 3, 16, 356.

Arran, Isle of, 60, 142, 415.

Art, the "Lonely", king of Tara, 189, 202.

Artaius, Mercurius, a Gaulish god, 274.

Arthur, 6, 8, 14, 155, 202, 222, 246, 258, 259, 271, 273, 274, 276, 296, 304, 306, 311, 312-320, 322, 323, 326, 327, 328, 329, 330-343, 348, 349, 351-360, 362, 364-366, 368, 371, 374-376, 392, 407; the mythical and the historical, 313, 314; assumes the attributes of Gwydion, 316; the Spoiling of Annwn by, 319-322; becomes head of the British Pantheon, 312-313; wins Olwen for Kulhwch, 343-353; in Geoffrey of Monmouth's *History,* 374, 375; leads the Wild Hunt, 392.

Arthurian Legend, Studies in the, Pro-

fessor Rhys's, 148, 158, 255, 257, 258, 269, 272, 274, 278, 285, 313, 314, 316, 321, 322, 323, 326, 327, 328, 329, 330, 331, 332, 333, 358, 359, 360, 364, 367, 368, 369, 370, 383, 387, 389.

Artur, son of Nemed, 274.

Aryans, 21, 31, 32, 247; common traditions of the, 32, 176, 189; Aryan languages, 21.

Astarte, worshipped at Corbridge, 275.

Astolat, 362.

Athens, 153.

Athlone, 175, 216.

Augusel, a king of Scotland, 375.

Aurelius, a British king, 325.

Avallach, see Avallon.

Avallon, a British god of the Underworld, 329, 359; Isle of, 374, and see Avilion.

Avebury, the "castle" of, 29.

Avilion, 133, 315, 329, 332, 334, 335, 390, 394.

Aynia, a fairy queen of Ulster, 245.

Babylon, 178.

Badb, a Gaelic war-goddess, 52, 53, 72, 117, 119, 245; the name often used generically, 53; description of a, 53.

"Badger in the bag", the game of, 285, 303.

Badon, battle of, 338.

Baile, love-story of, 188-189.

Baile's Strand, 186, 188.

Bajocassus, Temple of the sun-god Belinus at, 276.

Bala lake, 265.

Balan, 276, 357, 364.

Balder, 33.

Balgatan, a mountain near Cong, 73.

Balin, 276, 357, 358, 364.

Ballymagauran, village of, 38.

Ballymote, Book of, 10, 38, 123, 138, 229, 231.

Ballysadare, 75.

Balor, a king of the Fomors, 48-49, 50, 79, 83, 84, 90, 112, 113, 120, 233-239, 269, 324, 341, 345, 371; his evil eye, 49; kills Nuada and Macha, 112; is blinded by Lugh, 112; tales of, in modern folklore, 233-239.

"Balor's Hill", 69, 90.

Ban, king of Benwyk, 356, 360, 362.

Banba, a goddess representing Ireland, 125; an ancient name of Ireland, 126, 153.

Banshee, meaning of the word, 137.

Baoisgne, Clann, 209, 217.

Bards, 32, 42.

Bardsey Island, 326.

Barrow, river, how it got its name, 62.

Barrule, South, 242.

Barry, the, 246.

Basque race, 19.

Bath, 228, 275, 276, 338, 381.

Bathurst's *Roman Antiquities in Lydney Park*, 254.

Battle of Achren, 305; of Badon, 338; of Camlan, 222, 315, 334, 337, 375, 376; of Clontarf, 53; of Gabhra, 222, 223, 225, 315; of Mag Rath, 52; of Moytura Northern, 107–117, 407; of Moytura Southern, 72–75; of the Trees, 123, 305–308.

Bayeux, temple of Belinus at, 276.

Bean, curious passage relating to the, 306, 307.

Becuma of the Fair Skin, 202.

Bedivere, Sir, 6.

Bedwini, Arthur's bishop, 337.

Bedwyr, a follower of Arthur, 343, 344, 349.

Belacatudor, a war-god worshipped in Britain, 275.

Belgæ, 23, 76.

Beli, a British god, 120, 252, 260, 268, 295, 313, 335, 376.

Belinus, a Celtic sun-god, 276, 358, 364; as a king of Britain, 276, 384, 385.

Belisama, the Latin name of the Ribble, 413.

Beltaine, the Gaelic May-day, 41, 65, 287, 406, 408, 409, 410.

Berber race, 19.

Beth, an Iberian god, 64.

Bettws-y-coed, 7.

Beuno, Saint, sacrifices of cattle to, 413.

Big-Knife, Osla, 352, 353.

Bilé, father of the Gaelic gods and men, 51, 65, 120, 121, 122, 252.

Billingsgate, origin of name, 385.

Birds, of Rhiannon, the, 273, 294, 296; Dechtiré and her maidens changed into, 169.

Black Book of Caermarthen, the, 11, 255, 311, 312, 335.

Bladud, mythical founder of Bath, 381.

Blathnat, daughter of Mider, 55, 179.

Bliant, Castle, 358.

Blodeuwedd, wife of Lleu Llaw Gyffes 265, 266, 268.

Blood-fines among the Celts, 30; blood-fine paid for Cian, 94–97.

Boann, wife of the Dagda, 55, 139, 141.

Boar, wild, of Bengulben, 221; the Boar Trwyth, 347–353.

Bodb the Red, son of the Dagda, 60, 133, 140, 141–145, 157, 205, 208; is made king of the Tuatha Dé Danann, 140; his swineherd, 164; marries nis daughter Sadb to Finn, 208.

Bogles, 393, 403, 405.

Bonfires in Celtic ritual, 409–412.

Boreadæ, 42.

Bordeaux, Sir Huon of, 7.

Borrach, 193, 195, 200.

Bors, king of Gaul, 360.

Bors, Sir, 368, 369.

Boyne, river, 55, 56, 129, 136, 137, 158, 210, 213, 230.

Brahmans, 32.

Bran, son of Febal, an Irish king, 134, 135, 224.

Bran, Finn's favourite hound, 213.

Brân, British god of the Underworld, 258, 271–272, 276, 289–294, 296, 306, 308, 313, 328, 329, 331, 338, 356, 357, 360, 364, 366, 384, 386, 387, 389, 394; fights the battle of Achren, 306; becomes the "Wonderful Head", 296; in Geoffrey of Monmouth's *History*, 384, 385; in the Morte Darthur, 356, 357; introduces Christianity into Britain, 386.

Brandegore, King, 272, 356.

Brandegoris, King, 356.

Brandel, Brandiles, Sir, 356.

Branwen, British goddess of love, 271, 289–294, 387.

Brazil, 133.

Brea, ford of, Finn killed at the, 222.

Breasal's Island, 133.

Brécilien, Forest of, 361.

Bregon, 121.

Brennius, a mythical British king, 5, 276, 384, 385.

Brennus, 385.

Bress, son of Elathan, a Fomor, 50, 78–80, 82, 83, 90, 108–111, 115–116, 269; his beauty, 50; marries Brigit, and is made king over the Tuatha Dé Danann, 78; is forced to abdicate, 83; makes war on the Tuatha Dé Danaan, 83; is defeated and captured, 115–116.

Brian, son of Tuirenn, 90, 91, 92, 94, 99–102, 103, 105, 106.

Briareus, 326.

" Bridge of the Cliff ", the, 163.

Bridget, Saint, 7, 56, 228.

Brigantes, a North British tribe, 277.

Brigantia, a British Minerva, 277.

Brigindo, a Gaulish goddess, 277.

Brigit, Gaelic goddess of fire, poetry, and the hearth, 56, 78, 109, 110, 228, 269, 277, 387; is married to Bress, 78; is canonized as Saint Bridget, 228, 387.

Bri Leith, the *sīdh* of Mider, 136, 148, 152, 332.

Brindled ox, the, 320.

Britain, ancient names of, 292, 323.

British Goblins, Mr. Wirt Sikes', 389, 393, 415.

Britons, ancient, who were the, 18–23.

Britonum, Historia. See Historia, Geoffrey, Nennius.

Brittany, 24.

Briun, son of Bethar, 113.

Brownies, 248, 393 403.

Brude, king of the Picts, 401.

Brugh-na-boyne, 136, 139, 160, 213, 214.

Brutus, 121, 374.

Brythons, 21, 22, 23, 24, 35.

Buarainech, father of Balor, 48.

Buinne, the Ruthless Red, son of Fergus, 193, 196, 197.

Bull, the Brown, of Cualgne, 164, 165, 168, 175; the White-horned, of Connaught, 165, 175.

Bwbachod, 393.

Cadbury, the supposed site of Camelot, 335.

Cader Idris, 305.

Caemhoc, Saint, 146.

Caer, daughter of Etal Ambuel, 141.

Caer Arianrod, 252, 264.

Caer Badus, 381.

Caer Bannawg, 367.

Caer Colvin, 275.

Caer Dathyl, 308, 310.

Caer Golud, 320.

Caer Llyr, 270.

Caer London, 376.

Caer Myrddin, 324.

Caer Ochren, 320.

Caer Pedryvan, 319, 356, 367.

Caer Rigor, 319.

Caer Sarrlog, 386.

Caer Sidi, 319, 321, 322, 368.

Caer Vandwy, 257, 320.

Caer Vedwyd, 319.

Caer Wydyr, 320.

Caesar, Julius, 5, 8, 18, 22, 23, 25, 27, 30, 35, 38, 119, 204, 376, 399, 412, 417.

Cairbré, son of Cormac, 206, 222, 315.

Cairn of Octriallach, 110.

Cairpré, son of Ogma, bard of the Tuatha Dé Danann, 58, 82, 83, 87, 139.

Calais, 383.

Calatin the wizard, 171, 172; daughters of Calatin, 178–181.

Caledonians, 22.

Camelot, 314, 335.

Camlan, battle of, 222, 315, 334, 337, 375, 376.

Camulodunum, the Roman name of Colchester, 276.

Camulus, a Gaulish god of war and the sky, 51, 204, 275, 323.

Caoilte, a Fenian hero, 63, 146, 208, 212, 217, 222, 227, 246.

Caractacus, Carataca, 271, 386, 387.

Caradawc of the Strong Arms, son of Brân, 271, 291, 295, 338, 386, 389.

Carbonek, 357, 367.

Carmarthen, 324.

Carnac, 114.

Carnarvon, 310.

Carrowmore, 114.

Cassibellawn, Cassivelaunus, 376.

" Cassiopeia's Chair ", 252.

Castell y Moch, 310.

Castle of Arianrod, 252, 264.

Castle Bliant, 358.

Castle of Gwydion, 253.

Castle Hacket, 244.

Castle of Revelry, 366, 367.

Castle of Riches, 367.

"Castles", Celtic, 29.

Caswallawn, son of Beli, 295.

Cath Godeu. See the "Battle of the Trees".

Cathbad, druid of Emain Macha, 161, 162, 174, 178, 181, 190, 198, 200.

Cathubodva, a Gaulish war-goddess, 276.

Cauldrons in Celtic mythology; the Dagda's, 54, 71, 366; of Ogyrvran the Giant, 366; of Diwrnach the Gael, 346, 349; cauldron given by Brân to Matholwch, 290, 293, 366; cauldron stolen from Mider by Cuchulainn, 176, 366; cauldron kept in Annwn by the chief of Hades, 273, 319, 366; the legend of the Holy Grail founded upon Celtic myths of a cauldron of fertility and inspiration, 365-370.

Celtæ, 22.

Celtic mythical literature the forerunner of mediæval romance, 184.

Celtic strain in modern Englishmen, 3.

Celts: the, 19, 20, 21, 25-44, 70, 119, 121, 124, 136, 138, 261, 262, 278, 283, 329, 404, 407, 412.

Cemmes, a parish in Pembrokeshire, 394.

Cenn Cruaich, 41.

Cermait, i.e. "Honey-mouth", a title of Ogma, 57.

Cethé, son of Diancecht, 62, 90.

Cethlenn, wife of Balor, 90.

"Chain, Lugh's", 62; "chief's", 93.

Champion of the Tuatha Dé Danann, 59, 276; Champions of the Red Branch, see Red Branch; "The Champion's Prophecy", 201.

Chariots, war, of the Celts, 25, 27, 28.

Charon, 403.

Chaucer, 2, 12.

Chess, Mider's game with Eochaid Airem, 149; Ossian's game with Finn, 220.

Children of Dôn, Nudd, and Llyr, 252.

Christianity, introduced into Britain by Brân, 386, 387; conquers Druidism, 400, 401; adopts harmless heathen cults, 416, 417.

Cian, son of Diancecht, 62, 63, 78, 84, 90-94, 106, 235-237, 239, 269, 345, 371.

Ciaran, Saint, 10.

Cichol the Footless, a Fomor, 66.

Cilgwri, the Ousel of, 349.

Clann Baoisgne, 209, 217, 222.

Clan Chattan, 415.

Clann Morna, 209, 211, 218, 232.

Clann Neamhuinn, 216, 218.

Clann Ronan, 218.

Clas Myrddin, an old name for Britain, 323.

Claudius, Roman emperor, 387.

Cliodna, fairy queen of Munster, 244.

Clontarf, battle of, 53.

Clûd, goddess of the river Clyde, 284, 285.

Cluricanes, 248.

Cnoc Miodhchaoin, 97.

Cnucha, battle of, 209.

Coblynau, 393.

Cocidius, a war-god worshipped by a Dacian colony in Cumberland, 275.

Coed Helen, 310.

Coel, a mythical king of Britain, 275, 323.

Coir Anmann, the "Choice of Names", an old Irish tract, 50, 54, 61, 245, 270.

Colchester, 276.

"Cole, Old King", 276.

Collen, Saint, 389, 390, 391.

Columba, Saint, 12, 240, 401, 417.

Comes Britanniæ, 313.

Comes Littoris Saxonici, 314.

Comyn, Michael, a Gaelic poet, 223.

Conairé the Great, high king of Ireland, 152, 157.

Conall the Victorious, 163, 177, 183, 192, 193, 197, 198.

Conan, a Fenian hero, 209, 218.

Conann, son of Febar, a king of the Fomors, 67.

Conchobar, king of Ulster, 29, 147, 154-156, 158, 160-162, 166-168, 173, 174, 179, 185, 190-192, 193, 195-198, 200, 201, 204, 227; his treachery towards the sons of Usnach, 192-200; his tragical death, 155.

Condates, a war-god worshipped in Britain, 275.

Cong, village of, 73, 76.

Conlaoch, son of Cuchulainn, 177, 178.

Conn the Hundred Fighter, 201, 202.

Conn, son of Lêr, 143.

Conn, son of Miodhchaoin, 105.
Connaught, 73, 75, 76, 165, 168.
Connla, son of Conn the Hundred Fighter, 202.
Contemporary Review, the, 241.
Contrary Head, 242.
Conway, river, 262.
Cooking-places of the Fenians, 206.
Cooking-spits of the women of Fianchuivé, 96; at Tara, 98.
Cooley, see Cualgne.
Coranians, a mythical tribe of dwarfs, 377-379.
Corb, an Iberian god, 64.
Corbridge, 275.
Corc, son of Miodhchaoin, 105.
Corca-Duibhne, 70.
Corca-Oidce, 70.
Cordeilla, daughter of Leir, in Geoffrey of Monmouth's *History*, 381-383.
Cordelia, daughter of Shakespeare's *King Lear*, 259, 381.
Coritiacus, a war-god worshipped in Britain, 275.
Cormac, "the Magnificent", 201, 202, 203, 206, 215, 222, 315.
Cornwall, 3, 23, 294, 296, 327, 334, 353, 382, 384.
Coronation Stone, the, 71.
Corrib, see Lough Corrib.
Corspitium, see Corbridge.
Corwenna, mother of Brennius and Belinus, 385.
Count of Britain, 313; of the Saxon Shore, 314.
Court of Dôn, the, 252, 317.
Cow, Balor's Gray, 235, 236, 237, 240; Mider's three cows, 57, 176.
Cow, Book of the Dun, 10, 12, 14, 37, 156, 164, 175, 184, 202, 227.
Credné, the bronze-worker of the Tuatha Dé Danann, 85, 86, 109.
Crete, 153.
Creudylad, daughter of the British sky-god Lludd, 256, 258, 259, 332, 348, 381, 407.
Criminal Resolutions of Britain, the Three, 334.
Crom Croich, 40.
Cromm Cruaich, 38, 39, 41, 154, 402.
Cronos, 63, 65, 326.
"Croppies' Grave", the, at Tara, 72.

Cruind, the river, 165.
Cu, son of Diancecht, 62, 90.
Cualgne, a province of Ulster, 164, 165, 175.
Cuan, head of the Munster Fenians, 218.
Cuchulainn, chief hero of the Ultonians, 10, 11, 14, 27, 154, 155, 156, 158-188, 192, 193, 202, 204, 210, 217, 223, 227, 274, 366; is the son of Lugh, 159-160; obvious solar character of, 158-159; how he obtained his name, 160-161; fights in the Táin Bó Chuailgne, 164-175; his wooing of Emer, 184-186; his raid upon the Other World, 175-176; his death, 183; is raised from the dead by Saint Patrick, 227.
Culann, chief smith of the Ultonians, 161; "Culann's Hound", 161, 166.
"Culture-King", 153.
Cumhal, father of Finn, 204, 209, 210, 275.
Cunedda, a North British king, 373.
Cunobelinus, king of Britain, 387.
Curoi, king of Munster, 147, 154, 179.
Custennin, 343, 344.
Cuthbert, Saint, bulls sacrificed to, 413.
Cwm Cawlwyd, the Owl of, 349.
Cwn Annwn, the "Hounds of Hell" 391, 392.
Cwy, 320.
Cymbeline, Shakespeare's, 387.
Cymri, 255, 373.

Dagda, the, Gaelic god of the Earth, 54, 78, 79, 87, 98, 107-109, 116, 117, 122, 132, 135, 136, 138-141, 156, 157, 211, 213, 228, 230, 240, 243, 269, 346, 366; his dress, arms, and harp, 54; his porridge-feast, 108; is cheated by his son Angus, 139; resigns the kingship of the Tuatha Dé Danann, 140; his last appearance, 157.
Dairé of Cualgne, owner of the Brown Bull, 165.
Dalân, druid of Eochaid Airem, 392.
Danes, the, 230.
Danu, the mother of the Gaelic gods, the same as Anu, *q.v.*, 44, 50, 51, 70, 245, 252, 407.
Dart, river, 414.
Dartmoor, 392.
Darvha, Lake, 143-145.

Deaf Valley, the, 180.

Dechtiré, mother of Cuchulainn, 156, 159, 160, 181.

Dé Danann, see Tuatha Dé Danann.

Dee, river, 413.

Deimne, the first name of Finn, 210.

Deirdre, 190-200; Deirdre's Farewell to Alba, 194-195; Deirdre's Lament over the Sons of Usnach, 199-200.

Demetia, Roman province of, 273, 278.

Demetrius, an early traveller in Britain, 326.

"Demon of the air", Aeifé changed into a, 145.

Derivla, a sacred well in the island of Inniskea, 415.

Desmond, fourth Earl of, nicknamed "the Magician", 245.

"Destiny, laying a", a Celtic custom, 262-265, 340.

Devon, 312, 392.

Devwy, the dales of, 320.

Dialogue of the Elders, the, 205, 222, 404; Dialogues of Patrick and Ossian, 226-227.

Diancecht, the Gaelic god of medicine, 61, 62, 78, 80, 81, 82, 84, 85, 86, 90, 110, 141, 232, 269; makes a silver hand for Nuada, 78; kills his son Miach, 81-82; presides over the "Spring of Health", 110; prescriptions of Diancecht, 232.

Diarmait O'Duibhne, the Fenian Adonis, 209, 212, 215-221, 315.

Dinadan, Sir, 328.

Dinas Dinllev, 264.

Dinas Emrys, 324, 381.

Dingwall, Registers of the Presbytery of, 412.

Dinnsenchus, 38, 40, 132, 154.

Dio Cassius, 387.

Diodorus Siculus, 41, 42, 325.

Dionysus, rites of, 410.

Dis Pater, 51, 120, 252, 383.

Dissull the Giant, 348-349.

Diwrnach the Gael, the cauldron of, 346, 349.

Dobhar, king of Sicily, 96, 98, 102, 103.

Doctrine of the transmigration of souls, 36, 37.

Domnann, Fir, *i.e.* men of Domnu. See Fir Domnann.

Domnu, a goddess, mother of the Fomors, 48, 70, 112; meaning of the name, 48; gods of Domnu, 48, 70; men of Domnu, 70.

Dôn, the British equivalent of the Gaelic Danu, 44, 252, 260, 268, 269, 273, 295, 308, 310, 316; euhemerized into a king of Dublin, 372-373.

Donn, son of Milé, 126-131, 246.

"Donn's House", 246.

Dormarth, the hound of Gwyn son of Nudd, 257.

Dowth, 137-138.

Dragon, Red, of Britain, 378; White, of the Saxons, 378.

"Dragon-mouth", a lake called, 141.

Dream of Rhonabwy, the, 260, 312, 337, 338.

Drogheda, 137.

Drowes, river, 110.

Drudwyn, the whelp of Greid the son of Eri, 347.

Druidism, the religion of the Celts, 35, 43; possibly non-Aryan in origin, 36; in Gaul, 34; derived from Britain, 35; suppressed by the Romans, 399, 400.

Druids, 18, 33-37, 84, 111, 115, 151, 179, 180, 182, 188, 202, 399-401, 411, 412, 417; origin of the name, 33; in Gaul, 34; in Britain, 35; human sacrifices of the druids, 37, 412; the druids of Brude, king of the Picts, 401.

Drumcain, an old name for Tara, 126.

Dublin, 66, 372.

Duke of the Britains, the, 313.

Dulachan, 247, 248.

Dul-dauna, the, 237.

Dun Cow, Book of the. See Cow.

Dundalk, 177.

Dundealgan, 177, 181, 188, 189.

Dún Scaith, 175-176.

Dux Britanniarum. See Duke of the Britains.

Dwynwen, Saint, 388.

Dyfan, Saint, 386.

Dyfed, or Demetia, a province of South Wales, 273, 278, 279, 281, 282, 286, 298-301, 303, 304, 309, 310, 394.

Dylan, a British god, 261, 262, 322, 335, 360, 364, 371.

Eagle, of Gwern Abwy, 350; Lleu changed into an, 266–268.
Earl Gerald, 245.
Easal, king of the Golden Pillars, 96, 103.
Eber, son of Milé, 129–131, 146, 153.
Eber Scot, 120.
Eboracum, Roman name of York, 275.
Edeyrn, son of Nudd, 260.
Edinburgh, the Advocates' Library at, 11.
Eel, the Morrígú takes the shape of an, 169; transformation of the rival swineherds into eels, 165.
Egypt, 120.
Eigen, the first female saint in Britain, 386.
Eildon Hills, Arthur living beneath the, 335.
Elaine, 362.
Elathan, a king of the Fomors, 49, 50, 78, 83, 90, 116, 269.
Elayne, 358.
Elberich, 392.
Elders, Dialogue of the. See *Dialogue.*
Elen Lwyddawg, wife of Myrddin, 323, 362.
Eleutherius, Pope, 386.
Ellylion, the Welsh elves, 393.
Elton's *Origins of English History*, 6, 8, 25, 26, 70, 228, 327, 413.
Elves, 393.
Elysium, Celtic. See Other World, Celtic.
Emain Macha, the capital of ancient Ulster, 28, 29, 158, 160, 161, 162, 164, 173, 174, 179, 180, 183, 188, 192, 194, 196, 200, 201, 204.
Emer, wife of Cuchulainn, 162, 164, 177, 184–188.
Emer, the Wooing of, an old Irish saga, 28, 29, 37, 184.
Emperor, a title given in Welsh legend to Arthur, 314, 338.
Emrys, a title of Myrddin, 324, 329, 360, 369.
Englishmen, Celtic strain in, 3.
"Entertaining of the Noble Head", the, 296.
Eochaid, son of Erc, king of the Fir Bolgs, 69, 73, 74, 75.
Eochaid Airem, see Airem.
Eochaid O'Flynn, an Irish poet, 231.

Erc, king of Tara, 179, 182, 183.
Eremon, son of Milé, and first king of Ireland, 40, 129, 130, 131, 132, 146, 153, 154.
Erin, 97, 98, 99, 102, 104, 126, 193, 225, 231; meaning of the word, 126.
Eriu, a goddess representing Ireland, 125, 126, 128, 129.
Eros, the Gaelic, 56, 140. See Angus.
Essyllt, wife of March, or Mark. See Iseult.
Etain, wife of Mider, 57, 139, 147–152, 154, 224, 331–333.
Etair, a vassal of King Conchobar, 147.
Etal Ambuel, father of Caer, 141.
Etan, wife of Ogma, 62, 87, 239.
Ethnea, a name of Ethniu in modern folklore, 238.
Ethniu, daughter of Balor, 62, 79, 84, 90, 269, 371.
Ethnology in Folklore, Mr. G. L. Gomme's, 35, 69, 412, 413, 414, 416.
Etirun, "an idol of the Britons", 294.
Etive, Loch, 193.
Etruscans, the, 20; Etruscan mythology in modern Italian folklore, 403.
Ettard, 358.
Ettarre, Pelleas and, Tennyson's idyll of, 358.
Euhemerism of Gaelic gods, 227–230; of British gods, 372–389.
Euskarian race, 19.
Evelake, King, 359.
Evnissyen, son of Penardun, 290, 292, 293.

Failinis, the hound of the king of Ioruaidhé, 96, 97, 104.
Fairie Queene, Spenser's, 7, 389.
Fairies, the, 4, 137, 242–248, 389–393, 403, 404, 409, 418; the old gods are remembered as "fairies", 243–248, 389–393; two varieties of fairy in folklore, 403; Irish and Welsh fairies identical in nature, 404; king of the Irish fairies, 136; king of the Welsh fairies, 392; size of the fairies, 404; fairy money, 377; fairy food, 391; the "fairy hills", 135–139, 394.
Fal, the stone of. See Stone of Destiny.
"Falcon of May", 369; "Falcon of Summer", 369.

Falga, Isle of, 57, 175.

Falias, a city of the Tuatha Dé Danann, 71, 72.

Fand, wife of Manannán son of Lêr, 186–188, 202.

Faraday, Miss, her translation of the *Táin Bó Chuailgné*, 164.

Fata Morgana, 395.

Fate of the Children of Lêr, 142–146; of the Sons of Tuirenn, 90–105; of the Sons of Usnach, 190–200.

Fea, a war-goddess, wife of Nuada, 52.

"Feast of Age", Manannán's, 61, 98, 143.

Feast of Lugh, see Lugnassad.

Feast of St. John, 409.

Fec's Pool, on the Boyne, 210.

Fedlimid, vassal to King Conchobar, 190.

Fenians, the, 11, 17, 155, 201, 203–209, 211–215, 217–219, 220–223, 225, 226, 314, 315; real or mythical, 203–205; origin of, 206; duties of, 206; accomplishments of, 207; chief heroes of, 207–209; destruction of, at the battle of Gabhra, 222; stories of, 209–226; the Fenian sagas possibly non-Aryan, 70.

Fenius Farsa, 120.

Ferdiad, a warrior slain by Cuchulainn, 172, 173, 184.

Fergus, son of Finn, 208.

Fergus, son of Roy, an Ulster hero, 14, 166, 167, 170, 171, 175, 192–196, 198, 200.

Fergusson, Dr. James, 76, 114, 137, 138.

Festivals, Celtic solar or agricultural, 405–412.

Ffordd Elen, 324.

Fiacha, son of Conchobar, 197, 198.

Fiachadh, king of Ireland, 206.

Fiachra, son of Lêr, 143.

Fianchuivé, submarine island of, 97, 104.

Fianna Eirinn, see Fenians.

Figol, son of Mamos, druid of the Tuatha Dé Danann, 90.

Findabair, daughter of Medb, 168.

Findias, a city of the Tuatha Dé Danann, 71, 72.

Finn mac Coul (Cumhail), 4, 11, 16, 37, 146, 155, 201, 203, 204, 206, 207, 208, 209, 210–218, 220–222, 224, 226, 246,

(B 219)

254, 274, 314, 315; his upbringing and boy-feats, 209–210; reorganizes the Fenians, 211; is killed at the Ford of Brea, 222; is reborn as Mongan, an Ulster chief, 37; is he historical or mythical, 204; parallels between Finn and Arthur, 314–315.

Finn mac Gorman, compiler of the Book of Leinster, 10.

Finn the Seer, 210.

Finola, daughter of Lêr, 143.

Finvarra, king of the Irish fairies, 243, 244, 405.

Fiona Macleod, Miss, 241.

Fionn, see Finn.

Fionnbharr, the *sídh* of Meadha assigned to, 136; his appearance in the Fenian sagas, 212; becomes fairy king of Ireland, 243.

Fir Bolgs, an Iberian tribe, 68–70, 72–78, 114, 125, 229, 230, 407.

Fir Domnann, an Iberian tribe, 68–70, 76, 172.

Fir Gaillion, an Iberian tribe, 68–70, 76.

Fish, sacred, 416.

Fly, Etain changed into a, 147; Lugh takes the form of a, 159; a sacred, 416.

Folklore, Ethnology in. See *Ethnology*.

Folk-tales, Irish, 233–240; Welsh, 371.

Fomors, Gaelic deities of Death, Darkness, and the Sea, 11, 48–50, 67, 70, 76, 83, 86, 88, 89, 90, 98, 107–117, 120, 122, 157, 205, 225, 229, 230, 252, 269, 274, 327, 406; meaning of the name, 48; their war with the Tuatha Dé Danann, 107–117; are the Lochlannach in the Fenian sagas, 205.

Forgall the Wily, father of Emer, 162, 163, 164, 184.

Fotla, a goddess representing Ireland, 125; an ancient name of Ireland, 126.

"Four Ancient Books of Wales", the, 11, 15. See also Skene.

"Four Branches of the Mabinogi", the, 14, 15, 251, 278, 289, 312, 355.

"Four-cornered castle", the, 366.

Frazer's *Golden Bough*, 33.

"Frivolous Battles of Britain, The Three", 334.

Frogs, sacred, 416.

Fury, Great, and Little Fury, two swords of Manannán, 60, 217.

2 E a

Gabhra, battle of, 222, 223, 225, 315.

Gabius, a Roman consul, 385.

Gabriel Hounds, the, 392.

Gae bolg, Cuchulainn's spear, 170, 173, 178.

Gaels, 68, 69, 70, 71, 76, 93, 108, 119, 124, 149, 183, 203, 204, 230, 357.

Gaiar, son of Manannán, 202.

Gaillion, Fir. See Fir Gaillion.

Galahad, Sir, 362, 368, 369.

Galan-mai, Welsh spring festival, 408.

Gan Ceanach, 247.

Garden of the Hesperides, the, 95, 98, 99.

Gargantua, Rabelais', 386.

Gast Rhymri's cubs, 347, 349.

Gaul, 22, 274, 276, 383, 384, 385.

Gauls, the, 22, 23, 119, 230.

Gavida, 238, 239.

Gavidjeen Go, 235.

Gawain, Sir, 360, 363, 364, 369, 375.

Geasa, taboos among the Irish Celts, 177, 195, 216.

Genii locorum, 43.

Geoffrey of Monmouth, 9, 121, 251, 254, 259, 276, 323, 324, 330, 336, 372, 373–376, 381, 384.

George's Hill, Saint, 29.

Geraint, 312, 387.

Gildas, a British writer, 400.

" Glamour, the Realm of", an old name for Dyfed, 279.

Glamour put on Cuchulainn by Cathbad, 178 ; by the daughters of Calatin, 179, 180; put on the sons of Usnach, 198; on Arianrod, 264, 265; on Dyfed, 298.

Glass Castle, of the Fomors, 67; a synonym for the other world, 320, 367.

Glastonbury, 260, 329.

Glastonbury Tor, 272, 390.

Glenn Faisi, 130.

Glora, Isle of, 144, 145, 146.

Glyn Cûch, 279, 281.

Gobhan Saer, the, 232, 235, 240.

Goibniu, Gaelic god of smithcraft, 61, 84, 86, 98, 109, 110, 141, 231, 232, 238, 239, 261, 371; forges the weapons of the Tuatha Dé Danann, 61, 109; kills Ruadan, 110; his ale, 61; survives in tradition as the Gobhan Saer,

q.v.; as a character in folk-tale, 232–240. See Gavida and Gavidjeen Go.

Goidel, a mythical ancestor of the Irish, 120.

Goidels, the, 21, 22, 23, 24, 35.

Golden bough, the mistletoe the, 33.

Golden Pillars, king of the. See Easal.

Goll, 209, 211, 222.

Gomme, Mr. G. L., 20, 35, 69, 412, 413, 414, 416.

Gonorilla, daughter of Leir, 381, 382.

Gore, 357. See Gower.

Goreu, Arthur's cousin, 317, 338.

Gorias, a city of the Tuatha Dé Danann, 71, 72, 97.

Govannan son of Dôn, British god of Smithcraft, 261, 313, 316, 345; kills his nephew Dylan, 261; assists Kulhwch, 345.

Gower regarded as part of the other world, 272, 356, 357, 373.

Grail, the Holy, 2, 7, 273, 357–359, 365–370.

Grainne, 209, 215–221, 315.

Graves of the Warriors, the Verses of the, 272, 311, 334.

Gray of Macha, Cuchulainn's horse, 174, 181, 182, 183.

Greece, 1, 20, 68, 99, 100, 101, 155.

Greek mythology, ancient, 1, 2, 4; modern, 403.

" Green Meadows of Enchantment", the, 394.

Gregory, Lady, 159, 201.

Greid, the son of Eri, 347, 350.

Gresholm Island, 294, 356, 394.

Grianainech, the "sunny-faced", an epithet of Ogma, 59.

Grianan Aileach, grave of Nuada at. See Aileach.

Gronw Pebyr, 265, 266, 268.

Guanius, Gwyn as a mythical king of the Huns, 375.

Guest, Lady Charlotte, 253, 255, 268, 278, 289, 295, 298, 308, 317, 337, 339, 340, 348, 350, 369, 377.

Guinevere, Arthur's queen, 315, 334, 357, 359, 365, 375, 407.

Gunvasius, king of the Orkneys, 376.

Gurgiunt Brabtruc, king of Britain, 385.

Guyon, Sir, in Spenser's *Fairie Queene*, 7, 389.

Gwalchaved, 369.

Gwalchmei, 323, 330, 334, 335, 338, 343, 360, 364, 368, 369, 375.

Gwales, island of, 294, 296, 356.

Gwarthegyd, son of Kaw, 337.

Gwawl, son of Clûd, Pwyll's rival for Rhiannon, 284, 285, 303, 362, 380.

Gweddw, owner of a magic horse, 347.

Gweir, a form of the name Gwydion, *q.v.*, 319, 321, 322.

Gwenbaus, Sir, 359.

Gwern, son of Matholwch and Branwen, 291, 292, 293.

Gwinas, Sir, 359.

Gwlgawd Gododin, the drinking-horn of, 346.

Gwragedd Annwn, 393.

Gwrhyr, a companion of Arthur, 343, 349, 350, 351.

Gwri of the Golden Hair, 287.

Gwrnach the Giant, 346, 348.

Gwyar, wife of Lludd, 323, 338, 369.

Gwyddneu Garanhir, his dialogue with Gwyn, 255-258; his magic basket, 346.

Gwyddolwyn Gorr, the magic bottles of, 346.

Gwydion son of Dôn, the British Mercury, 260-268, 305, 306, 308-311, 316, 317, 322, 327, 330, 335, 358, 360, 364, 371, 372, 373, 377; druid of the gods, 260; father of the sun-god, 261; fights the "Battle of the Trees", 306; is the British equivalent of the Teutonic Woden, 260; his place taken in later myth by Arthur, 316.

Gwyl Awst, the Welsh August festival, 409.

Gwyllion, 393.

Gwyn son of Nudd, British god of the Other World, 7, 254-259, 272, 313, 315, 329, 332, 348, 359, 365, 371, 372, 376, 389-393, 405, 407; attributes of, 255; his dialogue with Gwyddneu Garanhir, 255-258; contends with Gwyn for Lludd's daughter Creudylad, 259; is made warder of Hades, 254-255; prominent in the Arthur legend, 359; becomes king of the Welsh fairies, 392; his interview with Saint Collen, 389-391.

Gwynas, Sir, 359.

Gwyngelli, a companion of Arthur, 352.

(B 219)

Gwynhwyvar, 315, 226, 331-333, 334, 364. See Guinevere.

Gwynn Mygddwn, the horse of Gweddw, 347.

Gwynwas, a form of the name Gwyn, *q.v.*, 332, 359.

Gwyrd Gwent, father of one of the three Gwynhwyvars, 331.

Gwyrthur, son of Greidawl, contends with Gwyn for Creudylad, 258, 259, 348, 407; father of one of the three Gwynhwyvars, 331.

Hacket, Castle, 244.

Hades, the Celtic. See Other World, Celtic.

Hades, the Greek god, 152, 260.

"Hades, Head of", a name given to Pwyll, 278, 282.

Hallowe'en, 40, 153, 407, 410.

Hamitic languages, 19.

"Happy Plain", the, 133, 135, 186. See Mag Mell.

Hare held sacred by the Ancient Britons, 417.

Harlech, 289, 294, 295, 296.

Harp of the Dagda, 54, 346; of Angus, 56; of Teirtu, 346.

Havgan, a king of Annwn, 279, 281.

Hawthorn, chief of Giants, father of Olwen, 340, 341, 343-345, 349, 353.

Heifer, a black-maned, called "Ocean", 80, 117, 240; the Morrígú takes the shape of a, 169-170.

Hengist, 325.

Henuinus, Duke of Cornwall, 382, 383.

Hephæstus, the Gaelic, 61, 63, 233.

Heracles, 158, 276.

Heré, 263.

Hereford, 299.

Hergest, the Red Book of, 11, 258, 260, 312, 328, 336, 369.

Herimon, 40. See Eremon.

"Hero-light", Cuchulainn's, 177, 183.

"Hero's salmon-leap", Cuchulainn's, 163.

Hesiod, 65.

Hesperides, garden of the. See Garden.

Hesus, a Gaulish god, 52.

Hevydd the Ancient, father of Rhiannon, 283, 285.

Hi Dorchaide, 70.

2 E a 2

Hibbert Lectures (for 1886) on *Celtic Heathendom*, Professor Rhys's, 41, 43, 48, 51, 54, 57, 59, 90, 120, 205, 238, 253, 254, 258, 262, 264, 268, 271, 277, 282, 284, 307, 313, 318, 324, 325, 331, 377, 408.

Hill of Uisnech, 69, 324.

Historia Britonum of Nennius, 9, 336; of Geoffrey of Monmouth, 9, 251, 323, 324, 336, 372, 373, 374, 375, 376, 381, 384, 386.

Hittites, the, 20.

Holy Families of Britain, the Three Chief, 386.

Holy Grail, the. See Grail.

Holy wells, 414–415.

Homeric and Celtic civilization compared, 25, 29.

Hoodie-crow, 52, 53, 169, 271.

Horse of Manannán mac Lir, 60, 88, 98; of Gweddw, 347; of Gwyn son of Nudd, 255, 256, 348.

"Hound of Culann", the, 161, 166; hound of Lugh, 63; of the king of Ioruaidhé, 104; hounds of Finn mac Coul, 213; hounds of Celtic myth, 225, 280, 391, 392.

Hull, Miss Eleanor, her *Cuchullin Saga*, 155, 156, 159, 184, 190, 199, 227.

Human sacrifices of the Druids, 37, 38; to Cromm Cruaich, 38, 39, 40, 400; symbolical, 405, 410, 411.

Huon of Bordeaux, Sir, 7.

Huxley, Professor, 19.

Hy-Breasail, 133.

Iberians, the, 19, 20, 21, 22, 23, 35, 68, 69, 70, 76, 230, 248, 278; their physique, 19; language, 19; original home, 19; state of culture, 20; gods, 43, 44, 64.

Iddawc, the Agitator of Britain, 337, 338.

Ilbhreach, son of Manannán, 136, 140, 211, 222.

Iliad, the, 75, 156.

Illann the Fair, son of Fergus mac Roy, 193, 196–198.

"Illusion, the Land of", an old name for Dyfed, 279.

Indech, son of Domnu, a king of the Fomors, 48, 70, 83, 90, 108, 112.

Inniskea, the Lonely Crane of, 146; stone worship in, 415.

Invasions, the Book of, 121.

Ioldanach, the "Master of All Arts", a title of Lugh, 63, 85, 237, 239.

Iolo Morganwg, bardic name of Mr. Edward Williams, 372.

Iolo MSS., the, 269, 270, 372, 373, 387, 388, 389.

Iona, Adamnan, Abbot of, 401.

Ioruaidhe, 96, 97, 104.

Ireland, old names of, 125, 126, 150. See also Iweridd.

Iseult, wife of King Mark, 327, 338.

Island, submarine, 97, 104.

"Island of the Mighty", a bardic name for Britain, 292.

Islands, sacred, 326.

Ith, 121, 122; Ith's Plain, 66, 122.

Iuchar, son of Tuirenn, 90–106.

Iucharba, son of Tuirenn, 90–106.

Iweridd, *i.e.* "Ireland", wife of the British sea-god Llyr, 258, 270, 271.

Janus, 383.

Javelin, Red, one of Manannán's spears, 60, 217.

John, Feast of Saint, 245, 407, 411.

Jones, the Rev. Edward, on apparitions, 391.

Joseph of Arimathea, 358, 359, 366.

Jubainville, M. H. d'Arbois de, 25, 34, 37, 48, 54, 67, 68, 72, 77, 78, 107, 120, 124, 128, 132, 158, 188, 202.

Judgment of Amergin, the, 127.

Julius Caesar, see Caesar.

Kacmwri, the servant of Arthur, 352, 353.

Kaerlud, 376.

Kai, 326, 327, 338, 343, 348, 349, 350, 351.

Karitia, see Calais.

Kay, Sir, 6, 326.

"Keening" invented, 110.

Kelli Wic, 334.

Keltic Researches, Mr. Nicholson's, 3.

Kenmare, river, 121.

Kieva, wife of Pryderi, 289–301.

Kildare, shrine of St. Bridget at, 228.

Killaraus, Mount, 324.

Killarney, Lake, 223, 247.

" Kingly Castle", see Caer Rigor.
Kirwans of Castle Hacket, the, 244.
Knights, King Arthur's, 6, 7, 8, 155, 251, 274, 358, 371.
Knockainy, 245.
Knockers, 393, 403.
Knockma, fairy hill of, 136, 243, 244.
Knockthierna, 247.
Knowth, 137, 138.
Kulhwch, 340, 341, 343, 344, 345, 347, 353.
Kulhwch and Olwen, the tale of, 258, 259, 260, 313, 321, 327, 339, 340-353, 369, 407.
Kyndellig, 343.
Kynedyr Wyllt, 348, 352.

Labhra, Mider's leech, 213.
Labraid of the Quick Hand on Sword, 202.
Lady of the Lake, 361.
Laeg, Cuchulainn's charioteer, 169, 181, 182, 186.
Laegaire the Battle-winner, 163.
Lakes, twelve chief, of Ireland, 88.
Lamias, 403.
Lammas, 407.
Land of Illusion, 279; of Happiness, 119, 133; of the Living, 133, 335; of Promise, 133, 217, 337; of Summer, 119, 329; of the Young, 133, 225.
Laon, 277.
Larminie, Mr. William, 233.
Launcelot, Sir, 7, 328, 333, 358, 359, 362, 365.
Lear, King, Shakespeare's, 5, 7, 259, 270, 381.
Lecan, the Book of, 10, 38, 123, 229; the Yellow Book of, 10, 164.
Leicester, 270, 383.
Leinster, 179, 189.
Leinster, Mount, 140, 211, 212.
Leinster, the Book of, 10, 38, 55, 56, 121, 132, 139, 155, 156, 157, 190, 199, 204, 229.
Leir, Geoffrey of Monmouth's King, 381-383.
Leodogrance, father of Guinevere, 357.
Leprechaun, 247, 248, 393, 403.
Lêr, the Gaelic sea-god, 60, 140, 142-144, 146, 205, 211, 212, 222, 252, 269;

his rebellion against Bodb the Red, 140; their reconciliation, 142; the fate of the children of, 142-146; is killed by the Fenian hero Caoilté, 146, 222.
Levarcham, 196.
Leyden, 277.
Lia Fáil, see Stone of Destiny.
Liban, 186, 202.
Lismore, the Book of, 10.
Lla Lluanys, the Manx August festival, 409.
Llacheu, son of Arthur, 258, 326.
Llandwynwyn, the church of Dwynwyn (Branwen), in Anglesey, 388.
Lleminawg, 319.
Lleu (Llew) Llaw Gyffes, the British sun-god, 261-268, 276, 305, 306, 322, 323, 325, 330, 335, 360, 364, 369, 370; his birth, 261; and naming, 263; takes part in the Battle of the Trees, 306; is changed into an eagle, 266; his place taken in later myth by Gwalchmei, 323; and in the Arthurian legend by Sir Gawain, 360.
Llevelys, king of France, 378.
Lloegyr (Loegria), Saxon Britain, 258, 299, 300, 384.
Lludd Llaw Ereint, the British Zeus, 252, 253, 254, 259, 312, 315, 323, 329, 332, 350, 359, 364, 375-381, 407; his wife Gwyar, 323; puts an end to the "Three Plagues of Britain", 377-380; founds London, 376; appears in the Morte Darthur as King Lot of Orkney, 359.
Llwyd, son of Kilcoed, avenges Gwawl, son of Clûd, 303, 304.
Llwyr, son of Llwyrion, the magic vessel of, 346.
Llyn Llyw, the salmon of, 350.
Llyr, the British sea-god, 252, 259, 269, 270, 271, 273, 289, 290, 304, 313, 316, 338, 381, 383, 386; possibly borrowed from the Gaels, 270; becomes the "King Leir" of Geoffrey of Monmouth, 381; and the "King Lear" of Shakespeare, 270, 381; founds a family of saints, 386; his tomb or temple at Leicester, 383.
Llyr-cestre, 270, 283.
Llys Dôn, 252, 317.

Llywarch Hên, a sixth-century British poet, 11.

Loch, a warrior slain by Cuchulainn, 169-170.

Lochlann (Lochlin), 97, 205, 372; Lochlannoch, the, 205, 211.

London, 294, 296, 376, 377.

Londres, 376.

Lot or Loth, king of Orkney, 359, 364, 375.

Loucetius, a war-god worshipped in Britain, 275.

Lough Corrib, its Shores and Islands, Sir William Wilde's, 76.

Lough Gur, 246.

Lucan, the Roman poet, 52.

Luchtainé, the carpenter of the Tuatha Dé Danann, 61, 84, 86, 109.

Lud, king of Britain, 5, 7, 376-381.

Ludesgata, Ludgate, 5, 254, 376.

Lugaid, son of Curoi, 179, 182, 183.

Lugh Lamhfada, the Gaelic sun-god, 62-63, 84-90, 93-97, 103, 105, 106, 111-113, 115-117, 136, 139, 156, 157, 160, 170, 201, 230, 233, 238-240, 262, 276, 325, 339, 344, 345, 370, 371; his spear, 63, 71, 97; his hound, 63, 97; his rod-sling and chain, 62; his first appearance at Tara, 84; gains the title of *Ioldanach*, 85; avenges his father's murder upon the sons of Tuirenn, 94-106; leads the Tuatha Dé Danann against the Fomors, 111; prophecies to Conn the Hundred Fighter, 201.

Lugnassad, "Lugh's Commemoration", 277, 409.

Lugudunum, "town of Lugus", 277, 409.

Lugus, the Gaulish sun-god, 42, 276, 409.

Lundy Island, 272, 322.

Lydney, temple of Nodens at, 254; monograph upon it, 254.

Lyons, 277, 409.

Mab, Queen, 246.

Mabinogi, the Four Branches of the, 14, 15, 355.

Mabinogion, 12, 14, 16, 356, 372, 377, 403, 407. See also Guest, Lady Charlotte.

Mabon, a British sun-god, 276, 328, 330, 335, 338, 347, 349-352, 387.

Macaulay, 22.

Mac Cecht, a king of the Tuatha Dé Danann, 122, 125, 126, 130.

Mac Cuill, a king of the Tuatha Dé Danann, 122, 125, 126, 130.

Mac Gee, Thomas D'Arcy, 232.

Mac Greiné, a king of the Tuatha Dé Danann, 122, 125, 126, 130.

Mac Kineely, 238-239.

Mac Moineanta, a king of the Irish fairies, 242.

Mac Nia, an old Irish poet, 138.

Mac Oc, "Son of the Young", a title of Angus, 56, 139.

Mac Pherson's *Ossian*, 203.

Mac Samthainn, 238.

Macha, a war-goddess of the Gaels, 52, 72, 112; meaning of her name, 52; "Macha's acorn-crop", 53; is killed by Balor, 112.

Macleod, Miss Fiona, 241.

Maelmuiri, scribe of the Book of the Dun Cow, 10.

Maelon, 388.

Maenor Alun, 310; Maenor Penarth, 310.

Maen Tyriawc, the grave of Pryderi, 311.

Maglaunus, Duke of Albania, 382, 383.

Mag Mell, the "Happy Plain", a name for the Celtic Elysium, 133, 135.

Mag Mon, the "Plain of Sports", a name for the Celtic Elysium, 134.

Mag Slecht, human sacrifices at, 38-40, 132, 154.

Mag Tuireadh, see Moytura.

Magog, 229.

Malory, Sir Thomas, 323, 328, 330, 333, 354-357, 359-364, 367, 368.

Malvasius, king of Iceland, 376.

Man, Isle of, 23, 24, 57, 60, 175, 241, 261, 272, 273, 408, 409.

Manannán son of Lêr, a Gaelic god, 60-61, 89, 98, 129, 134, 136, 140, 143, 157, 186, 188, 199, 202, 203, 205, 217, 224, 233, 235-237, 239, 240-242, 270, 371, 405; his armour, 60, 88; weapons, 60, 217; horse, 60, 89, 98; mantle, 61, 129, 188, 217, 221; pigs, 61, 98; his "Feast of Age", 61, 143; lord of the Celtic Paradise, 134; his wife Fand in love with Cuchulainn, 186–188; his friendship with Cormac, king of Ireland, 203; his message to Saint Columba, 240–241; his connection with the Isle of Man, 60, 241–242.

Manawyddan son of Llyr, his British analogue, 270, 271, 273, 289, 290, 293, 294, 296, 298–304, 313, 315, 317, 321, 338, 352, 373; his attributes, 270–271; accompanies Brân to Ireland, 289–294; marries Rhiannon, 298; defeats the magic of Llwyd, son of Kilcoed, 301–304; constructs the bone-prison of Oeth and Anoeth, 270; helps Arthur in the chase of Twrch Trwyth, 352.

Maponos, a Gallo-British sun-god, 276, 328.

March, a British god of the Under World, 316, 327, 329, 335, 338.

Mark, King, 327, 328.

Mars, 51, 204.

"Master of All Arts", see *Ioldanach*.

Mâth, a British god, brother to Dôn, 260, 265, 266, 268, 308, 310, 322, 329, 360, 361, 364; meaning of his name, 260; teaches magic to Gwydion, 260; rules from Caer Dathyl, 308; compared with Merlin, 360, 361, 362.

Matholwch, king of Ireland, 289–293.

Mâthonwy, father of Mâth, 260, 308.

Matière de Bretagne, the, 363, 365.

Matthew Arnold, 3, 16, 356.

May Day, 123, 259, 287, 407.

May Eve, 377, 407.

Maypole, 408.

Meadha, the *sídh* of, 136, 212, 243.

Meath, 179.

Medb, queen of Connaught, 147, 154, 164–168, 170, 171, 172, 175, 178, 179, 183, 200, 246; makes war on Ulster to get the Brown Bull of Cualgne, 165–166; becomes a fairy queen, 246; is perhaps the original of "Queen Mab", 246.

Mediterranean race, 19; *Mediterranean Race, The*, Prof. Sergi's, 20.

Medrawt, 315, 323, 332, 333, 334, 337, 360, 364.

Meleaus, or Melias, de Lile, Sir, 359.

Melga, king of the Picts, 375.

Meliagaunce, or Meliagraunce, Sir, 359, 365, 407.

Melwas, 329, 332, 359, 365, 407.

Menai Straits, the, 262, 264.

Menw, 343, 344, 351.

Mercurius Artaius, a Gallo-Roman god, 274, 313.

Mercury, 274, 313.

Merlin, 324, 325, 339, 360, 361, 364. See Myrddin.

Mesgegra, king of Leinster, 147, 154.

Meyer, Dr. Kuno, 38, 134, 154, 184, 190.

Miach, son of Diancecht, 62, 80–82, 232.

Midas, the British, 328.

Mider, Gaelic god of the Under World, 56, 57, 117, 136, 140, 142, 147–151, 154, 157, 175, 179, 205, 211–213, 224, 243, 331–333; rebels against Bodb the Red, 140; gambles with Eochaid Airem for possession of Etain, 149; is besieged in his *sídh*, and helped by the Fenians, 211–213.

Midsummer Day, 75, 406, 407.

Midsummer Eve, 242.

Milé, the ancestor of the Gaels, 122, 123, 126, 129, 130, 132, 146, 153.

Milesians, the, 76, 125–127, 129, 145, 153, 229, 230, 243.

"Milky Way", the, 62, 253, 268.

Minerva, 275, 277, 413.

Minos, 153.

Miodhchaoin, 97, 105, 106.

Mistletoe, 18, 33.

Mithras, a Persian sun-god worshipped at York, 275.

Mochdrev, 310.

Mochnant, 310.

Modron, wife of Urien and mother of Mabon, 328, 338.

Mona, see Anglesey.

Mongan, an Ulster prince, a reincarnation of Finn mac Coul, 37.

Monmouth, Geoffrey of. See Geoffrey.

Morc, son of Dela, a king of the Fomors, 67, 327.

Mordred, Sir, 315, 334, 360, 364, 374, 375.

Morgawse, sister to Arthur, 323.

Morrígú, the, Gaelic goddess of war, 52, 53, 72, 87, 98, 107, 113, 117, 139, 157, 168–170, 323; description of, 52; her dealings with Cuchulainn on the Táin Bó Chuailgne, 168–170.

Morte Darthur, Sir Thomas Malory's, 7, 272, 276, 323, 328, 334, 354, 362, 364–368, 372, 407.

"Mound, Lord of the", 41, 403.

Mountains of Ireland, the twelve chief, 87.

Mourie, "Saint", 413.

Mouse, Manawyddan and the, 301–304.

Moyle, Sea of, 144, 145.

Moytura, Northern, Battle of, 11, 107–117, 157, 407; Southern, Battle of, 72–77, 114.

Muirthemne, 90, 93, 166, 181.

Munster, 69, 164, 218, 244, 245.

Murias, a city of the Tuatha Dé Danann, 71, 72.

Mur y Castell, Lleu's palace near Bala Lake, 265, 268.

Myrddin, a British Zeus, 323–325, 329, 360, 362, 369; gave its first name to Britain, 323; his wife Elen, 323; his town Carmarthen, 324; appears in Geoffrey of Monmouth and in the Morte Darthur as Merlin, *q.v.*

Myrddin, a sixth-century British bard, 11.

Mythology, importance of, 1; Greek, 1, 2, 4, 403; Scandinavian, 3; Celtic, its influence on English literature, 6, 7; on mediæval chivalric romance, 184.

Name, ancient British superstitions with regard to, 263.

Names, Choice of, The. See *Coir Anmann.*

Names, early of Britain, 292, 323; of Ireland, 126, 150, 151.

Nant Call, 310.

Nant y Llew, 267.

Naoise, son of Usnach, 191–193, 195–198.

Narberth, 279, 281, 282, 283, 288, 298, 300.

Navan Fort, 158.

Neamhuainn, Clann, 216, 218.

Neath, Vale of, 255, 335, 392.

Nedd, river, 405.

Neevougi, a stone worshipped at Inniskea, 415.

Nemed, 67–69, 274; the race of, 229, 230, 327, 406.

Nemetona, a war-goddess worshipped at Bath, 275, 276.

Nemon, a Gaelic war-goddess, wife of Nuada, 52, 276.

Nennius, his *History of the Britons*, 9, 336.

Nentres, King, 357, 362.

Nereids, 403.

Nêt, an Iberian god, 64.

New Grange, 137–139.

Nia, the Plain of, 73.

Niamh of the Golden Hair, daughter of Manannán, 223–225.

Nicholson's *Keltic Researches*, 3.

Niebelungenlied, 393.

Nimue, 358, 361, 362.

Nissyen, son of Penardun, 290, 293.

Niul, 120.

Noah, descent of the Gaelic gods and men from, 329.

Nodens, a temple to, at Lydney, 253.

"Northern Crown", constellation of the, 252.

Nos galan-gaeof, the Welsh winter festival, 408.

Nuada of the Silver Hand, a Gaelic Zeus, 51, 52, 74, 75, 78, 80, 81, 83–86, 93, 94, 105, 122, 157, 230, 253, 276, 323; his sword, 51, 71; his wives, 52; his hand cut off in battle, 75; a silver hand made for him by Diancecht, 78; his own hand renewed by Miach and Airmid, 81; his death at the hands of Balor, 112; his tomb at Grianan Aileach, 122, 157.

Nudd, British god, 252, 253, 254, 313; to be identified with Lludd, *q.v.*

Nutt, Mr. Alfred, 12, 37, 38, 134, 154, 158, 164, 318, 348.

Nwyvre, 322, 364.

Nynniaw, son of Beli, 268, 269, 313.

Oak, held sacred by the Druids, 33.

Oberon, 7, 392.

"Ocean", a black-maned heifer called, 80, 240.

Ochall Ochne, king of the Sídhe of Connaught, 164.

Ochren, battle of, 305; Caer, 320, see Achren.

Octriallach, son of Indech, 110; the "Cairn of Octriallach", 110.

O'Curry, Eugene, 37, 56, 63, 72, 78, 89, 93, 111, 113, 137, 138, 146, 151, 152, 155, 188, 201, 204.

Odin, 260.

O'Donaghue, the, 247.

O'Donovan, 238.

Oeth and Anoeth, the Bone-prison of, 270, 271, 317, 373.

O'Flynn, Eochaid, an old Irish poet, 231.

Ogam, writings in, 58, 93, 151, 189.

Ogma, Gaelic god of Literature and Eloquence, 57–60, 79, 80, 82, 84, 85, 112, 116, 117, 122, 136, 139, 157, 276; his wife and children, 57; his epithets of "Cermait" and "Grianainech", 57, 59; his great strength, 59; kills Indech in the battle of Moytura, 112; inventor of the ogam alphabet, 58.

Ogmios, a Gaulish god, 276.

O'Grady, Standish Hayes, Mr., 28, 159, 201, 203, 205, 207, 213, 215, 222.

Ogyrvran, a British god of the Under World, father of Gwynhwyvar, 329–331, 357, 366.

O'Herlebys, wooden idol of the, 413.

Old Plain, the, 66.

Old Sarum, 29, 386.

Olwen, 340, 341, 343, 345, 353.

Onagh, queen of the Irish fairies, 243, 244.

Origins of English History, Mr. Elton's, 6, 8, 25, 26, 70, 228, 327, 413.

Orkneys, 386; King Lot of Orkney, 359.

Oscar, son of Ossian, 208, 212, 217, 222, 246, 315.

Osla Big-Knife, 352, 353.

Ossian, MacPherson's, 203.

Ossian, son of Finn mac Coul, 11, 208, 212, 214, 215, 217, 220, 223–227, 246, 318, 337.

"Ossianic ballads", 205, 208, 213; Ossianic Society, see *Transactions*.

Other World, the Celtic, 65, 68, 71, 98, 119, 121, 133–136, 150, 151, 175, 176, 201, 202, 203, 224, 252, 255, 270, 271, 272, 273, 278, 279, 281, 305, 307, 316, 317, 318–322, 329, 334, 336, 366, 387, 389, 395; different names of, 133, 318–320; descriptions of, 136, 150–151, 224; variously imagined as upon the sea, 202, 224, 272, 394; under the sea, 305; under the earth, 135–136; upon earth, 271, 272, 273, 278, 279; original abode of men, 119; visited by Cuchu-lainn, 175–176, 186; Conn, 201; Connla, 202, Ossian, 224; Pwyll, 281; Gwydion, 305; Arthur, 317–320. See also Annwn, Avilion, Happy Plain, Mag Mell, Mag Mon, Land of Happiness, of the Living, of Promise, of Summer, of the Young.

Ousel of Cilgwri, 349.

Ovid's *Metamorphoses*, 393.

Owain, son of Urien, 328, 330; Sir Owain, 363.

Owl, of Cwm Cawlwyd, 349; Blodeuwedd changed into an, 268.

Ox, the brindled, 320, 321; oxen, magic, 345.

Oxford, 379.

Paradise, the Celtic. See Other World, Celtic.

Parthludd, 254, 376.

Partholon, 65–68, 386; race of, 229, 230, 406.

Patrick, Saint, 8, 40, 41, 132, 145, 222, 225, 226, 227, 242, 401, 402.

Paul's Cathedral, Saint, 254.

Pausanias's *Description of Greece*, 36.

Pedigree of the gods, 229; of Finn mac Coul, 204.

Pedryvan, Caer, 319, 356, 367.

Peel Castle, 242.

Peibaw, son of Beli, 268, 269, 313.

Pelasgoi, 20.

Peleur, King, 368.

Pellam, King, 358, 364.

Pellean, King, 358.

Pelleas, Sir, 358, 368; *Pelleas and Ettarre*, Tennyson's Idyll of, 358.

Pelles, King, 357, 362, 367.

Pellinore, King, 362.

Pembroke, County Guardian, the, 394.

Pembrokeshire, 273, 278, 394.

Pen Annwn, the "Head of Hades", a title of Pwyll, 278, 282.

Penardun, daughter of Beli and wife of Llyr, 269, 270, 289, 290, 293.

Pendaran Dyfed, 288, 295.

Pendragon, meaning of the word, 330.

Pennant, 409.

Percivale, Sir, 359, 363, 368, 369.

Peredur, 330, 368, 369.

Perilous glens, the, 163.

Persephoné, the British, 259, 260.

Persia, 274; Pisear, king of, 96, 97, 101–103.

Petrie, Dr., 72, 98, 114.

Picts, 23, 230, 401, 417.

Pigs, in the Celtic Other World, 136; of Manannán, 61, 63; of Easal, king of the Golden Pillars, 96, 97, 103; of Pryderi, 308, 316, 327; of March, 316, 327; of Angus, 214; Cian changed into a pig, 91.

Pigskin of King Tuis, the, 96, 99, 100.

Pillars, king of the Golden. See Easal.

Pisear, king of Persia, 96, 97, 101–103.

Pixies, 393.

Plain of Ill Luck, 163; of the Sea, 72; of Adoration, 38; the Old, 66.

Pliny, 33, 35, 400.

Plutarch, 326.

Pluto, the Gaelic, 57; the Cambrian, 260.

Poetry, the Gaelic goddess of, 56; cauldron of inspiration and, 365–370.

Policy of the Christian Church towards objects of pagan worship, 417.

Pookas, 247, 248, 393, 403, 405.

Porsenna, a Roman consul, 385.

Poseidon, 52, 260; the Gaelic, 60; the British, 269.

Posidonius, 26.

Prophecy of Badb, 117–118; of Eriu, 125–126; of the seeress to Queen Medb, 166; of Lugh to Conn the Hundred-Fighter, 201–202; of Cathbad concerning Cuchulainn, 161, concerning Deirdre, 190–191.

Pryderi, son of Pwyll and Rhiannon, 273, 286–288, 289, 294, 295, 298–301, 303–305, 308, 309–311, 313, 315, 316, 319, 321, 327, 335, 358, 364, 366, 368, 377, 407; is stolen at birth, 286; meaning of his name, 288; accompanies Brân to Ireland, 289–294; is spirited away by Llwyd and recovered by Manawyddan, 300–304; receives a present of pigs from Annwn, 308; is killed by Gwydion, 311; appears in Arthurian legend, 358.

Prydwen, Arthur's ship, 319, 320, 352.

Puck, 393.

Puffin Island, 322.

Pursuit of Diarmait and Grainne, The, 215–221.

Pwccas, 393.

Pwyll, Prince of Dyfed and "Head of Annwn", 273, 274, 278–288, 298, 303, 304, 305, 308, 316, 319, 329, 357–358, 366, 367, 380; changes shapes with Arawn, king of Annwn, 281; his wooing of Rhiannon, 282–286; is owner of a magic cauldron in Hades 321; and keeper of the Holy Grail in the Morte Darthur, 357–358.

Pwynt Maen Dulan, 262.

Queen Guinevere, 315, 334, 357, 359, 365, 375, 407.

"Queen Mab", 246.

Queen of the Irish fairies, 243, 244; of the fairies of Munster, 244; of the fairies of North Munster, 244; of the fairies of South Munster, 244.

Queene, The Fairie, Spenser's, 7

Quicken-tree, the magic, 219.

Races of Britain, the, 19–21.

Rathconrath, 69.

"Realm of Glamour, The", a name for Dyfed, 279.

Re-birth of Cuchulainn, 37; of Finn mac Coul, 37.

Red Book of Hergest, see Hergest.

Red Branch Champions of Ulster, the, 4, 147, 157, 167, 183, 191, 192, 204, 227, 314.

Red Branch House, the, 29, 196, 197.

Red Dragon of Britain, the, 378.

Redynvre, the stag of, 349.

Regan, daughter of King Leir, 381, 382.

Religion, Aryan, 32, 47.

Retaliator, the, the sword of Manannán mac Lir, 60, 198.

Revelry, the Castle of, 319, 366.

Revolving Castle, the, 319, 366.

Revue Celtique, 40, 53, 78, 107, 117, 142, 158, 184, 190, 201, 241, 246.

Rhiannon, a British goddess, 273, 282–288, 298, 300, 301, 303, 304, 358, 361, 362, 407; her three magic birds, 273, 294, 296; her name afterwards corrupted into Nimue and Vivien, 358, 361.

Rhinnon Rhin Barnawd, the magic bottles of, 346.

Rhonabwy, 336, 337, 338; The *Dream of Rhonabwy*, 312, 337, 338.

Rhyd y Groes, a ford on the Severn, 337.

Rhys, Professor, 22, 23, 35, 41, 44, 64, 68, 158, 205, 254, 256, 262, 282, 289, 307, 313, 316, 318, 319, 324, 331, 335, 352, 363, 370, 395, 404, 413, 414. See also *Arthurian Legend* and *Hibbert Lectures*.

Ri, Roi, an Iberian god, 64.

Ribble, the river, 413, 414.

Riches, the Castle of, 367.

Rience, King, 357.

Rigor, Caer, 319.

Rigosamos, a war-god worshipped in Britain, 275.

Ritual, remains of Celtic, 405–412.

Rivers, the twelve chief, of Ireland, 88.

Rivers, the worship of, 413, 414.

Rodrubân, the *sidh* of Lugh, 136.

Romans, the, 23, 24, 25, 373, 385, 386, 399, 413.

Rome, 5, 155, 274, 315, 317.

Ronan, Clann, 218.

Round Table, King Arthur's, 6, 314.

"Round Towers", the, attributed to Goibniu, 233.

Rowan-tree, 219, 410.

Ruadan, son of Bress and Brigit, 109–110.

Rude Stone Monuments, Fergusson's, 76, 114, 137, 138.

Ryons, King, 357.

Sacred animals, 406, 416, 417; islands, 326; fish, 416; frogs, 416; stones, 406, 415, 417; trees, 406, 415; wells, 414–416.

Sacrifices of animals, 406, 412; human, 18, 37-40, 399; symbolical human sacrifices, 405, 410, 411.

Sadb, daughter of Bodb the Red, and mother of Ossian, 208.

"Sage's seat", the, 85, 86.

St. Catherine's Hill, 29; St. George's Hill, 29.

St. Gall MS., the, 232.

Saints, transformation of Celtic gods into, 6, 228, 229, 372, 386, 389.

Salisbury Plain, 325.

Salmon of Knowledge, the, 55, 210; of Llyn Llyw, 350.

Samhain, the Celtic winter festival, 40, 42, 67, 107, 108, 286, 406, 407, 408, 410, 411.

Samhanach, 408.

Sarn Elen, 324.

Sarrlog, 386; Caer Sarrlog, 386.

Satires, magical, 83, 87, 172, 182.

Scathach the Amazon, 163, 164, 172, 173, 176.

Scêné, the river, 121.

Scot, Eber, a mythical ancestor of the Gaels, 120.

Scota, 120.

Scotti, 357.

Sea, Celtic ideas regarding the, 48, 261, 270.

Second Battle of Moytura, The, the Harleian MS. called, 50, 54, 72, 78, 107.

Seint Greal, the, 322, 326, 368.

Senchan Torpeist, 14.

Sen Mag, see Old Plain.

Serapis worshipped at York, 275.

Setanta, original name of Cuchulainn, 160, 161.

Severn, the river, 254, 337, 350, 352, 353.

Sgeolan, one of Finn's hounds, 213.

"Shadowy Town, or City", 175, 366.

Shakespeare, 5, 259, 270, 381, 393, 408.

Shannon, the river, 88, 165, 292.

"Shape-shifting", 37.

Sharvan the Surly, 219.

Shield, Conchobar's magic, 197.

Shony, a Hebridean sea-god, 410.

Shouts on a hill, the three, 94, 97, 105, 106.

Sicily, 96, 102.

Sidh Airceltrai, 136; Bodb, 136; Eas Aedha Ruaidh, 136; Fionnachaidh, 136, 140, 142, 146, 222; Meadha, 136, 243; Rodrubân, 136.

Sidhe, "fairy mounds", 135, 136, 139, 181.

Sidhe, The, the Gaelic gods, or fairies, 136, 223, 244, 246.

Sidi, Caer, 319, 321, 322, 368.

Silures, tribe of the, 22.

Silurian race, the, 19.

Silver Hand, Nuada's, 51, 78, 81, 253: Lludd's, 253.

Sinann, goddess of the Shannon, 56.

Skene, Dr. W. F., 71, 123, 256, 258, 311, 312, 316, 317, 319, 328, 334.

Skye, Isle of, 163.

Slecht, Mag. See Mag Slecht.

Slieve Bloom, 209; Slieve Fuad, 136; Slieve Mish, 130.

Smallpox, goddess of the, 413.

Snowdon, 267, 305, 335, 380.

Sol Apollo Anicetus, a sun-god worshipped at Bath, 275.

Solar festivals of the Celts, 41, 405-412.

Solinus, Caius Julius, 228.

Somerset, 329.

"Son of the Young", see Mac Oc.

Sore, the river, 383.

Sorrowful Stories of Erin, The Three, 106.

Spain, 22, 121; used as an euphemism for the Celtic Other World, 68, 120, 121, 230, 386.

Spear of Lugh, 62, 97; of Pisear, king of Persia, 96, 97, 101, 103.

"Spearman with the Long Shaft", 369.

Speech, Aryan, 21, 31.

Spenser, 7, 389.

Spey, the river, 414.

"Splendid Mane", the horse of Manannán mac Lir, 60, 88, 98.

Spoiling of Annwn, The, a poem of Taliesin, 306, 317-321, 366.

"Spring of Health", the, 110.

Sreng, a warrior of the Fir Bolgs, 75.

Stag of Redynvre, the, 349.

Stokes, Dr. Whitley, 40, 50, 72, 78, 107, 152, 190, 203, 417.

Stone, Black, of Arddhu, 305; Coronation, 71; of Destiny, 72; of Kineely, 239.

Stones, worship of, 406, 415.

Stonehenge, 42, 324, 325.

Strabo, 22, 399.

Strachey, Sir Edward, 356.

Study of Celtic Literature, Matthew Arnold's, 3, 16, 356.

Sualtam, the mortal father of Cuchulainn, 159, 160, 173, 174.

Suir, the river, 165.

Sul, a goddess worshipped at Bath, 228, 275.

"Summer, the Land of", *i.e.* the Celtic Other World, 119, 329.

Sun, worship of the, 41, 42; Cuchulainn a personification of the, 158-159.

Swans, Caer and Angus take the forms of, 141-142; the children of Lêr changed into, 143; Mider and Etain become, 151.

Sword, of Manannán, 60, 198; of Nuada, 51; of Gwrnach the Giant, 346, 348.

Swinburne, 6.

Swineherds, the rival, 164-165.

Table Round, the, 6, 354, 371.

Taboos, Celtic. See Destiny, *Geasa*.

Tacitus, 22, 24, 387, 400.

Tailtiu, the Gaelic gods defeated by the Milesians at, 130.

Táin Bó Chuailgné, 10, 14, 28, 159, 164, 175.

Taliesin, 11, 123, 124, 261, 271, 273, 294, 296, 306, 317, 318, 320, 321, 328, 356, 366, 367.

Taliesin, the Book of, 11, 123, 261, 271, 273, 306, 317, 318, 321, 328.

Tallacht, burial-place of Partholon's people, 66.

Tara, 29, 72, 84, 93, 98, 105, 125, 126, 129, 147, 153, 189, 190, 216, 230.

Taran, 294.

Taranis, 294.

Tathlum, a sling-stone, 112, 113.

Tawë, a river in South Wales, sacred to Gwyn ap Nudd, 257, 279, 392, 405.

Tegla's well, Saint, 415.

Teirnyon Twryf Vliant, 287, 288, 358, 407.

Teirtu, the harp of, 346.

Telltown, see Tailtiu.

Temple of Nodens at Lydney, 253-254; St. Paul's cathedral occupying the site of a, 254; sacrifices of cattle on the site of a, 413; ancient British temples still standing in the sixth century, 400.

Tennyson, 6, 133, 260, 274, 297, 312, 354, 355, 358, 361, 362.

"Terrace cultivation", 20.

"Terrestrial gods and goddesses", 156.

"Terrible Broom, The", name of the banner of Oscar's battalion, 209.

Tethra, a king of the Fomors, 83, 90.

Teutates, a god of the Gauls, 51, 52.

Thames, the river, 254.

Theseus, 153.

Thirteen Treasures of Britain, the, 313, 326, 339, 340.

Three Birds of Rhiannon, the, 273, 294, 296.

Three Chief Holy Families of Britain, 386.

Three Counselling Knights of Arthur, 312.

Three Cows of Mider, 57, 176.

Three Cranes of Denial and Churlishness, 57.

Three Criminal Resolutions of Britain, 334.

Three Etains, 331.

Three Frivolous Battles of Britain, 334.

Three Generous Heroes of Britain, 253.

Three Gwynhwyvars, 333.

Three Paramount Prisoners of Britain, 350-351.

Three Plagues of Britain, 253, 377-380.

Three shouts on a hill, 94, 97, 105, 106.

Three Sorrowful Stories of Erin, 106.

Three War-knights of Arthur, 312.

Three Wicked Uncoverings of Britain, 297,

Tiberius, the Emperor, 400.

Tigernmas, a mythical Irish king, 153-154.

Tighernach, an old Irish chronicler, 204.

Tir nam beo, see Land of the Living.

Tir nan og, see Land of the Young.

Tir Tairngiré, see Land of Promise.

Titania, 393.

Tomb of the Dagda, 138.

Tombs of the Tuatha Dé Danann, 138-139.

Torpeist, Senchan. See Senchan.

Tory Island, 49, 67, 238.

Toutates, a war-god worshipped in Britain, 275.

Tower Hill, Brân's head buried at, 294, 296, 331.

Transactions of the Ossianic Society, 124, 127, 128, 201, 203, 211, 213, 215, 223, 226.

Transmigration of souls, 36; of the swineherds, 164-165.

Treasures of Britain, the Thirteen, 313, 326, 339, 340.

Trees, the Battle of the, 123, 305-308.

Trees, worship of, 406.

Triads, 11, 253, 273, 331, 334, 350, 351.

Trim, 175.

Trinity Well, the source of the Boyne, 55.

Trinovantum, *i.e.* New Troy, a mythic name of London, 376, 385.

Tristrem, Sir, 6, 327, 363.

Trouveres, the, 363.

Troy, 374.

Tuatha Dé Danann, the gods of the ancient Gaels, 11, 17, 48, 50, 51, 58, 59, 60, 65, 70-79, 82-86, 91, 95, 97, 104, 108-112, 114, 115, 117, 123, 125, 126, 129, 132, 136-138, 140, 141, 145, 153, 154, 156, 157, 205, 211, 214, 217, 219, 222, 225, 228, 229-231, 243, 246, 252, 269, 276, 312, 330, 393, 403, 404, 406, 410; their arrival in Ireland, 71, 72; their battle with the Fomors, 108-117; are conquered by the Milesians, 130; retire into underground palaces, 135, 136; and become the fairies of Irish belief, 137.

Tuirenn, son of Ogma, 57, 90, 106.

"Tuirenn, the Fate of the Sons of", 90-106.

Tuis, king of Greece, 96, 98, 102.

' Turning Castle", 322.

Tweed, the river, 23, 414.

Twr Branwen, 289.

Twrch Trwyth, the hunting of, 347-353.

Tylwyth Teg, the Welsh fairies, 255.

Tynwald Hill, 412.

Tyrian Hercules worshipped at Corbridge, 275.

Uaman, *sídh* of, 141.

Uaran Garad, spring of, 165.

Uffern, the "Cold Place", a name for Annwn, 319.

Uisnech, the hill of, 69, 324.

Ulster, 29, 57, 64, 69, 76, 158, 164, 165, 166, 171, 174, 175, 180, 183, 188, 189, 190, 191, 192, 217, 245.

"Undry", the name of the Dagda's cauldron, 54, 366.

Unius, the river, 107.

Unsenn, the river, 112.

Urddawl Ben, see Venerable Head.

Urien, an Under World king, 328, 329, 357, 376; Uriens, Urience, King, in the Morte Darthur, 357; Urianus, King, in Geoffrey of Monmouth' *History*, 376.

Usnach, the sons of, 191–200.
Uther Ben, the "Wonderful Head", a name for Brân, 296, 330, 356.
Uther Pendragon, Arthur's father, 330, 356.

Val des Fées, in the forest of Brécilien, 361.
Vandwy, Caer, 257, 320.
Varro, 26.
Vedwyd, Caer, 319.
"Venerable Head, The", 296.
Verses of the Graves of the Warriors, The, 272, 311, 334.
"Victor, son of Scorcher". See Gwyrthur, son of Greidawl.
Vita Columbæ, Adamnan's, 401, 417.
Vivien, 358, 361.

Wales, the Four Ancient Books of, 11, 15. See Skene.
Walgan, 375.
Wall, Roman, 25, 273, 274, 400.
War-chariots, 27; Cuchulainn's, 28.
Warrefield, 242.
"Water-dress", Brian's, 104.
Waves, the Four, of Britain, 261.
"Wave-sweeper", Manannán's boat, 60, 98, 104.
Weapons of the Celts, 27.
Wells, worship of, 414, 415; holy, 414.
Welsh fairies, 255, 392–394.
Westminster, 407; Westminster Abbey, 71.
White Dragon of the Saxons, 378.
White-horned Bull of Connaught, 165, 175.
White Mount in London, see Tower Hill.
White-tusk, king of the Boars, 346, 349.

Wild Huntsman, the, 255.
Wilde, Sir William, his *Lough Corrib*, 76; Lady Wilde's *Ancient Legends of Ireland*, 243, 409.
Williams, Mr. Edward. See Iolo Morganwg.
Wish Hounds, the 392.
Woden, 260.
Wolf, the Morrígú takes the shape of a, 170.
Women, position of, among the Celts, 30.
"Wonderful Head", the, 296, 330.
"Wood of the Two Tents", the, 216.
Wordsworth, 4, 5.
Wren, Lleu and the, 263; a bird of augury among the druids, 417.
Wydyr, Caer, 320.
Wye, the river, 352.

Yeats', Mr., The *Wanderings of Oisin*, 223.
Yell, or Yeth, Hounds, the, 392.
Yellow Book of Lecan, the, 10, 164.
"Yellow Shaft", one of Manannán's spears, 60, 217.
Ynys Avallon, 329. See Avilion, Glastonbury.
Ynys Branwen, 295.
Ynys Wair, 322. See Lundy Island.
York, 275.
Young, Land of the, 133, 225; Son of the, see Mac Oc.
Yspaddaden Penkawr, see Hawthorn, Chief of Giants.

Zeus, 65, 260, 261; the Gaelic, 41, 51, 253; the British, 5, 324.
Zimmer, Professor, 152.

TABLE OF PRONUNCIATION
FOR THE MORE DIFFICULT WORDS

A. Stress is of four kinds, and marked here: (1) - (weak stress).

        (2) ɪ (medium).

        (3) ' (strong).

        (4) ; (emphatic).

B. Cymric words of more than one syllable have the stress regularly on the antepenult (although there are some words with the stress on the last; and the negative prefix *an* often takes full stress).

Cymric wy = ui; ðð = th in English *th*en; ll (ʜ) = a broad buzzed l, i.e. like the French l unvoiced, sounds like *hl*, and is unilateral (right side) with the tongue in the *i* position. The thorn letter þ = voiceless sound as in English wi*th*.

C. Nasality of vowels marked with (◠) underneath the vowel.

Interdental (ṭ, ḍ, ḷ, ṇ) marked with dot underneath.

l mouillé, i.e. palatal, marked ᵗ.

n   ,,   ,,   ,,   ñ (cf. Colo*gn*e).

ε = open *e*; e = close e; ɔ = o open; o = o close.

r = thin *r* (i.e. r after e, i).

œ = the mid-front narrow round (close); cf. German ö.

ə = mid-mixed indefinite sound at end of unstressed syllables, often alternating with mid-back (close) vowel a, which is the sound of u in Gaelic ag*u*s; the *a* has the sound of *a* in f*a*ther, but it occurs both long and short. Doubling of vowels indicates length. a is a more obscure sound.

ɪ = high-mixed open *i*; ɪ̈ = high-front open *i*; i itself is in Gaelic a high-front narrow, i.e. close sound.

For basis cf. H. Sweet's *Phonetics*.

dʒ approximately like *dg* in English ju*dg*e.

tʃ (*tch*), the voiceless sound of preceding.

pb is to indicate the peculiar quality of Gaelic initial *b*, which begins voiceless and ends voiced.

h stands for breath-glide, on or off, according as it precedes or follows the consonant concerned.

ç like *ch* in standard pronunciation of German i*ch*, "I". It is the forward palatal position of the guttural *ch*, here marked *x*. It is in Gaelic associated with thin or clear vowels (i.e. e, i).

c = forward palatal position of *k*.

447

ȝ = voiced form of the voiceless *x*: it is ordinarily written *gh*, while the
voiceless sound is written *ch* in the ordinary script. In the later
form of Mag (a plain) it passes into *gh*, i.e. Ma*gh*, and is often
but feebly felt, in which cases it is Moy in place names, c.f.
Moylena.

Aberffraw (-abˑɛr-frau).
Abergeleu (ˑabarˈgɛl-oï).
Achill (ˈaç-ïl).
Achren (ˈaxrən).
Adamnan (ˈadam-nan).
Aebh (ˈeev).
Aed (ˈeeṭ).
Aedh (ˈee). In Scotland
  y, e.g. y Mˈy = Hugh
  Mackay.
Aeife (eeif-ə).
Aerfon (ˈairvon).
Aes Sídhe (ˈees ˑʃïï-hə).
Ailbhe (ˈɛlᵉv-ə).
Ailech (ˈaɫ-ɛx).
Ailill (ˈaɫ-ïɫ).
Ailinn (ˈaɫ-ïñ).
Ailioll (aɫ-jŭl).
Aine (ˈɑɑ-ñə).
Airceltrai (ˈerˈkɛlṭrai).
Airem, Eochaid (ˈaïr-em,
  ɛɔx-atʃ).
Airmid (ˈair-mïtʃ).
Alaw (ˈal-au).
Alba (aḷə-pa).
Allobroges
  (-alˈlo-brog-ɛs).
Amaethon (-amˈaïþ-on).
Amergin, G. Amorgin,
  Amorgene
  (ˈamor-gïn).
Amlwch (ˈam-lux).
Ana (ˈaɑṇa).
Aneurin (-aˈnoï-rïn).
Annwn (ˈanˈnuun).
Aoibhinn (ˈoïv-ïñ).
Aoife (ˈoïf-ə).
Aranon (arˈan-on).
Arawn (ˈarˈaun).
Ardan (ˈaarṭ-an).
Ard Chein (-aarṭ ˈçeeñ).
Arddu (ˈarðï).

Argetlám (ˈarc-ɛṭˈlʰaav).
Arianrod (ariˈan-rod).
Armagh (-arˈmah), from
  Ard Macha (-aarḍ
  ˈmaaxa), i.e. Altitudo
  Machae,   Macha's
  Height.
Arran (ˈarr-an).
Art (arᵉṭ).
Arthur (ˈarþ-ïr).
Artur (ˈarᵉt-ar).
Avallach (avˈaɫ-ax).
Aynia *v.* Aine.

Badb (pbav).
Badon (ˈbad-on).
Baile (pbai-lə).
Bala (ˈbaal-a).
Balin (ˈbal-ïn).
Ballymagauran
  (-pbalə-maˈgaur-an).
Ballymote
  (G. Baile an mhóta,
  -pbal-ən ;vooṭ-ə).
Ballysadare
  (G. Baile-easa-Dara,
  -pbal-esa ;ḍhara).
Balor (ˈpbaḷ-or).
Banba (ˈpbanᵉ-va).
Baoisgne (ˈpbœœʃc-ñə).
Beltaine (ˈpbjauḷḷ-ṭïñ).
Bettws-y-coed 1. (ˈbetus
  kooyd), 2. (-bɛts-əˈkoïd).
Beuno (ˈboi-no).
Bilé (ˈpbil-ə).
Blathnat (ˈpbḷaa-naṭ).
Blodeuwedd
  (ˈblod-oï;u-eðð).
Boann (ˈpboo-aṇ).
Bodb (pbov).
Borrach (ˈpborr-ax).
Branwen (ˌbranˈu-en).

Brea (pbree).
Brian (ˈpbrï-an).
Brigit (ˈpbrïï-tʃ).
Bri Leith (-pbrï ˈlhɛɛh).
Buarainech
  (ˈpbuuar-añɛx).
Bwbachod (-buˈbax-od).

Caemhoc (-kïïvˈɔɔk).
Camulodunum
  (kamuloˈduun-aṁ).
Caswallawn
  (-kasˈuaʰl-aun).
Cian (kiian).
Ciaran (kiiaran).
Cichol (ˈkixol).
Clann Chattan (klan
  ˈxatt-an).
Clann Neamhuinn (klan
  ˈñeviñ).
Clontarf (klonˈtarf).
Coblynau (-kobˈlyn-oï).
Conchobar (ˈkona-xar).
Conlaoch (ˈkǫo-ḷœœx).
Connaught (ˈkon-aht).
Connla (ˈkǫo-ḷa).
Cruind (kruⁿïñ).
Cualgne (ˈkuⁿaɫ-ñə).
Cuchulainn (-kuˈxuḷ-iñ).
Culann (ˈkuḷ-an).
Cumhal (ˈkụh-al).
Curoi (-kuˈrɔɔi).
Custennin (kustˈɛnin).
Cwm Cawlwyd (-kum
  ˈkaul-uïðð).
Cwy (kui).

Daire (ḍhai-rə).
Dechtire (ˈdʒeç-tʃïrə).
Dé Danann (dʒe
      ˈḍan-aṇ).
Deimne (ˈdʒem-ñə).

Deirdre ('dʒeɹ-dɹə).
Devwy ('dɛv-ui).
Diancecht ('dʒian;ɔjɛxt̩).
Diarmait O'Duibhne
('dʒiiar-mitʃ-o·d̩hui-ñə).
Dinas Dinḷḷev ('diinɑs
'dïn-hlɛv).
Dinas Emrys ('diinɑs
'ɛm-rïs).
Dingwall ('ding-wɑl).
Dinn-senchus
('dʒijü;hɛn-xüs).
Diwrnach ('dʒurn-ɑx).
Dobhar ('d̩ov-ɑr).
Domnann ('d̩om-naṉṉ).
Dundalk (-dun-dɒk).
Dundealgan
(d̩uun-dʒɑlᵃg-ɑn).

Eriu ('eeɹ-iu).
Essyllt (-ɛss·ïʰlt).
Etain ('et-qɑñ).
Evnissyen (-ev'nïss-jen).

Ferdiad (-fɛɹ'dʒiiɑ).
Ffordd Elen ('forð̆ð̆
'ɛl-ən).
Fionnbharr('fjüṉṉ-vɑrr).

Gabhra ('gɑu-ra).
Gaillion, Fir ('gɑɫ-i-on,
fïɹ).
Govannon (-gov'ɑnn-on).
Gwalchaved
(-guɑl'xɑv-eð̆ð̆).
Gwalchmei ('guɑlx-mei).
Gwarthegid
(-guɑrþ'ɛg-ið̆ð̆).
Gwawl ɪ. ('guɑul),
2. ('ᵍwaul).
Gwlgawd Gododin
(gul'gɑuð̆ð̆ -god'od-ïn).
Gwragedd Annwn
(-gur'ɑg-eð̆ð̆ -ɑn'nuun).
Gwrhyr ('gur'hïr).
Gwyngelli (guïn'gɛl-lï).
Gwynhwyvar
(-guïn'huïɪvar).

Hi Dorchaide
(hi 'd̩orx-ɑdʒ-ə).
Hy Breasail(hi ·bree-sal).
Iddawc ('ïð̆ð̆-auk).
Inniskea ('iñ-ïsh-cjee).
Iolo Morganwg (ɪi'olo
-mor'gɑn-ug).
Iseult (-ï'sœlt).
Iuchar ('ïu-xɑr).
Iweridd (-ïu'ɛɹ-ïð̆ð̆).

Killarney (-ciɫ'ɑɑɹñə).
Knockainy
(-krohk'ɑɑñə).
Kulhwch ('kœl'huch).

Laeg (ḻœœk).
Laegaire ('ḻœœk-aɹə).
Ler ('ɫeɹ).
Levarcham ('ɫevar-xam).
Lia Fáil ('ɫiiɑ 'fɑɑl).
Lismore (-ɫïs'moor).
Llevelys (-hlev'ɛl-ïs).
Lloegyr ('hloigür).
Lludd (hḻüð̆ð̆).
Llyr (hḻïr).
Lochlann ('ḻox-ḻaṉṉ).

Mabinogion
(mab-ïn'og-ï-on).
Mac Cecht(-mɑʰk'cjɛxt̩).
MacCuill(-mɑʰk'cʰuᵘït̩).
Mac Gréine
(-mɑʰk'crʰee-ñə).
Mac Kineely
(-mɑʰk ɪcʰïñ'eel-i).
Mac Moineanta
(-mɑʰk 'moïn-ɑnt-ə).
Mac Nia (-mɑʰk 'ñïïa).
Mac Oc (-mɑʰk 'ook).
Mac Samthainn
(-mɑʰk 'sav-hïñ).
Macha (mɑɑx-ɑ).
Maelmuiri
(-mœœl'mur-i).
Maenor Alun ('mɑi-nor
-ɑl-ün).

Maen Tyriawc (ɪmɑin
-tïr'ï-auk).
Manawyddan
(man-ɑu'yð̆ð̆-ɑn).
March ('mɑrx).
Matholwch
(-maþ'ol-ux).
Mathonwy (-maþ'on-uï).
Meadha ('mɛh-a).
Medb ('mæ̞ɛv).
Melwas (ɪmɛl;u-ɑs).
Menw (mɛnu).
Mesgegra (-mɛs'gɛg-ra).
Miach ('mii-ɑx).
Mider ('mïï-tʃəɹ).
Míle ('mïï-lə).
Mochdrev ('mox-drɛv).
Mochnant ('mox-nant).
Morrígu ('mor-riig-u).
Moytura (ɪmoi'tʰuur-ɑ).
Muirthemne
(ɪmur;hɛm-ñə).
Myrddin ('mərð̆ð̆-ïn).

Nant y Llew (ɪnant -ə
'ḥloi).
Neevougi (-neev'ook-ə).
Niamh (ñï̈av).
Nos galan gaeof (-nos
-gɑl-ɑn 'gɑï-of).
Nwyvre ('nuïv-rə).
Nynniaw (ɪnïn'ï-au).

Oeth, Anoeth
('oiþ, 'anɪoiþ).
Ossian ('oʃ-an) (Irish,
-ïʃ'ïïn).

Pryderi (-prï'de-rï).
Prydwen ('prəd-wɛn).
Pwyll ('pui-ɫ).

Queen Guinevere
(-kgïn-ɛ'veer).

Rhiannon (-ʰrï'an-non).
Rhyd y Groes (-ʰrïð̆ð̆ -ə
'grois).

Sadb (saɑv).
Samhain ('sạv-ïñ).
Scathach ('skɑh-ɑx).
Scêne ('scjee-ne).
Senchan Torpeist ('ʃen-xɑn 'thor-peeʃt).
Sen Mag (ʃen maʒ).
Sgeolan ('skjoo-lɑn).
Sídh (ʃïïh).
Sinann ('ʃïn-ɑṇ).

Tailtiu ('tɑɑl-tʃu).
Táin Bó Chuailgné ('tʰɑɑñ pbo 'xualc-ñə).
Taliesin (-tal-i'ess-ïn).
Tallacht ('tʰaḷ-ɑxṭ).
Tathlum ('tʰaḷ-əm).

Tawë ('tau-ə).
Teirnyon Twryf Vliant (-teir'nï-on 'tur-ïf 'vlï-ant).
Tethra ('tʃɛ-ra).
Tigernmas ('tʃïh-ərn-mɑs).
Tighernach (tʃïh-ərn-ɑx).
Tir nam beo ('tʃïïr -nam -bɛɔɔ).
Tir nan og ('tʃïïr -nan 'ook).
Tir Tairngire ('tʃïïr 'ṭhairñ-cïrə).
Tuatha Dé Danann ('tʰuⁿah-a ːdʒə ;dan-aṇ).

Twr Branwen (ːtuur 'bran-wɛn).
Twrch Trwyth (ːturx 'truïþ).
Tylwyth Teg (ːtəl-uïþ 'tɛg).
Uisnech ('uʃ-ñɛx).
Unsenn ('un-ʃeṇ).
Urddawl Ben ('urðð-aul 'bɛn).
Wydyr ('uïðð-ər).
Yspaddaden Penkawr (ïsp-aðð'ad-ɛn 'pɛn-kaur).